# Critical
## *Issues* in
# Early Childhood
# Professional
# Development

# *Critical Issues* in
# Early Childhood Professional Development

edited by

**Martha Zaslow, Ph.D.**
Child Trends
Washington, D.C.

and

**Ivelisse Martinez-Beck, Ph.D.**
Child Care Bureau
Washington, D.C.

·P·A·U·L·H·
BROOKES
PUBLISHING CO. ®

Baltimore • London • Sydney

**Paul H. Brookes Publishing Co.**
Post Office Box 10624
Baltimore, Maryland 21285-0624

www.brookespublishing.com

Typeset by Auburn Associates, Inc., Baltimore, Maryland.
Manufactured in the United States of America by
Versa Press, Inc., East Peoria, Illinois.

**Library of Congress Cataloging-in-Publication Data**

Critical issues in early childhood professional development / edited by Martha
Zaslow and Ivelisse Martinez-Beck.
    p.    cm.
    Includes bibliographical references and index.
    ISBN-13: 978-1-55766-825-7 (pbk.)
    ISBN-10: 1-55766-825-6 (pbk.)
    1. Early childhood teachers—Training of—United States.   2. Early child-
hood educators—United States.   I. Zaslow, Martha J.   II. Martinez-Beck,
Ivelisse.
LB1775.6.C745 2006
372.21—dc22
                                                        2005024239

British Library Cataloguing in Publication data are available from the British
Library.

# Contents

# About the Editors

**Martha Zaslow, Ph.D.,** Vice President for Research and Content Area Director for Early Childhood Development, Child Trends, 4301 Connecticut Avenue, NW, Suite 350, Washington, DC 20008

Dr. Zaslow is Vice President for Research at Child Trends, a nonpartisan, nonprofit research organization in Washington, D.C., that focuses on research and statistics on children and families in the United States. She also heads the Early Childhood Content Area at Child Trends. She received her doctoral degree in personality and developmental psychology from Harvard University, Cambridge, Massachusetts. Dr. Zaslow's research takes an ecological approach, considering the role of multiple contexts in children's development, including the family, early care and education settings, and programs and policies for families with young children. She is especially interested in understanding how to strengthen quality in early care and education settings and in how children's experiences in such settings contribute to school readiness. She is grateful for the opportunity that this book has given her to focus in depth on the characteristics and qualifications of the early childhood workforce as a facet of quality and contributor to children's development.

**Ivelisse Martinez-Beck, Ph.D.,** Social Science Research Analyst and Research Coordinator, Child Care Bureau, Administration for Children and Families, U.S. Department of Health and Human Services, Switzer Building, Room 2046, 330 C Street, SW, Washington, DC 20447

Dr. Martinez-Beck received her doctoral degree in developmental psychology and linguistics from the University of Michigan, Ann Arbor, and joined the Child Care Bureau in 2000 as a Society for Research in Child Development Executive Branch Policy Fellow. Her work as Research Coordinator and Research Team Leader for the Child Care Bureau involves planning and designing the Child Care Bureau's research agenda, managing research grants and contracts, studying topics related to child care subsidy policies, implementing child care quality initiatives (including efforts to improve the knowledge, skills, and competencies of the early care and education workforce), and evaluating the initiatives' effects on quality of care and child outcomes. She is a member of the steering committee of the Child Care & Early Education's *Research Connections* project and is Project Officer of the recently funded Quality

Interventions in Early Care and Education (QUINCE) project, a study led by researchers at the FPG Child Development Institute at The University of North Carolina at Chapel Hill, and the Center on Health and Education at Georgetown University in Washington, D.C., to study the effectiveness of training interventions for family child care providers and center-based teachers to improve quality of care, caregiving practice, and child outcomes.

# Contributors

**W. Steven Barnett, Ph.D.**
Director
National Institute for Early
  Education Research
Rutgers, The State University of
  New Jersey
120 Albany Street, Suite 500
New Brunswick, NJ 08901

**Daniel Berry**
Harvard Graduate School of
  Education
Larsen Hall, Room 715
Appian Way
Cambridge, MA 02138

**Heather Biggar, Ph.D.**
Professional Development Specialist
National Association for the
  Education of Young Children
1509 16th Street, NW
Washington, DC 20036

**Elena Bodrova, Ph.D.**
Senior Researcher
Mid-continent Research for
  Education and Learning
2550 South Parker Road, Suite 500
Aurora, CO 80014

**Joanne P. Brady, M.Ed.**
Vice President
Education Development Center, Inc.
Director
Center for Children & Families
55 Chapel Street
Newton, MA 02458

**Richard N. Brandon, Ph.D.**
Director
Human Services Policy Center
Evans School of Public Affairs
University of Washington
Box 354804
1107 45th, NE
Seattle, WA 98195

**Barbara Bristow, M.S.**
Extension Associate
Cornell University
292 Martha Van Rensselaer Hall
Ithaca, NY 14853

**Joanna Cannon, B.A.**
Graduate Research Assistant
Developmental Psychology
Teachers College
Columbia University
TC BOX 118
525 West 120th Street
New York, NY 10027

**Richard M. Clifford, Ph.D.**
Senior Scientist
FPG Child Development Institute
Campus Box 8040
Chapel Hill, NC 27599

**Maria I. Cordero, Ed.D.**
Special Project Manager
Administration for Children's
  Services
Division of Child Care
66 John Street, 8th Floor
New York, NY 10038

**Stephanie M. Curenton, Ph.D.**
Assistant Professor
Department of Family and Child
  Sciences
Florida State University
212 Sandels Building
Tallahassee, FL 32306

**David K. Dickinson, Ed.D.**
Professor
Teaching and Learning Department
Peabody College
Vanderbilt University
Box 330
Nashville, TN 37235

**Janet G. Eisenband, B.A.**
Doctoral Candidate
Educational Psychology Human
  Cognitive Studies in Education
Teachers College
Columbia University
TC BOX 118
525 West 120th Street
New York, NY 10027

**V. Jeffery Evans, Ph.D., J.D.**
Director of Intergenerational
  Research
Demographic and Behavioral
  Sciences Branch
National Institute of Child Health
  and Human Development
6100 Executive Boulevard, Room
  8B07
Bethesda, MD 20892

**Cathie C. Feild, M.A.**
FPG Child Development Institute
University of North Carolina
516 South Greensboro Street
Carrboro, NC 27510

**Michelle Galanter, M.A.**
Doctoral Candidate
Developmental Psychology
Teachers College
Columbia University
TC BOX 118
525 West 120th Street
New York, NY 10027

**Herbert P. Ginsburg, Ph.D.**
Jacob H. Schiff Foundations
  Professor of Psychology and
  Education
Department of Human
  Development
Teachers College
TC BOX 184
525 West 120th Street
New York, NY 10027

**Susan Hegland, Ph.D.**
Associate Professor
Department of Human
  Development and Family Studies
Iowa State University
4380 Palmer Hall
Ames, IA 50011

**Becky Houf, B.S.W.**
Early Childhood and Prevention
  Services Program Manager
Missouri Department of Social
  Services
Post Office Box 1527
Jefferson City, MO 65102

**Marilou Hyson, Ph.D.**
Senior Advisor for Research and
  Professional Practice
National Association for the
  Education of Young Children
1509 16th Street, NW
Washington, DC 20036

**Rochelle Goldberg Kaplan, Ph.D.**
Professor
Department of Elementary and Early
  Childhood Education
William Paterson University
1600 Valley Road
Wayne, NJ 07470

**Naomi Karp, M.Ed.**
Early Childhood Education Policy
  Consultant
3600 North Camino Rio Soleado
Tucson, AZ 85718

**Pamela J. Kelley, M.S.W.**
Research Associate
National Institute for Early
  Education Research
Rutgers, The State University of
  New Jersey
120 Albany Street, Suite 500
New Brunswick, NJ 08901

**Deborah J. Leong, Ph.D.**
Professor
Metropolitan State College of Denver
Post Office Box 173362
Denver, CO 80217

**Kelly L. Maxwell, Ph.D.**
Scientist
FPG Child Development Institute
University of North Carolina
Campus Box 8040
Chapel Hill, NC 27599

**Lana Messner, M.A.**
Project Director
Infant Toddler Initiative
Kansas Association of Child Care
  Resource and Referral Agencies
112 West Iron
Salina, KS 67401

**Martha Moorehouse, Ph.D.**
Director
Division of Children and Youth Policy
Office of the Assistant Secretary for
  Planning and Evaluation
U.S. Department of Health and
  Human Services
200 Independence Avenue, SW,
  Room 404E
Washington, DC 20201

**Melissa Morgenlander, M.A.**
Doctoral Candidate
Educational Psychology; Human
  Cognitive Studies in Education
Teachers College
Columbia University
TC BOX 118
525 West 120th Street
New York, NY 10027

**H. Elizabeth Peters, Ph.D.**
Professor
Department of Policy Analysis and
  Management
117 Martha Van Rensselaer Hall
Cornell University
Ithaca, NY 14853

**Carla Peterson, Ph.D.**
Associate Professor
Department of Human Development
  and Families Studies
Iowa State University
58 Le Baron Hall
Ames, IA 50011

**Robert C. Pianta, Ph.D.**
Novartis US Foundation Professor of
  Education
University of Virginia
350 Old Ivy Way, Suite 100
Charlottesville, VA 22903

**H. Abigail Raikes, M.P.H.**
Senior Research Assistant
Center on Children, Families, and
the Law
University of Nebraska–Lincoln
121 South 13th Street, Suite 302
Lincoln, NE 68588

**Helen H. Raikes, Ph.D.**
Professor
Family and Consumer Sciences
University of Nebraska–Lincoln
257 Mabel Lee Hall
Lincoln, NE 68588

**Craig T. Ramey, Ph.D.**
Founding Director, Georgetown
Center on Health and Education
Distinguished Professor of Health
Studies
School of Nursing and Health
Studies
Georgetown University
Box 571107
3700 Reservoir Road, NW
Washington, DC 20057

**Sharon Landesman Ramey, Ph.D.**
Susan H. Mayer Professor of Child
and Family Studies
Director, Georgetown Center on
Health and Education
Georgetown University
Box 571107
3700 Reservoir Road, NW
Washington, DC 20057

**Colleen Rathgeb, M.P.P.**
Senior Social Science Analyst
Office of the Assistant Secretary for
Planning and Evaluation
U.S. Department of Health and
Human Services
200 Independence Avenue, SW,
Room 404E
Washington, DC 20201

**Catherine A. Rosemary, Ph.D.**
Associate Professor
John Carroll University
20700 North Park Boulevard
University Heights, OH 44118

**Kathleen Roskos, Ph.D.**
Professor
John Carroll University
20700 North Park Boulevard
University Heights, OH 44118

**Jacqueline Scott, Ph.D.**
Senior Policy Research Analyst
Center for Family Policy and Research
University of Missouri
1400 Rock Quarry Road
Columbia, MO 65211

**Sandra Scott, B.A.**
Program Specialist
Nebraska Health and Human
Services Department
Post Office Box 95044
Lincoln, NE 68509

**Kyle L. Snow, Ph.D.**
U.S. Department of Health and
Human Services
National Institutes of Health
National Institute of Child Health
and Human Development
6100 Executive Boulevard, Room
4B05
Bethesda, MD 20892

**Kathy Thornburg, Ph.D.**
Professor
Department of Human
Development and Family Studies
Director, Center for Family Policy
and Research
University of Missouri–Columbia
1400 Rock Quarry Road
Columbia, MO 65211

**Julia C. Torquati, Ph.D.**
Associate Professor
Child Development Research
Coordinator
University of Nebraska–Lincoln
135 Mabel Lee Hall
Lincoln, NE 68588

**Kathryn Tout, Ph.D.**
Senior Research Associate
Child Trends
4301 Connecticut Avenue, NW,
Suite 350
Washington, DC 20008

**M. Heidi Varner, M.Ed.**
Educational Consultant
John Carroll University
20700 North Park Boulevard
University Heights, OH 44118

**Melissa Welch-Ross, Ph.D.**
Affiliated Associate Professor
Department of Psychology
George Mason University
David King Hall
4400 University Drive
Fairfax, VA 22030

**Anne Wolf, Ed.D.**
Society for Research in Child
Development (SRCD) Policy
Fellow
Office of the Assistant Secretary for
Planning and Evaluation
U.S. Department of Health and
Human Services
200 Independence Avenue, SW,
Room 404E
Washington, DC 20201

# Foreword

*Critical Issues in Early Childhood Professional Development* grew out of the collaboration among federal agencies participating in the Science and the Ecology of Early Development (SEED) consortium. As such, it represents one of the best examples of how a collaborative effort, characterized by a shared purpose among a diverse set of agencies, can yield important dividends. SEED is a consortium of federal agencies that aims to integrate the various elements of research and policy expertise needed to respond to emerging questions in the field of early childhood development. Through dialogue, keen awareness of both the research and policy issues affecting the field of early childhood care and education, and a shared vision of how to integrate resources to move forward, the SEED consortium agreed that professional development was a common focus and that a forum was needed to take stock of the evidence, identify areas where our knowledge is strong, and provide a vision for next steps.

The first step toward integrating science across federal agencies occurred in 1996 when a small group of agency representatives—Martha Moorehouse (Office of the Assistant Secretary for Planning and Evaluation [ASPE], U.S. Department of Health and Human Services [DHHS]), Louisa Tarullo and Helen Howerton (Administration on Children, Youth and Families [ACYF]), Donna Hinkle (National Institute on Early Childhood Development and Education, Office of Educational Research and Improvement [OERI]), Pia Divine (Child Care Bureau [CCB]), Naomi Karp (National Institute on Early Childhood Development and Education, OERI), Ed Bran (the Centers for Disease Control and Prevention), Jerry West (U.S. Department of Education), V. Jeffery Evans, and I (National Institute of Child Health and Human Development [NICHD])—met and decided to create a collaborative effort to address issues of national importance that cut across the singular mission of the different agencies. In addition to the individual commitment of these people, SEED would not have been created if not for the generous support and encouragement of Duane Alexander, Director of NICHD; Ann Segal, then at the Office of the Assistant Secretary for Planning and Evaluation, DHHS; and Chris Bacharach, Chief of the Demographic and Behavioral Sciences Branch, NICHD. They provided institutional support and resources to make SEED a reality. However, V. Jeffery Evans's intellectual integrity, vision, and complete belief that the advancement of science depends on the collective strength of several partners formed the engine of SEED.

SEED provides a flexible and efficient mechanism for integrating the various elements of research and policy expertise needed to respond to emerging questions in the field of early childhood development. The consortium's over-arching goal is to foster integrated research on the multiple contexts of child development—family, child care settings, schools, communities, and broader cultural and policy contexts—especially for children from low-income families. Part of this goal is to bridge the gap between researchers and policy makers by fostering activities that not only translate research for policy makers but also serve to guide and inform the questions that researchers seek to answer.

SEED has fulfilled many parts of its goal in different ways. Some accomplishments have been made possible by pooling resources across participating agencies and others by providing the scientific rationale, sharing ideas, and encouraging agencies to be part of a collective research agenda. For example, SEED added supplements to existing NICHD grants that analyze time diaries, collected from teachers or child care providers and parents, to examine time use and after-school care and the stability of child care among the working poor. It provided funds to add a father study to the National Early Head Start Evaluation. It established a partnership among NICHD's extramural and intramural programs, ACYF, and the Ford Foundation to support a study of newborns and their parents who are part of the Early Head Start evaluation. To stimulate innovative and cutting-edge research, SEED organized the 1997 workshop *Poverty and Children* to take stock of the knowledge base on developmental trajectories of children from low-income families. This workshop identified a set of research objectives, gaps in the literature, and directions for research that formed the basis for the first SEED program announcement, released in 2001. (A second SEED program announcement was issued in 2004.) In addition, SEED sponsored several high-profile, multidisciplinary meetings that highlighted the role of child care in state welfare evaluations and showcased emerging research findings on subsidies, regulations, and quality of care in the context of policy makers' concerns and needs for research that can guide and inform public policies.

This book is based on the third SEED-sponsored meeting. *Early Childhood Professional Development and Training and Children's Successful Transition to Elementary School,* which was held February 25–26, 2003, addressed two goals: 1) to present emerging research on the links between children's successful transition to elementary school and professional development and training in the early childhood workforce across the range of care and education settings and 2) to identify meaningful directions for further research on this topic. This meeting identified research already underway on early childhood professional development that could be fruitfully extended to study the transition to elementary school and at the same time provide a map for future research. In keeping with SEED's mission, all of the agencies participated in planning and running the meeting, with the CCB and ASPE playing a lead role in this particular meeting.

In turn, *Critical Issues in Early Childhood Professional Development* accomplishes two important goals. First, it identifies key emerging issues in the research on early childhood professional development and highlights links across areas of research that focus on laying the groundwork for school readiness. At present, a great deal of state and federal effort is devoted to preparing children to enter elementary school with an ability to engage positively with adults and other children in a formal school setting, openness to and eagerness for learning, and enough basic knowledge from which to build. Part of this task is to highlight research that can tell us how multiple aspects of early childhood experiences, including the professional development of those who educate and care for children, can foster a successful transition to elementary school. Hence, this book also highlights the current extent and nature of the early childhood workforce's education and training. Second, in the context of this research focus, *Critical Issues in Early Childhood Professional Development* pays tribute to the integrity, scientific creativity, vision, and humanity that are represented by the collaborative nature of SEED. In so doing, it offers a model for future collaborations in which the stakes are high and the risks are many but the payoffs are extremely gratifying because they offer the hope of improving the contexts for development of the country's most precious resource—our children.

*Natasha J. Cabrera, Ph.D.*
*Assistant Professor*
*Human Development Department*
*University of Maryland, College Park*

# Acknowledgments

The co-editors thank the members of the federal interagency Science and the Ecology of Early Development (SEED) workgroup for the planning and support they provided for the meeting that served as the basis for this book. In particular, the co-editors are grateful for the leadership of Shannon Christian, Associate Commissioner, Child Care Bureau, U.S. Department of Health and Human Services; Karen Tvedt, Director of Policy Division, Child Care Bureau, U.S. Department of Health and Human Services; and Martha Moorehouse, Director of Children and Youth Policy, Office of the Assistant Secretary for Planning and Evaluation, U.S. Department of Health and Human Services.

# CHAPTER 1

# Introduction

*The Context for Critical Issues in*
*Early Childhood Professional Development*

IVELISSE MARTINEZ-BECK AND MARTHA ZASLOW

This book identifies a series of problems and gaps in the understanding of early childhood professional development, specifically in knowledge of the characteristics and size of the early childhood workforce, in understanding how early childhood professional development contributes to the quality of early care and education, in the evidence on strategies to strengthen the qualifications of this workforce, and in the methods available to assess the costs and benefits as well as market effects of differing approaches to strengthening professional development. Each chapter in this book aims to go beyond the identification of problems and gaps, however, to identify new methodological and substantive approaches. Our aim throughout is to build from the identification of critical issues in early childhood professional development to the identification of strategies to move both research and practice forward.

This introduction attempts to provide a context for the chapters that follow. In particular, it identifies the *Good Start, Grow Smart* initiative as a key policy context fostering greater emphasis on early childhood professional development as a means to enhance children's school readiness. This initiative addresses issues across all major types of early care and education (what we refer to as *sectors*): home- and center-based child care, Head Start, and pre-kindergarten. Although it would be far easier to focus on only one sector of early care and education (e.g., to make progress in measuring the size and qualifications of the child care workforce alone), a theme throughout the book will be the need to address research and practice to strengthen professional development across all sectors. To provide a context for this focus on all early care and education sectors, the chapter briefly summarizes recent findings on the numbers of young children participating in each of the types of early care and education and the extent of the public investment in each type. Then it turns to an overview of the facets of early childhood professional development examined in the different sections of this book, briefly previewing each chapter and the critical issues it raises.

## POLICY CONTEXT:
## THE *GOOD START, GROW SMART* INITIATIVE

Information on the characteristics of the early care and education workforce and the professional development experiences that contribute to their skills and competencies is essential for programs serving children and families. Although this need has been identified in previous research (Bowman, Donovan, & Burns, 2000; Isenberg, 2000; National Institute of Child Health and Human Development [NICHD] Early Child Care Research Network, 1996, 2000), it has reached a new level of importance since the passage of the No Child Left Behind (NCLB) Act of 2001 (PL 107-110) and its complementary early childhood presidential initiative, *Good Start, Grow Smart.* Early childhood programs funded through state and federal dollars are putting new emphasis on the professional development of the early care and education workforce in recognition that children's early experiences with those who care for them inside and outside the home are critical to their early healthy development and their readiness for school. Under NCLB, states are held accountable for providing children with the experiences necessary to succeed in school and, more specifically, to show progress in those areas that will better equip them to pursue other educational goals and to become successful and responsible citizens. This focus on accountability underscores the need for children to arrive in school with the necessary skills and competencies to engage productively, to progress, and to succeed, putting more pressure on those who share the responsibility of providing children with opportunities for learning and development prior to school entry.

*Good Start, Grow Smart* was launched in April 2002 as the early education reform companion of NCLB. The Department of Health and Human Services (DHHS), the Department of Education (ED), and the White House Office of Domestic Policy are partners in this effort to improve school readiness for young children in all types of early care and education settings. The initiative charges the Head Start Bureau (HSB/DHHS), the Child Care Bureau (CCB/DHHS), and the Office of Elementary and Secondary Education (OESE/ED) with specific activities in support of the vision for improving young children's early learning. It asks these programs to strengthen Head Start; bring research-based information to teachers, caregivers, and parents; and partner with the states to improve early childhood education.[1]

In addition, *Good Start, Grow Smart* calls for federally funded programs to formulate early learning guidelines—goals for the skills and competencies

---

[1]The CCB supports the goals of *Good Start, Grow Smart* through the quality provisions of the Child Care and Development Block Grant (CCDBG) Act of 1990. This legislation requires states to coordinate the provision of child care services with other federal, state, and local partners and use a portion of the funding they receive to improve the quality of early care and education programs.

that preschool-age children should accomplish before starting school. The articulation of early learning guidelines is then seen as serving as a framework for both practice (what are the competencies and skills that should be emphasized in early childhood settings) and early childhood assessment (how should these skills and competencies be measured).

The initiative calls for those caring for children to have the qualifications needed to support the skills and competencies identified in the early learning guidelines. It asks for programs to lay out professional development plans that will foster the development of competencies in early childhood caregivers and teachers that will, in turn, support young children's early learning. The initiative also asks that diverse delivery systems work together to ensure congruency, continuity, and better use of funds, including the identification of efforts by private and nonsecular organizations. These efforts have been framed in terms of standards or guidelines at the level of the child (learning standards) and at the level of the system (professional development and program standards). Research yielding a greater understanding of professional development of the early childhood workforce and how this contributes to children's early learning can clearly help inform the *Good Start, Grow Smart* initiative.

An important underpinning of the *Good Start, Grow Smart* initiative is the emerging body of evidence underscoring the importance of children's early experiences for their future healthy development. For example, as summarized by the Committee on Integrating the Science of Early Childhood Development in the influential book *From Neurons to Neighborhoods* (Shonkoff & Phillips, 2000), the research points to implications over time of children's early brain development, the quality of their relationships with the adults who care for them, the early capacity for emotional as well as attentional self-regulation, and their early learning processes. *From Neurons to Neighborhoods* emphasized the importance of the characteristics and quality of the diverse care environments that young children spend time in spanning care by parents; relatives; friends; family child care providers; and formal, center-based programs (Shonkoff & Phillips, 2000). In addition, research on the experiences of school-age children while in nonparental care and the conditions that lead to school failure and risky behaviors points to the need for better understanding of the characteristics of those who care for school-age children and the types of supports they need to offer children enriching and stimulating experiences (Halpern, 1999; Vandell & Su, 1999).

The body of research on early childhood development emphasizes the relationship between the child and the caregiver as the central feature of quality in early care and education settings and as a predictor of children's eventual readiness for school. Whether the caregiver is the grandmother, an unrelated baby sitter, or a center-based teacher, positive caregiver–child interactions involve language-stimulating interactions in which the caregiver is warm, engaged, and responsive.

Critical to sustaining high-quality child care for young children are the providers' characteristics—notably their education, specialized training, and attitudes about their work and the children in their care—and the features of child care that enable them to excel in their work and remain in their jobs—notably better ratios, group sizes, and compensation (Shonkoff & Phillips, 2000). Findings from new research looking at the relationship between providers' characteristics and structural features of early care environments will help clarify which combinations of variables matter the most for which children, in which environments.

## THE NEED TO FOCUS ON PROFESSIONAL DEVELOPMENT IN MULTIPLE SECTORS OF EARLY CARE AND EDUCATION

As noted next, the evidence indicates that substantial numbers of young children in the United States participate regularly in nonparental care and that their hours in care are distributed across different types of early childhood care and education. Children tend to experience different forms of care as they grow older, and a proportion of children experience multiple types of care simultaneously. Furthermore, children from differing socioeconomic backgrounds tend to rely on different types of care. Therefore, efforts to strengthen professional development need to be addressed to the early childhood workforce across different sectors or types of care if children's school readiness is to be fostered through early care and education experiences.

### Estimates of Children in Different Types of Nonparental Care

The U.S. Census Bureau (2000) estimated that the percentage of mothers with children under 6 years old who were in the workforce more than doubled between 1970 and 2000, from 30.8% in 1970 to 61.9% in 2000. Close to 20 million children under the age of 13 are in nonparental care arrangements while their parents work (National Survey of America's Families, 2002).

The National Household Education Survey (NHES; National Center for Education Statistics [NCES], 2001) provided national estimates of the types of nonparental care experiences of children birth through 6 years who were not yet in kindergarten. Approximately half (52%) of children ages 0 to 2 years are in some form of nonparental care arrangement as compared with 74% of 3- to 6-year-olds. Not surprisingly, younger children (0 to 2 years) are more likely than older children (3 to 6 years) to receive nonparental home-based care and less likely to receive center-based care. In addition, the child care arrangements of preschool-age children are more complex than those of younger children, with just under one third of 3- to 6-year-olds participating in multiple care arrangements as compared with one fifth of children ages 0 to 2 years. Although a large number of children ages birth through 6 years from families of all income levels are participating in nonparental care arrangements, there are differences across family income levels in the types of care arrangements children are using. For example, data from the NHES (2001) showed that children living in poverty (below 100% of the federal poverty level) are more likely to receive home-based care from their relatives than children living above poverty (above 150% of poverty level). Furthermore, a higher percentage of children living above poverty (19%) receive home-based care from nonrelatives than children living in or near poverty (10% and 13% respectively). In addition, 37% of children living above poverty use center-based care as compared with just over a quarter (27%) of those living in or near poverty (Kinukawa, Guzman, & Lippman, 2004).

## Public Investments in Early Care and Education

The federal government, as well as state and local governments, are making large investments in programs to support families and children by providing both direct services through early care and education programs, such as Head Start and prekindergarten, and through provision of child care subsidies for parents to be able to afford child care and early education for their children while they work. Estimates of state and federal spending in 2003 on child care and early childhood education programs (e.g., subsidies for child care and Head Start) serving children birth through age 13 was close to $18.1 billion.[2] In addition, state and federal funding for public prekindergarten, or programs offered through the public schools systems and other community-based programs for children ages 3 and 4, has increased to unprecedented levels—approximately $2.54 billion in 2002–2003 (Barnett, Hustedt, Robin, & Schulman, 2004). Prekindergarten programs targeting children who are 4 years old are on the agenda of many state legislatures, with at least 38 states working on or offering some kind of prekindergarten initiative (Barnett et al., 2004). These programs served nearly 740,000 children, or 10% of the nation's population of 3- and 4-year-old children, in school year 2002–2003 (Barnett et al., 2004).

*Child Care and Development Fund*    The Child Care and Development Block Grant Act, as amended by the Personal Responsibility and Work Opportunity Reconciliation Act (PRWORA) of 1996 (PL 104-193) and the Balanced Budget Act of 1997 (PL 105-33), authorizes the Child Care and Development Fund (CCDF).[3] Including funds transferred by states from

---

[2]The number includes spending from CCDF, Head Start, TANF, SSBG, and other programs targeting children who are at risk.

[3]CCDF is administered at the federal level by the CCB of the Administration on Children, Youth and Families (ACYF) of the Administration for Children and Families (ACF) in collaboration with ACF regional offices. States, territories, and tribes are responsible for ensuring that their CCDF grants are administered in compliance with statutory and regulatory requirements. In administering CCDF, states have significant discretion in how funds will be used and where emphasis will be placed in achieving the overall goals of CCDF.

Temporary Assistance for Needy Families (TANF) to CCDF, this is a significant source of federal support to improve the affordability, supply, and quality of child care in the United States. CCDF assists low-income families, including families receiving or transitioning from temporary public assistance, in obtaining child care so the adults can work or, at state option, attend training or pursue further education. In fiscal year 2003, $4.8 billion in CCDF funding was made available through block grants to all 50 states, the District of Columbia, five territories, and 259 tribal grantees (representing approximately 500 Native American tribes). Including required state contributions (state matching and maintenance of efforts funds) and TANF dollars transferred to CCDF or spent directly by states on child care services, an estimated $11.4 billion in CCDF and TANF funds was available for child care services in 2003. This compares with $3.2 billion in 1996. CCDF funds are used primarily to provide subsidized child care services through vouchers or certificates to low-income working families with children under age 13. In 2003, approximately 1.75 million children received child care subsidies for child care services from CCDF and TANF transfer funds. Of those children, approximately 79% came from families below 150% of the federal poverty level.

Nationally, more than one quarter (29%) of the children served through CCDF are infants and toddlers, more than one third (36%) are preschool and kindergarten age, and another third are school age. Parents may select any legally operating child care provider—including child care centers, family members, neighbors, family child care homes, after-school programs, and faith-based programs. In 2003, the majority of children from birth to 6 years who were served through CCDF received care in child care centers (58%), more than one third were served in home-based care in the provider's home (35%), and 7% were served in the child's own home. States make decisions about the education and professional development levels they will require caregivers to have to be eligible to participate in the child care subsidy program.

### Head Start and Early Head Start

Head Start and Early Head Start are comprehensive child development programs that serve children from birth to 5 years and pregnant women and their families. These programs focus on increasing school readiness for children from low-income families. Head Start[4] was authorized under the "Head Start Act," which is part of the Omnibus Budget Reconciliation Act of 1981 (PL 97-35), and reauthorized in 1998. Children from low-income families are eligible for Head Start if their families' incomes are below the federal poverty level or if their families are eligible for

---

[4]The Head Start program is administered by the HSB, ACYF, ACF, DHHS. Grants are awarded by the ACF regional offices and the HSB's American Indian–Alaska Native and Migrant and Seasonal Program Branches directly to local public agencies, private organizations, Indian Tribes, and school systems for the purpose of operating Head Start programs at the community level.

public assistance. In 2003, Head Start was appropriated more than $6.7 billion dollars for programs, technical assistance, research, and other activities.

Head Start has a long tradition of delivering comprehensive services designed to foster healthy development in children from low-income families. Head Start grantee and delegate agencies provide a range of individualized services in the areas of education and early childhood development; medical, dental, and mental health; nutrition; and parent involvement. In addition, the entire range of Head Start services is intended to be responsive and appropriate to each child's and family's developmental, ethnic, cultural, and linguistic heritage and experience. All Head Start programs must adhere to program performance standards. The program performance standards define the services that Head Start programs are to provide to the children and families they serve and constitute the expectations and requirements that Head Start grantees must meet. They are designed to ensure that the Head Start goals and objectives are implemented successfully, that the Head Start philosophy is manifested in programs, and that all grantee and delegate agencies strive to improve and maintain quality in the provision of Head Start services. One way to improve quality of services was introduced in the 1998 Head Start Reauthorization legislation, which required that at least 50% of teachers in Head Start programs obtain an associate's degree or a higher degree in early childhood education by 2002. In fact, Head Start programs met and surpassed the goal that year.

Head Start and Early Head Start programs served more than 900,000 children in approximately 50,000 classrooms in 19,000 centers in 2002. Of those children, 74% were eligible to attend Head Start because of their poverty status. As noted previously, the Head Start Act allows enrollment if children are eligible for public assistance, and 19% of children fell into that category in 2001–2002. The program also allows up to 10% of enrollment outside of poverty level eligibility, and 7% of children with family incomes that fell above the poverty level were accepted in the program in 2001–2002. Children in Head Start and Early Head Start attended different types of programs, but almost half were in full-day center-based programs operating 5 days a week. Approximately 400,000 children attended that type of program. Another 194,000 attended part-day programs (less than 6 hours per day), 5 days a week; 200,000 attended part-day programs, 4 days a week; and another 83,000, mainly Early Head Start children, attended home-based, combined (i.e., center-based as well as home-based), or locally designed program options.

In the 2001–2002 school year, it was determined that 447,294 of the children enrolled in Head Start and Early Head Start needed full-year, full-day care because of the education or work needs of their parents. Those children received care in a variety of settings, either only in Early Head Start or Head Start centers (232,564) or in Head Start/Early Head Start along with other community-based facilities, including prekindergarten programs. In addition, approximately 99,000 of the children enrolled in Head Start received a child care subsidy, either voucher or contracted slot, whether the care was provided through Head Start or another provider.

**Prekindergarten**    The public school systems in the United States are an important part of the child care and early childhood education system that provides early educational experiences to preschool-age children in order to prepare them for entry into school. These systems have access to federally and state-funded programs that focus on children who are at risk, including children from low-income families, families that do not speak English at home, or families that have other disadvantages. These funding streams include Individuals with Disabilities Education Act (IDEA) funds targeting children with disabilities and Title 1 funds for children who are educationally disadvantaged. A proportion of prekindergarten programs operating in public elementary schools received some form of federal or state funds targeting children at economic risk, including funds from Head Start and child care subsidy programs (in the 2000–2001 school year, 13% and 11% of schools received such funds respectively; NCES, 2003). Excluding funding from Head Start and CCDF, it is estimated that approximately $13.8 billion was available to public school districts and other eligible programs from appropriations in 2003 for IDEA, Title 1, or other programs.

Prekindergarten programs offered through the public schools are operated by the school districts, and roughly 80% of these programs receive funds from state or local education agencies. In addition to the programs offered by states through their public school systems, states are implementing their state-funded prekindergarten programs through a variety of community-based early care and education settings. Although, on average, 86% of prekindergarten teachers in programs in the public schools have a bachelor's degree or higher (NCES, 2003), only 13 of the 38 states funding one or more prekindergarten initiatives controlled by the state in the 2002–2003 school year required teachers to have both a bachelor's degree and specialized training in early childhood education (Barnett et al., 2004).[5]

During the 2000–2001 school year, 822,000 children participated in prekindergarten programs offered by 19,000 public elementary schools in approximately 58,000 classrooms (NCES, 2003). These represented 35% of all schools in the United States. More than 10,000 public elementary schools offered half-day programs and 7,280 offered full-day programs, although

---

[5]Many states report using combined funding to help support services for children participating in prekindergarten programs, and they are often unable to provide complete, specific data on the number of children benefiting from each source. Funding levels reported in this chapter are estimates taken from diverse sources, and both levels of funding and number of children served through each program do not represent unduplicated numbers.

some schools offered both types. The majority of the prekidergarten classes in the United States were located in schools where 75% or more of the student population came from low-income families, based on whether the students were eligible to receive free or reduced-priced lunch.

**Participation in More than One Type of Early Care and Education Program**    Data collected by the Head Start Program Information Report (PIR; 2002) indicated that about half of the children in Head Start attended part-day or part-week programs. In addition, more than half of the prekindergarten programs offered through the public school system offer services for half a day (NCES, 2003). At least half of the families in Head Start, and probably a good proportion of those whose children attend public prekindergarten, need full-year, full-day care arrangements in order to work. Many of these children are already linked to the subsidized child care system through shared funds; others may not receive subsidies but are probably attending the same care settings as children who receive subsidies mainly because they share demographic characteristics and reside in the same neighborhoods as the children who receive subsidies. The numbers of children served by each program described previously are not unduplicated numbers because many children participate in more than one of these programs simultaneously. These findings again underscore the need to consider professional development of the early childhood workforce across sectors rather than within any one sector.

## THE NEED FOR GREATER PRECISION IN THE RESEARCH ON PROFESSIONAL DEVELOPMENT

There is increased public attention to the professional development of the early childhood workforce given the renewed policy focus on the early childhood years as laying the groundwork for school readiness and the specific emphasis in the *Good Start, Grow Smart* initiative on professional development of the early childhood workforce as a factor that can contribute to early learning and school readiness. This attention is further encouraged by the substantial public investments in early care and education and the substantial numbers of children participating in nonparental care on a regular basis.

Policy makers and practitioners alike are turning to the research on professional development of the early childhood workforce and asking a series of very precise questions. However, their questions are often much more specific than the precision in the existing research. This book attempts to identify critical issues in early childhood professional development where progress is needed to move toward addressing the more precise and incisive questions that will be informative to policy and practice. It also attempts to identify emerging research approaches that can help move the work in this area in a direction of greater usefulness.

Here are examples of the kinds of questions that policy makers and practitioners are posing that often outstrip the research base.

- How many early childhood workers do we actually have in our state, looking across all the different sectors of early childhood care and education providers (including family, friend, and neighbor care; licensed family child care; center care; Head Start; and prekindergarten)? If we are to expand the number of early childhood workers, what is our starting point, and what is the extent of the growth that is needed in terms of numbers?

- In expanding our early childhood workforce, what is the most important investment? Will we gain the most from assuring that the early childhood workforce has specific types of training offered through community organizations (e.g., resource and referral agencies)? Is it a degree in an institution of higher education that will matter most? Or are both valuable investments in terms of quality of care and children's school readiness?

- What is the most important content to include in the preparation of the early childhood workforce, whether offered through a community organization or an institution of higher education? Is school readiness best supported by content focused specifically on early literacy development? What about other content areas such as early mathematical skills? Kindergarten teachers often stress children's ability to cooperate and to focus. Should social skills and self-regulation be the primary content area in which early childhood professionals prepare?

- Are there other important dimensions of professional development than training and education that predict better early education environments and outcomes for children? What about experience or exposure to certain kinds of supervision? Attitudes about caring for children?

- What systems need to be in place to support early childhood professional development? How can such systems ensure that professional preparation translates into practices in the early childhood classroom or group; that sequences of training and/or education have the specific content that will help children progress toward school readiness?

- How expensive is it to implement different approaches to early childhood professional development? What is the benefit relative to the cost of differing approaches?

The chapters in this book identify limitations in the existing research that have made it difficult to address such precise questions and identify ways for the research base to progress to match the emerging needs for information. For example, the first question points to the importance of accurate estimates of the workforce as a necessary first step toward assessing the needs for an expanded early childhood workforce; an estimate that includes care and education providers from all sectors. Yet, as Chapter 3 points out, existing data collection approaches often focus only on one sector, such as Head Start or center child care. It is difficult to create a composite picture when the data collection instruments for different sectors of early care and education do not ask for the same information or do so in the same way. Furthermore, existing data collection efforts at both the state and national level tend to have a "blind spot" with respect to those who do not identify themselves as teachers or professionals, including those who are not paid for caring for children. Yet, to exclude such providers from efforts at support, training, or education would be missing an important component of the workforce—families, friends, and neighbors are caring for substantial numbers of young children. Chapter 3 goes beyond identifying these critical issues in the measurement of the workforce to proposing very specific steps that national and state data collection efforts could take to ask questions in ways that would encompass all sectors of the workforce.

Turning to the second question, the research on the effects of early childhood professional development lacks precision in regard to the issue of investing in different types of training and education. Chapter 2 points to a lack of agreement in definitions that creates serious impediments to summarizing findings across studies. For example, some studies use the term *training* to refer to any courses or workshops as long as they include some content pertaining to early childhood development, whereas others use the term to refer strictly to community-based training, reserving the term *education* to courses taken in institutions of higher education. If a state early childhood task force is consulting the research to determine whether to invest in community-based training, in strengthening institutions of higher education with a focus on early childhood, or both, then this blurring of definitions creates barriers to finding the needed information. Chapter 2 goes beyond the "diagnosis" of the problem to very specific recommendations for creating clear and consistent definitional distinctions.

Even if researchers were to use consistent definitions, research is lacking on some aspects of early childhood professional development. For example, Chapter 4 addresses the linkages between qualifications and the quality of early care and education environments utilizing the definitional distinctions recommended in Chapter 2. The term *training* is used for workshops and courses taken outside of formal educational settings, and the term *education* is used for courses within formal education. Once the definitions become distinct, it becomes clear that the research to date focuses heavily on education, providing very limited information on the potential importance of training, which has been considered primarily in family child care settings. Yet, the potential importance of training is a significant issue across types of early care and education. Again underscoring the lack of precision in the existing research base, Chapter 4 notes that the research to date tends to ask the question, "Is *more* professional development *better?*" rather than, "Are there key *thresholds* for professional development? Is it clear, for example, that the quality of the environment or children's outcomes differ when an early childhood professional has a bachelor's degree as opposed to some college?" In addition, the research tends to stop at an examination of the relation of professional development to the quality of the early childhood environment, rather than asking whether professional development is related to children's development.

Turning to the third question noted previously, the research on professional development is lacking in precision in the sense that it has not focused extensively on effective strategies for covering specific content areas, such as early literacy or mathematical skills. Chapter 11, which focuses on the new standards for early childhood professional development of the National Association for the Education of Young Children (NAEYC), provides historical context for this gap. Two instructional approaches for young children have traditionally been seen as antithetical—an approach in which the child's play and exploration provide the impetus for development (and the role of the early childhood professional is to support play and exploration) and an approach involving direct instruction (in which the role of the early childhood professional is instruction). Focusing on content areas such as early mathematics or literacy was seen as useful only for direct instruction approaches, which in turn have not been seen as developmentally appropriate.

Chapter 11 points to the progress being made to set aside the perspective that child-led and teacher-led instructional approaches are entirely antithetical. It discusses a perspective that encourages an integration of both approaches—for example, through intentional structuring of the care and education environment to encourage children's exploration of specific content. Furthermore, this chapter underscores the support in the newly revised NAEYC standards for preparation of early childhood professionals in specific content areas.

Exciting new steps are being taken to create and evaluate professional development approaches focusing on such content areas as early literacy development, early mathematical skills, and children's social and emotional development. Chapters 6, 7, and 8 identify critical issues emerging in the new work in each of these content areas. Specific preparation approaches are described along with the evidence from evaluations, although in some instances the approaches are so recent that evaluations are ongoing or just now being launched.

As noted in the fourth question, policy makers may ask the question of whether their focus should be only on strengthening education and training or whether other aspects of early childhood professional development should also be strengthened. Chapter 5 suggests that it would be useful to broaden the "window" on professional development to include such assets as membership in a professional organization and exposure to certain forms of supervision.

This chapter presents research from four Midwestern states indicating that a certain number of assets predicts quality, raising the possibility that assets may be able to cumulate to substitute for others. This work takes a major step toward identifying which assets alone and in combination predict quality.

States will be concerned not only about what types of approaches to invest in to increase the number and skills of their early childhood workforce, but also what *systems* to put in place to expand and improve their workforce, as noted in the fifth question. Newly emerging research is beginning to suggest approaches that can be implemented as systems. For example, Chapter 9 proposes that a system of preparation should focus immediately and directly on providing feedback to early childhood educators on the practices they are implementing in the classroom. It suggests that the adoption of curricula or attainment of certification or degrees do not assure implementation; that these are distal rather than immediate or proximal indicators of professional development. This chapter describes new research focusing on a system emphasizing observation and feedback on instructional quality and emotional climate in the early childhood classroom.

Chapter 10 identifies the alignment between early learning goals for young children that a state may have articulated in its early learning guidelines and the actual content of coursework in early childhood that qualifies for a Child Development Associate (CDA) credential, associate's (AA), or bachelor's (BA) degree as a critical issue. The authors pioneer a methodology for assessing the degree to which the content of a course of study within a state corresponds to its goals for young children's learning and development. They caution that there is variation even within a level of professional development, such as the AA, in the degree to which specific content is covered and the way in which it permits the integration of knowledge and practice. Although the pilot study they describe focuses on early literacy, the methodology can readily be applied to other content areas within a state's early learning guidelines. Here again, a gap is identified and a course for future practice and research is identified.

Turning to the final question, because state budgets are tight, policy makers and those implementing professional development approaches are very likely to be concerned about the cost of differing strategies for increasing the size and skills of their workforce relative to the benefits that can be expected from alternative strategies. Although economic approaches such as cost-benefit analysis have certainly been implemented in research on early childhood development, this has occurred primarily in assessing intensive early childhood interventions. As Chapter 12 notes, tools for cost–benefit analysis are available but have not been applied to the issue of early childhood professional development. The chapter provides a guide to how cost–benefit analysis and related strategies could be applied to help decide among alternative approaches to strengthening and expanding the early childhood workforce.

An economic perspective suggests the importance of thinking not only about strategies directly targeting professional development but also about the possibility that market strategies, or strategies aimed at affecting the supply or demand for child care, may indirectly affect professional development. Strategies aimed at providing parents with better information about child care quality, such as through systems providing ratings of child care facilities, have the potential to affect the demand for higher quality care. Early evidence from an evaluation of such a strategy in New York state, described in Chapter 13, suggests that child care providers begin to work toward meeting the criteria for higher ratings when they volunteer to have their facilities included in the rating system. Such efforts may result in child care facilities improving the qualifications of their workers. The critical issue raised in this chapter is the need to think more broadly about how improvements in professional development might be brought about—to consider market effects of broader quality improvement strategies as well as more targeted approaches.

Taking all of these questions into account, what are the most important challenges that will need to be addressed to move forward both practice and research concerning early childhood professional development? The concluding chapters of the book take a step back and provide a perspective on overarching issues. Chapter 14 proposes that addressing three issues will be central to improving the quality of early childhood care and education across sectors: using a definition of quality that is applicable across all sectors, moving toward an understanding of the qualifications of early childhood workforce that rests on directly observed behavior with children, and developing a system for monitoring quality on an ongoing basis. Chapter 15 focuses on specific steps that can be taken to enhance the applied utility of future research on professional development of the early childhood workforce for both policy and practice. The utility of research requires an understanding of the multiple policies that pertain to early care and education and of the points in the process of formulating and implementing policy in which research is most useful. The application of research in policy and practice will also depend on the rigor of the research (e.g., utilization of experimental designs when possible) and on formulating research questions that are of importance to those making and implementing policy. Given that key policy and practice decisions in early care and education are made at the state and local as well as national levels, the chapter underscores the need for research at the state and local levels as well as research that is national in scope.

This book, then, identifies critical issues in early childhood professional development with the aim of moving both research and practice forward. The book is organized into four sections in which emerging work is identifying new approaches. A concluding section provides an overview of the implications of this new set of approaches for research and for policy.

- Section I focuses on *defining and describing the workforce* as a key step toward assessing the needs for expansion and improvement. Following a section introduction, chapters in this part of the book focus on how best to make progress in terms of defining and measuring the workforce (Chapter 2); on improving efforts to get accurate estimates of the size and characteristics of the workforce (Chapter 3); on the findings to date, gaps, and next steps in the research looking at the linkages between qualifications and the quality of the early care and education environment (Chapter 4); and on the full set of assets that could be considered in describing the workforce and how these work together to predict quality (Chapter 5).

- Section II describes *strategies for going beyond a focus on extent of preparation to a focus on the content of preparation* in strengthening the early childhood workforce. Following the Section II introduction, chapters focus on the progress being made in developing and evaluating professional development approaches specifically focusing on early language and literacy (Chapter 6); on early mathematical skills (Chapter 7); and self-regulation as a key component of children's social and emotional development (Chapter 8).

- Section III moves to the issue of *systems or models for improving professional development of the early childhood workforce.* After an introductory overview, chapters in this part of the book address the possibility of implementing a model focusing directly on teacher–child interaction (Chapter 9); on a methodology piloted in the state of Ohio for assessing the alignment between goals for early learning and the specific content covered in early childhood professional development at different levels of certification or higher education (Chapter 10); and on the new NAEYC standards for early childhood professional development as a framework for assessing professional development in institutions of higher learning through the National Council for Accreditation of Teacher Education (NCATE) review and accreditation process (Chapter 11).

- Section IV turns to the role of *economic analysis* in weighing differing approaches to expanding and improving early childhood professional development. The section introduction notes the importance of economic analyses in this field of work. Chapters then focus on how cost–benefit analysis could be used to guide decisions on strengthening the early childhood workforce (Chapter 12) and how approaches focusing on affecting dynamics in the early childhood care and education market have the potential to affect professional development of the workforce (Chapter 13).

- Section V focuses on the *implications of the findings for policy and practice as well as research.* The section introduction notes how the gaps in the research identified throughout the book can be used to build toward new directions. Chapters address the steps that the authors perceive as necessary in order to improve the quality of early care and education in general and the qualifications of the early childhood workforce more specifically (Chapter 14), as well as identify steps to ensure that research in this area has both rigor and utility (Chapter 15).

## REFERENCES

Administration for Children and Families, Head Start Bureau. (2002). *Program information report.* Retrieved May 4, 2005, from http://www.acf.hhs.gov/programs/hsb/programs/pir

Balanced Budget Act of 1997, PL 105-33.

Barnett, W.S., Hustedt, J.T., Robin, K.B., & Schulman, K.L. (2004). *The state of preschool: 2004 state preschool yearbook.* Rutgers: The National Institute for Early Education Research, The State University of New Jersey.

Bowman, B., Donovan, M.S., & Burns, M.S. (Eds.). (2000). *Eager to learn: Educating our preschoolers.* Washington, DC: National Academy Press.

Halpern, R. (1999). After-school programs for low-income children: Promises and challenges. *The Future of Children: When School Is Out, 9*(2), 81–95.

Isenberg, J.P. (2000). The state of the art in early childhood professional preparation. In *New teachers for a new century: The future of early childhood professional preparation* (pp. 17–48). Jessup, MD: U.S. Department of Education, ED Publishing.

Kinukawa, A., Guzman, L., & Lippman, L. (2004). *National estimates of child care and subsidy receipt for children ages 0 to 6: What can we learn from the National Household Education Survey?* Washington, DC: Child Trends.

National Center for Education Statistics. (2001). *National Household Education Survey: Early childhood program participation.* Washington, DC: Institute of Education Sciences, U.S. Department of Education.

National Center for Education Statistics. (March, 2003). *Prekindergarten in U.S. public schools: 2000–2001.* Washington, DC: Institute of Education Sciences, U.S. Department of Education.

National Institute of Child Health and Human Development Early Child Care Research Network. (1996). Characteristics of infant child care: Factors contributing to positive caregiving. *Early Childhood Research Quarterly, 11,* 269–306.

National Institute of Child Health and Human Development Early Child Care Research Network. (2000). Characteristics and quality of child care for toddlers and preschoolers. *Applied Developmental Science, 4*(3), 116–135.

National Survey of America's Families. (2002). *Assessing the new federalism.* Washington, DC: Urban Institute.

No Child Left Behind (NCLB) Act of 2001, PL 107-110, 20 U.S.C. §6301 *et seq.*

Personal Responsibility and Work Opportunity Reconciliation Act of 1996 (PRWORA), PL 104-193, 42 U.S.C.

Shonkoff, J.P., & Phillips, D.A. (Eds.). (2000). *From neurons to neighborhoods: The science of early childhood development.* Washington, DC: National Academy Press.

U.S. Census Bureau. (2000). *P54: Presence of own children under 18 years by age of own children and employment status for females 16 years and over.* Washington, DC: Author.

Vandell, D.L., & Su, H. (1999). Child care and school-age children. *Young Children, 54*(6), 62–71.

# Toward Better Definition and Measurement of Early Childhood Professional Development

STEPHANIE M. CURENTON

The *Good Start, Grow Smart* initiative has asked states to examine their training and educational plans for early childhood professionals across both formal and informal care and education environments. At the same time, federal policy makers have asked researchers to help identify how to invest most effectively in early childhood professional development. Unfortunately, the research literature pertaining to the early childhood workforce precludes researchers from making confident and consistent recommendations to policy makers because the literature is riddled with a fundamental problem: poor definition and measurement of the early childhood professional workforce. The chapters in Section I describe the problems with definition and measurement and identify suggestions to increase clarity and agreement.

Chapter 2 turns from the issue of who should be included when defining the early childhood workforce to the problem of what criteria researchers should use to measure professional development. Across studies there is little consistency regarding measurement approaches, which hinders the field from determining what aspects of professional development matter most for promoting quality care environments and positive child outcomes.

The authors of Chapter 2 conducted a detailed classification of measurement approaches used in large federal studies and studies published in peer-reviewed journals. The authors characterize professional development as having three components: 1) education (professional development that occurs within the formal educational system), 2) training (professional development that occurs outside of the formal education system—e.g., through child care resource and referral agencies), and 3) certification (the attainment of specific state and local credentials with specified requirements). They note problems with measuring all three of these components, but the most serious problems are in the measurement of training. Although researchers often collect detailed information (e.g., the number of workshops, number of course credit hours, training hours), there is no standard method to summarize the amount of training a provider has received. As a result, researchers often collapse the more detailed information into simple binary categories such as training and no training. Furthermore, there is a lack of agreement as to what the term *training* encompasses. One researcher may use it to refer to both community-based workshops and to higher education degrees in early childhood; on the contrary, another researcher may use *training* to refer only to community-based workshops. As suggested later (in Chapter 4), such measurement problems prevent researchers from reaching appropriate conclusions regarding training when summarizing results across studies.

Chapter 3 notes that it is essential to have accurate estimates of the size of the early childhood workforce in order to effectively determine how many professionals are needed to care for children younger than age 6. It is also important to have an accurate estimate of the characteristics of the workforce in order for policy makers to strategize about how to strengthen professionals' knowledge and skills. Across both national and state data collection, however, there is a lack of consensus as to who should be included when defining the early childhood workforce. For instance, should estimates include only those working in the role of primary and assistant caregivers/teachers, or should estimates also include early childhood specialists, such as those helping children with special needs?

These definitional issues are compounded by the fact that researchers conducting state and national surveys may word questions in a manner that inadvertently excludes individuals in particular sectors of the early care and education field. For example, questions specifically addressing teachers may unintentionally exclude providers who do not self-identify as teachers or educators, such as paid friends and relatives or family child care providers.

Many states have collected data to estimate the size and characteristics of their early childhood workforces, but there is a lack of agreement in the categories and definitions used across state surveys, which prevents the use of state surveys to arrive at a cross-state picture. In addition, the authors' review of the state level surveys indicates that some surveys have low response rates and that states do not frequently update the survey information.

The two final chapters in this section examine the links between professional development and the quality of care and education settings. Chapter 4 applies the Chapter 2 distinctions among education, training, and certification to the existing research. When the terms for the components of professional development are used in a clear and consistent way, the gaps in the existing research become much more clear. It becomes evident, for example, that researchers have focused on education rather than on training. This review points to the need for research to address different questions, going beyond the issue of "Is more professional development better?" to "What types of professional development are most effective?"

Building on data collected by a consortium of Midwestern states, Chapter 5 examines the links between provider-level qualifications and quality of early childhood environments. The chapter authors use the metaphor of a bread basket to describe 14 markers of professional development. Their research indicates that at least eight servings from the bread basket are needed in order to observe higher quality in early childhood settings. They suggest that it may not be necessary to have particular markers of professional development but, rather, to surpass a threshold in terms of the total number.

The chapters in Section I clearly delineate the problems with defining and measuring professional development in the early childhood workforce, and the authors provide insightful suggestions for future directions. Chapter 2 suggests gaining further insight into the measurement of professional development by carrying out new analyses with existing datasets where the raw data on professional development were quite detailed. Another proposed suggestion, put forth in Chapter 3, is to extend the federal and state data collection efforts on the early childhood workforce to involve all sectors of the workforce, including those paid family, friend, and neighborhood providers who do not label themselves as teachers. Because so many children receive care from family, friends, and neighbors, researchers and policy makers need to understand the characteristics and needs of these providers in order to successfully reach and support them. Chapter 4 suggests the need to examine thresholds, or levels, of professional development, rather than continuing to simply examine whether more is better. Finally, Chapter 5 introduces the important concept that specific facets of professional development need to be studied in combination.

Stakeholders from both the research and policy communities need to continue the discussion of how to define and measure professional development more effectively in order to agree on what next steps need to be taken. In February 2004, the Child Care Bureau and the Office of the Assistant Secretary for Planning and Evaluation of the Department of Health and Human Services sponsored *Defining and Measuring Early Childhood Professional Development.* This workshop articulated potential future directions that have become the focus of a steering committee consisting of policy makers, practitioners, and researchers. This committee includes representatives from federal agencies as well as the National Association of Child Care Resource and Referral Agencies (NACCRRA), the National Association for the Education of Young Children, the National Registries Alliance, Council for Professional Recognition, and researchers with background in federal and state surveys and administrative data. Specific steps being explored include an effort by the National Registries Alliance to develop a consistent categorization of the content of training, and NACCRRA's development of a survey for child care resource and referral agency directors that focuses on the nature and extent of training activities. Such work has the potential to improve our estimates of the early childhood workforce, to increase our understanding of which components of professional development contribute most to quality, and to enhance our design of a career lattice that will facilitate the progress of individuals in the workforce.

CHAPTER 2

# Defining and Measuring Professional Development in Early Childhood Research

KELLY L. MAXWELL, CATHIE C. FEILD, AND RICHARD M. CLIFFORD

This chapter provides a foundation for the rest of the book by examining a very basic yet critical question: How is professional development defined and measured in early childhood research? Before the other chapters address the more complex questions of the relationships among professional development, quality care and education, and child outcomes, one must understand how *professional development* itself is defined and measured. The deceptively simple question regarding definitions and measurement belies the complexity and, sometimes, confusion evident in the early childhood research. This chapter, based on early childhood research, seeks to address the question by undertaking a review of studies and their measures in the areas of education, training, and credentials.

## SELECTION OF STUDIES FOR REVIEW

We identified studies by conducting literature searches using the Education Index, Education Resources Information Center (ERIC), and PsycINFO databases and by reviewing reference lists of published articles. Studies in the review were published between 1988 and 2003, and they measured professional development of lead teachers or family child care providers. We focused the review on studies reported in peer-reviewed articles as a means of quality control; we assumed that studies reported in peer-reviewed journals had undergone a rigorous review process and met high standards of research quality. We limited the review to those studies that included at least 50 teachers or family child care providers because we wanted to focus the review on major studies with relatively large samples of teachers or providers. We limited the studies to those conducted in the United States because we were interested in examining how professional development was defined and measured in this country. Studies of community-based child care, public school preschool, Head Start, and family child care were included. Children served in these settings included infants, toddlers, and preschoolers.

This chapter was partially supported by the Foundation for Child Development. The views expressed in this chapter are those of the authors and may not reflect those of the funding agency.

Measure is the unit of analysis for this review. As a first step in the review process, we requested copies of the measures used to obtain information about the professional development of teachers and providers for each study that met the previously described criteria. *Study* was defined as a single overall data collection effort. There could be multiple peer-reviewed articles published from one study. A list of each measure, along with its corresponding article(s), is provided in this chapter's appendix. Of the 23 studies that met the inclusion criteria, 5 were excluded because the measures were not available. The remaining 18 studies yielded 16 measures that were included in the analysis. In 14 studies, there was a one-to-one correspondence between measure and study; that is, one measure was used in one study. The National Institute of Child Health and Human Development (NICHD) Early Child Care Research Network Study (1996, 1999, 2000, 2002; also Clarke-Stewart, Vandell, Burchinal, O'Brien, & McCartney, 2002) used three different measures that included questions about professional development: one for family child care providers, one for center-based staff serving children 15–36 months, and one for center-based staff serving children 54 months. These measures had some small differences but were generally similar and, thus, were considered as one measure and counted only once in the analysis. Three other studies—the Family Child Care Study (Burchinal, Howes, & Kontos, 2002), Adding Two School Age Children Study (Howes & Norris, 1997), and Family Child Care Training Study (Kontos, Howes, & Galinsky, 1996)—used the same measure; this measure was coded only once. Thus, 16 measures were analyzed for this chapter.

We also reviewed nine measures from "studies of note." We included the measures from these studies, such as the national Head Start Families and Child Experiences Survey (FACES; Zill et al., 2001) because we believe the studies are important to the early childhood field, are either national or multistate in scope, and meet all of the inclusion criteria except that they have not been published in peer-reviewed journals. For eight of these studies, there was a one-to-one correspondence between measure and study. The ninth study, the Profile of Child Care Settings (Kisker, Hofferth, Phillips, & Farquahar, 1991), used two different versions of measures: one for center-based teachers and one for family child care providers. We considered these versions as one measure because the professional development questions were very similar. The measures and reports from these studies of note are also listed in the appendix.

Finally, it is important to note that the unit of analysis—measure—for this chapter is different from the unit of analysis in other chapters. Chapter 4, for example, uses results published in peer-reviewed articles as the unit of analysis. This difference reflects the distinct purposes of the chapters.

## Defining Professional Development

Based on the review, no common definition of *professional development* exists. Researchers did not provide explicit statements about the meaning of various professional development terms in the text of articles and reports. They instead implicitly defined the terms by operationalizing them in their measures. The terms were defined by the way the professional development questions were asked in the measures—information to which most readers of the articles and reports would not have access. Because no explicit definitions were provided, we analyzed the original measures themselves to determine how researchers addressed the topic of professional development. When analyzing the measures, we developed and applied our own definition of *professional development* because no common implicit definition emerged from the measures themselves.

We identified three components of professional development: education, training, and credential. *Education* is defined as the professional development activities that occur within a formal education system. Most measures addressed two aspects of education: overall level of education and content-specific education (including both academic major and coursework). *Training* is defined as the professional development activities that occur outside the formal education system. Training activities do not lead to a degree and may sometimes be referred to as *in-service* or *informal training*. *Credential* does not clearly fall into either the education or training category because the organizations that grant credentials are typically not the same ones that provide the requisite knowledge. Thus, *credential* is described as a third component of professional development.

The research itself is not nearly as neat as these definitions suggest. The three categories were often intermixed in the measures, and the terminology was not used consistently. We recognize the limitations of imposing definitions onto a body of research but believe that this is the best way to describe adequately how professional development is defined and measured in the early childhood field.

The next three sections of this chapter focus on the three components of professional development. For each component, we describe how it is measured and summarize key findings from the review. The final section draws broader conclusions from the review and makes recommendations for future directions.

## EDUCATION

*Education* is defined in this chapter as the professional development activities occurring within the formal education system. Two major aspects of education are described: levels of education and content of education. These two fundamentally different approaches to measuring education reflect the substantive issue in the field of whether it is overall educational attainment—regardless of content—or attainment of education about young children that matters to the quality of the environment and children's development.

## Levels of Education

A question about the general level of education obtained, without respect to the content of that education, was included in 15 of the 16 measures (94%, plus all measures from the nine studies of note). Of the 15 studies that included a general question about education level, 13 (87%) limited the question to the highest level attained. This is an efficient way to collect the data because the highest level of education achieved usually encompasses all lower levels.

The categories of education levels measured varied greatly but generally can be grouped into eight areas: 1) less than a high school diploma or general equivalency diploma (GED), 2) high school diploma or GED, 3) more than high school but less than college, 4) some college but no degree, 5) associate's degree, 6) bachelor's degree, 7) more than a bachelor's degree but less than a master's degree, and 8) master's or higher degree. The range of categories was wide, with most measures including a full spectrum of choices from less than a high school diploma to a graduate degree. Table 2.1 presents the number of measures that collected information about various levels of education.

Across measures, several different phrases were used to determine participants' levels of education. For instance, for the category "less than a high school diploma," the most commonly asked question was whether teachers or providers had some high school education but no degree. Measures from one peer-reviewed study, the National Early Childhood Teachers Study (Saluja, Early, & Clifford, 2002), and three studies of note—FACES (Zill et al., 2001), Head Start Family and Child Care Evaluation Study (Faddis, Ahrens-Gray, & Klein, 2000), and the National Center for Early Development and Learning (NCEDL) Multi-state Study of Pre-Kindergarten (Clifford et al., in press)—asked specifically about education levels at eighth

**Table 2.1.**   Levels of education measured

| Level of education | Peer-reviewed studies | Studies of note |
|---|---|---|
| Less than a high school diploma | 11 of 15 (73%) | 6 of 9 (67%) |
| High school diploma or GED | 15 of 15 (100%) | 7 of 9 (78%) |
| More than high school, less than college | 2 of 15 (13%) | 5 of 9 (56%) |
| Some college, but no degree | 12 of 15 (80%) | 5 of 9 (56%) |
| Associate's degree | 11 of 15 (73%) | 7 of 9 (78%) |
| Bachelor's degree | 14 of 15 (93%) | 9 of 9 (100%) |
| More than a bachelor's degree, less than a master's degree | 11 of 15 (73%) | 2 of 9 (22%) |
| Master's degree or higher | 14 of 15 (93%) | 7 of 9 (78%) |

grade or less. General terminology such as "have not completed high school" or "less than high school" was used sometimes. In these instances, one does not know the highest grade completed (e.g., fifth or eleventh grade). A few of the measures in peer-reviewed studies listed a GED separately from a high school diploma.

Two measures from peer-reviewed studies and five from studies of note included education categories for vocational or technical school beyond high school, although two additional measures combined vocational school with some college or an associate's degree (i.e., NICHD Caregiver Interview and the Family Day Care Provider Questions). This highlights one of the difficulties in categorizing and quantifying the information obtained from the measures—the categories cannot be disaggregated to investigate the relationship of more precise levels of education to other variables.

All of the studies in peer-reviewed journals and studies of note that measured education included questions about college experience or degrees. As seen in Table 2.1, most of the measures asked about terminal degrees (e.g., associate's, bachelor's). However, many also included a category for some college but no degree. Researchers may include this "some college" category because they believe teachers or providers who have taken some college courses, even if they do not have a degree, are different from those who have not. The "some college" category, however, may include people who have taken just one college course as well as those who are one course away from having a bachelor's degree.

For one of the studies of note that gathered information about public school prekindergarten programs (Smith, Kleiner, Parsad, & Farris, 2003), only one question about formal education was included: how many prekindergarten teachers did not have a bachelor's degree. This suggests that some of the variation in measures may be due to assumptions about the study participants. In public school settings, one would assume that most teachers have a bachelor's degree. Finally, many measures listed options beyond a bachelor's degree, ranging from "at least one year of coursework beyond a bachelor's degree" to "doctoral degree" or, in one, case "law degree."

***Reported versus Measured***    All but one study reported education categorically, similar to how the data were gathered. The Early Childhood Job Satisfaction Study (Jorde-Bloom, 1988) assigned values to these categories and reported mean level of education. None of the studies that separated GED from high school diploma in the measures reported these two categories separately. Overall, slightly fewer degree categories were reported than measured. The most frequently reported categories of education in peer-reviewed articles were: 1) less than a high school degree, 2) high school degree or GED, 3) some college, 4) associate's degree, 5) bachelor's degree, and 6) bachelor's degree or higher.

## Content of Education

Two aspects of the content of formal education—major and coursework related to early childhood education—were analyzed for this review. All of the measures for studies published in peer-reviewed journals and those for seven of the nine studies of note included at least one question about the content of education. A question about education major was included in 13 of 16 (81%) measures from peer-reviewed studies, as well as in 6 of 9 measures from studies of note. Seven of 13 (54%) peer-reviewed studies (and 1 study of note) asked about major at the highest degree obtained only, and 6 of 13 (46% and 8 studies of note) asked about major for each degree obtained (i.e., if respondents had multiple degrees, such as associate's, bachelor's, and master's degrees). Table 2.2 shows the different approaches used to measure major.

The other aspect of education identified when reviewing measures was coursework—content, amount, and timing. Questions about coursework were included in 13 of 16 (81%) measures from peer-reviewed studies and in 3 of 9 measures from studies of note. The questions typically asked whether respondents had taken *any* coursework related to early childhood education/child development (ECE/CD) or, less frequently, asked more specifically about the content of the ECE/CD coursework (e.g., curriculum planning, working with parents, health and safety). Table 2.3 indicates the number of measures that asked about various aspects of coursework.

***Reported versus Measured*** A little more than half of the studies that measured early childhood education (i.e., majors or coursework) reported it in one or more peer-reviewed articles. The broad category of early childhood, child development, or a related area was the most frequently reported education content category. Only one study (Snider & Fu, 1990) reported more specifically on topics covered within early childhood coursework. Most articles reported early childhood education at the level of bachelor's degree, associate's degree, some college courses, or high school. Few studies reported

**Table 2.2.** Approaches used to measure education major

| Education major options | Peer-reviewed studies | Studies of note |
| --- | --- | --- |
| Early childhood education/ child development (ECE/CD)– related major only | 5 of 13 (38%) | 3 of 6 (50%) |
| ECE/CD–related major plus fill in the blank option | 3 of 13 (23%) | 0 |
| Multiple majors from which to select, such as elementary education or psychology | 2 of 13 (15%) | 2 of 6 (33%) |
| Fill in the blank only | 3 of 13 (23%) | 1 of 6 (17%) |

**Table 2.3.**    Approaches used to measure coursework

| Coursework questions | Peer-reviewed studies | Studies of note |
|---|---|---|
| Asked one question about ECE/CD (early childhood education/ child development)–related coursework in general | 11 of 13 (85%) | 3 of 3 (100%) |
| Included a question about the specific content of ECE/CD coursework | 2 of 13 (15%) | 0 |
| Included a student teaching or practicum question | 3 of 13 (23%) | 0 |
| Asked about where the coursework occurred (e.g., high school, community college, university) | 12 of 13 (92%) | 2 of 3 (67%) |
| Asked about coursework taken in the past year | 3 of 13 (23%) | 1 of 3 (33%) |
| Asked about coursework taken ever | 10 of 13 (77%) | 2 of 3 (67%) |
| Asked about the number of course hours taken | 1 of 13 (8%) | 1 of 3 (33%) |

data about early childhood education at the graduate level. Most studies that measured both general education and early childhood education reported both (instead of focusing solely on one). Approximately one fourth of the studies that obtained information on both general education and early childhood education reported only early childhood education data.

## Key Findings

All of the studies reviewed measured some aspect of education. All of the measures included categories of education (e.g., high school degree, bachelor's degree), rather than years of education (e.g., 12, 16). The number and range of categories varied across studies. This mirrors the wide range of levels of education present among caregivers and teachers in the early childhood field. Nationally, there is no standard education requirement for early childhood teachers outside the public school system. The wide range of categories was evident in studies of family child care, center-based child care, and Head Start. No categories were uniformly used across all measures.

The degree categories were sometimes very general or vague and may not have accurately captured information regarding teachers' or providers' formal education level. The "some college" category is most ambiguous, which may limit researchers' ability to test the effects of having some college education. If researchers hypothesize that teachers or providers with 3 years of college, for example, provide different environments for children compared with teachers or providers who have taken only one college-level course, then it would be important to measure college education at a more detailed level. In addition, some measures combined "some college" with "associate's degree" or "associate's degree" with "vocational school" to make one category, which prohibits an examination of the differential affects of these educational experiences.

The same point applies to various high school categories. If researchers hypothesize that teachers or providers with less than a high school diploma have similar effects on the environment and children, then the general category of "less than high school" is sufficient. If not, then a more detailed measurement of education may be needed. Also, a GED and high school diploma were often combined into one category when reported. If researchers are likely to combine these two categories in their analysis, either because there are very few teachers or providers in their studies who have GEDs or because the researchers do not hypothesize that providers with GEDs differ from those with high school diplomas, then the GED and high school diploma categories could be combined in the measurement question.

With regard to the content of education, most measures included at least one question regarding an early childhood education degree. A little more than half of the peer-reviewed studies asked about content for the highest degree only; the rest asked about content at various levels of education. Limiting the question to the highest degree only may bias the information obtained. If, for example, a teacher had an associate's degree in early childhood education and a bachelor's degree in business administration, then using the highest degree only would not permit researchers to know that he or she had a degree in early childhood education. The majority of studies also gathered information about early childhood coursework, although it was typically in the form of one general question about whether the participant had taken any coursework in early childhood education or a related area.

The information about education reported in peer-reviewed articles was less exhaustive than the information gathered in the measures. For example, a little more than half of the studies that measured early childhood education reported it in a peer-reviewed article. If the field wants to better understand the impact of the content of teachers' or providers' education, then researchers need not only to measure but also to analyze and report data about the content of early care and education. To test hypotheses such as whether general educational attainment or educational attainment in early childhood education matters most to children's development, more researchers must measure, analyze, and report data on the content of education.

It would also be helpful if the measures and analyses went beyond a simple "has" or "has not had" any early childhood education to a more detailed level about the type and extent of early childhood education. This more detailed level may help the field develop better theories about the relationships among teacher or provider knowledge and behavior, quality environments, and children's outcomes. The more detailed level of measurement will be challenging, though, because most research relies on self-reported information about course content. If course content is thought to be especially important, then the feasibility of other strategies for collecting these data may need to be explored (e.g., reviewing transcripts).

The range and combination of education categories measured and reported makes it difficult to compare findings across studies. Reducing variability in how education is measured and reported would increase the ability to compare findings across studies. As one possible strategy, the field could develop a core set of questions that researchers would agree to include in all of their study measures. If this core set of questions were small, researchers could easily supplement it with other questions related to their particular area of interest. For example, a core education question about highest degree obtained could include five response options: high school or GED, associate's degree, bachelor's degree, master's degree, and doctoral degree. If a researcher was interested in 1-year technical degrees, then he or she could add this category to the core question or include a separate question about this topic.

## TRAINING

No clear definition or consistent use of the term *training* emerged from the review of the literature. Often training was included with questions about education. For example, a measure might ask a teacher to select the highest level of early childhood education and training he or she had received, offering a list of options such as workshops, college courses, and associate's degree. Other measures included questions such as, "Have you had any early childhood courses or training workshops?" For these studies, the term *training* seemed to be used in the broadest sense to encompass professional development opportunities specific to early childhood that occur either inside or outside the formal education system. Less frequently, measures included a separate question about in-service or informal professional development opportunities.

Because of the varied use of the term *training* in the literature, we developed our own definition and applied this definition to the analysis of measures. As noted, *training* is defined as the professional development experiences that take place outside the formal education system. When both education and training were addressed in one question, we coded each separately when the data could be disaggregated. For questions that combined both elements in a way that could not be disaggregated (e.g., "Have you had any early childhood courses or training workshops?—Yes or no"), we coded them as training. Thirteen of 16 (81%) measures collected data about training (as did measures for 6 of 9 studies of note). Four general areas of training were covered: type, content, amount, and timing of training. Each of these is discussed next.

## Type of Training

The types of training most frequently measured were in-service training (7 of 13 or 54%, plus 3 of 6 studies of note), workshops (6 of 13 or 46%, plus 1 study of note), and conferences or workshops (4 of 13 or 31%, and no studies of note). Eight of the 13 measures from peer-reviewed studies (62%, plus 4 of 6 studies of note) asked about multiple types of training, ranging from two to eight different types. Of the 5 measures from peer-reviewed studies (38%) that listed only one type of training, most used a broad phrase such as "in-service training" or "conferences or workshops." Table 2.4 lists some of the

**Table 2.4.**   Descriptors of types of training found in measures reviewed

In-service training (at preschool or center)
Informal training
Correspondence or television course
Parent education class
Workshops at professional meetings
Training by referral or government agency
Workshops in the community (or other)
Conferences or workshops
Government agency or program
Internet
Resource library
Child care courses or workshops
Supervision and feedback
Visits to other child care programs
Teacher training
County-level professional organization meetings
State-level professional organization meetings
National-level professional organization meetings
Workshops in the county
College or agency
Videotapes and study materials in the home/center
Conferences
Support person who comes to center/home
Regional, state, or national professional meetings or conferences
Nurses' training or health courses
Teleconferencing or ICN distance learning
Continuing education or in-service training, type not specified
Other (fill in the blank)

descriptions of training found in the measures. Categories that combined elements of education and training, such as "college or agency" and "child care courses or workshops," were coded as training.

   ***Reported versus Measured***    Most of the studies with measures that included a question about the type of training reported something about this topic in a peer-reviewed article. However, most studies gathered more detailed training information than they reported. Very few reported information on more than one type of training. In addition, no single type of training was reported in more than two peer-reviewed articles—most likely because so many different phrases were used to capture the training information. For example, workshops were variously reported as in-service workshops, workshops in the community, workshops at professional meetings, or simply as workshops. Sometimes the articles reported information about training and education in a combined manner, such as "high school education plus a few workshop trainings in child development" (Howes, 1997).

## Content of Training

Of the 13 measures from peer-reviewed studies that collected data about training, 12 (92%, plus 5 of 6 from studies of note) gathered information about the content of training. Five of the 12 (42%, plus 2 of the 5 studies of note) asked about only one general topic: child development or early childhood related training. One measure from the peer-reviewed studies asked about Child Development Associate (CDA) training only. The remaining 6 measures from peer-reviewed studies included between 2 and 11 different content areas from which participants could choose. Table 2.5 lists some of the descriptors used to measure training content.

   ***Reported versus Measured***    Less than half of the studies that measured training content reported it in a peer-reviewed article. When training content was reported, the most common way of presenting the information was by collapsing all of the various training categories measured into one category: whether teachers or providers had no specialized training in early childhood.

## Training Amount and Timing

Of the 13 measures that asked about training, 5 (38%, plus 2 of 6 studies of note) asked about training within the past year only. Four of the 13 measures (31%, and 1 study of note) included a question about training both within the past year and ever. The remaining 4 measures (31%, plus 3 studies of note) asked about training ever, either explicitly by including the word *ever* in the

**Table 2.5.**   Training content areas measured in studies

Child development: cognitive/intellectual/language

Child development: social-emotional

Child development: physical

Child development: general/early childhood education

Curriculum planning/educational programming

Health and safety

Working with parents

Classroom or behavior management

Program administration

Working with staff

Child abuse

Domestic/family violence

Substance abuse

Stress reduction

Play

Parenting

Education

Child assessment and evaluation

Child care food program

Child's health issues (e.g., immunizations, childhood diseases)

Children with special needs

Multicultural education/curriculum/sensitivity

Related to your family child care program

CDA training

Providing case management services to families

Family health issues (e.g., AIDS, asthma)

Mental health issues

Advocacy

Family needs assessment/evaluation

Work/family conflict

Working with other agencies to assist families

Involving parents in program activities

Providing supervision to staff

Head Start principles and practices

CPR

Physical care of children

Social services

Discipline practice

*Key:* CDA = Child Development Associate credential; CPR = cardiopulmonary resuscitation.

question or implicitly by not mentioning any time period. Eight of the 13 measures (62%, plus 3 studies of note) tried to quantify the amount of training received by asking, for instance, the number of workshops or the number of hours of training received.

**Reported versus Measured**    Few of the studies that gathered information about amount of training reported the information in a peer-reviewed article. Among the 4 studies that asked about training within the past year *and* ever, 2 reported both findings in at least one peer-reviewed article.

## Key Findings

There was no consensus in the measures and literature reviewed regarding the definition of training. Sometimes the term *training* was used to describe in-service or informal professional development opportunities. Other times, *training* was used in a broad sense that encompassed professional development activities both within and outside the formal education system. Confusion about use of the term *training* was apparent in the measures as well as in the articles and reports.

Using our definition of *training* (i.e., professional development experiences that take place outside of the formal education system), almost all of the measures reviewed collected data on some aspect of training. Generally, training questions covered the type (e.g., workshop, on-site technical assistance) and content (e.g., child development) of training. More emphasis was given to training type than content in terms of the number of measures that covered the topic, the range of categories measured, and the items that were reported. The types of training measured varied widely, and terms or phrases were not used consistently.

Training content was most frequently analyzed and reported in the literature as a dichotomous variable—having or not having any specialized early childhood training. If the field wants to understand the impact of training content on teacher and provider behavior, environments, and child outcomes, then it may be useful to analyze and report two levels of training content. The first level could be the previously described general category—whether the person has had any specialized training. The second level could then provide more detailed information about the content of training (e.g., child development, health and safety).

We believe that much of the confusion in defining and measuring training is due to a lack of clear hypotheses about the impact of training on teachers, caregivers, classrooms, and children. Little research to date has provided the foundation needed to understand the impact of training and to develop specific hypotheses about training. Does the type of training really matter? If so, what type is better than another? Is on-site training, for example, better than off-site training? Does a workshop at a professional meeting differ from a workshop in the community? Similarly, what differences do researchers expect among teachers who have had certain training content? Other factors about training such as quality—a factor that is rarely measured—may matter more than either type or content.

The broader context of training is also important but not frequently measured. It is difficult to understand whether a particular amount of training is better or worse than expected without understanding the training requirements of employers and state agencies. Fifteen hours of training may mean something very different in a state that requires 5 hours per year as compared with a state that requires 30 hours per year. Only one of the peer-reviewed studies asked whether the employer or state required training.

## CREDENTIAL

Like the other aspects of professional development, credential was not defined or clearly operationalized in the early childhood research reviewed. The terms *credential, certificate,* and *license* were often used interchangeably, although they are not necessarily the same. This chapter uses the term *credential* because it is the broadest of the three terms, encompassing certification of individuals and accreditation of institutions as well as occupational licensing. Although each term means something slightly different, all three convey a certain status to the holders and provide some assurance to consumers that the holders are qualified to provide designated services. Usually, professional boards or associations are responsible for certification and state governments oversee occupational licensing (Jacobs, 1996). Darling-Hammond, Wise, and Klein noted a distinction between licensing in other professions and in teaching:

> Whereas professional boards establish standards for education and entry in professions such as medicine, nursing, architecture, accounting, and law, until fairly recently such boards have been absent in teaching. Instead, hundreds of individual state mandates have controlled what is taught—as well as the standards that are used to grant a teaching license. (1995, p. 9)

Certification, or licensing, in early childhood education is complicated by the bifurcated nature of the field. Certification for those working with children younger than age 5 is often handled by state departments of health and human services, whereas certification for those working with children in the early childhood age range of 5–8 years (or those working in public school preschool classrooms) is usually governed by state departments of education. Some have referred to the early childhood system as trifurcated because the federal government sets standards for Head Start teachers (Goffin & Day, 1994). The inconsistencies in certification and licensing requirements across states and agencies make it very difficult to understand the meaning of a particular certificate or license. People unfamiliar with the state or agency requirements would not know the amount or type of education received by a licensed person.

In our review, measures usually contained one or more questions about credentials, certificates, or licenses. Researchers used many different phrases to capture this information. Among the 16 measures reviewed, 14 (88%) included some type of credential question, as did measures for 8 of 9 studies of note. Some measures listed nine or more different types of credentials from which to choose, whereas others listed only one. To illustrate, Table 2.6 lists the different phrases used to capture credential information from the measures used in these four studies.

The variation in measuring credentials is not surprising, given the multiple ways these terms are used across states and agencies. For example, some of the options listed for credentials in the early childhood age range were: "early childhood certificate" and "state certificate in nursery/prekindergarten education." Some options were difficult to interpret, such as "college early childhood education certificate," or were very broad, such as "a teaching certif-

**Table 2.6.** Credential phrases from the National Child Care Staffing Study (NCCSS), National Institute of Child Health and Human Development (NICHD), National Early Childhood Teachers Study (NECTS), and the Early Childhood Job Satisfaction Study (ECJS).

|  | NCCSS | NICHD | NECTS | ECJS |
|---|---|---|---|---|
| State certificate or license in early childhood education | X | X | | |
| State certificate in nursery/prekindergarten education | | X | | |
| State elementary education certificate | X | X | | |
| State special education certificate | X | X | | |
| State secondary education certificate | X | X | | |
| Child Development Associate (CDA) credential | X | X | X | |
| Any teaching certificate or credential (fill in blank) | | | | X |
| Any kind of certificate or credential in early childhood education or child care | | X | | |
| Nursing license (RN or LPN) | X | | | |
| Social worker certification or license | X | | | |
| Certificate of Clinical Competence/ speech pathologist | X | | | |
| Psychologist certification or license | X | | | |
| Another state education certificate | X | X | | |
| Other credential, certificate, or license | X | X | | |

icate that requires at least a bachelor's degree." The wording for most of the state credentials did not permit one to distinguish across various state agencies; one could not tell whether the state credential was from the state department of education or the state department of health and human services.

The most frequently listed credential across measures was the Child Development Associate (CDA) credential. Among the 16 measures used in peer-reviewed studies, 14 asked about credentials; 11 (79%) of these included the CDA, as did 6 of the 8 studies of note that asked about credentials. Measures from 2 of the studies of note (FACES, NCEDL) included a question about the CDA separate from other types of credentials. For half of the measures in peer-reviewed studies (7 out of 14), the CDA was the *only* credential listed. The CDA was likely the most frequently mentioned credential because it is a national credential specifically designed for teachers of young children from birth to age 5, has existed for more than 25 years, and has been awarded to over 160,000 people since its inception (Council for Professional Recognition, 2003).

Although the CDA was the credential most frequently included in measures, the wording used in the CDA questions sometimes made it difficult to determine the intent of the question. Sometimes the phrase *CDA training* was used instead of *CDA* or *CDA credential*. *CDA training* could be interpreted to mean that the person has completed some of the training required for a CDA, has completed all the required training but has not completed other requirements, or has obtained the CDA credential. For purposes of this chapter, *CDA training* was coded as training and *CDA* and *CDA credential* were coded as receipt of credentials.

In reviewing the credential questions in measures, we also examined how researchers conceptualized credentials in relation to the other two components of professional development (i.e., education and training). Eight of 14 measures (57%) used in peer-reviewed studies that included some type of credential question (and 3 of 8 measures used in studies of note) separated the credential question from the other two categories of education and training. In other words, these measures included a question that asked solely about credentials. Credentials were listed as one of the options under an education question in 5 of the 14 measures (36%, plus 3 studies of note). The CDA credential was the only credential listed under an education question in 4 of 5 measures, suggesting that the CDA credential sometimes may be thought of as an education degree.

***Reported versus Measured***    Information about credentials was reported far less frequently than was collected. Although 14 measures asked about credentials, only 7 studies from peer-reviewed journals (plus 3 studies of note) reported data about credentials. Most of these reported the number of participants with the CDA credential. The credential information was combined with education in 3 of these 7 studies. For instance, one of the articles from the Cost, Quality, and Child Outcomes Study reported "Associate's degree or CDA" (Burchinal, Cryer, Clifford, & Howes, 2002), and one article from the NICHD study included in its analysis a category of "certification, vocational/adult education training or degree in related field" for the variable "specialized training" (Clarke-Stewart et al., 2002, p. 64). The NICHD study exemplifies the confusion among the use of all three terms—certification was combined with education for a variable called *specialized training.*

## Key Findings

The terms *credential, certificate,* and *license* were not used consistently in the reviewed early childhood research literature. Researchers sometimes used state-specific credential terms in the measures, which makes it difficult for people unfamiliar with the state to understand the credential. Most measures used in early childhood studies gathered data on some aspect of credential. The CDA credential was the most frequent type of credential included in measures, although the range of credentials varied across studies and included other early childhood-related credentials, as well as credentials in other areas such as nursing. About half of the measures included a separate question about credentials. The other half either included credentials with education or, less frequently, combined all three components—education, training, and credentials.

As stated previously, the term *credential* can encompass both certification and licensing, and professional boards or associations are usually responsible for certification whereas state governments are responsible for occupational licensing. Thus, a credential is not usually obtained during education or training; instead, it is the result of an additional effort undertaken after a person has received requisite education or training. In addition, the education component of some credentials (e.g., the CDA) may be completed through either educational or training experiences (Council for Professional Recognition, 1999). As a result, it may be useful for researchers to ask a separate question about credentials, rather than combining it with education or training. Within the credential question, it is also recommended that researchers use terminology consistently. For example, *CDA credential* is clearer than *CDA training.*

As requirements for early childhood teachers rise (e.g., Head Start standards, state prekindergarten standards) and move toward the bachelor's degree with some type of teacher licensure, it may be useful to include questions that specifically address teacher licenses granted by state departments of education. It is important to develop questions that include the state-specific language and yet can be understood by people outside the state. For example, the term *birth–kindergarten certificate* is more widely understood than *B–K certificate* (used in North Carolina to indicate that a person has specialized education to teach children from birth through kindergarten). Cross-state studies may provide direction for this task. If states have different credentials available from different agencies, then it is important to ask about each specifically (e.g. license from state department of education to teach children younger than age 5, certificate to work as a lead teacher in a child care center). However, as long as the field requires different credentials for teachers of young children depending on the age of the children and the settings in which they are served, it will be difficult to devise simple questions to accurately capture this information. Finally, researchers may want to carefully consider the options they include in the credential questions. As early childhood education credentials increasingly are available and required, it may not be as relevant to ask about credentials in other fields such as nursing or psychology.

## CONCLUSIONS AND RECOMMENDATIONS

Several conclusions can be drawn from the review of how professional development is defined and measured in early childhood research. This section presents the conclusions and suggests some recommendations for future directions.

### Conclusions

*There are no common definitions of professional development terms.* Our review indicated that the terms *education, training,* and *credential* were not explicitly defined or used consistently. None of the articles or reports reviewed provided explicit statements about the meaning of these terms. Rather, they were implicitly operationalized by the way the questions were asked in the measures. Of the three terms, general level of education is the area in which there was most agreement. Most measures, for instance, included a fairly standard list of education levels from which to choose (e.g., high school, some college, associate's degree, bachelor's degree). There was much less consistency in the measurement of training, credentials, and the content of education. For example, sometimes all three elements were evident in the same question (e.g., workshops, degrees in early childhood education/child development, CDA credential).

*Without common definitions, the measurement of professional development cannot be consistent.* The topics covered, the number and range of categories used, and the wording of questions and categories varied considerably across instruments. With such wide variability on so many aspects, it is difficult to analyze data or synthesize findings across studies. Finally, the variability in wording may negatively affect the quality of data gathered. If study participants are not clear on the definitions of terms used (e.g., vocational training, some college), then they cannot be expected to accurately report the information.

*The lack of consensus is problematic for policy makers and practitioners as well as researchers.* Researchers sometimes use particular professional development terms because they are commonly used and known within a particular state.

In these cases, the confusion originates in anchoring the definition in specific state policies without providing the information about this context. One needs to know much more information than the title of the credential, such as the number and content of courses required to receive the credential, to understand the implications of having a particular credential. Practitioners, policy makers, and researchers may have difficulty interpreting findings in the literature if they do not fully understand how professional development was defined and measured in the study.

Confusion among the professional development components also exists outside the research arena. The CDA credential, for instance, includes examples of both training (e.g., through child care resource and referral agencies) and education (e.g., courses at community colleges) activities that can be used to meet the requirement of "120 clock hours of *formal education* [italics added]" (Council for Professional Recognition, 1999, pp. 11–12). Thus, resolving issues about definitions requires collaboration among researchers, policy makers, and practitioners.

*Of the three areas of professional development, training is the most problematic.* The term *training* was sometimes used in the literature to 1) describe specialized education in early childhood (e.g., college training in early childhood education), 2) encompass professional development activities within and outside of the formal education system, or 3) describe only informal or in-service professional development activities. Measurement of training was also inconsistent. Information about the types and content of training varied considerably across studies. Measuring training is problematic, in part, because of the relatively little research available to guide researchers' hypotheses. Most measures included more questions about type of training (e.g., workshops, on-site technical assistance) than content and often ignored other areas that may be more important, possibly because they are more difficult to measure (e.g., quality and quantity of the training).

*Researchers gather more data than they report.* Comparisons of the data collected in the study measures with the information reported in peer-reviewed articles showed that the information in the articles was always less extensive than the information collected. At some level, summarizing and condensing data are a necessary part of writing. However, the research reviewed for this chapter suggests that researchers consistently gather more data than they report. One might hope for a better balance between data collected and reported. This does not necessarily mean that researchers should report more data than they currently report. It may, in fact, suggest that researchers gather too much or too detailed data. Finally, although it may be tempting to recommend "mining" existing data sets because there are more data available than reported in the literature, we do not recommend this approach because we believe that an analysis of existing data would be severely limited by the wide variety of definitions and measurement questions used across studies.

*Professional development measures rely on self-report.* All of the measures reviewed relied on study participants to answer questions about their professional development activities through either written surveys or interviews. Accuracy of reporting and interpretation of the questions can be problematic for self-reported data and cannot be ignored as a potential bias in the research on professional development. How accurate is recall for questions such as the number of courses *ever* taken in early childhood education? Is there a better method for gathering this information? If not, then researchers may need to limit information gathered to topics and a time period that one can reasonably expect people to remember with relative accuracy. For surveys, respondents must interpret the research question before answering it. Some categories, such as "vocational education" or a "state credential in early childhood" may not be interpreted the way researchers intended. Both of these self-report issues potentially bias the research base on professional development.

*Problems are not restricted to any one early care and education setting.* There generally was no consistency within a type of child care setting, and there were no major systematic differences evident across settings (e.g., Head Start versus other center-based programs, center-based programs versus family child care, preschool versus infant toddler care). The variability in definitions and measurement was evident across studies regardless of the early care and education setting. Thus, it does not seem that the lack of consensus in definitions and measurement is due to different vocabularies and practices within different child care settings but rather to a lack of consensus within and across all child care settings.

## Recommendations

Based on our review of the measures used in research studies, we make the following recommendations for improving the definition and measurement of professional development in the early childhood field.

*Develop definitions and use them consistently.* Although it is difficult to encourage a large group of people to use terms similarly, common definitions and recommended uses of professional development terms would be beneficial. In this chapter, we present one proposed set of definitions for education, training, and credentials and hope that the broader early childhood field will use this work as a starting point for discussion. Federal and state agencies that fund early childhood research can help promote consistency by encouraging their staff and funded researchers to use similar definitions.

*Work toward consistency in measurement across studies.* Researchers will always need to adapt measurement tools to their particular study and research questions. However, it may be possible for a group of researchers to agree on a small common core of questions to measure particular aspects of professional development. Education is the area for which agreement will likely be easiest.

Defining terms similarly and including common questions in data collection instruments of different studies will greatly enhance the generalization of findings across studies. Public and private agencies that fund research could develop consortia to address these issues and develop agreements to use some common measurement approaches across studies. Developing a common core set of questions for professional development would increase comparability across studies, and keeping the core set of questions small would increase the likelihood of researchers using the core because they could then supplement it with their own research questions of interest.

*Expand data collection to include the context of professional development activities.* Our review of the measures and studies suggests that more must often be known about the context of professional development activities before appropriately interpreting the data, especially with regard to training and credentials. If researchers report the number of training activities in which a teacher or provider participated, readers typically know only whether that is better or worse than the sample mean. It may be more important to know whether the teacher or provider participated in the minimum required training or received much more training than required by the employer or state. Among all of the studies reviewed (i.e., peer-reviewed and studies of note), only one asked whether training was required by the employer or the state.

With regard to credentials, researchers typically used either very general terms (e.g., *early childhood credential*) or very specific terms (e.g., *North Carolina Child Care Credential*). Both types are problematic. General terms rely on the respondent to determine whether his or her particular credential fits the more general category. State-specific credentials are easily recognized by respondents in the state but are not known by respondents outside the state and readers of the research who are not familiar with the state. With most credential terms, readers of the research often do not know the particular requirements associated with the credential. For example, does the North Carolina Child Care Credential require a certain amount of college coursework or simply passing a state exam? Interpretation of the findings and cross-study comparisons would be easier if researchers provided additional contextual information in articles and reports.

*Use hypotheses to drive instrument development.* Researchers should clearly link their hypotheses to each question in their measures so that 1) unnecessary data are not collected and 2) data are collected in a way that allows researchers to test specific hypotheses about professional development issues. The development of a standard, core set of professional development questions with flexibility for researchers to add others may help minimize the collection of unnecessary data and maximize researchers' ability to test hypotheses and compare findings across studies. The current knowledge base could be used to develop consensus around promising hypotheses about professional development from which the core set of research questions could be developed. If researchers have hypotheses that are not addressed by these questions, then they could supplement the core with additional questions to meet their needs.

*Conduct additional research regarding the impact of professional development on teachers' behavior, the quality of care and education, and child outcomes.* Our review suggests that the variability evident in the measurement of education, training, and credentials is due in part to a lack of solid research regarding the effects of specific professional development activities on important teacher, caregiver, classroom, and child variables. Researchers may be casting their net widely, so to speak, because they are not sure what to expect. For example, what components of training matter most—type, content, quality, or quantity? The field needs additional, specific research that examines these types of important questions. Without such research, it will be difficult for researchers to develop specific hypotheses and narrow the scope of their measures. This future research could help refine the core professional development questions.

In closing, we realize the difficulty in moving toward consensus on the various professional development terms and on standard measurement approaches, but any move toward consensus is better than the current quagmire. Understanding the terms and ways in which they are measured is the foundation on which all research knowledge about early childhood professional development is built. Other chapters in this book review the research on important questions such as, "What is the impact of professional development on classroom quality?" This chapter serves as a warning to interpret these research findings carefully due to the lack of consensus and the wide variability in measuring the basic components of professional development—education, training, and credentials.

## REFERENCES

Abbott-Shim, M., Lambert, R., & McCarty, F. (2000). Structural model of Head Start classroom quality. *Early Childhood Research Quarterly, 15*(1), 115–134.

Bellm, D., Burton, A., Whitebook, M., Broatch, L., & Young, M. (2002). *Inside the pre-K Classroom: A study of staffing and stability in state-funded prekindergarten programs.* Washington, DC: Center for the Child Care Workforce.

Burchinal, M., Cryer, D., Clifford, R., & Howes, C. (2002). Caregiver training and classroom quality in child care centers. *Applied Developmental Science, 6,* 2–11.

Burchinal, M., Howes, C., & Kontos, S. (2002). Structural predictors of child care quality in child care homes. *Early Childhood Research Quarterly, 17,* 87–105.

Burchinal, M., Roberts, J., Riggins, R., Zeisel, S., Neebe, E., & Bryant, D. (2000). Relating quality of center child care to early cognitive and language development longitudinally. *Child Development, 21,* 339–357.

Buysse, V., Wesley, P., Bryant, D., & Gardner, D. (1999). Quality of early childhood programs in inclusive and noninclusive settings. *Exceptional Children, 65*(3), 301–314.

Clarke-Stewart, K.A., Vandell, D.L., Burchinal, M., O'Brien, M., & McCartney, K. (2002). Do regulable features of child-care homes affect children's development? *Early Childhood Research Quarterly, 17,* 52–86.

Clifford, R., Barbarin, O., Chang, F., Early, D., Bryant, D., Howes, C., Burchinal, M., & Pianta, R. (in press). What is pre-kindergarten? Trends in the development of a public system of pre-kindergarten services. *Applied Developmental Science.*

Cost, Quality, and Child Outcomes Study Team. (1995). *Cost, quality, and child outcomes in child care centers: Public report.* Denver: University of Colorado at Denver.

Council for Professional Recognition. (1999). Assessment system and competency standards for preschool caregivers. Washington, DC: Author.

Council for Professional Recognition. (2003). *About CDA national credentialing program.* Retrieved April 28, 2005, from http://www.cdacouncil.org/cda/whatis.htm

Darling-Hammond, L., Wise, A., & Klein, S. (1995). *A license to teach.* Boulder, CO: Westview Press.

Epstein, A. (1999). Pathways to quality in Head Start, public school, and private nonprofit early childhood programs. *Journal of Research in Childhood Education, 13*(2), 101–119.

Faddis, B., Ahrens-Gray, P., & Klein, E. (2000). *Evaluation of Head Start family child care demonstration, final report.* Washington, DC: U.S. Department of Health and Human Services, Administration on Children, Youth and Families.

Gable, S., & Halliburton, A. (2003). Barriers to child care providers' professional development. *Child and Youth Care Forum, 32*(3), 175–193.

Gilliam, W.S., & Marchesseault, C.M. (2005a). *From capitols to classrooms, policies to practice: State-funded prekindergarten at the classroom level.* New Haven, CT: Yale University Child Study Center.

Gilliam, W.S., & Marchesseault, C.M. (2005b). *From capitols to classrooms, policies to practice: State-funded prekindergarten at the classroom level. Part 1: Who's teaching our youngest students? Teacher education and training, experience, compensation and benefits, and assistant teachers.* New Haven, CT: Yale University Child Study Center.

Goffin, S., & Day, D. (Eds.). (1994). *New perspectives in early childhood teacher education: Bringing practitioners in the debate.* New York: Teachers College Press.

Holloway, S.D., Kagan, S.L., Fuller, B., Tsou, L., & Carroll, J. (2001). Assessing childcare quality with a telephone interview. *Early Childhood Research Quarterly, 16,* 165–189.

Howes, C. (1997). Children's experiences in center-based child care as a function of teacher background and adult:child ratio. *Merrill-Palmer Quarterly, 43,* 404–425.

Howes, C., & Norris, D. (1997). Adding two school age children: Does it change quality in family child care? *Early Childhood Research Quarterly, 12*(3), 327–342.

Howes, C., & Smith, E.W. (1995). Relations among child care quality, teacher behavior, children's play activities, emotional security, and cognitive activity in child care. *Early Childhood Research Quarterly, 10*(4), 381–404.

Howes, C., Whitebook, M., & Phillips, D. (1992). Teacher characteristics and effective teaching in child care: Findings from the National Child Care Staffing Study. *Child and Youth Care Forum, 21,* 399–414.

Jacobs, J.A. (1996). *Association law handbook* (3rd ed.). Washington, DC: American Society of Association Executives.

Jorde-Bloom, P. (1988). Factors influencing overall job satisfaction and organizational commitment in early childhood work environments. *Journal of Research in Childhood Education, 3*(2), 107–122.

Kisker, E., Hofferth, S., Phillips, D., & Farquahar, E. (1991). *A profile of child care settings: Early education and care in 1990.* Princeton, NJ: Mathematica Policy Research.

Kontos, S., Howes, C., & Galinsky, E. (1996). Does training make a difference to quality in family child care? *Early Childhood Research Quarterly, 11,* 427–445.

Kowalski, K., Pretti-Frontczak, K., & Johnson, L. (2001). Preschool teachers' beliefs concerning the importance of various developmental skills and abilities. *Journal of Research in Childhood Education, 16*(1), 5–14.

National Institute of Child Health and Human Development Early Child Care Research Network. (1996). Characteristics of infant child care: Factors contributing to positive caregiving. *Early Childhood Research Quarterly, 11*(3), 269–306.

National Institute of Child Health and Human Development Early Child Care Research Network. (1999). Child outcomes when child care center classes meet recommended standards for quality. *American Journal of Public Health, 89*(7), 1072–1077.

National Institute of Child Health and Human Development Early Child Care Research Network. (2000). Characteristics and quality of child care for toddlers and preschoolers. *Applied Developmental Science, 4*(3), 116–135.

National Institute of Child Health and Human Development Early Child Care Research Network. (2002). Child-care structure–process–outcome: Direct and indirect effects of child-care quality on young children's development. *Psychological Science, 13*(3), 199–206.

Phillipsen, L., Burchinal, M., Howes, C., & Cryer, D. (1997). The prediction of process quality from structural features of child care. *Early Childhood Research Quarterly, 12,* 281–303.

Raikes, H., Wilcox, B., Peterson, C., Hegland, S., Atwater, J., Summers, J., Thornburg, K., Torquati, J., Edwards, C., & Raikes, A. (2003). *Child care quality and workforce characteristics in four Midwestern states.* Lincoln: University of Nebraska–Lincoln, The Center on Children, Families, and the Law.

Saluja, G., Early, D., & Clifford, R. (2002). Demographic characteristics of early childhood teachers and structural elements of early care and education in the United States. *Early Childhood Research and Practice, 4*(1), 1–19.

Smith, T., Kleiner, A., Parsad, B., & Farris, E. (2003). *Prekindergarten in U.S. Public Schools: 2000–2001* (NCES 2003-019). Washington, DC: U.S. Department of Education, National Center for Education Statistics.

Snider, M., & Fu, V. (1990). The effects of specialized education and job experience on early childhood teacher's knowledge of developmentally appropriate practice. *Early Childhood Research Quarterly, 5,* 69–78.

Whitebook, M., & Sakai, L. (2003). Turnover begets turnover: An examination of job and occupational instability among child care center staff. *Early Childhood Research Quarterly, 18*(3), 273–293.

Zill, N., Resnick, G., Kim, K., McKey, R., Clark, C., Pai-Samant, S., Connell, D., Vaden-Kiernan, M., O'Brien, R., & D'Elio, M. (2001). *Head Start FACES: Longitudinal findings on program performance—third progress report.* Washington, DC: U.S. Department of Health and Human Services, Administration on Children, Youth and Families.

# Studies Reviewed

This appendix lists the studies and associated measures reviewed for Chapter 2. Peer-reviewed studies are listed first, followed by studies of note. For the studies that have only one peer-reviewed article, the appendix includes the reference for the article followed by the measure(s) reviewed from that study. For the few studies that have multiple peer-reviewed articles, the appendix includes the study name, followed by the peer-reviewed articles and measure(s). In all but one case, measures were obtained from the study authors. For the one study in which measures were obtained from the Internet, the web address is provided.

## PEER-REVIEWED STUDIES

Abbott-Shim, M., Lambert, R., & McCarty, F. (2000). Structural model of Head Start classroom quality. *Early Childhood Research Quarterly, 15*(1), 115–134.

*Measure:* Research Center on Head Start Quality, Demographics Information Questionnaire (Georgia)

Burchinal, M., Howes, C., & Kontos, S. (2002). Structural predictors of child care quality in child care homes. *Early Childhood Research Quarterly, 17,* 87–105.

*Measure:* Family Day Care Study: Family Day Care Provider Questions[a]

Burchinal, M., Roberts, J., Riggins, R., Zeisel, S., Neebe, E., & Bryant, D. (2000). Relating quality of center child care to early cognitive and language development longitudinally. *Child Development, 21,* 339–357.

*Measure:* Preschool to School Classroom and Teacher Questionnaire

Buysse, V., Wesley, P., Bryant, D., & Gardner, D. (1999). Quality of early childhood programs in inclusive and noninclusive settings. *Exceptional Children, 65*(3), 301–314.

*Measure:* Smart Start Evaluation Child Care Director Interview

*Cost, Quality and Child Outcomes Study*
Burchinal, M., Cryer, D., Clifford, R., & Howes, C. (2002). Caregiver training and classroom quality in child care centers. *Applied Developmental Science, 6,* 2–11.

Howes, C. (1997). Children's experiences in center-based child care as a function of teacher background and adult:child ratio. *Merrill-Palmer Quarterly, 43,* 404–425.

Phillipsen, L., Burchinal, M., Howes, C., & Cryer, D. (1997). The prediction of process quality from structural features of child care. *Early Childhood Research Quarterly, 12,* 281–303.

*Measure:* Cost, Quality and Child Outcomes Staff Questionnaire

---

[a]This measure was used in three different studies.

Epstein, A. (1999). Pathways to quality in Head Start, public school, and private non-profit early childhood programs. *Journal of Research in Childhood Education, 13*(2), 101–119.

*Measure:* High/Scope Educational Research Foundation Study of Teacher Training and Early Childhood Programs: Teacher telephone interview

### Florida Quality Improvement Study

Howes, C. (1997). Children's experiences in center-based child care as a function of teacher background and adult:child ratio. *Merrill-Palmer Quarterly, 43,* 404–425.

Howes, C., & Smith, E.W. (1995). Relations among child care quality, teacher behavior, children's play activities, emotional security, and cognitive activity in child care. *Early Childhood Research Quarterly, 10*(4), 381–404.

*Measure:* Teacher questionnaire

Gable, S., & Halliburton, A. (2003). Barriers to child care providers' professional development. *Child & Youth Care Forum, 32*(3), 175–193.

*Measure:* Child Care Provider Training Needs Assessment–Phone Survey

Holloway, S.D., Kagan, S.L., Fuller, B., Tsou, L., & Carroll, J. (2001). Assessing child-care quality with a telephone interview. *Early Childhood Research Quarterly, 16,* 165–189.

*Measure:* Growing Up in Poverty Project: Caring for Children Study, Family Day Care/Informal Provider Pack

Howes, C., & Norris, D. (1997). Adding two school age children: Does it change quality in family child care? *Early Childhood Research Quarterly, 12,* 327–342.

*Measure:* Family Day Care Study: Family Day Care Provider Questions[a]

Howes, C., Whitebook, M., & Phillips, D. (1992). Teacher characteristics and effective teaching in child care: Findings from the National Child Care Staffing Study. *Child and Youth Care Forum, 21,* 399–414.

*Measure:* National Child Care Staffing Study Interview, Section E: Educational Background

Jorde-Bloom, P. (1988). Factors influencing overall job satisfaction and organizational commitment in early childhood work environments. *Journal of Research in Childhood Education, 3*(2), 107–122.

*Measure:* Early Childhood Job Satisfaction Survey

Kontos, S., Howes, C., & Galinsky, E. (1996). Does training make a difference to quality in family child care? *Early Childhood Research Quarterly, 11,* 427–445.

*Measure:* Family Day Care Study: Family Day Care Provider Questions[a]

Kowalski, K., Pretti-Frontczak, K., & Johnson, L. (2001). Preschool teachers' beliefs concerning the importance of various developmental skills and abilities. *Journal of Research in Childhood Education, 16*(1), 5–14.

*Measure:* The Child Development Project: Preschool Teacher Survey

---

[a]This measure was used in three different studies.

### National Institute of Child Health and
### Human Development, Early Child Care Research Network

Clarke-Stewart, K.A., Vandell, D.L., Burchinal, M., O'Brien, M., & McCartney, K. (2002). Do regulable features of child-care homes affect children's development? *Early Childhood Research Quarterly, 17,* 52–86.

National Institute of Child Health and Human Development (NICHD) Early Child Care Research Network. (1996). Characteristics of infant child care: Factors contributing to positive caregiving. *Early Childhood Research Quarterly, 11*(3), 269–306.

National Institute of Child Health and Human Development (NICHD) Early Child Care Research Network. (1999). Child outcomes when child care center classes meet recommended standards for quality. *American Journal of Public Health, 89*(7), 1072–1077.

National Institute of Child Health and Human Development (NICHD) Early Child Care Research Network. (2000) Characteristics and quality of child care for toddlers and preschoolers. *Applied Developmental Science, 4*(3), 116–135.

National Institute of Child Health and Human Development (NICHD) Early Child Care Research Network. (2002). Child-care structure-process-outcome: Direct and indirect effects of child-care quality on young children's development. *Psychological Science, 13*(3), 199–206.

    *Measures:* 1) NICHD Caregiver Interview, Center Version, 54 months; 2) NICHD Child Caregiver Center Version, Long Form (15, 24, 36 month); and 3) NICHD Child Caregiver Interview, Home Version, Long Form (15, 24, 36 month)— retrieved January 28, 2003, from http://secc.rti.org/forms.cfm

Saluja, G., Early, D., & Clifford, R. (2002). Demographic characteristics of early childhood teachers and structural elements of early care and education in the United States. *Early Childhood Research and Practice, 4*(1), 1–19.

    *Measure:* Questions for a Preschool Teacher

Snider, M., & Fu, V. (1990). The effects of specialized education and job experience on early childhood teacher's knowledge of developmentally appropriate practice. *Early Childhood Research Quarterly, 5,* 69–78.

    *Measure:* Teacher Information Report

Whitebook, M., & Sakai, L. (2003). Turnover begets turnover: An examination of job and occupational instability among child care center staff. *Early Childhood Research Quarterly, 18*(3), 273–293.

    *Measure:* Then & Now interview questions Section B: Who Are You?

## STUDIES OF NOTE

Bellm, D., Burton, A., Whitebook, M., Broatch, L., & Young, M. (2002). *Inside the Pre-K Classroom: A Study of staffing and stability in state-funded prekindergarten programs.* Washington, DC: Center for the Child Care Workforce.

    *Measure:* Pre-Kindergarten Director Interview

Clifford, R.M., Barbarin, O., Chang, F., Early, D., Bryant, D., Howes, C., Burchinal, M., & Pianta, R. (in press). What is pre-kindergarten? Characteristics of a public system of pre-kindergarten services in six states. *Applied Developmental Science.*

*Measure:* National Center for Early Development and Learning Multi-State Study of Pre-Kindergarten, Teacher Questionnaire, Fall of Pre-Kindergarten (2001)

Faddis, B., Ahrens-Gray, P., & Klein, E. (2000). *Evaluation of Head Start family child care demonstration, final report.* Washington, DC: Administration on Children, Youth and Families, U.S. Department of Health and Human Services.

*Measure:* Evaluation of Head Start Family Child Care Demonstration, Caregiver Characteristics Interview (Fall 1994)

Kisker, E., Hofferth, S., Phillips, D., & Farquahar, E. (1991). *A profile of child care settings: Early education and care in 1990.* Princeton, NJ: Mathematica Policy Research.

*Measures:* Profile of Child Care Settings Center Instrument and Profile of Child Care Settings Family Provider Questionnaire

### National Prekindergarten Study

Gilliam, W.S., & Marchesseault, C.M. (2005a). *From capitols to classrooms, policies to practice: State-funded prekindergarten at the classroom level.* New Haven, CT: Yale University Child Study Center.

Gilliam, W.S., & Marchesseault, C.M. (2005b). *From capitols to classrooms, policies to practice: State-funded prekindergarten at the classroom level. Part 1: Who's teaching our youngest students? Teacher education and training, experience, compensation and benefits, and assistant teachers.* New Haven, CT: Yale University Child Study Center.

*Measure:* Survey of lead teachers

### National Study of Child Care for Low Income Families conducted by Abt Associates Inc. (Jean I. Layzer, Project Director)

Report or article in peer-reviewed journal not available.

*Measure:* Family Child Care Provider Interview

Raikes, H., Wilcox, B, Peterson, C., Hegland, S., Atwater, J., Summers, J., Thornburg, K., Torquati, J., Edwards, C., & Raikes, A. (2003). *Child care quality and workforce characteristics in four midwestern states.* The Center on Children, Families, and the Law, University of Nebraska–Lincoln.

*Measure:* Midwest Child Care Study, CRT (The Gallop Organization)

Smith, T., Kleiner, A., Parsad, B., & Farris, E. (2003). Prekindergarten in the U.S. *Prekindergarten in U.S. Public Schools: 2000–2001* (NCES 2003-019). Washington, DC: U.S. Department of Education, National Center for Education Statistics.

*Measure:* Survey of Classes That Serve Children Prior to Kindergarten in Public Schools: 2000–2001 (FRSS 78, 2001)

Zill, N., Resnick, G., Kim, K., McKey, R., Clark, C., Pai-Samant, S., Connell, D., Vaden-Kiernan, M., O'Brien, R., & D'Elio, M. (2001). *Head Start FACES: Longitudinal findings on program performance, third progress report.* Washington, DC: Administration on Children, Youth and Families, U.S. Department of Health and Human Services.

*Measure:* Head Start Family and Child Experiences Survey (Educational Background and In-Service Training)

# CHAPTER 3

# Estimating the Size and Characteristics of the United States Early Care and Education Workforce

Richard N. Brandon and Ivelisse Martinez-Beck

This chapter considers the current status of estimates of the size and characteristics of the early care and education (ECE)[1] workforce, addressing conceptual challenges and presenting estimates of the number of paid ECE workers in the United States. Our estimates distinguish the settings in which paid caregivers work and the ages and other characteristics of children in care. The chapter summarizes what is known from multistate and federal program statistics about the educational attainment of child care workers in different settings. It concludes that the ECE workforce is large—constituting about one third of the United States' instructional corps—and culturally diverse, but has lower educational qualifications than those recommended by many experts. Recommendations include further clarification of workforce concepts, improved federal and state data collection, and analyses of the degree to which children of certain demographic or developmental characteristics are concentrated in specialized ECE facilities and the degree to which this may impede or improve their development.

## PURPOSES OF EARLY CARE AND EDUCATION WORKFORCE ESTIMATES

This chapter considers the size and characteristics of the ECE workforce—the individuals who are paid to directly provide care on a regular basis for children ages birth through 5 years but not during the hours they are in kindergarten. There are many purposes for which national, state, and local policy makers require knowledge of the size and characteristics of the ECE workforce. Improving the quality of ECE caregivers and teachers through profes-

---

Louisa B. Tarullo, formerly in the Office of Planning, Research and Evaluation, DHHS, provided important information and insights about the Head Start workforce.

[1]This chapter uses the term *early care and education,* which encompasses a wide range of early childhood workers and reflects the dual purpose of their activity. However, when cited literature refers to *child care* workers, we present that term to accurately reflect the cited works.

sional development and training is recognized in the quality set-aside specifications of the Child Care Development Fund (CCDF), in the federal Head Start Program Performance Standards and in many decisions made by states regarding the minimum required qualifications of teachers providing services through state- and federally funded prekindergarten programs. Since 1998, the Head Start authorizing statute requires that a majority of teachers hold associate's or bachelor's degrees in early childhood, and 21 states require prekindergarten teachers to have a bachelor's degree (Barnett, Robin, Hustedt, & Schulman, 2003). Efforts to improve the quality of the ECE through professional development require knowledge of how many teachers are working in various settings and caring for children of different ages, because appropriate skills and knowledge vary by a child's age. Implementing appropriate curricula and care for children with special learning, physical, or emotional needs requires knowing how many teachers are caring for such children and should thus receive special training and support. Assuring that children with limited English language proficiency or from diverse cultures have appropriate and responsive care also requires knowing how many teachers with appropriate skills and backgrounds must be recruited and trained. The question of maintaining diversity in the ECE workforce raises the issue of whether to require formal, preservice training or to provide opportunities for in-service education and training of teachers. The disparity between the proportion of minority children and teachers in public school has been cited as a contributor to educational disparities (Dee, 2003; Ferguson 1998). There appears to be a rough equivalence of cultural background between children and caregivers in the current child care workforce (Kisker, Hofferth, Phillips, & Farquhar, 1991; Salujah, Early, & Clifford, 2002) that could be lost if a high level of formal education was set as a standard for job entry, rather than allowing college degrees to be earned over time. In 2002–2003, 23% of all Head Start teachers were enrolled in an early childhood degree program (U.S. Department of Health and Human Services [DHHS], 2002–2003), which shows the viability of increasing educational qualifications while on the job.

As policy makers struggle with decisions related to the financing of ECE to allow improvements in quality and groups advocate for better quality ECE and attempt to improve public understanding of the issues, they need reliable data to indicate the size and characteristics of the workforce. In addition, the level of compensation necessary to recruit and retain a qualified workforce is a key factor in determining the cost of quality ECE for young children (Brandon, Maher, Li, & Joesch, 2004). Accurate workforce estimates are also essential for economic impact analysis showing the contribution of the ECE sector to the economy.

Figure 3.1 suggests the level of detailed workforce information that is ultimately required for planning improvement strategies, showing that care-

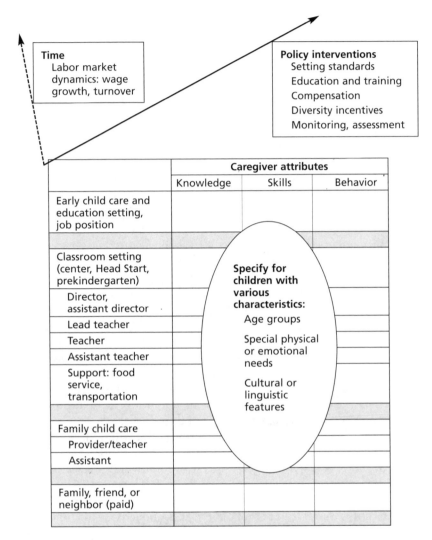

**Figure 3.1.**    Early care and education workforce policy framework.

giver attributes and policy interventions may well have to be specified separately for different job positions and children of different ages and characteristics. Effective design of policy interventions to improve the quality of ECE will thus require detailed knowledge of the characteristics of the ECE workforce, including their education and skills, their cultural backgrounds, their responses to economic incentives, and the characteristics of the children for whom they are responsible.

## ESTIMATING THE SIZE OF THE WORKFORCE
## USING FEDERAL DATA AND STATISTICAL MODELS

There are serious limitations on the applicability and detail of current data concerning the size and characteristics of the ECE workforce. These limitations stem from both a lack of conceptual clarity and inadequate labor force data collection systems. The lack of conceptual clarity in the field centers on which individuals to include in the ECE or child care workforce. Previous work by the Center for the Child Care Workforce and the Human Services Policy Center (CCW & HSPC, 2002) has distinguished between the *child care occupation* (those individuals who are directly responsible for the care of children or who supervise those caregivers) and the *child care sector* (all those individuals who work for organizations providing child care, including accounting and support staff). However, it is not clear whether to include some individuals (e.g., food service or transportation workers) who interact with children on a regular basis but for a limited number of hours in the occupation or sector. Nonparental caregivers may include directors, lead teachers, teachers and assistant teachers in center-based settings, and providers/teachers and assistant teachers in family child care homes; family, friends, and neighbors providing care in their own homes or in the child's home; and nannies or babysitters. In Head Start, social and health services are part of the basic program model, and nutrition coordinators, mental health consultants, family support workers, and case managers are often center staff members and interact regularly with children and parents. Are they part of the child care workforce or only part of the larger child care sector? How important is the worker's self-identification? If a relative is paid and spends 20–40 hours per week caring for a child, but believes she is doing so to help a family member rather than to make money, then is she part of the workforce? Language in the field often reflects the lack of conceptual clarity. For example, the term *provider of care* is sometimes used to refer to an organized entity, such as a child care center, and sometimes to the individual caregiver. In the case of a family child care provider, the entity and the caregiver are the same.

Until it is clear whom to count in the ECE workforce, neither the number of workers nor the distribution of different levels of skills and educational attainment can be known. More important, the likely policy applications of the estimates require clarity on these issues. For example, education and skills standards should vary between classroom teachers and food service workers in a center, even though both need some knowledge of, and sensitivity to, child development concerns. Family child care providers caring for children of diverse ages may need skills to meet the developmental needs of infants, toddlers, and preschoolers, including skills needed to support the school readiness of preschoolers through early literacy and numeracy. Similarly, adults nurturing children with special learning, physical, emotional, or linguistic needs require different training and support to be effective.

Decisions on such conceptual questions have been made on an ad hoc basis to address particular questions in research studies or to address information needs in the implementation of programs. However, for policy purposes, it is useful to have databases that are consistent over time and across geographic areas to track trends and analyze what factors are related to differences in workforce size and characteristics. To develop such databases will require an agreement on such conceptual issues as to who is to be included in the workforce. Achieving consensus will require further research on the impact of different workers' interactions with children on their development, plus a collaborative process involving researchers and policy officials.

## Federal Data Sources

Although federal agencies currently collect a significant amount of useful data about the ECE workforce, their data systems are not designed to generate a portrait of its overall size and characteristics and cannot perform this function. Our intent here is to urge continuation and expansion of agency efforts to address these issues. We hope to encourage improvement of the data systems by laying out the specific limitations of current data sources and what modifications would be required to generate the kind of information we believe is necessary. We particularly want to see adequate standard data regarding the number and characteristics of workers and the settings in which they work.

For other occupations and economic sectors, workforce data are collected at the federal level by the Bureau of Labor Statistics (BLS) and the Census Bureau. Standard workforce data for most sectors are collected by the BLS from firms and by the Census Bureau from households. Although these agencies collect data relevant to ECE for other purposes, their definitions and methods do not yield data that allow for a determination of the overall size and characteristics of the workforce. A central problem is that the ECE workforce is a mixture of firms and individuals, so data collection aimed at only one or the other may not capture the full mixture. Furthermore, many individuals who are paid on a regular basis to care for children do not label themselves as ECE workers and are therefore missed in surveys based on workers' self-identification.

More specifically, the BLS workforce dataset collected from firms or employers contains two categories: preschool teachers and child care workers. The preschool teacher category includes school-based programs but does not include such similar operations as nursery schools or Head Start programs that may not be located at schools. The child care worker category covers employees of center-based programs, nannies, and assistants at family child care homes. However, it neither includes the proprietors of family child care homes who provide the bulk of such care, nor does it include those individuals—family, friends, or neighbors—who are paid on a regular basis to care for other peoples' children but who do not work for a firm. Some research suggests that such individuals are paid amounts comparable to what licensed care providers are paid and that a substantial share are paid for 30–40 hours a week—the equivalent of a full-time job (Brandon, Maher, Joesch, & Doyle, 2002).

Data collected by the Census Bureau do not meet our desire to describe the size and characteristics of the ECE workforce for similar reasons. They combine preschool and kindergarten teachers in a single category, adding in workers who care for older children while potentially missing some in nursery schools or other center-based arrangements caring for younger children. Assistant teachers, family child care providers, and in-home workers are included. However, license-exempt but paid family, friend, and neighbor care-givers are excluded.

In addition to the general population data collected by the BLS and the Census Bureau, federal agencies collect useful data on workers employed by the early childhood programs they fund or operate. However, because these programs only serve a small portion of the population, such data are not reflec-tive of the overall workforce in either size or composition.

Data from the federal/state Child Care and Development Fund (CCDF) program yield a partial picture of the number of entities employing the ECE workforce. Although CCDF collects unduplicated, monthly average numbers of participants and provider organizations, the focus is restricted to services to low-income families receiving subsidies. Therefore, the data collected do not encompass all teachers and caregivers employed in providing ECE. Moreover, they reflect the number of employing entities but not the number of individ-uals who work for those entities.

Another federal data source focuses specifically on Head Start program staff. The annual Program Information Report (PIR) for 2001–2002 reported 95,563 center-based teachers and assistant teachers in preschool Head Start. Approximately 6% of these were staff in community child-care centers part-nering with Head Start, which follow program performance standards and serve children who are funded through Head Start. Another 1,326 staff were family child care providers, whereas 2,916 were home visitors and 445 pro-vided care under the home-based option within the Head Start program. In addition, there were 6,663 child development supervisors, including direc-tors, as well as managers for child development and education, health services, and family and community partnerships. Thus, during the 2001–2002 pro-gram year, 106,913 staff people were identified as child development profes-sionals working in the Head Start preschool program. Child development staff were culturally diverse, and approximately 27% reported proficiency in a lan-guage other than English.

The 2001–2002 PIR also reported 7,463 Early Head Start center-based teachers and assistant teachers. About a quarter of these were staff of com-munity child care facilities that provide center-based care for Early Head Start children and follow the performance standards. Another 868 Early

Head Start staff were family home providers and 2,386 staff were home visitors. Among Early Head Start staff there were also 3,404 directors; managers for education and child development, health, and community partnerships; and direct supervisors of teaching and home visiting staff. Thus, during the 2001–2002 program year, Early Head Start identified 14,121 staff carrying out the program.

These Head Start and Early Head Start data highlight the conceptual and definitional issues discussed previously in this chapter. It is not clear whether staff working in health services, family and community partnerships, or home visiting should be included in the ECE workforce because they are not directly interacting with children during most of their work hours, although they are certainly part of the ECE economic sector.

A further issue that the field is starting to recognize is the lack of parallel lead agencies at federal and state levels charged with collecting ECE workforce data. By way of contrast, the U.S. Department of Education's National Center for Education Statistics (NCES) directly collects and maintains many datasets and conducts a periodic Schools and Staffing Survey that yields reliable data on the characteristics and attitudes of school personnel. It also encourages state education agencies to report a Common Core of Data on K–12 education, which includes data on the number of teachers. Standard definitions allow states to collect and report data in a way that permits the NCES to aggregate state data into reasonably reliable national statistics. Development of the Common Core required a collaborative process that took into account state differences and constraints as well as national opportunities. These types of data do not currently exist for child care and early education programs or for the ECE workforce. State agencies responsible for regulating child care providers and planning services for the population currently lack such standard data systems for their own use or for contributing to a national system. There is some discussion of developing a comparable approach to ECE data that would build on the experiences of developing and operating the Common Core; this would be an important advance.

***Including All Components of the ECE Workforce***    Current federal data systems fail to capture some components of the ECE workforce, particularly those in license-exempt settings. The importance of reflecting workers in all ECE settings is demonstrated by Figure 3.2, which shows the percent of nonparental care hours that children ages birth through 5 years spend in each type of setting. The underlying data are derived from parent responses to the National Household Education Survey: Early Childhood Program Participation (HSPC, 2004). Eighteen percent of paid child care hours are in family, friend, and neighbor care, and 26% are in nonrelative family child care in the provider's home. Fifty-six percent of such hours are in center-based settings, including Head Start and preschool.

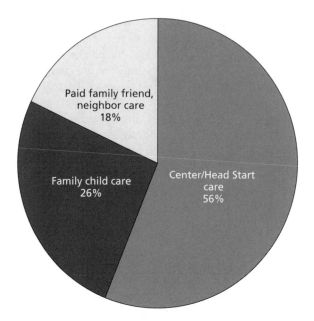

**Figure 3.2.** Percent aggregate nonparental care hours by setting for U.S. children birth through age 5. (*Source:* Human Services Policy Center, 2004.)

Similarly, 2001 administrative data from the CCDF showed that only 58% of the children birth through 5 years who received subsidies funded with federal and state dollars used center-based care, whereas the remainder used family child care provided by relatives and nonrelatives or were cared for by relatives and nonrelatives in the child's own home. Because child–adult ratios are much lower for family child care and family, friend, or neighbor care than for center-based care, the number of workers in each of these settings is substantially greater than those working in centers.

Thus, the fact that major federal population-based data systems do not include paid ECE caregivers working outside formal employment entities leads them to generate underestimates of the size of the ECE workforce. Because the characteristics of such caregivers are likely to differ from those employed in more formal settings, estimates of caregiver characteristics drawn from such sources are also likely to be inaccurate.

## State Data Sources

Most states do not currently maintain data systems, either through administrative datasets or periodic surveys able to produce reliable ECE workforce information. The workforce data sources that do exist tend to be inconsistent across states (Stahr-Breunig, Brandon, & Maher, 2004). However, there are several opportunities to obtain useful data of which only a few states are taking advantage. For example, most states have program licensing or registration data systems that list the provider organization (e.g., center, family child care home) and the allowable capacity (i.e., number of children). States could record the number of staff members on which the allowable capacity was based, plus the current staff and their qualifications, and be able to derive an estimate of workers in those portions of the workforce. Such data would be most consistent for center-based programs, which are regulated in all states, though with widely divergent definitions of what constitutes a center. For example, half-day programs at public schools and church-based center care are exempt from licensing in some states, even though they meet other characteristics of licensed centers and their paid staff should be considered part of the child care workforce. Because states vary widely in whether and how they require noncenter type care to be registered or licensed, consistent data are not likely to emerge unless national guidelines are established and data can be collected on providers not subject to licensing.

Some resource and referral agencies, which provide information to parents about the availability of child care and early education services in local communities, collect consistent data on family child care providers as well as centers. In addition, states are required to conduct market rate surveys to establish reimbursement rates for child care subsidies, reporting the prices charged by a representative sample of ECE providers. Inclusion of questions in these surveys about the number and characteristics of staff could add useful data on the characteristics of the ECE workforce at little additional cost. The value of such an effort would be enhanced by developing consistent definitions and categories to be used across states. Research has also found that states often do not keep licensing data updated and purged of inactive providers (Stahr-Breunig et al., 2004). Updated licensing data provide another important source of information about the workforce, especially if those data include information about the numbers and characteristics of staff working in programs. Several states that have conducted surveys of the ECE workforce to determine its characteristics have been able to assure that they are sampling a representative population of providers by having an external research group purge and supplement the official licensing lists. If the sample of providers is representative and the response rate is sufficient, then the responses can then be generalized into an estimate of the workforce employed in licensed facilities. However, only general population surveys of the type conducted by the state of Oregon can estimate the number of workers outside the licensed sector (Stahr-Breunig et al., 2004).

### Estimating Workforce from Demand Surveys
Alternative ECE workforce estimation methods have emerged in response to the lack of complete federal and state survey and administrative data regarding the

number and characteristics of the ECE workforce. A project conducted by the CCW and the HSPC and funded by the Child Care Bureau (CCB) proposed a set of relatively clear conceptual definitions of the workforce. The researchers developed a methodology to estimate the number of paid child care workers caring for children birth to 5 years, who were not in kindergarten, from representative sample household surveys of ECE utilization (CCW & HSPC, 2002). This effort applied two central concepts. First, it focused on the occupation, rather than the sector, because the primary objective identified was to support policies to improve the quality of caregiver–child interaction, regardless of setting. Second, it defined an ECE worker as anyone who is paid to care for someone else's child on a regular basis or someone who supervises such caregivers. The researchers used a relatively narrow conceptualization of the workforce, excluding such individuals as family support workers, food service personnel, or transportation workers. Unpaid caregivers were also excluded. However, they recognized that there may be other purposes for which it would be appropriate to consider the size of the child care sector, such as economic impact studies, in which case their methodology would have to be modified accordingly. This conceptualization focused on the nature of the work and the financial transaction but did not limit the setting or relationship of the caregiver to the child. Thus, they included family, friends, or neighbors who are paid to care for someone else's child, whether in the adult's or the child's home. This approach produced a significantly larger workforce estimate than would be derived from BLS or Census Bureau data.

The CCW/HSPC demand-based methodology for ECE workforce estimation is explained in detail in their report (CCW & HSPC, 2002). The essential logic of their approach is that if a representative sample of parents report how many hours their children spend in each type of paid care in a typical week, and how many adults and children are present, then, with a variety of statistical adjustments, it is possible to estimate how many adults must be employed to care for them. The adjustments included correcting for parent misreporting of center care ratios and taking account of average hours caregivers work per week. Because many of the policy applications of the estimates—such as planning professional development initiatives—involve knowing how many individuals are employed in ECE through the course of a year rather than at a single point of time, the researchers used estimates of occupational turnover rates to move from the number of individuals employed in a typical week to the number employed in the course of a year. Applying their demand-based methodology and the relatively narrow concept of paid caregiver, CCW and HSPC (2002) estimated that in 2001, there were 2.5 million paid ECE workers in the United States caring for children birth through 5 years. As shown in Figure 3.3, this compares with 3.5 million elementary and secondary school instructional staff and 1.7 million postsecondary instructional staff. ECE therefore accounts for about one third of the total United States instructional

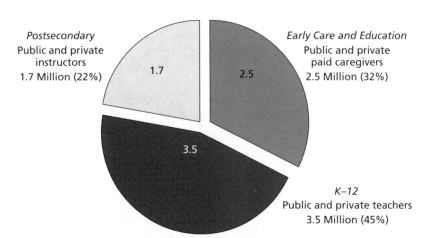

Millions of Paid Instructors

*Postsecondary*
Public and private
instructors
1.7 Million (22%)

*Early Care and Education*
Public and private
paid caregivers
2.5 Million (32%)

*K–12*
Public and private teachers
3.5 Million (45%)

**Figure 3.3.**   U.S. Teaching Corps, 2001.

corps. As shown in Figure 3.4, CCW and HSPC (2002) estimated that of the 2.5 million paid ECE workers, only about half work in center-based or formal family child care settings.

A benefit of estimating the ECE workforce from demand surveys is that it allows estimates not only of the workers employed at various settings, but also of how many workers are caring for diverse children based on a variety of information reported on the demand survey: child's age, household income, limited English proficiency, special needs status, and racial/ethnic group. These characteristics of children can all affect the number of ECE staff with different skills and characteristics who must be recruited and trained to ensure that children receive an appropriate experience. For example, a survey of public elementary and secondary school teachers indicated that 82% were teaching students with an individualized education program (IEP) for special needs, but only 31% had a basic level of training on how to do so; similarly, 41% were teaching students with limited English proficiency, but only 13% had relevant training (Gruber, Wiley, Strizek, & Burian-Fitzgerald, 2002). Collecting data about such characteristics of children and the number of workers caring for them is necessary to support effective policies to assure that there are sufficient training opportunities for ECE workers to respond effectively to the needs of children.

Applying their demand-based methodology, CCW and HSPC researchers estimated that 49% of the paid workforce is caring for toddlers (ages 19–36 months), 29% for infants, and 22% for preschool-age children (3–5 years). The high percent engaged with toddlers is due to the fact that

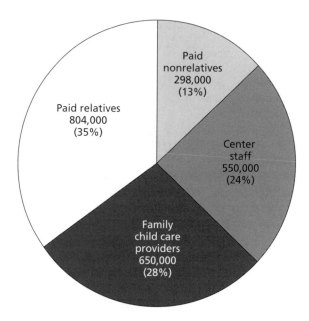

**Figure 3.4.** Number of child care workers by child care setting or provider type. (From Center for the Child Care Workforce & Human Services Policy Center. [2002]. *Estimating the size and components of the U.S. child care workforce and caregiving population* [p. 18]. Washington, DC: Center for the Child Care Workforce; Seattle: Human Services Policy Center, University of Washington; reprinted by permission.)

child–adult ratios are still relatively low at this age, whereas the percent of children in nonparental care increases compared with that for infants.

However, an interesting challenge arises when attempting to apply the demand-based estimation methodology to determine the number of workers caring for children with limited English proficiency (LEP), special needs, or in various racial/ethnic groups. It is not possible to estimate the degree to which these children are concentrated or dispersed in ECE entities. Thus, for example, if four children with special needs are in a designated room with one special needs teacher, then there is one special needs teacher per four children. However, if those same four children are dispersed in settings, with each one in a setting with typically developing children, and parents report the same 4 to 1 ratio, then four teachers will require the skills to care for those same four children with special needs. Moreover, the skills required to work effectively with a group of children of mixed abilities may differ from those required for a homogeneous group of children with special needs. The same logic applies with LEP and racial/ethnic groups. If such children are highly concentrated in certain provider entities, then a smaller number of teachers will be interacting with them than if they are dispersed across many places. Thus, the concentration or dispersion of children with limited English proficiency or from particular cultural backgrounds will greatly affect the number of ECE teachers who must have bilingual skills, multicultural competence, or reflect various cultural backgrounds. The wide range of estimates yielded by different assumptions about concentration of children with these characteristics in each setting are shown in Table 3.1. The large size of the midpoint estimates highlights the importance of this issue. Studies to determine the degree of concentration or dispersion of children of selected characteristics in various ECE settings is thus an important research priority that emerges from this work. It is important not only for estimating the number of caregivers for children of selected characteristics, but also for considering the type of preparation and recruitment policies necessary to assure that children with these characteristics receive appropriate care. In addition, because these are potentially overlapping characteristics, the degree to which children may fall into more than one group of interest must also be ascertained.

Because much ECE policy, including professional development initiatives, is planned and implemented at the state level, reliable state and substate level workforce estimates are necessary. The same BLS and Census Bureau data available nationally are available for states but with the same limitations. Reliable demand surveys have been conducted for states, and the same estimation method developed for national estimates can be applied. HSPC has found about 20 states for which adequate demand surveys are available, including the 13 states oversampled in the National Survey of American Families (NSAF) and four additional states with a standard survey developed by HSPC. As noted previously, augmented licensing or market rate survey data could also provide useful estimates for the licensed ECE sectors.

## Estimating the Levels of Professional Qualifications and Training for Different Components of the Workforce

The level of professionalization and the specific skills, competencies, and qualifications required for ECE staff to be effective in nurturing children constitute a major policy issue. Varying experts have reached different conclusions from research and practice about what is most appropriate. A National Academy of Sciences committee recommended that each center classroom should have at least one teacher with a bachelor's degree with an emphasis on early childhood (Bowman, Donovan, & Burns, 2001). Another working group of nationally recognized ECE experts recommended a mix of staff, varying by age of child, that would average out to about two thirds of center teachers and one half of family child care providers having at least a bachelor's degree with an emphasis in early childhood (Kagan, Brandon, Ripple, Maher, & Joesch, 2002). These recommendations are based on research literature that has demonstrated significant relationships between care-givers' education level and specific skills training on the nature of care-

**Table 3.1.** Paid workforce caring for selected groups of children ages birth to 5 years

| | Center-based Staff | Family Child Care Providers | Paid Relatives | Paid Nonrelatives | Total Workforce, All Types (Mid-point Estimate) |
|---|---|---|---|---|---|
| African American children | 132,000–1,037,000 | 156,000–539,000 | 203,000–300,000 | 12,000–37,000 | 1,208,000 |
| Latino children | 63,000–478,000 | 70,000–200,000 | 209,000–365,000 | 34,000–79,000 | 749,000 |
| Children with disabilities | 84,000–629,000 | 78,000–262,000 | 115,000–177,000 | 32,000–73,000 | 725,000 |
| Children with limited English proficiency | 20,000–161,000 | 22,000–56,000 | 93,000–169,000 | 10,000–19,000 | 275,000 |

From Center for the Child Care Workforce & Human Services Policy Center. (2002). *Estimating the size and components of the U.S. child care workforce and care-giving population* (p. 23). Washington, DC: Center for the Child Care Workforce; Seattle: Human Services Policy Center, University of Washington; reprinted by permission.

Ranges reflect different levels of assumed concentration of children of each characteristic in each care setting.

giver–child interaction and child outcomes (Administration for Children and Families [ACF], 2003b; Phillips, Mekos, Scarr, McCartney, & Abbott-Shim, 2000, Shonkoff & Phillips, 2000). This literature is mostly correlational, indicating that caregivers with certain education and training have more desirable interaction with children. There is a potential that such correlations may be an artifact of the background, motivation, beliefs about the nature of learning, or other concomitant variables associated with caregivers who are better educated that also result in better quality of care. There has not, to our knowledge, been a careful sorting out of how different levels of caregiver education and skills affect children of different ages cared for in different settings (see Chapter 4). Not only is it hard to gather information on the number of ECE workers providing care for children, but it is also hard to get a complete picture of their qualifications. Therefore, it is necessary to consider which data sources are available and how they might be improved.

## Data from Surveys of Early Care and Education Providers

Researchers at the CCW and the HSPC reviewed the literature on the characteristics of the ECE workforce and selected a set of studies that had the most representative samples (nationwide or multistate) and the most reliable methods. The researchers then reported a range of educational levels found for workers in center-based and family child care settings. Findings for center-based caregivers and teachers are summarized in Table 3.2 (CCW & HSPC, 2002). There are several challenges embedded in this summary data. Although several are multistate studies, only the Profile of Child Care Settings (PCCS) is a representative national sample, and the PCCS findings are considerably different from the rest of the literature. The PCCS found that in 1990, 47% of center teachers had a bachelor's degree or higher. The other studies, which were conducted in multiple states between 1990 and 1995, estimated that 31–33% of center teachers had a bachelor's degree. Head Start PIR data show a similar 30% of teachers with bachelor's degree or higher, but that is for a program with higher standards and serving a somewhat older group of children than the full universe of center-based ECE. The overall increase in utilization of paid care, the impact of substantial increases in funding and growth of subsidized services in the mid to late 1990s, and the related impacts on staff qualifications are therefore not reflected in those data. In 2001, the Midwest Child Care Research Consortium surveyed caregivers in four Midwestern states and estimated that approximately 22% of center-based caregivers had a bachelor's degree or higher (Raikes, 2003). There is suggestive evidence that the average level of qualifications of center teachers may have declined since the 1990s (Whitebook, Sakai, Gerber, & Howes, 2001). However, there is no representative national estimate of qualifications since 1990, so both the current level and the trend remain unknown.

**Table 3.2.**  Education levels of center teachers

| Study | Percent with High School or Less | Percent with Some College | Percent with Bachelor's Degree or Advanced Degree |
|---|---|---|---|
| Profile of Child Care Settings Willer, Hofferth, Kisker, et al. (1991) | 13 | 39 | 47 |
| National Child Care Staffing Study (Whitebook, Howes, & Phillips, 1990) | 26 | 44 | 31 |
| Cost, Quality and Child Outcomes Study (Cost, Quality and Child Outcomes Study Team, 1995) | 20 | 47 | 33 |
| Midwest Child Care Research Consortium (Raikes, 2003) | 24 | 54 | 22 |
| Head Start Bureau: Program Information Reports (U.S. Department of Health and Human Services, 2001–2002) | | 21 | 30 |

HSPC reviewed studies conducted at the state level and found several that have reasonably high response rates and a representative underlying sample of providers or individual caregivers (Stahr-Breunig et al., 2004). Table 3.3 summarizes the formal education levels reported in several of the reliable surveys identified in that study. Although this set of surveys was not conducted nationally, it has the advantage of being current and, in aggregate, reflects a diverse set of states. The researchers selected only surveys with at least a 50% response rate and no apparent biases in sampling or construction of questions. In some cases, they decided that the survey met criteria for one type of care and not others and only included results regarding the type of care meeting criteria.

It is difficult to generalize or make detailed comparisons because these surveys used a wide range of methodologies and definitions. However, they clearly suggest that the percentage of center teachers with bachelor's degrees is not likely to exceed 25%, and teachers with associate's degrees is not likely to exceed 30%. Thus, in some states, a slim majority of center teachers appears to have one or the other degree and, in others, less than one third have these degrees. This is well below the levels recommended by many experts (Bowman et al., 2001; Kagan et al., 2002). Educational attainment is somewhat higher for center directors, with 20%–80% having a bachelor's degree or higher and another 16%–37% holding an associate's degree.

**Table 3.3.**    State surveys of caregiver characteristics

| | Centers, Directors | | Centers, Teachers | | Family Child Care | |
|---|---|---|---|---|---|---|
| | Percent with Bachelor's Degree or Higher | Percent with Associate's Degree | Percent with Bachelor's Degree | Percent with Associate's Degree | Percent with Bachelor's Degree | Percent with Associate's Degree |
| Florida | 39 | 22 | 16 | 18 | N/A | N/A |
| Hawaii | 80 | 16 | 48 | 37 | N/A | N/A |
| Illinois | 33 | 37 | 24 | 30 | 10 | 10 |
| Massachusetts | N/A | N/A | 14 | 25 | N/A | N/A |
| Maine | 37 | 16 | 22 | 14 | 12 | 12 |
| Nevada | 20 | 18 | 8 | 11 | N/A | N/A |
| North Carolina | 32 | 16 | 12 | 10 | 10 | 10 |
| Oklahoma | 20 | 10 | 8 | 3 | 12 | 12 |
| Vermont | N/A | N/A | N/A | N/A | 15 | 15 |

The wide range of findings across states is striking. At the high end, 48% of Hawaii's center teachers have a bachelor's degree. At the other extreme, only 8% of the teachers in Oklahoma and Nevada have a bachelor's degree. It will be important for researchers to explore alternative possible explanations for this wide range, including differences in labor market dynamics, education levels in the overall population, regulatory structures, and the relationship of public school prekindergarten programs to the rest of the ECE delivery system. It would also be interesting to consider whether there may be state cultural factors, such as parental expectations or preferences, explaining this wide variation.

Information on the qualifications of family child caregivers is even more sparse than that for center staff. Kontos, Howes, Shinn, and Galinsky (1995) estimated 17% had bachelor's degrees or higher, but their sample was not fully representative. Data from the National Study of Child Care for Low Income Families (Layzer & Goodson, 2004) showed that approximately 9% of caregivers who serve children from low-income families in family child care homes hold a bachelor's degree or higher. In that sample, the majority of caregivers had some training in child care or child development and a minority had some teacher training. Again, there is no way of determining the degree to which caregivers serving low-income families are representative of the sector as a whole. For family child care providers, the percent with bachelor's or associate's degrees is not likely to exceed 10%–15% each, based on the state surveys summarized in Table 3.3. Thus, less than one third of family child care providers is likely to have some level of college. The data are even more scarce for family, friend, and neighbor caregivers, with data only from Washington state. The HSPC Washington study estimated that 11% of family, friend, and neighbor caregivers held an associate's degree and another 14% held a bachelor's degree (Brandon et al., 2002). These data suggested that the education level of these less formal caregivers is lower than for center-based teachers and close to that of family child care providers.

***Data from Major Programs***    Although data from programs serving only children from low-income families are not representative of the full ECE workforce, it is useful to policy makers to understand the status and potential workforce dynamics of major programs as they consider standards and requirements. Staff training and development are emphasized in the Head Start Program Performance Standards (U.S. DHHS, 1996), and the development of staff was further stressed as one of four cornerstones for the Early Head Start programs by the Advisory Committee for Services to Families with Infants and Toddlers (U.S. DHHS, 1994). The Head Start Amendments of 1998 (PL 105-285) required that by September 30, 2003, at least 50% of all Head Start teachers in center-based programs have an associate's, bachelor's, or higher degree in early childhood education or experience teaching preschool children if the degree was in a related field. Programs may hire teachers at this level of educational background or support less highly qualified teachers in educational endeavors. By the 2001–2002 program year, Head Start had already met the requirement. Thirty percent of lead teachers were reported to have an ECE-related bachelor's or graduate degree, and another 22% were enrolled in an ECE-related degree program (U.S. DHHS, 2001–2002).

According to the FACES 2000 study (ACF, 2003b), more Head Start teachers had obtained a graduate level degree in 2000–2001 than in 1997–1998. In 2000, Head Start teachers were also younger compared with those in 1997–1998, and more of them had been teaching in Head Start for 2 years or less. Newer teachers are also more likely to have a graduate degree. In 2000, more teachers had studied early childhood education or child development for their highest degree than teachers in 1997–1998, and more teachers belonged to a national professional association for early childhood educators (ACF, 2003b).

Head Start has been known as an employer of former Head Start parents. This continues to be a value in many programs together with other efforts designed to support educational and training endeavors of parents. For example, in 2001–2002, approximately 20% of Early Head Start staff and approximately 29% of Head Start staff were former or current Head Start or Early Head Start parents (U.S. DHHS, 2001–2002).

In 2001–2002, more than one third of Early Head Start head teachers had an associate's degree or higher. However, many teachers were in the process of advancing their education level; for example, 23% of all teachers were enrolled in an early childhood degree program. Moreover, nearly all Early Head Start lead teachers were reported to either have a Child Development Associate (CDA) credential/state equivalent or an associate's degree or higher and/or were enrolled in a program to attain one of these levels of certification or degree. In home-based programs, home visitors deliver core services. More home visitors than teachers had completed an associate's degree or higher; nearly two thirds of home visitors had this level of preparation. The number of home visitors with graduate degrees was also considerably higher than teachers (e.g., some Early Head Start programs require home visitors to have a master's degree in social work; U.S. DHHS, 2001–2002).

The NCES (2002a) estimated that 86% of teachers working in prekindergarten programs offered through the public elementary schools held a bachelor's degree or higher. However, it is interesting to note that in those schools in which 75% or more of the student population is considered low-income as measured by participation in the reduced lunch program, only 81% of teachers held a bachelor's degree or higher. It should be noted that in many states, prekindergarten programs are a mixture of public school and community-based programs. As demonstrated by Henry's work in Georgia (Henry, Gordon, Henderson, & Ponder, 2003; Henry, Henderson, et al., 2003), the percent for prekindergarten teachers in community-based programs was much lower than in public schools.

***Lack of Experimental Data***    Experimental studies that would indicate the degree to which various professional development interventions succeed in changing caregiver behavior and child outcomes are critically important for policy decision-making on the level of qualifications required for ECE caregivers. This is a high priority need that is being addressed by several major federally funded projects (e.g., Quality Interventions in Early Care and Education [QUINCE]) in which several models and delivery approaches to caregiver and teacher training and implementation of curricula are being tested for their effectiveness in improving professional preparation, skills, and competencies needed to support children's early learning. If specifying relevant qualifications is to be a major component of policy to improve early care and child outcomes, then a careful analysis is needed of two related potential outcomes. First, will recruiting a significant number of new entrants who have bachelor's degrees in early childhood produce a teaching corps with the desired behaviors and child outcomes? Second, will providing comparable educational enrichment and skills training to current members of the ECE workforce who lack these qualifications improve their interactions with children and result in better outcomes?

It is also unclear what level of compensation would be required to recruit and retain adequately qualified ECE staff. It is clear that the currently reported median wages of $7.90 and $9.53 per hour for child care workers and preschool teachers (U.S. Department of Labor, BLS, 2003) are insufficient.[2] Whitebook et al. (2001) have shown that among relatively high quality centers in California, higher compensation within the $12–$19 per hour range is associated with greater retention and quality of care. Average wage differences of about $3 per hour among equally trained staff seemed to make a significant difference in retention rates. Human services salaries are related to formal educational qualifications but with a wide range of variation. BLS data show that salaries for human services workers with a bachelor's degree plus certification range from about $16–$18 an hour for social workers, to $21 an hour for medical and clinical technologists, to $29 an hour for elementary school teachers. Human services workers who hold an associate's degree earn between $11 and $20 an hour (U.S. Department of Labor, BLS, 2003). Head Start teachers with bachelor's degrees had an annual salary averaging about $25,000 in 2002 (PIR, 2001–2002); those with an associate's degree and CDA certification averaged less than $19,000 a year. However, it is not clear how many hours a year Head Start teachers work—some are only employed during the school year, whereas others are employed year round—so a clear hourly salary comparison is not possible. It should also be noted that most child care workers have minimal health and retirement benefits, whereas public school teachers and health professionals have benefits that add another 20%–30% to the value of their compensation. This wide range of potential salary levels to recruit and retain appropriately qualified ECE staff suggests that experimental data are required to determine the impact of different compensation levels in different labor markets.

## CULTURAL CONGRUENCE

Cultural congruence between children and teachers is an important issue to be addressed in a research agenda regarding ECE workers. Experience in elementary and secondary education has indicated that the mismatch between the cultural backgrounds of public school teachers (approximately 84% Caucasian; NCES, 2002b) and students (approximately 40% non-Caucasian; NCES, 2004) may be a significant contributor to differences in student aspirations and achievement (Ferguson, 1998). Although data regarding the educational background of ECE caregivers are scarce, date are more scarce regarding the racial/ethnic background of caregivers and teachers. How these characteristics relate to the educational achievement of children is also lacking examination. It is known that educational attainment and access to professional training are related to socioeconomic status and cultural background. It is reasonable to

---

[2]Note that these data do not include all comparable workers, but there is no reason to believe that the excluded workers have higher salaries.

infer that if professionalization of the ECE workforce were to be achieved by rapidly setting high levels of preservice education and certification, as is done for K–12 teachers, it would be likely to produce a similar cultural mismatch between children and caregivers. Studies referenced earlier suggested that there is a reasonable consistency of backgrounds between young children and their caregivers and teachers (Kisker et al., 1991; Salujah et al., 2002).

Relevant data available from the federal Head Start program are shown in Figure 3.5. Child development staff in Early Head Start are culturally diverse, and approximately 20% are proficient in a language other than English—a number that corresponds closely to the number of parents in Early Head Start for whom English is not their primary language (Administration on Children, Youth and Families [ACYF], 1999). These data suggest that a carefully structured combination of hiring practices—including outreach to parents of children in the program who are interested in becoming ECE workers, providing in-service educational opportunities, and assuring that institutions of higher education are welcoming environments for adult learners of varying backgrounds—can produce a child care workforce that both displays higher education qualifications and maintains cultural diversity. Exploring this potential in the broader ECE field should be an important part of the research agenda.

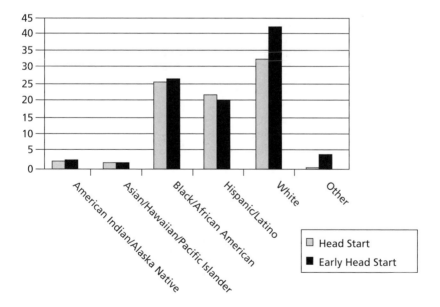

**Figure 3.5.** Percent of Head Start and Early Head Start child development staff by race/ethnicity, 2001–2002.

We do not know of any published literature regarding the degree to which cultural similarity of caregivers and young children affects their interaction and outcomes. Some research findings indicate the degree to which matching cultural backgrounds affect parents' choice of caregivers (Brandon et al., 2002)—a significant factor reported by a small percent (1%–3%) of parents. However, the research has found that knowing and trusting the caregiver is the primary factor in selecting care arrangements (Brandon et al., 2002; Hofferth, Shauman, Henke, & West, 1998; Pungello & Kurtz-Costes, 1999), and this may encompass aspects of cultural congruence. More exploration of the interaction of caregivers' cultural, racial, and ethnic backgrounds and their impact on the relationships among children, caregivers, and parents is needed.

Estimates indicate that large numbers of child care workers are caring for children whose characteristics require them to have particular knowledge and skills: children with special learning, physical, or emotional needs; children with limited English language proficiency; and children of minority cultural groups. However, policy could be greatly improved if research were conducted to examine the degree to which such children are concentrated together in particular ECE programs or diffused among the many programs. The degree to which social and economic segregation or integration in ECE settings facilitates or impedes young children's development is a critical area for research that could lead to important policy discussions concerning reimbursement systems and quality improvement strategies.

Although the primary concern of many ECE policies is with the developmental outcomes of children, it is important to recognize that ECE provides entry level jobs for many immigrant women and those from low-income families. If a policy of professionalization is pursued that closes off that entry into the workforce, then it could be detrimental to these women and their children. If, however, a strategy that recognizes this concern and offers opportunities for additional education, training, and advancement for these women is implemented, then the effects could be positive. The need for experimental research on the impacts of in-service training for ECE caregivers suggested previously is reinforced by these concerns about the impact on low-income, minority, and immigrant families.

## CONCLUSIONS AND RECOMMENDATIONS

Developing effective policies to improve the quality of ECE for young children in the United States requires clearly understanding the number and characteristics of individuals who are paid to work directly with children. Federal data systems are not designed for or adequate to the task, and they reflect limited or inconsistent concepts regarding who is to be included in the workforce. Neither federal nor state data systems are able to count or estimate the number of paid workers in the ECE occupation or the larger ECE economic sector. The situation could be improved if the BLS, the U.S. Census Bureau, and ECE experts in the DHHS and Department of Education sponsored necessary background studies and sharpened the definition of data categories to reflect the operational realities and policy needs of ECE. Federal agencies are currently sponsoring some ECE workforce studies that should help provide relevant information for young children. The following efforts already underway provide an opportunity to improve ECE workforce data.

- The HSPC, under sponsorship of the federal CCB, developed a demand-based methodology for estimating the number of ECE workers. This method shows the distribution of the workforce by such key characteristics as children's age and the child care settings in which they receive care. These estimates are available for the United States and for 17 states for which demand data are available. Applying the concept that the ECE workforce is comprised of those individuals paid to supervise or directly provide care for a child age birth through 5 years (but not in kindergarten) on a regular basis, it has been estimated that the child care workforce is comprised of about 2.3 million individuals at any point of time and about 2.5 million through the course of the year. This amounts to about one third of the paid United States instructional corps across ECE, elementary, secondary, and postsecondary education. The number of paid ECE workers is equivalent to two thirds the number of elementary and secondary school teachers. This suggests that efforts to improve the quality of caregiver–child interaction will require a large-scale, long-term investment.

- It is also clear that a large share of staff are working with children who have special physical or emotional needs and require appropriate skills and supports to provide effective care. A similar situation occurs for children with limited English language proficiency. However, additional data on the concentration or dispersion of such children across ECE entities is necessary to gauge the number of staff who must be recruited and retained to assure that children receive ECE from caregivers with the requisite skills.

- Estimation models have also indicated the distribution of paid workers by child care setting or arrangement and by the age of children in their care. These analyses show that the paid ECE workforce is about evenly split between those working in such formal settings as center-based arrangements and licensed and unlicensed family child care and such license-exempt arrangements as care by family, friends, or neighbors. This indicates that professional development opportunities should be designed to enhance the quality of adult–child interaction in all components of the ECE market. Controlled evaluations are required to determine which types of professional development training or support actually enhance caregiver knowledge, skills, and behavior in different settings.

- Demand-based estimates also show that about half of the paid workforce is caring for toddlers—children age 1.5 to 3 years. Policies and professional development, training, and support initiatives should therefore be sure to include core competencies that focus on the best practice for children in this age group. Personnel practices should also recognize the stresses and rewards of caring for toddlers.

- Data from the federal Head Start program suggest that it is possible to increase professional qualifications within the current workforce while maintaining cultural diversity by encouraging and supporting increased education for current workers. This can include continuing to recruit current or former parents as child care workers. Policy makers and researchers should explore the applicability of this encouraging Head Start experience to the broader ECE delivery system.

- There are several state and multistate studies that include data on the qualifications of ECE workers. These studies show that the qualifications of the ECE workforce are not high, with only about 20%–30% of center teachers holding a bachelor's degree. There is much that remains to be understood about state policies or cultures that produce particularly high or low rates of college educated caregivers.

- Many states are collecting data from either licensed providers or the entire ECE workforce in the form of licensing data, market rate surveys, or special workforce surveys. If states were to adopt appropriate sampling methods; consistent definitions of ECE occupations, qualifications, and settings; and consistent time frames, then such data could form the basis of a national ECE workforce data system. The Common Core of Data collected by the NCES in the U.S. Department of Education provides a model for a cooperative 50-state system that provides such consistent definitions. The CCB is convening a work group to pursue this approach. Successful collection of workforce data by the Head Start program provides a model that can help in developing such a system.

Further conceptual and empirical analyses are required to explore the full range of workers potentially included in the child care workforce, to determine what level of engagement with children has a significant effect on their early learning and development, and to decide which categories of worker meet that criterion of engagement. We are optimistic that the interest of federal and state agencies to invest in solid data about the size and characteristics of the ECE workforce can produce needed improvements.

## REFERENCES

Administration for Children and Families. (2003a). *Pathways to quality and full implementation in Early Head Start.* Washington, DC: Department of Health and Human Services.

Administration for Children and Families. (2003b). *Head Start FACES 2000: A whole-child perspective on program performance.* Washington, DC: Department of Health and Human Services.

Administration on Children, Youth and Families. (1999). *Leading the way: Characteristics and early experiences of selected first-wave Early Head Start programs (Vol. 1).* Washington, DC: Department of Health and Human Services.

Barnett, W.S, Robin, K.B., Hustedt, J.T., & Schulman, L.L. (2003). *The state of preschool: 2003 state preschool yearbook.* New Brunswick, NJ: National Institute for Early Education Research.

Bowman, B.T., Donovan, M.S., & Burns, M.S. (Eds.). (2001). *Eager to learn: Educating our preschoolers.* Washington, DC: National Academies Press.

Brandon, R.N., Maher, E.J., Joesch, J.M., & Doyle, S. (2002). *Understanding family, friend, and neighbor care in Washington state: Developing appropriate training and support.* Seattle: Human Services Policy Center, University of Washington.

Brandon, R.N., Maher, E.J., Li, G., & Joesch, J.M. (2004). *Orchestrating access to affordable, high-quality early care and education for all young children.* Seattle: Human Services Policy Center, University of Washington.

Center for the Child Care Workforce & Human Services Policy Center. (2002). *Estimating the size and components of the U.S. child care workforce and caregiving population.* Washington, DC: Center for the Child Care Workforce; Seattle: Human Services Policy Center, University of Washington.

Cost, Quality and Child Outcomes Study Team. (1995). *Cost, quality, and child outcomes in child care centers.* Denver: University of Colorado, Economics Department.

Dee, T.S. (2003). *Teachers, race and student achievement in a randomized experiment.* Swarthmore, PA: Department of Economics, Swarthmore College, and National Bureau of Economic Research.

Ferguson, R. (1998). Teachers' perceptions and expectations and the black-white test score gap. In C. Jencks & M. Phillips (Eds.), *The black-white test score gap* (pp. 273–317). Washington, DC: The Brookings Institution.

Gruber, K.J., Wiley, S.D., Strizek, G.A., & Burian-Fitzgerald, M. (2002). *Schools and staffing survey, 1999–2000: Overview of the data for public, private, public charter, and Bureau of Indian Affairs elementary and secondary school.* Washington, DC: National Center for Education Statistics, U.S. Department of Education.

Head Start Amendments of 1998, PL 105-285, 42 U.S.C. 9843a (a)(2) § 648A.

Henry, G.T., Gordon, C.S., Henderson, L.W., & Ponder, B.D. (2003). *Georgia pre-K Longitudinal Study: Final report 1996–2001.* Atlanta: Andrew Young School of Policy Studies, Georgia State University.

Henry, G.T., Henderson, L.W., Ponder, B.D., Gordon, C.S., Mashburn, A.J., & Rickman, D.K. (2003). *Report of the findings from the Early Childhood Study: 2001–2002.* Atlanta: Andrew Young School of Policy Studies, Georgia State University.

Hofferth, S.I., Shauman, K.A., Henke, R.R., & West, J. (1998). *Characteristics of children's early care and education programs: Data from the 1995 National Household Education Survey.* Washington, DC: National Center for Education Statistics, U.S. Department of Education.

Human Services Policy Center. (2004). *Analysis of the National Household Education Survey, 1999.* Seattle: University of Washington, Human Services Policy Center.

Kagan, S.L., Brandon, R.N., Ripple, C.H., Maher, E.J., & Joesch, J.M. (2002). Supporting quality early childhood care and education: Addressing compensation and infrastructure. *Young Children, 57*(3), 58–65.

Kisker, E., Hofferth, S., Phillips, D., & Farquhar, E. (1991). *A profile of child care settings: Early education and care in 1990 (Vol. 1).* Princeton, NJ: Mathematica Policy Research.

Kontos, S., Howes, C., Shinn, M., & Galinsky, E. (1995). Does training make a difference to quality in family child care? *Early Childhood Research Quarterly, 11*(4), 427–445.

Layzer, J.I., & Goodson, B.D. (2004, April 15). *Care in the home: A study of family child care providers and the low-income families that use them.* Panel presentation at the 2004 Annual Meeting of the Child Care Research Consortium, Washington, DC.

National Center for Education Statistics. (2002a). *The condition of education 2002* (NCES 2002-025). Washington, DC: U.S. Government Printing Office.

National Center for Education Statistics. (2002b). *Digest of education statistics.* Retrieved April 6, 2005 from http://nces.ed.gov/programs/digest/d02/tables/dt068.asp

Phillips, D., Mekos, D., Scarr, S., McCartney, K., & Abbott-Shim, M. (2000). Within and beyond the classroom door: Assessing quality in child care centers. *Early Childhood Research Quarterly, 15*(4), 475–496.

Pungello, E., & Kurtz-Costes, B. (1999). Why and how working women choose child care: A review with a focus on infancy. *Developmental Review, 19,* 31–96.

Raikes, H. (2003). *Child care quality and workforce characteristics in four Midwestern states.* Lincoln: The Gallup Organization and the Center on Children, Families, and the Law, University of Nebraska.

Saluja, G., Early, D.M., & Clifford, R.M. (2002). Demographic characteristics of early childhood teachers and structural elements of early care and education in the United States. *Early Childhood Research and Practice, 4*(1) [on line]. Retrieved April 20, 2005, from http://ecrp.uiuc.edu/v4n1/saluja.html

Shonkoff, J.P., & Phillips, D.A. (Eds.). (2000). *From neurons to neighborhoods: The science of early child development.* Washington, DC: National Academies Press.

Smith, T., Kleiner, A., Parsad, B., & Faris, E. (2003). *Prekindergarten in U.S. public schools: 2000–2001.* Washington, DC: National Center for Education Statistics, U.S. Department of Education.

Stahr-Breunig, G., Brandon, R., & Maher, E. (2004). *Counting the child care workforce: A catalog of state data sources to quantify and describe child caregivers in the fifty states and the District of Columbia.* Report to the Child Care Bureau, Administration for Children and Families, and U.S. Department of Health and Human Services.

U.S. Department of Health and Human Services. (1994). *The statement of the advisory committee on services for families with infants and toddlers.* Washington, DC: Author.

U.S. Department of Health and Human Services. (1996). *Head Start program: Final rule.* Washington, DC: Author.

U.S. Department of Health and Human Services. (2001–2002). *Head Start Bureau: Program Information Reports.* Washington, DC: Author.

U.S. Department of Health and Human Services. (2002–2003). *Head Start Bureau: Program Information Reports.* Washington, DC: Author.

U.S. Department of Labor, Bureau of Labor Statistics. (2003). *May 2003 national occupation employment and wage estimates.* Washington, DC: Author.

Whitebook, M., Howes, C., & Phillips, D. (1990). *Who cares? Child care teachers and the quality of care in America. (Final report: National Child Care Staffing Study).* Oakland, CA: Child Care Employee Project.

Whitebook, M., Sakai, L., Gerber, E., & Howes, C. (2001). *Then and now: Changes in child care staffing, 1994–2000: Technical report.* Washington, DC: Center for the Child Care Workforce; Berkeley: Institute of Industrial Relations, University of California.

Willer, B., Hofferth, S., Kisker, E.E., et al. (1991). *The demand and supply of child care in 1990.* Washington, DC: National Association for the Education of Young Children.

## STATE WORKFORCE SURVEYS
## FOR EDUCATIONAL ATTAINMENT DATA

Essa, E. (2002). *Who cares for Nevada's children?: A profile of the demographic, economic, and quality aspects of child care in Nevada. Key findings from the Nevada Child Care Workforce Study.* Reno: University of Nevada.

Etheridge, W., McCall, R., Groark, C., Mehaffie, K., & Nelkin, R. (2002). *A baseline report of early care and education in Pennsylvania: The 2002 Early Care and Education Provider Survey.* Report prepared for the Governor's Task Force on Early Childhood Education. Pittsburgh, PA: University of Pittsburgh Office of Child Development and the Universities Children's Policy Collaborative.

The Gallup Organization and the Center for Children, Families, and the Law; University of Nebraska; & The Midwest Child Care Research Consortium. (2002). *Child care quality and workforce characteristics in four Midwestern states.* Draft report.

Good Beginnings Alliance. (in press). *Hawaii's Early Childhood Workforce Study.* Honolulu, HI: Author.

Maricopa County Office of Research and Reporting. (2001). *Arizona Wage and Benefit Survey of Child Care/Early Childhood Education Center Based Personnel.* A report for the Governor's Division for Children. Tempe, AZ: Association for Supportive Child Care.

Massachusetts Child Care Resource and Referral Network, with Bernstein, A. (2000). *Massachusetts Child Care Center and School Age Program Salary and Benefits Report.* Boston: Massachusetts Office of Child Care Services.

Mills, L., Boston, S., Breindel, H., Goodman, I., & Mohrle, K. (2002). *Maine Child Care Market Rate and Workforce Study.* A report for the Office of Child Care and Head Start, State of Maine. Concord, MA: Mills Consulting Group, Inc.

Mills, L., Weiss, D., Boston, S., Goodman, I., Mohrle, K., & Minardi, M., Mills and Pardee, Inc., and Goodman Research Group, Inc. (2001). *Vermont Child Care: A Study of Wages, Credentials, Benefits, and Market Rates.* Waterbury, VT: Child Care Services Division, Department of Social and Rehabilitation Services.

Mullis, A., Mullis, R., & Cornille, T. (2001). *Florida Child Care Workforce Study.* Final report to the Florida Children's Forum. Tallahassee: Florida State University.

Oregon Childhood Care and Education Data Project. (2002). *Data for community planning: 2000 Oregon population estimates and survey findings.* Albany: Oregon Child Care Research Partnership.

Penn, D. (2001). *2001 Child Care Rate Study for Oklahoma Department of Human Services Office of Child Care.* Norman, OK: Center for Economic and Management Research, University of Oklahoma.

Ramsburg, D., Montanelli, D., & Rouge, E. (2002). *FY 2001 Illinois Salary and Staffing Survey: Child Care Centers and Family Child Care Home Providers.* Urbana: Department of Human and Community Development, University of Illinois.

Russell, S., Lyons, J., Grigoriciuc, M., & Lowman, B. (2002). *Working in child care in North Carolina.* Chapel Hill, NC: Child Care Services Association.

# CHAPTER 4

# Quality and Qualifications

## Links Between Professional Development and Quality in Early Care and Education Settings

KATHRYN TOUT, MARTHA ZASLOW, AND DANIEL BERRY

$T$his chapter examines the evidence linking qualifications of the early care and education (ECE) workforce and the quality of ECE programs. Across the ECE field, professional development and workforce qualifications have taken center stage as essential components of program quality. In all sectors of ECE—state-sponsored prekindergarten programs, Head Start, and community-based child care—requirements for the educational background and ongoing training of the ECE workforce are receiving increased scrutiny, and a variety of efforts are underway to promote improvements in workforce qualifications.

In Head Start, for example, a congressional mandate that half of teachers in center-based classrooms hold an associate's degree or higher with specialization in early childhood education or a related field by September 2003 has resulted in a steady increase in teacher qualifications. In 2003, 57% of teachers met the mandated qualifications, up from 51% in 2002 (Hart & Schumacher, 2004; Schumacher & Irish, 2003). In addition, in 2002, 45% of teachers without degrees were enrolled in a degree program (Schumacher & Irish, 2003). States creating or expanding prekindergarten programs must also make decisions about staffing requirements. About half of the approximately 38 state-sponsored prekindergarten programs require that lead teachers have bachelor's degrees (Barnett, Robin, Hustedt, & Schulman, 2003). States seeking to expand their prekindergarten programs are confronting an insufficient supply of qualified early childhood teachers and are considering ways to substantially expand their early childhood professional development in order to meet the new demand (Maxwell & Clifford, in press).

As part of the *Good Start, Grow Smart* initiative, states have been required to include a state plan for providing training and education for child care and preschool teachers and administrators in their biennial plans for the Child Care and Development Fund (CCDF; see Chapter 1). There is little indication that states are responding to the requirement to have a professional development plan by increasing regulatory requirements for child care providers. Only a handful of states have increased preservice requirements for teachers in center-based care, and a majority of states have no preservice ECE training or education requirements for center care providers (LeMoine, 2004a) and family child care providers (LeMoine, 2004b). However, a substantial number of states have responded to the challenge of increasing the qualifications of the ECE workforce by providing financial assistance to caregivers so that they can gain access to training and educational opportunities. For example, 22 states actively participate in the T.E.A.C.H. program, a program founded in North Carolina that involves scholarships for professional development and incentives for early childhood teachers to increase retention (T.E.A.C.H. Early Childhood Project, 2004). A number of states are also developing career lattices that outline the specific milestones of improved qualifications and practice and identifying and addressing barriers to professional development such as lack of articulation agreements between 2- and 4-year institutions of higher education.

Given the focus on professional development as a critical contributor to program quality and the investments being made at multiple levels (federal, state, and community) in improving workforce qualifications, the need for an intensive examination of the research evidence linking professional development and quality is pressing. This chapter's goal is to conduct a rigorous review of the literature by using clear definitions of professional development and drawing on studies from all sectors of the ECE field. Reviews of the literature (Barnett, 2003a; National Research Council, 2001; Whitebook, 2003) have focused exclusively on research linking teacher education and quality in center-based preschool classrooms and have asked in particular whether a bachelor's degree and specialized education in ECE are necessary to ensure quality. This chapter includes this research in the current review but goes beyond it to include evidence from infant and toddler care and family child care as well as Head Start and prekindergarten programs. The chapter also weighs the evidence on qualifications and quality considering the full range of professional development categories (education, training, and certification) rather than evidence focusing primarily on formal educational levels. We feel this approach will help identify multiple layers of policy and practice issues across the professional development spectrum (from little or no background in ECE to advanced degrees in child development and ECE).

The chapter first describes the strategy that we used for selecting and reviewing articles and synthesizing research findings. Next, it describes findings from our review of the literature (which includes studies meeting certain selection criteria described next, as well as studies of note that do not meet the criteria but make important contributions to emerging knowledge). The review is broken into four primary sections: 1) findings from studies addressing formal education and its relation to program quality, 2) findings from an overlapping set of studies specifically examining coursework in ECE, 3) findings from studies of training that occurs outside the formal education system, and 4) findings from studies examining certification. To anticipate the key conclusions from this section of the review, we find that

- More education, particularly with specialization in early childhood development, is related to a higher quality of ECE programs and interactions between teachers and children.

- However, the research base is limited by the lack of examination of thresholds (i.e., whether the attainment of specific levels of education, certification, or training are of particular importance for observed program quality).

- The role of training in professional development and its links to program quality have not been extensively or rigorously examined. Although training does seem to be associated with higher quality in the limited available research, the work focusing on training is hindered by imprecise measurement (e.g., assessing whether a provider has *ever* attended training) and thus does not allow an understanding of how different types, content, and intensity of training are related to program quality or improvements. Promising findings in this area suggest the potential importance of a more careful examination of the extent and nature of training as a contributor to ECE quality.

The chapter then highlights issues and problems that we discovered in the literature. It notes the need for studies that rigorously evaluate differing approaches to improving qualifications rather than simply studying the associations of quality and qualifications. The prevalent approach of studying associations is subject to the problem that findings may reflect the characteristics of those who seek out further professional development as well as, or instead of, the effects of the professional development itself. The chapter describes emerging approaches to tightening the linkages between qualifications and quality in the ECE field to ensure that the content and quality of professional development initiatives actually result in the desired competencies and practices among the ECE workforce. Finally, the chapter discusses important next steps for research and practice.

## STRATEGY OF REVIEW

Chapter 2 lays the groundwork for this chapter by proposing definitions for different aspects of professional development. The definitions are vital given the wide variation across researchers in the use of terminology to describe professional development in the ECE workforce. This lack of agreement on terminology impedes attempts to look across studies to consider patterns of findings. Researchers often use the same terms to refer to different aspects of professional development, so to summarize simply on the basis of the terminology used in different studies would often mean combining unlike categories. For example, for some researchers the term *training* encompasses early childhood content obtained within or outside of the formal education system (e.g., Clarke-Stewart, Vandell, Burchinal, O'Brien, & McCartney, 2002), whereas others use the word *training* to refer to professional development that occurs outside of the formal education system through such contexts as in-service workshops, community workshops, and workshops at professional meetings (e.g., Burchinal, Cryer, Clifford, & Howes, 2002).

In order to summarize similar categories, we set aside the labels used by the researchers in individual studies linking professional development and environmental quality and have superimposed the terminology proposed by Maxwell and colleagues in Chapter 2. They propose distinguishing between two aspects of education: 1) level of formal education attained (usually measured by years of education or highest degree obtained) without respect to the content of the education and 2) formal education with early childhood content, such as an associate's, bachelor's, or master's degree in child development or a related field. They also distinguish two other forms of professional development: 1) certification (with the Child Development Associate [CDA] as the type of certification most often reported on in the published research) and 2) "pure" training, occurring entirely outside of the formal educational system (e.g., through workshops sponsored by a child care resource and referral agency). Researchers have sometimes created a hybrid category of early childhood content attained within and outside of the formal educational system (e.g., Howes, 1997) using a ladder structure—the lowest rungs involve lower levels of education (e.g., high school degree) combined with workshops held outside of educational settings, but the high rungs involve more advanced educational degrees with majors in early childhood. Because this category does not fit cleanly in our education with ECE content category or our pure training category, we have added another category called "combined ladder." As the higher rungs of the combined ladder involve education with ECE content, we analyze findings from studies using this measurement approach together with those that examine education with ECE content.

We also follow the precedents in Chapter 2 by reviewing the research in two groupings of studies. Maxwell and colleagues first reviewed studies that met the following criteria: the studies focused on early childhood care and education *within the United States,* involved *50 early childhood teachers or family child care providers* (so as to include a sufficient range of settings), and the work was *published in peer reviewed journals.* Beyond these published studies, Maxwell and colleagues included "studies of note." These studies, if published, might not have focused on samples in the United States or met the criterion of 50 early childhood teachers or family child care providers (e.g., Arnett, 1989; Pence & Goelman, 1991). They might also have been important studies that have not yet been published in peer reviewed journals (e.g., the Head Start Family and Child Experiences Surveys [FACES] [Administration for Children and Families (ACF), 2003; Administration on Children, Youth and Families (ACYF), 2001]; the National Center for Early Development and Learning [NCEDL] study of prekindergarten settings in six states [Bryant, Barbarin, Clifford, Early, & Pianta, 2004]; or the studies of child care in four Midwestern states [see Chapter 5 of this book] and in Massachusetts [Marshall et al., 2001; Marshall et al., 2003]). As noted previously, other reviews of the literature on professional development (e.g., Barnett, 2003a; Whitebook, 2003) have focused on formal center-based settings only (center child care, preschool, Head Start, and prekindergarten). The present review includes home-based as well as classroom-based early childhood settings. As will be seen, the studies that meet the criteria for our first category are generally studies of child care settings, whereas the studies of Head Start and prekindergarten thus far fall into the second category of studies of note. This is a reflection of the evolution of the research. We expect that the body of published work focusing on early childhood settings in the United States and with a sample of 50 or more teachers will soon include detailed reports of some of the Head Start and prekindergarten work that are summarized in the "Evidence from Studies of Note" section.

Our review was also influenced by Breunig, Brandon, and Maher (2004). Breunig and colleagues reviewed the adequacy of the available data for estimating the size of the early childhood workforce. They note not only a lack of national data collection focusing on specific components of the workforce (e.g., self-employed providers), but also frequently occurring methodological problems especially in state data collection that hinder the use of available data as a basis for measuring the size and qualifications of the workforce. Although Chapter 2 provides a lens that clarifies the importance of definitional issues in the literature, the work of Breunig and colleagues provides a second lens that underscores the importance of methodological issues. Using this lens, this chapter asks: What questions do the analytic approaches in the research really permit us to address? Do the analyses carried out actually address *thresholds* (such as whether providers with a bachelor's degree differ from providers with less education with respect to the quality of the early childhood environment)? Do analyses permit us to say whether training predicts better outcomes above and beyond (i.e., controlling for) level of education or whether education matters above and beyond training? Do existing studies shed light on why there might be associations between qualifications and quality?

Findings are discussed in four sections. The chapter turns first to the published studies meeting our criteria and simply identifies which of the categories of professional development have been most widely studied in work linking qualifications and quality. It then summarizes the evidence in the published studies for whether there are statistically significant associations between qualifications and environmental quality when considering formal education, education with early childhood content, pure training, and certification. In a third step, the chapter attempts to go beyond the evidence for association of qualifications and quality and considers the extent to which the available evidence in published studies permits further, more detailed questions to be addressed. Finally, it reviews findings in the studies of note, considering whether they support and extend the patterns identified in the published research.

## FINDINGS FROM PUBLISHED STUDIES THAT MET THE CRITERIA

Sixteen studies met the criteria described previously for published studies examining linkages between qualifications and environmental quality in early childhood settings in the United States. Each of the studies involved at least one of our categories for professional development, used direct observation to document the quality of the ECE environment, and linked the quality of care with qualifications of the ECE teacher or family child care provider. Two types of quality measures were used most frequently. The first type involves a global or summary measure of quality, typically an environmental rating scale such as the Infant/Toddler Environment Scale, original and revised (ITERS and ITERS-R; Harms, Cryer, & Clifford, 1990, 2003); the Early Childhood Environment Rating Scale, original and revised (ECERS and ECERS-R; Harms & Clifford, 1980; Harms, Clifford, & Cryer, 1998); the Family Day Care Rating Scale (FDCRS; Harms & Clifford, 1989); or the Child Care HOME Inventory used in family child care homes (adapted from the HOME inventory [Caldwell & Bradley, 1984] for use in the National Institute of Child Health and Human Development (NICHD) Study of Early Child Care and Youth Development). The scales are used in full, or subscale scores or factor scores are created. The second type involves a measure focusing specifically on the quality of caregiver–child interactions, usually the Caregiver Interaction Scale (CIS; Arnett, 1989). The Observational Record of the Caregiving Environment (ORCE; used in the NICHD Study of Early Child Care and Youth Development) also documents the quality of caregiver–child interactions using both ratings and frequencies of "positive caregiving." When applicable, patterns found for each type of measure are noted.

Table 4.1 provides a brief categorization of findings from the studies we reviewed (a more detailed version of this table is available from the authors on request). Separate columns note whether a study examined, and whether it found, a significant linkage with program quality for 1) level of formal education (considered without respect to early childhood content); 2) formal education with early childhood content; 3) "combined ladder"; 4) the CDA (with other forms of certification not studied frequently enough to summarize); and 5) "pure training," or training provided entirely outside of the formal education system. The first and second columns in Table 4.1 note the author(s) and

**Table 4.1.** Literature examining the link between different aspects of professional development and child care quality

| Study | Multi-use data | Formal education without respect to content | Formal education with ECE content | "Combined ladder": ECE content both inside and outside of formal education | CDA | "Pure training" outside of formal education setting |
|---|---|---|---|---|---|---|
| **Studies of center-based care** | | | | | | |
| Blau (2000) | Cost, Quality and Outcomes Study | ✓ | — | ✓ | — | — |
| Burchinal, Cryer, Clifford, & Howes (2002) | Cost, Quality and Outcomes Study | — | — | ✓ | — | ✓ |
| de Kruif, McWilliam, Ridley, & Wakeley (2000) | N/A | ✓ | — | ✓ | — | — |
| Honig & Hirallal (1998) | N/A | ✓ | — | ✓ | — | — |
| Howes (1997) | Cost, Quality and Outcomes Study and Florida Quality Improvement Study | — | — | ✓ | ✓ | — |
| Howes, Whitebook, & Phillips (1992) | Child Care Staffing Study | ✓ | ✓ | — | — | — |
| Phillips, Mekos, Scarr, McCartney, & Abbott-Shim (2000) | N/A | Not significant | — | ✓ | — | — |
| Phillipsen, Burchinal, Howes, & Cryer (1997) | Cost, Quality and Outcomes Study | ✓ | — | — | — | — |
| **Studies that include both center-based care and family child care** | | | | | | |
| NICHD ECCRN (1996) | NICHD | Not significant | ✓ | — | — | — |
| NICHD ECCRN (2000) | NICHD | ✓ | ✓ | — | — | — |

*(continued)*

**Table 4.1.** *(continued)*

| Study | Multi-use data | Formal education without respect to content | Formal education with ECE content | "Combined ladder": ECE content both inside and outside of formal education | CDA | "Pure training" outside of formal education setting |
|---|---|---|---|---|---|---|
| NICHD ECCRN (2002) | NICHD | – | ✓ | – | – | – |
| **Studies of family child care** | | | | | | |
| Burchinal, Howes, & Kontos (2002) | Family Child Care and Relative Study and California Licensing Study | Not significant | – | – | – | ✓ |
| Clarke-Stewart, Vandell, Burchinal, O'Brien, & McCartney (2002) | NICHD | ✓ | Not significant | – | – | ✓ |
| Kontos, Howes, & Galinsky (1996) | N/A | – | – | – | – | ✓ |
| Norris (2001) | N/A | ✓ | – | – | – | ✓ |
| Weaver (2002) | N/A | ✓ | ✓ | ✓ | – | – |

A check mark (✓) indicates the aspect was examined and was significantly associated with quality; a minus sign (–) indicates that the aspect was not examined; *Not significant* indicates that the aspect was examined but was not significantly associated with quality. *Key:* CDA = Child Development Associate credential; ECE = early care and education; NICHD ECCRN = National Institute of Child Health and Human Development Early Child Care Research Network.

whether the study relied on data from a major dataset that has been analyzed in multiple ways (e.g., the Cost, Quality and Outcomes Study; the National Child Care Staffing Study; NICHD Study of Early Child Care and Youth Development). Row headings indicate whether the study focused only on center care, only family child care, or on both types of care.

When looking at the findings from the set of studies meeting our selection criteria, we note that when multiple studies relied on the same data from a major dataset (e.g., half of the studies we reviewed on center care involved analyses with the Cost, Quality, and Outcomes dataset), different analytic approaches often led to slightly different conclusions, again underscoring the importance of analytic approach. Yet, even with differences in analytic approaches with a single dataset sometimes yielding differing results, we recognized the overlap of these studies and tried not to weigh the findings from one dataset too heavily in synthesizing across the studies. Our summary statements below always rely on findings from multiple datasets. In addition, when a single study provided both initial exploratory results (e.g., simple correlations) but then went on to report on multivariate analyses (e.g., analyses controlling for background characteristics of the providers or families or controlling for one type of professional development to more fully isolate the role of another), we rely on the multivariate results. When alternate models were reported and it is not clear which one should be viewed as final, we draw on and summarize the findings for multiple models.

## Coverage of the Different Aspects of Professional Development

This section first looks at how extensive the focus has been on each of the distinct aspects of professional development in the published studies meeting our criteria. In general, using the definitions proposed by Maxwell and colleagues (see Chapter 2), the existing literature permits greater consideration of education than of training. Education—studied through a general measure of educational level (that is, not specifying ECE content) or through a measure specifying education with ECE content—is almost always included in studies linking qualifications and quality. In some cases, the researchers noted that only one measure of education is included in the analyses because of high intercorrelations between measures of formal education and education with ECE content (e.g., Phillipsen, Burchinal, Howes, & Cryer, 1997). Other researchers included both types of education measures in analyses and acknowledge the potential overlap between them (Clarke-Stewart et al., 2002; Howes, Whitebook, & Phillips, 1992). Still others used the combined ladder approach to merge education with ECE content and training into one measure (e.g., Burchinal, Cryer, et al., 2002; Howes, 1997). Because level of formal education with ECE is already included at the upper levels in a combined ladder measure, some studies using a combined ladder do not include an additional measure of formal education in the analyses (e.g., Burchinal, Cryer, et al., 2002; see Blau, 2000, for an exception). These findings on when and how different aspects of education are included in analyses on qualifications and quality highlight the tremendous variation in approaches used in the published research. Table 4.1 shows how studies vary not only in terms of which aspects of professional development they focus on, but also in the number of different aspects considered simultaneously. There is also variation across studies in the extent to which analyses control for some aspects of professional development to more fully isolate the role of a particular aspect (e.g., controlling for formal education and education with ECE content to isolate the role of training).

Few studies we reviewed contain a measure of "pure" training that has occurred outside of formal education systems, and these studies were primarily from the family child care literature. Researchers often incorporated training into combined ladders. When considered as part of a combined ladder, it is not possible to ask whether training in particular is associated with environmental quality. Yet, a separate consideration of training is important for policy makers and practitioners seeking to determine how to invest professional development funds. For example, do workshops offered through community or professional organizations make a difference in the quality of care provided? Are ongoing training requirements effective in helping providers maintain their skills? What format and content of training are most useful to providers? These questions remain virtually unanswered in the existing literature.

Finally, the only form of certification examined in the studies we reviewed was the CDA (see Chapter 2 for a discussion of other types of certification). In addition, the CDA was generally studied as one component of the combined ladder approach. Although two studies we reviewed provided evidence regarding associations of the CDA with quality in family child care (Weaver, 2002) or in center care (Howes, 1997), the capacity to make general statements about the associations between the CDA and environmental quality is limited.

## Do Different Aspects of Professional Development Predict Observed Quality?

This section reviews the evidence from the published studies that met our criteria linking the categories of professional development with program quality. It discusses findings for the professional development categories separately to help clarify the strength of the evidence but also notes when significant linkages were found for multiple professional development categories within the same study. For example, if a study identified a statistically significant linkage between quality and education as well as with training, the findings are discussed together, noting the relative importance of each category. Tables

4.2–4.4 provide a distillation of the evidence regarding associations between different facets of professional development and environmental quality in early childhood settings (level of formal education in Table 4.2, education with early childhood content in Table 4.3, and pure training in Table 4.4). These tables note whether the study considered the particular facet of professional development and, if so, whether a statistically significant association was found between the particular facet of professional development and measures of quality in the most rigorous test used within the study. The evidence is noted separately for studies focusing on center-based care, home-based care, and studies encompassing both types of care.

**Levels of Formal Education (Without Specification of ECE Content)**    As can be seen in Table 4.2, in most of the published studies that have examined formal education, this facet of quality has been found to predict observed quality in both center and family child care settings. There

**Table 4.2.**    Examination of final statistical models reported for formal education alone

| Supporting evidence? | Study sample includes | | |
| --- | --- | --- | --- |
| | Center care | Both | Family child care |
| Yes | Blau (2000) | NICHD ECCRN (2000) (quality at 24 and 36 months but not 6 or 15) | Clarke-Stewart, Vandell, Burchinal, O'Brien, & McCartney (2002) |
| | de Kruif, McWilliam, Ridley, & Wakeley (2000) | | Weaver (2002) |
| | Honig & Hirallal (1998) | | Norris (2001) |
| | Howes, Whitebook, & Phillips (1992) | | |
| | Phillipsen, Burchinal, Howes, & Cryer (1997) | | |
| No | Phillips, Mekos, Scarr, McCartney, & Abbott-Shim (2000) | NICHD ECCRN (1996) (quality at 6 months) | Burchinal, Howes, & Kontos (2002) |
| Not examined | Burchinal, Cryer, Clifford, & Howes (2002) | NICHD ECCRN (2002) | Kontos, Howes, & Galinsky (1996) |
| | Howes (1997) | | |

*Key:* ECE = early care and education; NICHD ECCRN = National Institute for Child Health and Human Development Early Child Care Research Network

**Table 4.3.**    Examination of final statistical models reported for formal education with ECE content and "combined ladder" (ECE content through courses *and* workshops)

| Supporting evidence? | Study sample includes | | |
| | Center care | Both | Family child care |
| --- | --- | --- | --- |
| Yes | Blau (2000) | NICHD ECCRN (1996) (quality at 6 months) | Weaver (2002) |
| | Burchinal, Cryer, Clifford, & Howes (2002) | NICHD ECCRN (2000) (quality at 24 and 36 months but not 6 or 15) | |
| | Honig & Hirallal (1998) | | |
| | Howes (1997) | NICHD ECCRN (2002) | |
| | Howes, Whitebook, & Phillips (1992) | | |
| No | Phillips, Mekos, Scarr, McCartney, & Abbott-Shim (2000) | | Clarke-Stewart, Vandell, Burchinal, O'Brien, & McCartney (2002) |
| Not examined | de Kruif, McWilliam, Ridley, & Wakeley (2000) | | Burchinal, Howes, & Kontos (2002) |
| | Phillipsen, Burchinal, Howes, & Cryer (1997) | | Kontos, Howes, & Galinsky (1996) |
| | | | Norris (2001) |

*Key:* ECE = early care and education; NICHD ECCRN = National Institute for Child Health and Human Development Early Child Care Research Network

were, however, instances in which a linkage was not found (Burchinal, Howes, & Kontos, 2002; NICHD Early Child Care Research Network [ECCRN], 1996; Phillips, Mekos, Scarr, McCartney, & Abbott-Shim, 2000). When link-ages were found, formal education was related to both global environmental quality measures and measures of caregiver–child interaction.

The linkages between formal education and observed child care quality can be illustrated with findings from large-scale studies of both center and family child care. Howes et al. (1992) analyzed data from the National Child Care Staffing Study, a study of 227 child care centers in five metropolitan centers in different areas of the United States. Within each center, data were collected for both teachers or teacher-directors and an assistant or aide in a ran-domly selected infant, toddler, and preschool-age classroom. Observed class-

**Table 4.4.**    Examination of final statistical models reported for "pure training"

| Supporting evidence? | Study sample includes | | |
|---|---|---|---|
| | Center care | Both | Family child care |
| Yes | Burchinal, Cryer, Clifford, & Howes (2002) | | Burchinal, Howes, & Kontos (2002) |
| | | | Clarke-Stewart, Vandell, Burchinal, O'Brien, & McCartney (2002) |
| | | | Kontos, Howes, & Galinsky (1996) |
| No | | | Norris (2001) |
| Not examined | Blau (2000) | NICHD ECCRN (1996) | Weaver (2002) |
| | de Kruif, McWilliam, Ridley, & Wakeley (2000) | NICHD ECCRN (2000) | |
| | Honig & Hirallal (1998) | | |
| | Howes (1997) | NICHD ECCRN (2002) | |
| | Howes, Whitebook, & Phillips (1992) | | |
| | Phillips, Mekos, Scarr, McCartney, & Abbott-Shim (2000) | | |
| | Phillipsen, Burchinal, Howes, & Cryer (1997) | | |

*Key:* NICHD ECCRN = National Institute for Child Health and Human Development Early Child Care Research Network

room quality was best explained in models that entered level of formal education first and then education with early childhood content (which was found to be moderately correlated with level of formal education). Considering all classroom age groups together, and combining the data from teachers and teaching assistants, level of formal education was the most consistent predictor of caregiver sensitivity, harshness, and detachment using the CIS. It also predicted ratings on a summary scale of appropriate caregiving (based on factor analysis with data from the ITERS or the ECERS). Education with ECE content was also a predictor for appropriate caregiving for infants.

Analyses conducted by Clarke-Stewart et al. (2002) provided evidence of the linkages between formal education and observed quality in family child care using data from the NICHD Study of Early Child Care and Youth Development, which is a large-scale longitudinal study of children's development in the context of child care and in light of family experiences from the first years of life forward. The sample was selected from a large pool of mothers giving birth in specified time periods in 31 hospitals in 10 locations in the United States. Although the full sample includes children with a range of child care experiences, the present analyses focused on nonrelative caregivers who cared for two or more children in a home-based setting and received payment. Analyses controlling for family characteristics, study site, and child age found that caregiver's level of formal education (along with education with ECE content and training in the past year) predicted quality of the environment as measured by the Child Care HOME Inventory, a measure of the stimulation and support available to the child in a child care home setting. Caregiver's level of formal education and recent training (but not education with ECE content) remained significant predictors of the Child Care HOME Inventory in a model with measures of caregiver characteristics (caregiver professionalism, child-centered beliefs, depressive symptoms, own child present, and caregiver age) taken into account. This is important as these caregiver characteristics might have helped to explain which individuals sought out and received the further education or training. Controlling for these factors helps to eliminate the possibility that the linkages between quality and qualifications are a result of the characteristics of those motivated enough to pursue professional development rather than the effects of the professional development activities.

### Education Specifying a Focus on Early Care and Education

**Content**    Table 4.3 provides a summary of the findings regarding education with ECE content. We include those studies that looked separately at education with ECE content (e.g., degrees with a major in early childhood development) and studies using a combined ladder approach in which the higher rungs of the ladder involved education with ECE content. Linkages have been found between education with ECE content and quality, especially in studies focused on center care (Blau, 2000; Howes et al., 1992; Phillips et al., 2000) but also, albeit less often, in studies of family child care (Weaver, 2002) and in samples encompassing a range of settings (NICHD ECCRN 1996, 2000). Although the balance of the evidence supports the conclusion that there is better observed quality when caregivers have more education with ECE content (as with the pattern of findings regarding level of formal education), the evidence here is somewhat mixed. One study does not find a link between education with ECE content and the quality of the environment (Clarke-Stewart et al., 2002). In addition, although not shown in the table, it should also be noted that other studies sometimes find linkages with quality for some age groups but not others (e.g., Phillips et al., 2000).

Among the studies providing evidence of a link between education with ECE content and quality in center child care, Howes (1997) analyzed data from the Cost, Quality and Outcomes study as well as the Florida Quality Improvement Study. The Cost, Quality and Outcomes Study involved a sample of 655 classrooms in full-day full-year child care centers in California, Colorado, Connecticut, and North Carolina. The Florida Quality Improvement Study sample involved 410 classrooms in 150 child care programs in four Florida counties. In the Cost, Quality and Outcomes Study, teachers with more education with ECE content were rated as more sensitive, less harsh, and more responsive. In the Florida Quality Improvement Study, having more education with ECE content was related to greater sensitivity and responsiveness, more language play, and more positive management in the classroom.

As an example of work focusing on education with ECE content among family child care providers, Weaver (2002) studied 65 licensed family child homes in Wisconsin and found that providers with at least one college course in ECE had higher scores on the FDCRS than those without any coursework in ECE. College coursework in ECE remained a significant predictor of the quality of the family day care environment even with formal education, accumulated training, psychological well-being, and family income taken into account.

***Training***    Table 4.4 provides an overview of findings regarding pure training. Each of the studies that has focused on pure training has reported evidence of an association with observed quality. However the number of studies is limited and, as already noted, concentrated in family child care. Burchinal, Howes, and Kontos (2002) looked at data from two studies of family child care: the Family Child Care and Relative Care Study (with 226 families and providers in Charlotte, North Carolina; Dallas-Fort Worth, Texas; and San Fernando Valley, California), and the California Licensing Study (with 100 licensed family child care homes in California). Pooling data from the two studies, analyses found that providers who had participated in training workshops had higher scores on the FDCRS and lower detachment scores on the CIS.

The one study focusing on pure training in center settings among the published studies meeting our criteria raises the possibility that training may be a significant predictor of quality in formal settings as well, even when other qualifications are taken into account. In analyses of Cost Quality and Outcomes data, Burchinal, Cryer, et al. (2002) provided evidence that pure training contributes to environmental quality and caregiver–child interaction even after controlling for education with ECE content. They examined individually the linkages with quality of three types of pure training: in-service workshops, workshops in the community, and workshops at professional meetings. Each added significantly to the prediction of environmental ratings

(ITERS and ECERS scores) and caregiver–child interactions (CIS total score) after taking into account other characteristics of the classroom (including teacher education with ECE content). Training was related to modestly higher skills for all teachers, regardless of their educational qualifications. Yet, the analyses also showed that training alone did not bring teachers with lower ECE educational qualifications (i.e., less than a bachelor's degree) up to the level of sensitivity and classroom quality observed by teachers holding a bachelor's degree with ECE content.

These studies also suggest that regular participation in training is related to quality. For example, in the work of Burchinal, Howes, and Kontos (2002), analyzing data from 226 family child care homes in the Family Child Care and Relative Study as well as from 100 family child care homes participating in the California Licensing Study, caregivers who had participated in a workshop in the past year had significantly higher FDCRS scores and had lower CIS detachment scores. Norris (2001) studied the care in family child care homes of 70 licensed family child care providers randomly selected from the lists of licensed providers in five California counties. This study distinguished between those who had never completed a workshop, those who had participated intermittently (not in every period of employment as a family child care provider), and those who had participated continually (participated in at least one workshop per time period of employment). FDCRS scores were higher for those who had participated continually than for either intermittent participants or nonparticipants. This pattern held for specific FDCRS subscales as well (Learning and Activities subscale and Basic Care subscale).

**Certification**    The CDA was the only form of certification studied in the set of published studies that met the criteria. Yet, this aspect of professional development tended to be included as one level of a combined ladder rather than studied separately, and was even studied rarely as a rung on a combined ladder. Accordingly, we do not include a separate table providing a distillation of these findings. Some findings do, however, suggest that having a CDA is positively associated with quality in both center and family child care settings. It should be underscored, however, that the findings focusing on this aspect of professional development are sparse.

In the Howes (1997) study, sample size was sufficient to give separate consideration to having a CDA in the Florida Quality Improvement Study but not in the Cost Quality and Outcomes Study. In the former study, having a CDA was examined as part of a combined ladder in which the levels included having completed high school and participated in some child development–related workshops, having completed a CDA, having some college courses in ECE, and having a bachelor's degree or higher in ECE. Findings differed by the specific aspect of quality considered. Teachers with a bachelor's degree or higher in ECE were more sensitive than those with a CDA, who were, in turn, more sensitive than those with some college ECE or high school with workshops. In addition, teachers with a bachelor's degree or higher in ECE were more responsive than all other categories. However, teachers with a CDA were observed to make more positive initiations toward children than other teachers, and those with either a bachelor's degree or CDA were observed to engage in more language play and positive management than teachers with a high school education.

In Weaver's (2002) study, the CDA was examined as part of a combined ladder in which the lowest rung was less than 1 year of required training as a licensed provider, the fourth rung was 10 or more years of accumulated training, and the highest rung was having a CDA or accreditation. We have labeled this as a combined ladder rather than as a training measure because the required 120 hours of coursework for the CDA can occur either within or outside of the formal educational system. We note that the joint examination of CDA and accreditation makes it impossible to isolate the role of the CDA alone in these analyses. Analyses indicated that there was a significant association of this combined ladder variable and observed quality as measured by the FDCRS. Follow-up analyses indicated that those providers with a CDA or accreditation had higher average FDCRS scores than all other groups. Furthermore, when this measure was entered into analyses along with formal education and education with ECE (as well as family income and psychological well-being), the combined ladder variable was the strongest predictor of FDCRS scores, although as noted previously, formal education and education with ECE content also remained significant predictors.

There is a clear need for further rigorous examination of the role of the CDA in contributing to quality. The findings of Howes (1997) are intriguing because they suggest that a bachelor's degree in ECE stands alone in predicting some aspects of quality in early childhood environments. For other aspects of quality, however, the CDA functions at the same level as a bachelor's degree in ECE as a predictor of quality. A careful consideration of the role of the CDA in predicting quality should include whether the coursework was completed within the formal educational system. Furthermore, work should also distinguish clearly between the CDA and accreditation for family child care providers as well as the CDA and an associate's degree for all providers. Sample sizes in the Howes (1997) study did not allow a simultaneous consideration of an associate's degree and CDA, but this is a comparison that would be informative in future work.

### Going Beyond "More Is Better": Thresholds     Taken together, the evidence presented in this chapter thus far indicates that different aspects of professional development (level of formal education, education with ECE content, training and certification) are related to observed quality in ECE settings, although with substantially more research on education than on train-

ing and very little research to date focusing on certification. Although the evidence to date suggests that these aspects of professional development matter, and that more of these aspects of professional development bode well for the quality of care, the research is not as clear with respect to the threshold (or absolute level) of professional development needed to obtain a particular level of quality in the early childhood setting. Policy makers are interested in this idea of thresholds because if it were known, for instance, that obtaining a bachelor's degree in any subject (not necessarily with ECE content) was sufficient for achieving a desired level of quality, then requiring a bachelor's degree with ECE content might not be necessary. Similarly, if having a CDA consistently brought quality to a level similar to that of an associate's or bachelor's degree, then this information could guide investments in professional development initiatives and the development of requirements for professional development. Unfortunately, the evidence to date does not suffice to permit clear statements about the level or type of professional development required for particular levels of quality. Analyses in some studies ask, "If qualifications increase, then does quality increase?" (e.g., NICHD ECCRN, 1996, 2000, 2002), which answers the question of whether "more is better" but not whether one form of professional development is better than another. However, even analyses that attempt to distinguish among levels of professional development do not always yield consistent results.

The evidence sometimes indicates that a bachelor's degree (when formal education is considered without respect to content) or a bachelor's degree in early childhood (when education with ECE content is considered) stands apart from other levels of education in predicting quality, but this is not always the case. As noted next, results sometimes indicate that having a bachelor's degree (or a bachelor's degree with a major in ECE) groups together with having some college with ECE content or a CDA. Findings differ even within studies according to which specific measure of quality is the outcome (e.g., ECERS score, CIS sensitivity), the age of the children in the classrooms or groups considered (infants and toddlers or preschoolers), and how the analyses were conducted. Blau (2000) noted that "[The] estimates clearly indicate that education and training matter, but the precise form of education and training that is most productive depends on whether unobserved differences are accounted for" in analyses as well as the specific way in which they are accounted for (p. 143). Thus, variation in findings may in part reflect whether and which approaches are taken to control for other factors (including background characteristics of the caregivers and settings) that may also predict quality.

The lack of clarity in the research as to thresholds may also be attributable in part to the lack of specification about the extent and content of the ECE courses when "some college" or a "bachelor's degree with an ECE major" are being considered. According to Russell (2004), the founder of the T.E.A.C.H. program, the academic records the T.E.A.C.H. program has reviewed involving a bachelor's degree in early childhood education have encompassed a wide range in terms of credit hours in courses focusing on ECE, with one noteworthy example including only three credits for a bachelor's degree in ECE. Chapter 10 of this book documents some variation *within* educational levels (examining course requirements for three bachelor's degree programs, associate's degree programs, and CDA programs) in the state of Ohio with respect to the coverage of specific elements of instruction for early childhood literacy. This raises the question of how much the categories labeled "some coursework" at the college level and a "bachelor's degree majoring in ECE" actually differ in these studies and what ECE content has actually been included within each of these levels. Future work on the issue of thresholds should include direct measures of the extent and content of coursework rather than the summary labels of some coursework, an associate's degree, or a bachelor's degree in early childhood.

Burchinal, Cryer, et al. (2002) found that teachers who have a bachelor's degree produce higher quality child care environments. They analyzed data from the Cost, Quality and Outcomes Study and found that child care center teachers with a bachelor's degree in early childhood education had higher scores on both global quality (as measured by the ECERS or ITERS) as well as CIS scores for the sensitivity of interaction with children. Caregivers with a bachelor's degree in ECE were more likely to have high-quality classrooms. The magnitude of the difference on global quality scores for having a bachelor's degree in ECE as opposed to an associate's degree in ECE or some ECE courses at the college level was about a third of a standard deviation, and the differences on the CIS were similar in magnitude. The authors concluded that having a bachelor's degree in ECE was the best predictor of quality. Other studies singling out a bachelor's degree as particularly associated with higher quality on at least one quality measure include studies by de Kruif, McWilliam, Ridley, and Wakeley (2000); Honig and Hirallal (1998); and Phillipsen et al. (1997).

In other studies, however, a bachelor's degree grouped with other educational levels in the prediction of quality child care environments. For example, in analyses with the Child Care Staffing Study data, Howes et al. (1992) found that having either a bachelor's degree (with or without ECE content) or college-level ECE content (and no bachelor's degree) was linked to teacher sensitivity (so, a bachelor's degree *or* college-level education with ECE content was important). For a summary measure of appropriate caregiving for preschoolers, the linkages were similar (that is, either a bachelor's degree *or* college-level education with ECE content was important). However, for infants, education with ECE content appeared to be a more important factor in appropriate caregiving than education alone (i.e., a bachelor's degree was not enough to assure quality of caregiving for infants). This example highlights a pattern seen in a number of (though not all) studies: more formal education is better for the quality of care and caregiver–child interactions, yet simultaneous consideration of ECE content provides a more complex picture in which more formal education is not necessarily better *if* education at somewhat lower levels includes college-level ECE content.

Other studies in which the bachelor's degree has been found to group together with other educational levels in predicting quality include 1) the study by Blau (2000) using the Cost, Quality and Outcomes data in which having some college, a college degree, and a graduate degree were all found to predict higher quality in center care (these findings are for one of three analytic approaches taken in this study—an approach involving no fixed effects; the findings from the two fixed effects models differ somewhat but always show multiple education levels grouping together in predicting quality); 2) Clarke-Stewart's et al. (2002) analyses focusing on family child care homes within the NICHD Study of Early Child Care and Youth Development, in which scores on the Child Care HOME were significantly higher for those who had attended college compared with those who had not; and 3) Weaver's (2002) study of family child care in which FDCRS scores differed for those who had some versus no college coursework focusing on early childhood development. In our discussion of the CDA, we have already noted that in the work of Howes (1997), the bachelor's degree in ECE sometimes stood apart in predicting quality and sometimes grouped with a CDA (and in one instance an associate's degree in ECE) in predicting quality depending on the aspect of quality considered.

In sum, this body of work shows that more professional development is better, but where the dividing line should fall to delineate "more" is not entirely clear. This may reflect differences across (and sometimes within) studies in whether and how other predictors of quality are controlled. It may also reflect the lack of precision in the summary labels. That is, a bachelor's degree in ECE at different institutions of higher education may vary widely in requirements to the extent that they may actually overlap in terms of ECE coursework content with that of some associate's degrees in ECE, some college coursework in ECE, or even some CDAs.

### Going Beyond "More Is Better": Joint Consideration of Education and Training    One of the key questions that policy makers have is where to allocate limited funding for professional development. A particularly important issue is whether it is worthwhile to allocate resources to training (defined as community-based and outside of the formal educational system), to professional development through formal education, or to both.

A small set of studies looks at whether training still matters to quality of care with level of education controlled, and whether both education and training predict quality when they are considered simultaneously. These studies suggested that both training and education matter to quality. Thus, for example, studies by Burchinal, Howes and Kontos (2002) and Norris (2001) found differences in the quality of family child care (measured using the FDCRS and the CIS) in light of participation in training, even when formal education was taken into account. Focusing on family child care data in the NICHD Study of Early Child Care and Youth Development, Clarke-Stewart and colleagues (2002) found that both recent training and level of formal education predicted the Child Care HOME even with features of care that are difficult to regulate (e.g., caregiver experience, beliefs about child rearing, depressive symptoms) taken into account.

The pattern extends also to center-based care. With data from the Cost, Quality and Outcomes Study of center child care, Burchinal et al. (2002) looked simultaneously at training (attendance at in-service workshops, community workshops, and workshops at professional meetings) and education with ECE content (using a combined ladder measure starting with no ECE education or workshops only and proceeding up to a bachelor's degree in ECE). These researchers found that both training and education with ECE content predicted quality as measured by the ECERS or ITERS when they were considered simultaneously. This research found that a bachelor's degree in ECE was the best predictor of quality but that training through workshops continued to relate to higher quality at all levels of ECE education. The authors concluded that although both training and education with ECE content matter to quality, those with only training never reach the level of quality seen in those with a bachelor's degree in ECE.

We underscore that only a small set of studies to date give simultaneous consideration to education and training (largely because training has not been extensively studied) and that the definitions of training are imprecise. Nevertheless, findings from this initial set of studies suggest that both education and training contribute to quality. The work of Burchinal and colleagues (2002) with the Cost, Quality and Outcomes data raises the important caution that although both training and education with ECE may help to improve quality, the level of quality associated with higher levels of education with ECE content may be substantially higher. Further work, especially involving more careful consideration of the nature and intensity of *both* education with ECE content and training, would be extremely valuable.

## EVIDENCE FROM STUDIES OF NOTE

The studies of note included in this review confirm and extend the basic patterns described in previous sections. They not only share similar methods and analytic strategies, but also many of the same definitional problems noted in the set of studies reviewed previously (e.g., different definitions of training and lack of specification about the content of training and education; see Arnett [1989] for an exception). They point to significant linkages between professional development qualifications and quality but highlight that the linkages are loose in many cases. These studies point to additional factors that should be taken into account in an examination of qualifications and quality, including the range of qualifications studied; the content of education and training; contextual features of ECE environments (including center-level characteristics and broader policy and regulatory characteristics); and characteristics of teachers and providers, such as knowledge and attitudes, that play a role in the quality of care they provide. A number of these factors were identified in the studies previously discussed, but their presence in the studies of note solidifies their status as important variables to consider.

As described previously, some of the studies of note examine Head Start and prekindergarten programs. These ECE sectors were not represented in the studies meeting the selection criteria for published studies. Prekindergarten programs, particularly those that are associated with public schools, tend to have teachers who hold higher educational credentials than community-based child care programs. Estimates of prekindergarten teachers holding bachelor's degrees range from 70% (Bryant et al., 2004; Clifford et al., 2003) to 90% (Saluja, Early, & Clifford, 2002; U.S. Department of Education, 2004), depending on the auspice (with teachers in public school–based programs holding higher qualifications than teachers in community-based programs).

An example of the way in which range of educational qualifications might make a difference comes from a set of state-level studies conducted in Massachusetts. State representative samples were drawn of community-based preschools (i.e., full-day, full-year child care centers; Marshall et al., 2001), licensed family child care providers (Marshall et al., 2003), and publicly administered prekindergarten classes in public schools (Marshall et al., 2002). In both family and center child care, linkages were found between years of education and overall quality (as measured by either the FDCRS or ECERS-R). Education was also related to specific aspects of quality, including summary scores for stimulation, warmth, and sensitivity in family child care; stimulation, engagement, and an index of process quality; and, marginally, warmth and sensitivity in center child care. The range of education in the three sectors varied widely. In family child care, about one in six providers had an associate's degree in ECE or a higher degree. In community-based child care, about one quarter held an associate's degree, and nearly 50% held a bachelor's degree or higher. In contrast, all of the teachers in the prekindergarten classrooms had bachelor's degrees, and two thirds had master's degrees. Given this limited, high range of educational qualifications, formal education was not a predictor of classroom quality in the prekindergarten study. A relationship was found, however, between additional training in early childhood education and the language and reasoning stimulation observed in the prekindergarten classroom. Furthermore, average scores on the language-reasoning subscale of the ECERS-R for prekindergarten classrooms were a full point higher than the average scores for community-based center classrooms. These findings highlight the importance of training in ECE beyond the level of formal education attained by teachers in prekindergarten programs. Yet, they also point out the potential difficulty of generalizing findings on qualifications and quality between ECE sectors, given the variation in qualifications by sector.

Two additional studies from prekindergarten and Head Start are useful for clarifying the relationship between qualifications and quality by showing statistically significant but modest associations. The first is the NCEDL Multi-State Study of Pre-Kindergarten (Bryant et al., 2004). The study is being carried out in six states with samples of prekindergartens in 40 schools or centers in each state (stratified by whether the teacher had a bachelor's degree, whether the program was in or out of a school setting, and whether the program was full or part day). The majority of teachers in the sample had attained high levels of education: more than two thirds of the teachers had a four-year degree or more, with 22% holding a bachelor's degree, 16% some education beyond the bachelor's degree, and 31% a master's degree or beyond. Yet, the level of overall quality documented on the ECERS-R (mean score of 3.9) was below the good benchmark. Quality was also below the good benchmark on two factor scores from the ECERS-R: teaching and interacting (including teacher–child interaction, discipline, supervision, encouragement to use language; mean score = 4.5) and provisions for learning (including furnishings, room arrangement, equipment for gross motor activities and for different kinds of play; mean score = 3.7). According to the authors, "process quality is lower than would be predicted given the high level of structural quality in these pre-k programs" (p. 6 of presentation handout). Scores were also lower on the instructional and emotional climate scales of the Classroom Assessment Scoring System (CLASS; Pianta & LaParo, 2003). Further analysis of the teacher and program characteristics show that teacher education was related to CLASS emotional quality scores and higher ECERS provision scores. It was not related, however, to ECERS teaching and interaction and CLASS instructional climate, two dimensions of quality closely linked to children's academic experiences. The authors concluded that, "current models of professional development may need revision to attend more to proximal (e.g., attitude and practices) rather than distal (e.g., degrees) factors" (p. 11 of presentation handout).

The set of findings from the Head Start FACES (ACF, 2003; ACYF, 2001) provide additional evidence for the relationship between qualifications and quality and the importance of examining proximal factors as recommended by the NCEDL Multi-State Study authors. Compared with the NCEDL study, in both rounds of FACES data collection, fewer teachers had high levels of education—about a third of the lead teachers in Fall 1997, and 39% in FACES 2000 had a bachelor's degree or higher. Yet, average quality in Head Start classrooms in both rounds of data collection closely approached the "good" benchmark according to the ECERS-R, with average ratings of 4.9 in

1997 and of 4.8 in 2000. In both rounds, teachers with higher levels of education tended to be in classrooms rated higher on the language subscale of the ECERS-R as well as on sensitivity as measured by the CIS. Those with bachelor's or associate's degrees also tended to be in classrooms with better adult–child ratios, suggesting that "good things go together." Additional analyses from FACES 2000 found that the relationship between teacher education and classroom quality was indirect: teachers' knowledge and attitudes toward early education practice as well as the type of curriculum used and the teacher's level of experience were stronger predictors of quality than teacher's educational background. Children's gains on specific cognitive assessments during the Head Start year were linked with use of an integrated curriculum, higher teacher salaries, and teacher educational credentials (related to scores on a measure of early writing skills).

As the examples from FACES show, it is important to go beyond teacher education to understand the aspects of program infrastructure that bolster classroom quality. Although it is possible to examine the linkages between education and quality separately from other characteristics of teachers and of the ECE environment, the reality of early childhood settings is that education may work in a cumulative way with other aspects of ECE programs and providers. Raikes and colleagues (see Chapter 5) document a "culture of quality" or set of characteristics that combine to predict quality in child care settings in four Midwestern states. The total number from among 14 factors ("assets") present for a particular teacher/caregiver was more effective in predicting the overall quality of the setting than consideration of individual factors. The assets included the teachers' qualifications (highest level of education, clock hours of training in child care in the past year, participation in intensive training, completion of a CDA) but went beyond these to include such factors as whether the center or family child care home the teacher worked in participated in the USDA food program for child care, whether the teacher had current CPR certification, whether the teacher used a curriculum, and whether the teacher had held a formal conference with each parent about the child's development. Similarly, Whitebook, Sakai, Gerber, and Howes (2001) identified "background climate" (i.e., the percentage of staff with bachelor's degrees and college-level ECE courses), not just the education level of the lead teacher in the classroom where quality was rated, as a characteristic related to sustained quality (rating a 5 or higher on the ECERS in both 1996 and 2000).

The content of education and training is another aspect of professional development addressed in the studies of note. Arnett (1989) compared four groups of teachers (49 overall) with various levels of education and "training" in a college-level early childhood education program in Bermuda (hereafter we use our terminology of *ECE education* rather than the author's term *training;* this is one illustration of the varying use of terminology in the literature). He found clear differences between the teachers with a 4-year college degree in ECE and the three other levels that included teachers with no ECE education and teachers who had completed half (1 year) or all of a 2-year ECE program at Bermuda College. The teachers with 4-year degrees were less authoritarian and displayed more positive interaction/sensitivity, less detachment, and less punitive behavior than the other three groups. There was little difference between the two groups of teachers that had completed half or all of the Bermuda College program. Both groups were less authoritarian, more positive, and less detached than the group of teachers with no ECE education. Looking specifically at the content of the 2 years of the Bermuda College program, Arnett (1989) concluded that the coursework in the first year—communication (behavior management, fostering self-esteem, and talking in a developmentally appropriate manner) and child development (stages, processes, and milestones)—was more important for changing teachers attitudes, behaviors, and interactions than the second year of coursework that focused on health, nutrition, and curriculum. The findings imply that even 1 year of coursework with content focused on communication and child development could positively influence teachers' behaviors and interactions. The Arnett (1989) study also contributed to a better understanding of thresholds (though it is unclear how generalizable the findings are to education within the United States) and the levels *and* content that are linked to teacher's behaviors. A similar study carried out with an experimental design (perhaps offering lagged entrance to the college courses) would be extremely helpful in teasing apart the selection factors and the specific coursework and activities that are linked to changes in teacher behavior and classroom quality.

In sum, the studies of note contribute to evidence that teachers' educational credentials matter to the quality of the environment and, for Head Start, the gains that children make on specific academic outcomes. However, in studies such as the NCEDL, FACES, and Massachusetts Cost and Quality studies, in which the high qualifications of the teaching staff would imply a high level of classroom quality, the linkages between level of formal education and quality of the environment are loose rather than tight. For example, the high proportion of teachers holding a bachelor's degree in the NCEDL multistate study of prekindergarten classrooms did not suffice to assure high average observed quality. These studies further underscore the need to examine more closely the factors that help to assure that qualifications will translate into quality.

## TIGHTENING THE LINKAGES: THE EMERGENCE OF MULTIPLE PERSPECTIVES

A new body of work is emerging that has the potential to tighten the linkages between professional development and quality, helping to assure that specific forms of professional preparation translate into practice. Thinking of a very simple logic model, with professional development (as the input) contributing to overall classroom quality (as the outcome) through changes in classroom practices (the output), the new work focuses on providing greater clarity 1) with respect to the input through greater specification of the *content* of professional development; 2) with respect to the output, through greater specification of *desired classroom practices;* or 3) on the alignment of the inputs and outputs.

This book includes strong examples of each of these approaches to tightening the linkages. Work toward greater specification of the content of professional preparation is apparent in Chapter 6, which focuses on preparing ECE teachers to support children's early literacy development; Chapter 7, which focuses specifically on children's early mathematical skills; and Chapter 8, which focuses on preparing ECE teachers to foster children's emerging capacity for self-regulation. Each of these chapters underscores the need to provide ECE teachers with a more specific and differentiated understanding of the components of the content area. For example, Chapter 7 notes that children's early mathematical skills cover multiple topics, each with subtopics. These include an understanding of number (e.g., counting, ordinal positions, cardinal value), shapes (both plain figures and solid figures as well as symmetries), and spatial relations (including position—e.g., in front of or behind; navigation—e.g., moving three steps forward or backward; and mapping—e.g., creating a simple representation of objects in the classroom). Each chapter also stresses the importance of sharpening teachers' observational skills to be able to identify when children are spontaneously engaging in activities that support the development of skills in each area and how to foster or extend these activities through structuring of the environment and interacting with children.

Although in the past there has been substantial concern that active structuring of activities to support learning in specific content areas would undermine developmentally appropriate practice for young children Chapter 11 notes movement away from a dichotomization of child-initiated and teacher-initiated learning in the new NAEYC standards for early childhood professional preparation. The standards explicitly support professional preparation in specific content areas and emphasize the possibility of structuring learning experiences for children that involve active child exploration in the context of settings and engaging activities that have been structured to support learning of particular content.

Chapter 10 provides another important example of a strategy to increase the specification of content in early childhood professional preparation. Focusing on preparation in the state of Ohio in early literacy development, this chapter provides a methodology for reviewing course descriptions and syllabi for the extent to which courses at the CDA, associate's degree, and bachelor's degree levels are covering the specific content elements in state preschool and elementary school early literacy curricula. This approach focuses on assuring that courses and sequences of courses in institutions of higher education are including very specific elements of content in their coursework for early childhood professionals. Although the pilot focuses on early literacy coursework, the methodology could readily be applied to other content areas.

Chapter 9 shifts the focus to the other side of the logic model—to outputs, or assuring specific practices in ECE environments. It urges organizing professional preparation directly around classroom practices and particularly teacher–child interaction. It also describes professional preparation approaches involving observation and the provision of feedback to teachers on their interactions with children using well-validated observational measures. Current work focuses on the evaluation of changes in classroom practice when observation and feedback are carried out either directly or via Internet linkages.

NAEYC's standards for early childhood professional preparation encompass both sides of the equation and underscore the importance of alignment across preservice learning and direct interaction with children in the classroom (see Chapter 11). The standards emphasize both mastery of knowledge in specific content areas and the application of the knowledge in the creation of learning environments for young children. This balance of emphasis on both knowledge and practice can be seen, for example, in wording used in one of the standards: "Candidates integrate their understanding of and relationships with children and families; their understanding of developmentally effective approaches to teaching and learning; and their knowledge of academic disciplines, to design, implement, and evaluate experiences that promote positive development and learning for all children." This emphasis on the alignment of knowledge and practice will be part of the review of the implementation of the NAEYC standards in programs of ECE professional preparation at 4-year colleges and universities through the National Council for the Accreditation of Teacher Education (NCATE).

The emerging work with the potential to tighten the linkages between ECE professional development and the quality of early childhood environments is focusing heavily on formal early childhood settings, such as center classrooms and prekindergarten and Head Start programs. A challenge for the future will be to extend these new approaches to home-based settings so that all sectors of ECE are encompassed.

## CONCLUSIONS AND RECOMMENDATIONS

The emerging work places a strong emphasis on using research to guide next steps in early childhood professional preparation. For example, Chapter 6 lays out the ways in which research over the course of a period of years was used to shape and then reshape the content as well as mode of delivery used in an approach to ECE professional preparation in early literacy. The research also examines explicitly how effective approaches have been when moving from small-scale demonstration projects to larger scale implementation within a state. Using research to guide the development and refinement of specific approaches to ECE preparation, and the large-scale implementation of such approaches, will continue to be important as states seek to expand their early childhood workforces and strengthen their qualifications. We see several key next steps for research.

Little is known about processes of selection: What are the characteristics of members of the early childhood workforce that predict their enrollment in professional development activities and attainment of education? Little is known about the extent to which findings on the linkages between quality and qualifications reflect the motivations, beliefs, and prior knowledge of those who select to pursue more education or training. Although the ECE field urgently needs continued and better attempts to *control* for background characteristics of providers in research, this issue should not only be seen as a complicating factor in the research. Taking a careful look at the characteristics of those who enroll in training and education, when this does and does not involve fulfilling specific preservice or in-service training requirements, can help to guide efforts to draw further members of the early childhood workforce into pursuing professional development. Maxwell and Clifford (in press) have suggested that there are barriers to pursuing higher education among the members of the early childhood workforce who are older, members of minority groups, and members who are balancing family obligations. Research focusing explicitly on understanding and seeking to surmount some of the problematic selection issues would help to assure that opportunities for professional development are actually utilized by the full range of members of the early childhood workforce and draw in new members.

Furthermore, work by Howes and colleagues (Howes, James, & Ritchie, 2003) suggested that the ECE field needs research to understand the personal characteristics, experiences, and workplace contexts that are linked to "effective teaching" practices in the absence of preservice training or attainment of higher levels of formal education. In a nonrepresentative sample of primarily African American and Latino teachers in child care programs serving children from low-income families, Howes and colleagues found that experiences with a supportive mentor, feeling a responsibility to the community, and experiences with intensive supervision were linked to effective classroom teaching practices. It will be important to conduct similar studies in diverse samples to better understand how teacher characteristics and workplace practices such as mentoring or reflective supervision interact to produce high-quality classroom environments that are beneficial for children, even when teachers have not attained bachelor's degrees or higher levels of formal education.

In addition to seeking to understand how selection issues are operating and to address them in outreach or structuring of training and education opportunities, there is also a need for rigorous research to provide better tests of the effectiveness of differing approaches to professional development. Experimental evaluations of differing professional development approaches would help to eliminate the concern that linkages found between quality and qualifications are spurious, reflecting the characteristics of those who choose to pursue the preparation rather than the effects of the further education or training. The Quality Interventions for Early Care and Education (QUINCE) evaluation is one example of an experimental evaluation that has two components focusing on somewhat different approaches to training, particularly for family child care providers and entry level center care providers. This evaluation, funded by the Child Care Bureau and the Office of the Assistant Secretary for Planning and Evaluation of the U.S. Department of Health and Human Services, is being implemented by the FPG Child Development Institute and Georgetown University in collaboration with research organizations in multiple states. Such rigorous evaluations of a range of professional development approaches will substantially add to the ECE field's knowledge of which approaches are effective and worthy of investment. Our review underscores the importance of extending such rigorous evaluation approaches to efforts involving training and certification as well as education.

We have noted the limited research focusing on training and especially certification. Yet, these represent important options for states in expanding their professional development opportunities. Furthermore, the existing research suggests that quality can be affected by both training and certification. The ECE field urgently needs better specification of the features of training that are important to quality of the early childhood environment, including an examination of content, intensity, and the auspice offering the training. Chapter 5 suggests that high-intensity training rather than single session workshops and the overall number of clock hours of training in the past year predict observed quality in early childhood settings in the four Midwestern states. Additional work is necessary for developing and testing ways of measuring intensity and content in training. Similarly, work is needed that explicitly focuses on the CDA as a form of professional development and extends the work on certification to other state and local forms of certification. Such work should take care, again, to specify the underlying content and intensity of the preparation involved.

Finally, new research needs to go beyond the "more is better" approach to provide specific information on the thresholds of early childhood professional development that are linked with quality. Such work needs to proceed hand in hand with the emerging work that is providing better specification of the content of early childhood education and training. Although the work to date is clear that more education, more education with ECE content, and more training are each associated with better quality early childhood environments, the ECE field will only gain a clear understanding of the levels of each of these that are critical to quality when professional development terms (e.g., a bachelor's degree in ECE) are more specific about the content and extent of coursework that are needed and the requirements to demonstrate that knowledge translates into practice.

## REFERENCES

Ackerman, D.J. (2004). States' efforts in improving the qualifications of early care and education teachers. *Educational Policy, 18*(2), 311–337.

Administration for Children and Families (ACF). (2003). *Head Start FACES: A whole-child perspective on program performance.* Fourth progress report. Washington, DC: U.S. Department of Health and Human Services.

Administration on Children, Youth and Families (ACYF). (2001). *Head Start FACES: Longitudinal findings on program performance.* Third progress report. Washington, DC: U.S. Department of Health and Human Services.

Arnett, J. (1989). Caregivers in day-care centers: Does training matter? *Journal of Applied Developmental Psychology, 10,* 541–552.

Azer, S.L. (1999). *Child care licensing: Training requirements for roles in child care centers and family child care.* Boston: The Center for Career Development in Early Care and Education, Wheelock College.

Barnett, W.S. (2003a). Better teachers, better preschools: Student achievement linked with teacher qualifications. *Preschool Policy Matters, 2.* New Brunswick, NJ: National Institute for Early Education Research.

Barnett, W.S. (2003b). Low wages = low quality: Solving the real preschool teacher crisis. *Preschool Policy Matters, 3.* New Brunswick, NJ: National Institute for Early Education Research.

Barnett, W.S., Robin, K.B., Hustedt, J., & Schulman, K. (2003). *The state of preschool: 2003 state preschool yearbook.* New Brunswick, NJ: National Institute for Early Education Research.

Bellm, D., Burton, A., Whitebook, M., Broatch, L., & Young, M.P. (2002). *Inside the Pre-K classroom: A study of staffing and stability in state-funded prekindergarten programs.* Washington, DC: Center for the Child Care Workforce. (Available at http://www.ccw.org/pubs/ccw_pre-k_10.4.02.pdf)

Blau, D.M. (2000). The production of quality in child-care centers: Another look. *Applied Developmental Science, 4*(3), 136–148.

Breunig, G.S., Brandon, R., & Maher, E.J. (2004, February). *Counting the child care workforce: A catalog of state data sources to quantify and describe child caregivers in the fifty states and the District of Columbia.* Presentation at the Workshop on Defining and Measuring Professional Development of the Early Childhood Workforce, sponsored by the Child Care Bureau and the Office of the Assistant Secretary for Planning and Evaluation, U.S. Department of Health and Human Development, Washington, D.C.

Bryant, D., Barbarin, O., Clifford, R., Early, D., & Pianta, R. (2004, June). *The National Center for Early Development and Learning: Multi-State Study of Pre-Kindergarten.* Presentation at the National Association for the Education of Young Children's 13th National Institute for Early Childhood Professional Development, Baltimore.

Burchinal, M.R., Cryer, D., Clifford, R.M., & Howes, C. (2002). Caregiver training and classroom quality in childcare centers. *Applied Developmental Science, 6*(1), 2–11.

Burchinal, M.R., Howes, C., & Kontos, S. (2002). Structural predictors of child care quality in child care homes. *Early Childhood Research Quarterly, 17,* 87–105.

Caldwell, B.M., & Bradley, R.H. (1984). *Home observation for measurement of the environment.* Little Rock: University of Arkansas.

Campbell, N.C., Applebaum, J.C., Martinson, K., & Martin, E. (2000). *Be all that we can be: Lessons from the military for improving our nation's child care system.* Washington, DC: National Women's Law Center.

Cassidy, D.J., Buell, M.J., Pugh-Hoese, S., & Russell, S. (1995). The effect of teacher education on child care teachers' beliefs and classroom quality: Year one of the TEACH early childhood associate degree scholarship program. *Early Childhood Research Quarterly, 10,* 171–183.

Center for the Child Care Workforce, A Project of the American Federation of Teachers Educational Foundation (CCW/AFTEF). (2004). *Current data on the salaries and benefits of the U.S. early childhood education workforce.* Washington, DC: Author. (Available at http://www.ccw.org/pubs/2004Compendium.pdf)

Child Care Services Association. (2003). *Child Care Services Association Annual Report: 2002–2003 fiscal year.* Chapel Hill, NC: Author. (Available at http://www.childcareservices.org)

Clarke-Stewart, K.A., Vandell, D.L., Burchinal, M.R., O'Brien, M., & McCartney, K. (2002). Do features of child care homes affect children's development? *Early Childhood Research Quarterly, 17,* 52–86.

Clifford, R.M., Barbarin, O., Bryant, D., Howes, C., Burchinal, M., Pianta, R., Early, D., & Chang, F. (2003). *What is prekindergarten? Six states' efforts to develop a prekindergarten system.* Manuscript submitted for review.

de Kruif, R.E.L., McWilliam, R.A., Ridley, S.M., & Wakely, M.B. (2000). Classification of teachers' interaction behaviors in early childhood classrooms. *Early Childhood Research Quarterly, 15,* 247–268.

Early, D., & Winton, P.J. (2001). Preparing the workforce: Early childhood teacher preparation at 2- and 4-year institutions of higher education. *Early Childhood Research Quarterly, 16,* 285–306.

Harms, T., & Clifford, R.M. (1980). *The Early Childhood Environment Rating Scale.* New York: Teachers College Press.

Harms, T., & Clifford, R.M. (1989). *Family Day Care Rating Scale.* New York: Teachers College Press.

Harms, T., Clifford, R.M., & Cryer, D. (1998). *Early Childhood Environment Rating Scale–Revised Edition.* New York: Teachers College Press.

Harms, T., Cryer, D., & Clifford, R.M. (1990). *Infant/Toddler Environment Rating Scale.* New York: Teachers College Press.

Harms, T., Cryer, D., & Clifford, R.M. (2003). *Infant/Toddler Environment Rating Scale–Revised Edition.* New York: Teachers College Press.

Hart, K., & Schumacher, R. (2004). Moving forward: Head Start children, families, and programs. *Center for Law and Social Policy: Policy Brief (No. 5).* Washington DC: Center for Law and Social Policy.

Honig, A.S., & Hirallal, A. (1998). Which counts more for excellence in childcare staff—years in service, education level or ECE coursework? *Early Child Development & Care, 145,* 31–46.

Howes, C. (1997). Children's experiences in center-based child care as a function of teacher background and adult–child ratio. *Merrill-Palmer Quarterly, 43*(3), 404–425.

Howes, C., James, J., & Ritchie, S. (2003). Pathways to effective teaching. *Early Childhood Research Quarterly, 18,* 104–120.

Howes, C., Whitebook, M., & Phillips, D. (1992). Teacher characteristics and effective teaching in child care: Findings from the National Child Care Staffing Study. *Child & Youth Care Forum, 21*(6), 399–414.

Kontos, S., Howes, C., & Galinsky, E. (1996). Does training make a difference to quality in family child care? *Early Childhood Research Quarterly, 11*(4), 427–445.

LeMoine, S. (2004a). *Center child care licensing requirements: Minimum early childhood education (ECE) preservice qualifications, administrative, and annual ongoing training hours for directors.* Vienna, VA: National Child Care Information Center. (Available at http://nccic.org/pubs/cclicensingreq/cclr-directors.html and http://nccic.org/pubs/cclicensingreq/cclr-directors.pdf)

LeMoine, S. (2004b). *Child care licensing requirements: Minimum early childhood education (ECE) preservice qualifications, orientation/initial licensure, and annual ongoing training hours for family child care providers.* Vienna, VA: National Child Care Information Center. (Available at http://nccic.org/pubs/cclicensingreq/cclr-famcare.html and http://nccic.org/pubs/cclicensingreq/cclr-famcare.pdf)

LeMoine, S. (2004c). *Center child care licensing requirements: Minimum early childhood education (ECE) preservice qualifications and annual ongoing training hours for teachers and master teachers.* Vienna, VA: National Child Care Information Center. (Available at http://nccic.org/pubs/cclicensingreq/cclr-teachers.html and http://nccic.org/pubs/cclicensingreq/cclr-teachers.pdf)

LeMoine, S. (2004d). *Summaries of child care licensing requirements minimum preservice qualifications and annual/ongoing training hours in early childhood education.* Vienna, VA: National Child Care Information Center. (Available at http://nccic.org/pubs/licensingtables/index.html)

Marshall, N.L., Creps, C.L., Burnstein, N.R., Cahill, K.E., Robeson, W.W., Wang, S.Y., Keefe, N., Schimmenti, J., & Glantz, F.B. (2003). *Massachusetts family child care today: A report on findings from the Massachusetts Cost and Quality Study.* Wellesley, MA: Wellesley Center for Women and Abt Associates.

Marshall, N.L., Creps, C.L., Burnstein, N.R., Glantz, F.B., Robeson, W.W., & Barnett, W.S. (2001). *The cost and quality of full day, year-round early care and education in Massachusetts: Preschool classrooms.* Wellesley, MA: Wellesley Center for Women and Abt Associates.

Marshall, N.L., Creps, C.L., Burnstein, N.R., Glantz, F.B., Robeson, W.W., Barnett, W.S., Schimmenti, J., & Keefe, N. (2002). *Early care and education in Massachusetts public schools preschool classrooms.* Wellesley, MA: Wellesley Center for Women and Abt Associates.

Maxwell, K.L., & Clifford, R.M. (in press). Professional development issues in universal prekindergarten. In E. Zigler, W. Gilliam, & S. Jones (Eds.), *The case for universal preschool education.*

National Prekindergarten Center. (2004). *Prekindergarten policy framework.* Retrieved April 19, 2005 from http://www.fpg.unc.edu/~NPC/framework/index.cfm

National Research Council. (2001). *Eager to learn: Educating our preschoolers.* Washington, DC: National Academy Press.

National Institute of Child Health and Human Development Early Child Care Research Network (NICHD ECCRN). (1996). Characteristics of infant child care: Factors contributing to positive caregiving. *Early Childhood Research Quarterly, 11*(3), 269–306.

National Institute of Child Health and Human Development Early Child Care Research Network (NICHD ECCRN). (2000). Characteristics and quality of child care for toddlers and preschoolers. *Applied Developmental Science, 4*(3), 116–141.

National Institute of Child Health and Human Development Early Child Care Research Network (NICHD ECCRN). (2002). Child-care structure–process–outcome: Direct and indirect effects of child care quality on young children's development. *Psychological Science, 13*(3), 199–206.

Norris, D.J. (2001). Quality of care offered by providers with differential patterns of workshop participation. *Child & Youth Care Forum, 30*(2), 111–121.

Pence, A., & Goelman, H. (1991). The relationship of regulation, training, and motivation to quality of care in family day care. *Child & Youth Care Forum, 20*(2), 83–101.

Pianta, R.C., & La Paro, K.M. (2003). *Classroom Assessment Scoring System (CLASS).* Unpublished measure, University of Virginia, Charlottesville.

Phillips, D., Mekos, D., Scarr, S., McCartney, K., & Abbott-Shim, M. (2000). Within and beyond the classroom door: Assessing quality in child care centers. *Early Childhood Research Quarterly, 15*(4), 475–496.

Phillipsen, L.C., Burchinal, M.R., Howes, C., & Cryer, D. (1997). The prediction of process quality from structural features of child care. *Early Childhood Research Quarterly, 12,* 281–303.

Russell, S. (2004, September). Discussant's comments prepared for the conference *Creating a National Plan for the Education of 4-Year-Olds,* Brookings Institution, Washington, DC.

Saluja, G., Early, D.M., & Clifford, R.M. (2002, Spring). Demographic education in the United States. *Early Childhood Research and Practice [Online], 4*(1). Retrieved April 29, 2005, from http://ecrp.uiuc.edu/v4n1/saluja.html

Schumacher, R., & Irish, K. (2003). What's new in 2002? A snapshot of Head Start children, families, teachers, and programs. *Center for Law and Social Policy: Policy Brief (No. 2).* Washington, DC: Center for Law and Social Policy.

T.E.A.C.H. Early Childhood Project. (2004). *T.E.A.C.H. Early Childhood State Contacts.* Retrieved April 19 2005, from http://www.childcareservices.org/TEACH/T.E.A.C.H.-States.htm

Turner, P. (2002). *La Ristra: New Mexico's comprehensive professional development system in early care, education, and family support.* Albuquerque: University of New Mexico.

U.S. Department of Education. (2004). *Abstracts of the 2004 Early Childhood Educator Professional Development (ECEPD) Project Grantees. CFDA# 84.349A.* Available at http://www.ed.gov/programs/eceducator/index.html

Weaver, R.H. (2002). Predictors of quality and commitment in family child care: Provider education, personal resources, and support. *Early Education and Development, 13*(3), 265–282.

Whitebook, M. (2003). *Early education quality: Higher teacher qualifications for better learning environments—A review of the literature.* Berkeley, CA: Institute of Industrial Relations, Center for the Study of Child Care Employment.

Whitebook, M., Sakai, L., Gerber, E., & Howes, C. (2001). *Then & now: Changes in child care staffing, 1994–2000.* Washington, DC: Center for the Child Care Workforce.

CHAPTER 5

# Studying the Culture
# of Quality Early Education and Care

*A Cumulative Approach to Measuring Characteristics of the*
*Workforce and Relations to Quality in Four Midwestern States*

HELEN H. RAIKES, JULIA C. TORQUATI, SUSAN HEGLAND,
H. ABIGAIL RAIKES, JACQUELINE SCOTT, LANA MESSNER,
CARLA PETERSON, KATHY THORNBURG, BECKY HOUF, AND SANDRA SCOTT

This chapter discusses recent state-level studies that rely on 1) representative sampling; 2) description of the early care and education (ECE) workforce, including providers' professional development experiences; 3) observational assessments of quality; and 4) linkage of workforce characteristics with observed quality. Here, findings from a representative, randomized telephone survey[1] of 2,022 providers in Iowa, Kansas, Missouri, and Nebraska, including observations of 365 of the providers, are presented. Fourteen key variables associated with child care quality across all forms of care studied (infant/toddler center-based care, preschool center-based care, and family child care) were identified and cumulated to form an Index of Child Care Assets (Index), creating a "breadbasket" of features related to quality. Among providers with 8 or more of the 14 assets, the percentage providing "good" quality care (more than 5 on an environment rating scale) ranged from 63% to 71% (depending on type of care), but when providers had 3 or fewer assets, the chance of good quality care was around zero. Developed in the state context, the approach provides an alternative way of studying workforce development that is consistent with some states' quality enhancement efforts.

## BACKGROUND

Because the majority of the responsibility for influencing child care quality and workforce development falls to states, state-level policy makers and administrators seek research to guide decisions about enhancing child care quality.

[1]The study was conducted by the Midwest Child Care Research Consortium, a collaboration that includes researchers, state child care officials, and other early childhood professionals in U.S. Department of Health and Human Services Region VII (Iowa, Kansas, Missouri, and Nebraska). The authors express grateful appreciation to the Child Care Bureau, U.S. Department of Health and Human Services, and the Ewing Marion Kauffman Foundation of Kansas City, Missouri, for support of the research described in this chapter.

Specifically, states want to know what combinations of training, consultation, regulation, or wage enhancement policies will provide the greatest return when they invest federal Child Care and Development Fund (CCDF) quality enhancement funds in quality-promoting activities. (States are required to use at least 4% of CCDF block grant allotments for quality enhancements.) Although considerable research progress has been made since the 1970s in isolating and identifying factors that relate to child care quality, including identification of program structural features (e.g., group size, ratios), provider characteristics (e.g., education, training), and process features (e.g., adult–child interactions) as predictors of quality, it is still not clear what combination of professional development and other initiatives constitute the best quality enhancement investments at the state level. More specifically, it is not clear what investments will raise the watermark of child care quality within states and best enable states to build a child care workforce capable of providing quality child care over time. This chapter briefly reviews the literature highlighting a broad range of predictors of child care quality, discusses four problems that become apparent when traditional research on predicting child care quality is applied to state-level decision making about investing child care quality enhancement dollars, illustrates alternative approaches several states have undertaken, and presents data from one study, identifying and cumulating factors influencing child care quality.

## A CALL TO ACTION:
## WHAT DO QUALITY ENHANCEMENT DOLLARS DO?

The dilemma of state policy makers was underscored by a report prepared by the General Accouting Office (GAO [now the Government Accountability Office]; 2002) stating that little is known about the effectiveness of quality enhancement dollars spent by states. Using only highly rigorous random assignment design studies and representative survey samples that had at least 70% response rates, the report concluded that the knowledge base on effects of quality investments was small and, consequently, there is little to guide state quality enhancement initiatives. The GAO called for new experimental design studies to test effects of interventions and investments (now underway; Fenson, 2005; Ramey, 2005) and for studies conducted with representative sampling to gain a more accurate depiction of the results of quality enhancement efforts within states.

### Factors Influencing Child Care Quality

Beyond the limited number of experimental and highly representative studies identified by the GAO (2002), there is a body of research based on descriptive and associative data, suggesting pathways toward quality. This research has yielded broad parameters at multiple levels for states to consider when making investments in child care quality, although, typically, this research was not designed to evaluate CCDF quality enhancement efforts occurring at provider, program, and state levels. According to the GAO (2002), 13% of quality enhancement funds are used for provider training and education (on and off-site) and 12% for provider compensation. At the program level, 12% of funds are used for meeting state standards (often for becoming licensed), 8% for accreditation incentives, and 8% for safety equipment/improvement. At the state level, 13% of all funds are used for enhanced inspections. Another 20% of the funds are used by resource and referral agencies, which, in turn, offer provider-level training and program-level services, whereas 12% of the funds go for unspecified uses. Porter and colleagues (2002) also identified 104 initiatives of selected states and classified these initiatives as professional development, training, and compensation initiatives, and accreditation or rating systems. The following sections briefly review research at each level. The review is not comprehensive but rather its purpose is to illustrate a breadth of factors studied.

### Provider-Level Characteristics and Quality

Provider-level characteristics, such as education, training hours, membership in professional associations, attitudes, experience, and self-reported quality practices, are potential predictors of child care quality. Some studies have found higher levels of quality associated with higher levels of education (see Chapters 2 and 4 for reviews; see also Blau, 2000; Burchinal, Cryer, & Clifford, 2002; Sachs, 2000; Whitebook, Howes, & Phillips, 1990). In particular, caregivers with higher levels of education, and those who majored in a child-related field at higher educational levels, provide higher quality care than other providers (Burchinal et al., 2002; Dunn, 1993). However, other studies have found no role for provider education in predicting child care quality (La Paro, Sexton, & Snyder, 1998; Phillips, Mekos, Scarr, McCartney, & Abbott-Shim, 2000; Phillipsen, Burchinal, Howes, & Cryer, 1997), particularly when accounting for contextual factors such as state policy, tuition, and compensation in multivariate analyses. The role of training in the delivery of high-quality care is also complex, partly because training has been operationalized in many ways across studies (see Chapter 2). Many studies have found a positive relation between provider wages and quality (Ghazvini & Mullis, 2002; Phillips et al., 2000; Phillipsen et al., 1997; Sachs, 2000; Whitebook et al., 1990). Similarly, strong associations have been found between observed quality and availability of employee benefits (Whitebook et al., 1990).

Other studies have found relations between provider beliefs and child care quality, including intentionality, or a belief in the importance of child care work (Galinsky, Howes, Kontos, & Shinn, 1994), and caregiver beliefs about practices that promote child development (National Institute of Child Health and Human Development [NICHD], 2000). In addition, Holloway, Kagan, Fuller, Tsao, and Carroll (2001) found modest relationships between self-reported quality practices, such as using learning centers and holding formal conferences with parents, and observed quality.

*Program-Level Characteristics and Quality*   Center-based providers are nested in the programs in which they work. Thus, many features that relate to quality are the result of decisions made at the center level. Program-level features that have been associated with observed quality in previous studies include structural features of quality such as group size and adult–child ratio and characteristics of center directors (Whitebook et al., 1990) including use of supportive supervision and mentoring in centers (Howes, James, & Ritchie, 2003). National Association for the Education of Young Children (NAEYC) accreditation has been associated with greater caregiver sensitivity and better health and safety practices (Bloom, 1996; Harris, Morgan, & Sprague, 1996), better ratios, and smaller group sizes (Whitebook, 1996). Although there are studies of the nutrition-related effects of the Child and Adult Care Food Program, no studies were found linking participation in that program with global child care quality. Child care partnerships with Head Start/Early Head Start represent a relatively new phenomenon to extend the reach of the Head Start performance standards and the resources of Head Start into community child care (U.S. Department of Health and Human Services [DHHS], 1994); child care programs participating in such partnerships tend to make more investments in quality practices and to be of higher quality than is true for programs on average (Paulsell, Nogales, & Cohen, 2003; Administration for Children and Families (ACF), 2003b).

*State-Level Characteristics and Quality*   States introduce another set of influences on child care quality through their policies on regulation, subsidy, and quality enhancement. Multiple studies have linked higher regulatory requirements with observed quality in centers (Cost, Quality, and Child Outcomes Study Team, 1995; Gallagher, Rooney, & Campbell, 1999) and family homes (Raikes, Raikes, & Wilcox, in press). The relations between subsidy policies and observed quality, as is true for numerous other features of child care, are complex, but these influences are rarely studied. For example, we found that home providers who received subsidies offered lower quality care than providers who did not receive subsidies, but this relation was not found in center-based care (Raikes et al., 2003). Finally, two studies found an effect for state itself, meaning that there were differences between states beyond what could be attributed to variables in models designed to account for state differences, such as regulation (Phillips et al., 2000; Raikes et al., in press).

## Limitations of Current Approaches to Assessment of Quality Predictors

Although there is a knowledge base on factors that are associated with child care quality, the existing research does not necessarily translate well into the type of information that states need for making quality-enhancement investment decisions. In addition to the lack of causal models (GAO, 2002), there are four reasons why research to date may not answer states' questions. First, present studies tend to examine only one or a handful of variables in any given study, introducing some statistical problems and preventing assessment of whether the identified variables would be the "best" investment for a state. Second, some variables that influence quality may violate conventional assumptions for statistical analyses, such as having non-normal distributions. Third, study findings not based on representative samples are a problem for states, which must consider an entire workforce population. Fourth, the state context itself sets the parameters for child care quality through the presence and enforcement of child care regulations. Thus, relations between variables may be different for different states. The following discussions elaborate on each of the four concerns.

First, conventional approaches to understanding which features of the child care workforce predict quality tend to concentrate on a few variables at a time (Phillipsen et al., 1997). However, findings sometimes change depending on which variables are entered into equations (Phillips et al., 2000). Correspondingly, we note the sometimes reported phenomenon that "good things go together" in child care settings, with studies showing that a number of aspects of quality may be related to one another. For instance, providers with higher education also tend to have higher wages and care for children who pay higher tuition (Kontos, Howes, Shinn, & Galinsky, 1995). We contend that these findings belie both a problem and an opportunity. The problem is one of multicollinearity, or patterns of association between variables that occur when many variables are strongly associated with each other (e.g., provider education and wages). As a result of collinearity, results across studies can be inconsistent because they can be affected by which variable in a collinear group is entered into an equation. Varying results make it difficult to interpret findings across studies, let alone make recommendations to states about where to invest precious resources. However, if, in fact, "good things go together" to influence quality, the field is not only in danger of drawing false conclusions about what is driving quality based on what it chooses to examine (or not) in any one analysis but also may be missing the opportunity to understand what happens when several features that support quality cluster together in one provider, which often happens in reality.

Second, the distribution of some predictors of quality may not follow a normal distribution and thus violate mathematical assumptions necessary for testing linear models. Non-normal distributions happen when some predictors are common, such as complying with a state standard for CPR training, and some are quite rare, such as completing National Association for the Education of Young Children (NAEYC) accreditation. For example, in three

Midwestern states where licensing regulations require annual CPR certification, more than 90% of providers were certified. Yet, only 15% of the providers had at least a bachelor's degree, and 16% belonged to the NAEYC (Raikes et al., 2003). These factors may all be associated with quality, but the sample distribution does not lend itself to linear statistical modeling. Moreover, the collinearity described previously and distribution problems are not independent; in the previously mentioned study, providers who had a bachelor's degree were more likely to belong to NAEYC than those who did not.

A third limitation in the current understanding of predictors of quality is that findings and conclusions cannot be generalized to the entire child care workforce unless samples are representative of that workforce. Much of the knowledge base to date is based on truncated samples that do not include all providers. For example, education predicted quality in one sample of relatively highly educated providers, but the story changed with a sample of providers with lower mean levels of education (Howes, Whitebook, & Phillips, 1992). Providers at the lowest levels of education and those with the least regulation may not be represented in many studies of child care quality (Gallagher et al., 1999). As the GAO (2002) pointed out, few studies describing predictors of child care quality have used truly representative samples across the entire spectrum of the child care workforce, although many strive for representation within sectors studied, with varying degrees of success. Different samples (in turn, representing differing subsectors of the child care workforce) likely contribute to inconsistent findings across studies. However, a state must necessarily learn about quality and workforce enhancement across the entirety of its workforce.

Fourth, the regulatory and subsidy climate resulting from state policies may exert influences on child care quality that make states unique and limit the ability to apply findings from one state to another. For example, in a state where regulations allow group size to vary from six to 12 infants, group size may be linked to quality. However, studies in states where regulations limit the maximum group size to six, relations between group size and quality may not be apparent. Therefore, understanding the limits in the ranges of key predictors of child care quality imposed by the regulatory context helps explain inconsistencies in findings. Moreover, Phillips et al. (2000) and Raikes et al. (in press) have reported that the state where a study is conducted is a statistically significant variable accounting for additional variance in program quality even after other variables, including regulation, have been controlled. Although much progress has been made, the field has not yet discovered all of the ways that states influence child care quality. Taken together, the limitations of collinearity of predictors, non-normal distribution of variables, nonrepresentation, and state-specific influences indicate that testing new avenues for understanding quality would be useful.

# THE CURRENT STUDY WITHIN THE CONTEXT OF STATE EFFORTS TO DOCUMENT CHILD CARE QUALITY

A number of states are conducting new kinds of studies that, for the most part, are based on representative sampling, offer a description of the workforce (including descriptions of providers' professional development), and include observations of quality in order to more precisely define how quality enhancement initiatives and efforts aimed at increasing the qualifications of child care providers influence quality. Some of these states then link characteristics of the workforce to quality, either at a single point in time or over time.

## Midwest Child Care Study in Iowa, Kansas, Missouri, and Nebraska

This chapter describes an effort to document workforce characteristics and quality within and across four Midwestern states. The Midwest Child Care Research study, a representative sample of 2,022 providers conducted in Iowa, Kansas, Missouri, and Nebraska, will be described in greater detail in the chapter. First, the following sections briefly summarize other efforts to build toward as representative as possible a picture of ECE and providers in states.

*Pennsylvania*    Under the Governor's Task Force on Early Childhood Care and Education (2002), the University Children's Policy Collaborative completed a series of studies of 372 ECE facilities in Pennsylvania. The studies were designed to provide a baseline for the ECE services delivered in the Commonwealth of Pennsylvania. The study included 50 Head Start programs, 48 preschools, 111 child care centers, 109 family child care homes, 46 group homes, and 8 legally regulated relative/neighborhood care providers. Results indicated that Head Start and preschool programs provide higher levels of quality and that the provider's educational level and utilization of a curriculum are both related to quality, especially among family child care providers.

*Connecticut*    Connecticut analyzed all available information about the early child care and education workforce. The populations studied included licensed family child care providers, child care centers, Head Start programs, preschools and license-exempt informal caregivers (Child Health and Development Institute of Connecticut [CHDI], 2003). Connecticut has also conducted a pre-post design study of the effects of training on 103 center-based and 14 family child care settings (phase one) and 62 center-based, 37 family child care, and relative care providers (phase two). The training targeted entry-level providers and was associated with higher scores on the environment ratings scales and provider self-reported commitment to stay in the early childhood field (CHDI, 2003).

*Wisconsin*    Wisconsin perhaps best exemplifies use of state data over time to track changes in the workforce and, potentially, progress toward quality. The Wisconsin Child Care Research Partnership (2003b) compared results from a survey sent to 2,000 programs that received subsidies in 2001 to results obtained using similar procedures in 1980, 1988, and 1994. They reported changes in the child care workforce from 1994 to 2000 including increased diversity, lower average levels of education, decreasing wages relative to inflation, and increased job turnover, although teachers and directors in all surveys reported high job satisfaction. The Wisconsin Child Care Research Partnership (2003a) also completed child care quality observations in 174 classrooms in 28 subsidy-receiving centers and found that most care was rated in the "mediocre" category. Quality was found to associate positively with provider education (particularly at the bachelor's degree level) and wages. In addition, directors with higher levels of education employed teachers with more years of education and experience and paid them higher wages than directors with less education (Wisconsin Child Care Research Partnership, 2003a).

*Delaware*    In 2001, 201 programs, stratified for region, were identified for the Delaware study of child care quality. Researchers completed multiple observations within programs; a total of 576 quality observations were completed in family child care homes, center-based programs, Head Start/Early Head Start, and part-day programs. Characteristics of providers and quality varied across types of programs. For example, the majority of infant/toddler teachers reported their highest level of education was a high school degree (54.5%), but many part-time teachers (40.7%) held a bachelors' degree. The Delaware study identified areas for targeted improvements. For example, teacher–child interactions and curriculum-related areas of the observations were low across all types of care, and among infant/toddler programs, 70% were rated as "poor" in the area of personal care routines. The study also identified strengths. For example, more than 70% of the part-time programs were rated as "good" in the area of language and literacy, and more than 50% of Head Start or Early Head Start programs were rated as "good" in five or more of the seven subscales (Gamel-McCormick, Buell, Amsden, & Fahey, 2003).

*Nevada*    Nevada researchers completed a profile of demographic, economic, and quality aspects of child care within the state (Essa, 2002). The goals of the study were to gain a comprehensive picture of child care in the state, especially of the child care workforce; to provide guidance to policy makers regarding allocation of resources for child care; and to begin a data base for the establishment of a Child Care Registry, intended to provide information on work place characteristics and the education and training of those who work in licensed child care in the state. A quality observation was conducted in 103 settings in the Reno area (39), the Las Vegas area (34), and rural parts of the state (30), and assessments were administered to children in these child care settings. Information gathered included compensation of the child care workforce, providers' education and training, existing state child care quality initiatives, the cost of child care, state licensing and regulation of child care providers, job stability of child care staff, and parents' perceptions of quality and availability. The study also found the quality of child care was positively linked to child outcomes.

## The Midwest Child Care Research Study of Providers and a Cumulative Approach Using Assets

The Midwest Child Care Research study of providers relies on a representative sample from Iowa, Kansas, Missouri, and Nebraska; describes the child care workforce; and studies the relation of workforce variables, singly and cumulatively, to observed quality. The cumulative approach is consistent with state efforts to pursue multiple avenues for quality enhancement simultaneously. This chapter presents the Index that includes 14 features of child care found to be associated with quality across the four states; these features were then summed to make an index. Assets may be viewed as a "breadbasket" of provider-level and program-level features worthy of tracking over time given their association with observed quality. It is assumed that the collection of child care features associated with quality and, therefore in the "breadbasket," could be different in different regions of the country.

## METHOD

The data reported in this chapter were collected in 2001 from a survey sample of 2,022 child care providers selected following random, stratified sampling of licensed and subsidy-receiving providers in Iowa, Kansas, Missouri, and Nebraska, as well as an observational sample of 365 providers randomly selected from the larger sample of providers surveyed. The telephone survey was conducted by professional interviewers from the Gallup Organization, and the observations were conducted by trained observers from state universities.

### Sample

The study generalizes to full-time child care providers serving children from birth through kindergarten in center- and home-based settings across four Midwestern states. State lists of licensed and other providers who received subsidies provided the initial pool of 39,473 child care providers. A sample pool of 10,000 was drawn at random, stratifying for state, type of care (center-based infant/toddler, center-based preschool, licensed family child care, registered family child care, license-exempt family child care), and subsidy receipt. In addition, license-exempt center-based child care providers were drawn in Missouri, and in all states, the population of Early Head Start/Head Start child care partners was sampled. The 10,000 providers identified were mailed letters informing them that they could be called by Gallup. Letters were also sent by some state agencies, and articles about the study were included in state early childhood newsletters encouraging participation. From this pool of 10,000, 2,496 providers were selected at random (again, following sample stratification for state, type of care, and subsidy receipt) and called, yielding 2,022 completed interviews with eligible providers (full-time child care providers serving children from birth through kindergarten in center- and home-based settings). The response rate for eligible participants was 81%; 99% of the nonparticipants were registered or license-exempt family home providers and of these, 80% of the nonparticipation was due to a telephone barrier (e.g., answering machine or answering service, did not answer the phone, the line was busy, the respondent was not available at the time of the planned callback across the seven-call call-back design of the study). Table 5.1 includes further description of the study sample. At the end of the interview, providers were asked if they would be willing to be contacted again for more in-depth study; 87% of the providers said they would be willing to be contacted again, ranging from a high of 95% of center-based providers to 70% of license-exempt family providers. State university researchers contacted willing providers at random for follow-up observations. Three hundred sixty-five providers were observed in their natural child care settings (centers and homes). Center directors were also interviewed at the time of the observation.

## Instruments

The telephone survey was comprised of 28 general questions, eight demographic and one open-ended question. Items were selected if 1) they or related items had been found to predict observed quality or child outcomes in previous studies, 2) they were related to features of the labor force in other studies, or 3) they represented specific state quality-enhancement efforts. An effort was made to generalize questions to all states and all types of providers; however, the study was customized to some extent for type of provider or state. Completing the interview by telephone took 12.5 minutes on average.

Observations were completed using the Early Childhood Environment Rating Scale-Revised Edition (ECERS-R; Harms, Clifford, & Cryer, 1998), Infant/Toddler Environment Rating Scale (ITERS; Harms, Cryer, & Clifford, 1990), Family Day Care Environment Rating Scale (FDCRS; Harms & Clifford, 1989), and the Caregiver Interaction Scale (CIS; Arnett, 1989). For

**Table 5.1.**    Characteristics of the workforce and inputs to quality

| Item | Percentage "yes" (or mean) |
| --- | --- |
| **Education, training, and professional association** | |
| 13 years of education or more | 42% |
| Of those with a degree, major area of training | |
| Child development | 68% |
| Child Development Associate (CDA) credential | 17% |
| Training hours (clock hours) received during the previous year | |
| <12 | 23% |
| 12–24 | 32% |
| >24 | 46% |
| Received one type of intense[a] training | 43% |
| Received training during the previous year | |
| Videotapes | 59% |
| Training provided by director or other staff person | 39% |
| Support person who comes to program | 24% |
| Community workshops | 75% |
| Regional, state, or national conferences | 46% |
| Training for which you received credit | 47% |
| Internet | 18% |
| Teleconferencing or distance learning | 9% |
| Received training needed "to do the job right" | 61% |
| Certification or recertification within the past 2 years in | |
| Cardiopulmonary resuscitation (CPR) | 82% |
| First aid | 84% |
| Both CPR and first aid | 78% |
| Membership | |
| National Association for the Education of Young Children NAEYC) | 19% |
| National Association for Family Child Care | 7% |
| Division of Early Childhood | 6% |
| Council for Exceptional Children | 2% |
| National School Age Child Care Alliance | 2% |
| **Attitudes, experience, and self-reported quality practice** | |
| **Motivations for working in child care** | |
| (percent reporting "definitely" a reason) | |
| My career or profession | 63% |
| A stepping stone to a related career or profession | 29% |
| A personal calling | 61% |
| A job with a paycheck | 26% |
| Work to do while children are young | 36% |
| A way of helping others out | 39% |
| Years of experience | |
| Less than a year | 15% |
| 1–3 years | 26% |

*(continued)*

**Table 5.1.**    *(continued)*

| Item | Percentage "yes" (or mean) |
|---|---|
| 3–5 years | 37% |
| More than 5 years | 44% |
| How much time provider plans to stay in child care | |
| Less than a year | 6% |
| 1–2 years | 33% |
| 2–5 years | 26% |
| More than 5 years | 61% |
| Quality practices (self- or director report) | |
| Would choose other work, if possible | 15% |
| Greets each parent and child every day | 76% |
| Reads to each child every day | 81% |
| Talks formally with parents at least once a year | 80% |
| Areas in child care are set up to encourage learning | 85% |
| The facility has good indoor spaces for children | 83% |
| The facility has good outdoor spaces for children | 82% |
| Children have daily access to a good supply of toys/materials | 88% |
| At least twice a week provider is left alone with too many children | 3% |
| Uses a curriculum | 55% |
| Report using developmentally appropriate practices | 85% |
| **Wages, benefits, and workplace beliefs** | |
| Average earnings during the previous year | $14,130 |
| Receiving any employee benefit (center-based only) | 76% |
| Health insurance for self | 56% |
| Health insurance for family | 43% |
| Paid vacation days | 91% |
| Paid sick days | 77% |
| Paid days to attend professional meetings | 74% |
| No or reduced tuition for children | 63% |
| Retirement benefits | 39% |
| Gallup Q-12™ (percent strongly agree; center-based only) | |
| I know what is expected of me at work | 93% |
| I have the materials and equipment I need | 62% |
| I have the opportunity to do what I do best every day | 79% |
| I have received recognition or praise in the last 7 days | 51% |
| My supervisor or someone at work cares about me as a person | 75% |
| There is someone at work who encourages my development | 66% |
| At work, my opinions seem to count | 67% |
| The mission or purpose of my company makes me feel my job important | 74% |
| My associates or fellow employees are committed to doing quality work | 59% |

| Item | Percentage "yes" (or mean) |
|---|---|
| I have a best friend at work | 51% |
| In the last 6 months, someone has talked to me about my progress | 62% |
| This last year, I have had opportunities at work to learn and grow | 79% |
| **Program level** | |
| Continuity of care for infants (center-based only) | 59% |
| Program accredited by nationally recognized accrediting body | 3% |
| Program an Early Head Start/Head Start partner | 9% |
| Program participation in the USDA/State Food Program | 63% |
| Family child care home is licensed or registered (of family child care providers) | |
| Licensed | 33% |
| Registered | 25% |
| License exempt | 21% |

Note: [a]If the respondent completed any of the following forms of training targeted to child care providers, then credit was given for Intense Training: Montessori Certification; West Ed Training Program for Infant and Toddler Caregivers; High/Scope; Creative Curriculum; Project Construct (Missouri); Child Net (Iowa); Heads Up! Reading (Nebraska). See Table 5.2 for participation in these projects by state.

the environment rating scales, core observers in each state received training from the scales' authors or from someone who had received training from the authors and from a qualified trainer on the CIS. Careful attention was paid to inter-rater reliability, and a train-the-trainer model was implemented. Following procedures recommended by the environment rating scale developers, two observers from each state attained cross-state reliability on all observation instruments and served as "anchors" for reliability within their respective states. Each observer was required to reach agreement within one point per item for at least 85% of the items on each scale. Follow-up checks on reliability were conducted throughout the data collection.

## Analysis

Because there are many similarities in the characteristics of the four states (e.g., rural areas with several large metropolitan centers and 85%–90% Caucasian inhabitants) and to gain statistical power, data are pooled for the present set of analyses (state-specific reports are available at http://ccfl.unl.edu). First, characteristics of providers and observed quality are reported. Next, preliminary bivariate analyses are presented to illustrate relations between characteristics of providers and observed quality. Characteristics with higher bivariate relations across types of care are summed to create an index, and the relations between the index and good quality care in chi square and analyses of variance analyses are reported by type of care[2].

# RESULTS

## Characteristics of the Workforce in Four Midwestern States

The study found that the modal provider in the Midwest sample had a high school degree with some additional training (see Chapter 3 of this book), had completed a CPR-first aid training program, and viewed child care as a profession (see Table 5.1). For example, 78% of providers reported they had received 12 or more hours of training; 17% had completed a Child Development Associate (CDA) certificate; 75% had participated in a community workshop; 46% said they had attended a regional, state, or national conference; and 55% reported using a curriculum. Only 3% of providers reported their programs had received accreditation (e.g., NAEYC); 63% participated in the Child and Adult Care Food Program. We also measured participation rates in various specific training initiatives (see Table 5.2).

## Description of Observed Quality

We classified all observed care following conventions used in the child care quality literature whereby scores below 3 were rated as poor quality; scores in the 3–4.99 range were rated minimal; and 5 and above were rated good quality care. Across all forms of care, 17.6% of providers were in the poor quality range, 48.8% were in the minimal range, and 33.3% were in the good quality range.

Average quality in infant/toddler center-based settings, as assessed by the ITERS, was 4.38 across 114 observations; 8.4% of infant providers were rated as providing poor quality care, 62.7% minimal quality care, and 28.9%, good quality care. Preschool settings, assessed by the ECERS-R, averaged 4.57 across 115 observations, and the distribution included 9.7% poor quality, 51.3% minimal quality, and 38.9% good quality settings. Family child care averaged 4.41 on the FDCRS. FDCRS scores were significantly higher for licensed family child care providers ($n = 88$, averaging 4.63) than for registered family child care providers ($n = 30$, averaging 3.56) or licensed-exempt family child care providers ($n = 14$; 3.57 on average). Only 9.2% of licensed family providers were observed to be in the poor quality range, whereas 50.6% were in the minimal range and 40.2% were in the good quality range. How-

---

[2]Data were analyzed both unweighted and weighted to the child care provider population using conventional survey data weighting procedures. Due to the sampling and response rates, differences between findings when weighted and unweighted were small. Except for descriptive data, data reported here are weighted to the child care provider population in the four states. A comprehensive description of analytic approaches is available elsewhere (Raikes et al., 2003).

**Table 5.2.**    Participation in specific initiatives by state

| Initiative | Iowa | Kansas | Missouri | Nebraska |
|---|---|---|---|---|
| West Ed Training Program for Infant and Toddler Caregivers[a] | 3% | 4% | 1% | 1% |
| Creative Curriculum[a] | 30% | 37% | 39% | 24% |
| High/Scope[a] | 7% | 6% | 7% | 13% |
| Parents as Teachers[a] | 3% | 7% | 12% | 3% |
| Montessori Training[b] | 2% | 5% | 5% | 3% |
| Child Net (Iowa) | 7% | | | |
| Project Construct (Missouri) | | | 22% | |
| Heads Up! Reading (Nebraska) | | | | 11% |

*Note:* [a] = p < .001 and [b] = p < .01; that difference between states is not due to chance. Percent represents the percent of all providers who reported they had participated in the type of training queried. Table 5.2 shows there were significant differences across states in the types of initiatives that providers participated in. However, across the states, providers had fairly comparable opportunities to participate in *some* type of initiative. Providers who had attended one (or more) of the initiatives, were coded as having received "intense training," 1 of 14 assets.

ever, nearly half of the registered family providers were in the poor range (47.5%), with 32.5% in the minimal range and 20% in the good range. The figures for license-exempt family care were similar with 45.5% in the poor range, 33.3% in the minimal range, and 21.2% in the good range.

## Characteristics of Providers and Observed Quality

Bivariate analyses (see Table 5.3) were completed to determine relations between characteristics of providers and observed quality in three forms of care: 1) infant/toddler center-based; 2) preschool center-based; and 3) family child care, across licensed, registered, and license-exempt family child care providers).[3] Provider characteristics that were significantly associated with quality across at least two forms of care and had a positive relationship in the third are listed in Table 5.3. These were identified as "best bets" for features associated with quality. To examine quality across type of care, we created an omnibus measure, using scores on the ECERS-R, ITERS, and FDCRS. Although quality is scored comparably across different ratings scales, we could not assume comparability of scales and ratings. Therefore, we did not use the omnibus rating in our analyses except as a verification of the procedure we relied on and described previously. Accordingly, for the "best bets," characteristics that had a significant bivariate relation with the omnibus quality variable were retained in the pool of characteristics (not shown).

---

[3]Many Ordinary Least Square and Logistic Regression analyses were also conducted to determine best predictors of ECERS-R, ITERS, and FDCRS quality. Discriminant analyses were also performed. Due to collinearity discussed previously, outcomes from these analyses often varied according to which of many other variables were included in the equations. Thus, an alternative to models requiring assumptions of linearity was selected as presented here.

**Table 5.3.**   Bivariate relationships between selected provider characteristics variables and global child care quality by type of care

| | Infant/toddler center based | Preschool center based | Family child care |
|---|---|---|---|
| Education level | .166 | .149 | .358[a] |
| Child Development Associate (CDA) (Yes/No) | .501[a] | .338[a] | .452[a] |
| Training hours | .395[a] | .123 | .433[a] |
| Intense training | .252[b] | .291[b] | .348[a] |
| Attended a conference | .299[a] | .126 | .416[a] |
| First aid and cardiopulmonary resuscitation (CPR) | .199[b] | .328[a] | .213[b] |
| Earnings | .328[a] | .216[c] | .255[a] |
| Used a curriculum | .324[a] | .096 | .290[a] |
| Conference with parents annually | .284[b] | .307[a] | .117 |
| Early Head Start/Head Start partner | .233[a] | .190 | .322[a] |
| Accredited | .274[b] | .207[b] | .185[b] |
| Food program | .148[b] | .189[d] | .348[b] |
| Centers: Talked about progress | .080 | .247[a] | NA |
| Centers: Health insurance | .234[a] | .328[a] | NA |
| Family child care: Support person visited | NA | NA | .330[a] |
| Family child care: Licensed | NA | NA | .307[a] |

*Key:* [a] = p ≤ .001; [b] = p ≤ .01; [c] = p ≤ .05; [d] = p ≤ .10

## Assets

Fourteen provider characteristics met our criteria for variables that were significant correlates of quality across types of care. All were set to categorical variables, often using mean splits or meaningful cut points near mean splits. The categorical variables that were identified included 1) highest level of education (whether the provider had completed 1 year of schooling beyond high school versus less than 1 year beyond high school completed); 2) a CDA credential (yes/no); 3) total clock hours of training related to child care in previous year (24 or more hours of training/less than 24 hours of training); 4) current in first aid and CPR certification (yes/no); 5) completed an intense training program (yes/no);[4] 6) attended a child care-related state, regional, or national conference (yes/no); 7) used a curriculum (yes/no); 8) held a formal

---

[4]If the respondent completed any of the following forms of training targeted to child care providers, then credit was given for Intense Training: Montessori Certification; West Ed (PITC); High/ Scope; Creative Curriculum; Project Construct (Missouri); Child Net (Iowa); Heads Up! Reading (Nebraska). See Table 5.2 for participation in these projects by state.

annual conference with each parent about the child's development (yes/no); 9) previous year's earnings ($12,500 or more/less than $12,500); 10) worked in a center/home that had been accredited by a state-recognized accrediting body (yes/no);[5] 11) worked in a center/home that had a partnership with an Early Head Start/Head Start program to follow the Head Start Performance Standards (yes/no); 12) worked in a center/home that participated in the USDA Child and Adult Care Food Program (yes/no).

Two additional characteristics were unique to family child care providers: 13) licensed to provide family child care (yes/no) and 14) received visits by a mentor/support person (yes/no). Two characteristics were unique to center-based providers: 15) received health benefits (yes/no) and 16) reported that someone (generally the program director) had talked to the provider about progress (yes/no). Altogether, there were 14 characteristics that applied to family child care providers and 14 characteristics that applied to center-based providers. Contenders that were not included because they did not meet the inclusion criteria and/or because adding them to the assets list did not improve the ability of the model to predict quality included membership in a professional organization, other employee benefits, other types of training, whether the provider had a degree in child development, most self-reported quality practices, and many attitudinal features queried (Table 5.1).

Bivarate relations were computed to determine the extent to which the assets covaried with one another, within type of care. Of 42 variables (3 types of care by 14 variables), all but 8 had significant relations with at least one other (not shown). Some were significantly associated with many others. For example, for family child care providers, receiving more than 24 hours of training was significantly associated with nine other assets, whereas having a CDA and attending a conference were each associated with 8 others. Among infant/toddler center-based providers, intense training and income were each associated with four other assets, and among preschool center-based providers, having a director who "talked to me about my progress" was associated with five other assets.

## The Cumulative Value of Correlates of Quality: Index of Assets

The features that met our criteria for good association with observed quality were added to create an Index with a total possible score of 14. As noted, 12 of the items were common across all forms of care, and two were unique to each

---

[5] Both accreditation and Early Head Start/Head Start partnerships represent state efforts to affect quality. Although each of these efforts includes its own set of standards, states were eager to see if their efforts and investments in these areas as "good bets" for quality improvements in fact were associated with higher quality.

family child care and center-based care. Cumulating variables was selected as an alternative to linear approaches that failed to yield reliable predictors of child care quality. The average number of assets across all family child care providers was 6.0, for infant/toddler center-based providers was 5.5, and for preschool center-based providers was 6.9.

## Index of Child Care Assets and Observed Quality

Our primary interest was to determine if the Index was able to accurately forecast observed quality. Chi square analyses were conducted examining the relation between the number of assets and three levels of quality: poor (less than 3 on the ITERS, ECERS-R, or FDCRS); minimal (3 to 4.99) and good (5 or higher). Breaks in the data distribution suggested that we could collapse the Index into three levels: low ($\leq$ 3), medium (4–7), or high ($\geq$ 8). We were interested in determining whether the Index, with break points so conceived, had the sensitivity to identify good quality care providers and specificity to exclude poor quality providers. Chi square analyses showed that observed quality and asset levels were highly related to one another (see Figure 5.1). The Index demonstrated high levels of sensitivity: 66% of infant/toddler center providers; 63% of preschool providers, and 71% of family child care

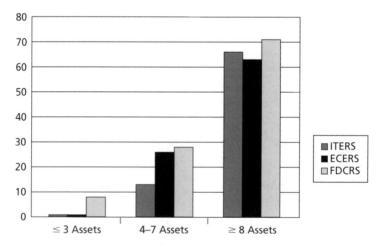

**Figure 5.1.**    Percent of providers with good quality (a 5 or higher) at three levels of assets across four states. Providers were evaluated on three environment rating scales: the Early Childhood Environment Rating Scale–Revised Edition (ECERS-R; Harms, Clifford, & Cryer, 1998), the Infant/Toddler Environment Rating Scale (ITERS; Harms, Cryer, & Clifford, 1990), and the Family Day Care Rating Scale (FDCRS; Harms, & Clifford, 1989). (*Key:* 3 or fewer = few assets, 4–7 = medium number of assets, and 8 or more = high number of assets.) (From Center on Children, Families and the Law, University of Nebraska–Lincoln. [n.d.]. *Child care aspects: What are 14 key assets of child care providers that support quality?* [Research Brief No. 1]. Lincoln: Author; reprinted by permission.)

providers with 8 or more assets were observed to be offering good quality care. The Index was also specific, successfully excluding providers with fewer assets from the good quality range. The chance that good quality care would be observed was almost nonexistent when providers had fewer than 4 assets, no center-based providers, and only 8% of the family child care providers with fewer than 4 assets were observed to be providing good quality care. The chances for good quality increased somewhat when providers had between 4 and 7 assets; 13% of infant/toddler center-based providers, 26% of preschool center-based providers, and 28% of family child care providers with assets in this midrange were observed to be providing good quality care.

Thus, it appears to take a substantial number of assets (8 or more) to create the critical mass that predicts good quality care (see Figure 5.1). The chi square statistics assessing level of assets for each type of care by level of quality were all significant at or beyond the .01 level. F statistics comparing number of assets among providers at poor, minimal, and good quality care were all significant at the .001 level.

It is reasonable to ask which assets were contributors to increments from one level of quality to another for each type of care. Separate logistic regression analyses were conducted to compare levels of quality (e.g., poor versus minimal, minimal versus good) for each type of care. Some assets were better predictors of increments in quality levels for a particular type of care than others. We report which assets, individually and not considering other assets, increased the odds at least 2 to 1 that the provider reached the next level of quality (e.g., good over mediocre). Table 5.4 shows that many assets contribute to quality increments and that they vary to some extent by type of care. However, food program participation and using a curriculum were common in predicting minimal versus poor quality across all types of care, and having a CDA and an education of 1 year beyond high school were common in predicting good versus minimal care. Other assets contributed to quality shifts but differently across types of care and/or quality levels.

## CONCLUSIONS AND RECOMMENDATIONS

The current study provides an example of a new wave of studies based on state-level representative sampling of providers and providing a description of the child care workforce and observational assessments of quality that link workforce characteristics to observed quality. In this study, 14 characteristics were cumulated to create an Index and demonstrated relations to quality. The probability of good quality was quite high (63%–71%) when 8 or more of the assets occurred together. We draw three conclusions from the study. First, there is value in identifying a short list or "breadbasket" of provider characteristics to track over time to determine if workforce development and qual-

**Table 5.4.**    Logistic regression analyses showing independent predictors for 1) poor versus mediocre and 2) mediocre versus good quality

| | Infant/toddler center-based | | Preschool center-based | | Family child care | |
|---|---|---|---|---|---|---|
| | P vs. M | M vs. G | P vs. M | M vs. G | P vs. M | M vs. G |
| Education level | | + | | + | + | + |
| Child Development Associate (CDA) credential (Yes/No) | | + | + | + | | + |
| Training hours | | + | | | | + |
| Intense training | | | + | | | |
| Attended a conference | + | + | | | + | |
| First aid and cardio-pulmonary resuscitation (CPR) | | | | + | | + |
| Earnings | | | | + | | |
| Used a curriculum | + | | + | | + | + |
| Parent conference | | | + | + | | + |
| Early Head Start/Head Start partner | | + | | | + | |
| Accredited | | | | | | |
| Food program | + | | + | | + | + |
| Centers: Talked about progress | | | | | | |
| Centers: Health insurance | | | | + | | |
| Family child care: Support person visited | | | | | | |
| Family child care: Licensed | | | | | + | |

Note: + means the predictor asset (Column 1) increased the odds of higher quality at least 2 to 1. One set of logistic regression analyses compared providers in the poor [P] quality group with those in the mediocre M group (i.e., P vs. M) by type of care (infant/toddler center-based, preschool center-based, and family child care). The second set compared providers in the mediocre group with those in the good [G] quality group (i.e., M vs. G) by type of care (infant/toddler center-based, preschool center-based, and family child care). Poor quality is defined as a score below 3 on the environment ratings scales, and good quality is defined as 5 or higher. Two assets (accreditation and having a support person visit a family child care home) did not independently predict quality level outcomes but were contributors to overall increments in quality based on total assets.

ity enhancement investments are paying off. Second, there are indications that what goes in the "breadbasket" should include a broad range of provider characteristics but also program factors not always considered (e.g., participation in the Child and Adult Care Food Program). Third, although our focus has been on state quality-enhancement accountability, the approach to characterizing the child care workforce described here may be useful for more general research on child care workforce development and child care quality.

## Identifying a Short List or "Breadbasket" of Provider Characteristics to Track Over Time

Some states, such as Wisconsin, collect representative provider data periodically and analyze trends deriving implications for quality. The representative telephone and observation study was designed to provide "baseline" data for subsequent studies in our states in which provider characteristics and quality would be measured in more cost-effective ways over time. Because it is very expensive to complete randomized studies of providers that include observations of quality, we were particularly interested in identifying a "short list" of predictors of quality that could be recommended to our states for data collection over time, as proxies for quality, with full representative studies involving observing quality occurring at anchor points, possibly every 10 years. In the Midwest Child Care Research Consortium, we have experimented with alternative ways to collect data, using a short list of key predictors of quality—the assets identified in this study and a few other variables. In one such study, licensing specialists collected data from all providers during routine visits in a typical month, distributing a survey that providers completed in approximately 3 minutes and sealed in envelopes to ensure confidentiality. Preliminary analyses show that this method of data collection provided data of comparable representativeness to that collected by professional telephone interviewers. These data are compared with those collected using alternative methods of data collection, such as data from voluntary registries.

## The "Breadbasket of Assets" and the Culture of Quality

We have reported that the short list of predictors of quality was particularly effective in forecasting quality when predictors of quality were cumulated to form an Index. We draw two conclusions: 1) what matters for workforce development and quality includes both provider- and program-level variables, and 2) the cumulative nature of the variables provides support for a "culture of quality," in which multiple forces create the climate for quality.

*Provider-Level Variables*    Approximately one half of the assets we identified in the current study related to workforce development (including provider education, receiving a CDA, and compensation; variables related to training; and on-site mentoring for family child care providers). Several components of workforce development suggest emphases for state initiatives in the future. First, *regarding education and compensation,* by linking provider educational attainment to compensation (modeled on projects such as Missouri's Workforce Incentive [WIN] Project and the T.E.A.C.H. program), states may be able to positively enhance the professional development of the child care workforce while reducing staff turnover due to low wages. Second, states can set forth *on-going systematic training* designed to address specific competencies desired for the child care workforce for providers at different levels of professional development (e.g., yearly training in first aid and CPR, training in one of several nationally recognized curricula). Third, our study found support for *on-site mentoring programs for family child care providers.* Because the family child care provider works in an environment affording little peer contact or training, states can support the professional development of these providers by developing on-site mentoring programs (examples include Educare in Missouri and the Child Care Resource and Referral Infant/Toddler Project in Kansas).

**Program-Level Variables**    Approximately one half of the identified 14 assets in this study potentially address *program* development (e.g., accreditation, participation in Early Head Start/Head Start partnerships, participation in the Child and Adult Care Food Program, promoting use of curriculum, formal conferences with parents, becoming licensed). Supportive policy initiatives might include providing *accreditation* aids for National Association for the Education of Young Children (NAEYC) accreditation process for centers or the National Association for Family Child Care (NAFCC) for family child care homes. Quality enhancement funds could be targeted to specific aspects of the accreditation process and could offer an incentive for accreditation by offering tiered reimbursement for accredited programs. Next, local, privately owned, or public early childhood programs that *partner with Head Start and Early Head Start* programs are able to benefit from the high-quality standards established by the federal government for those programs. Some states support these partnerships by providing partnership incentives to programs. Finally, states can provide *supports for more programs to receive Child and Adult Care Food Program monies* by encouraging resource and referral agencies to give information about the food program to providers and programs that do not use the resource. In our study, fewer connections were found between observed quality and directors' characteristics. We are hopeful that the new data will contribute to knowledge of the extent to which director characteristics may be added to the index.

**Culture of Quality**    The current research indicates it is the accumulation of assets at the individual provider and program levels that fosters a culture of quality for early childhood programs. This culture is further enhanced by improvements at the community, regional, or state levels—relations needing to be better understood. Such a conceptualization suggests using an ecological framework for understanding influences on the child care workforce (Bronfenbrenner, 1979) as has been suggested by others (Phillips et al., 2000). We found that achieving a "watermark" level of accumulated assets in several areas increased the probability of quality in the good range. The extent to which asset variables are relatively interchangeable will be a topic of future study. However, our analyses do demonstrate that some assets are more important in differentiating mediocre from poor care (e.g., food program participation, using a curriculum), whereas others seem to be more important in differentiating good from mediocre care (e.g., having a CDA, education beyond 1 year past high school).

## Implications for Research

The findings in the present study have implications for research methodology. Increased demands for accountability (e.g., GAO, 2002) have led several states to complete representative baseline studies of quality in order to assess the impact of quality improvement measures. However, multicollinearity, limited variability, and non-normal distributions limit the interpretation of bivariate correlations between structural variables and process quality. At the same time, the generalizability of a single index of quality, such as developed in the present study, may be an issue, and our Index may not be useful in other areas because of more or less stringent regulatory systems or other state differences. Some states may require different cut off scores in an index or different inputs altogether. Measuring the accumulation of assets is but another tool in the tool box for assessing and tracking workforce development and providing data to guide quality enhancement efforts and investment.

In sum, although some of the assets identified seem to go beyond the theme of professional development emphasized in the other chapters, many assets are relevant to the workforce due to a broader culture of quality that develops through workforce and quality improvements. Initial professional development efforts that seem to advance quality from poor to mediocre may be relatively simple—such as participation in the Child and Adult Care Food Program. Yet, the current study showed that many professional development features converge to move the watermark to higher quality, and thus, few single inputs into quality appear to move the workforce forward so much as multiple investments that facilitate providers reaching a critical mass of quality-enhancement efforts. In the Midwest, a relatively stable child care workforce provides potential for state efforts to result in upward trends in workforce development and higher quality of care for young children. Tracking key indicators—or assets, as we have called them—over time will help to tell whether this is the case.

## REFERENCES

Administration for Children and Families. (2003a). *Pathways to quality and full implementation in Early Head Start.* Washington, DC: Author.

Administration for Children and Families. (2003b). *The role of Early Head Start in addressing the child care needs of low-income families with infants and toddlers: Influences on child care use and quality.* Washington, DC: Author.

Arnett, J. (1989). Caregivers in day-care centers: Does training matter? *Journal of Applied Developmental Psychology, 10,* 541–552.

Blau, D.M. (2000). The production of child care quality in child-care centers: Another look. *Applied Developmental Science, 4*(3), 136–148.

Bloom, P.J. (1996). The quality of work life in early childhood programs: Does accreditation make a difference? In S. Bredekamp & B.A. Willer (Eds.), *NAEYC accreditation: A decade of learning and the years ahead* (pp. 13–24). Washington, DC: National Association for the Education of Young Children.

Bronfenbrenner, U. (1979). *The ecology of human development: Experiments by nature and design.* Cambridge, MA: Harvard University Press.

Burchinal, M.R., Cryer, D., & Clifford, R. (2002). Caregiver training and classroom quality in child care centers. *Applied Developmental Science, 6,* 2–11.

Center on Children, Families and the Law, University of Nebraska–Lincoln. (n.d.). *Child care aspects: What are 14 key assets of child care providers that support quality?* (Research Brief No. 1). Lincoln: Author.

Child Health and Development Institute of Connecticut. 2003, June). *A research perspective on the child care workforce in Connecticut.* Farmington, CT: Author.

Cost, Quality, and Child Outcomes Study Team. (1995). *Cost, quality, and child outcomes in child care centers: Public report.* Denver: University of Colorado.

Dunn, L. (1993). Proximal and distal features of day care quality and children's development. *Early Childhood Research Quarterly, 8,* 167–192.

Essa, L.E. (2002). *Who cares for Nevada's children? A profile of demographic, economic, and quality aspects of child care in Nevada.* Reno: University of Nevada, Reno.

Fenson, C. (2005, March 8–11). *Partnerships For Inclusion (PFI).* Presentation at the Annual Meeting of the Child Care Policy Research Consortium.

Galinsky, E., Howes, C., Kontos, S. & Shinn, M. (1994). *The study of children in family child care and relative care: Highlights of findings.* New York: Families and Work Institute.

Gallagher, J.J., Rooney, R., & Campbell, S. (1999). Child care licensing regulations and child care quality in four states. *Early Childhood Research Quarterly, 14,* 313–333.

Gamel-McCormick, M., Buell, M.J., Amsden, D.J., & Fahey, M. (2003). *Delaware Early Care and Education Baseline Quality Study executive summary.* Newark: University of Delaware, Center for Disabilities Studies.

General Accounting Office. (2002). *Child care: States have undertaken a variety of quality improvements, but more evaluations of effectiveness are needed* (GAO-02-897). Washington, DC: Author.

Ghazvini, A., & Mullis, R.L. (2002). Center-based care for young children: Examining predictors of quality. *The Journal of Genetic Psychology, 163,* 112–125.

Governor's Task Force on Early Childhood Care and Education. (2002, November). *Early care and education: The keystone of Pennsylvania's future—Preparing our children for success.* Retrieved May 2, 2005, from http://www.openminds.com/indres/early education12-2002.htm

Harms, T., Cryer, D., & Clifford, R. (1990). *Infant/Toddler Environment Rating Scale (ITERS).* New York: Teachers College Press.

Harms, T., & Clifford, R. (1989). *Family Day Care Rating Scale (FDCRS).* New York: Teachers College Press.

Harms, T., Clifford, R. M., & Cryer, D. (1998). *Early Childhood Environment Rating Scale–Revised Edition (ECERS-R)*. New York: Teachers College Press.

Harris, L., Morgan, G., & Sprague, P. (1996). Facilitated accreditation project. In S. Bredekamp & B.A. Willer (Eds.), *NAEYC accreditation: A decade of learning and the years ahead* (pp. 83–96). Washington, DC: National Association for the Education of Young Children.

Holloway, S.D., Kagan, S.L., Fuller, B., Tsou, L., & Carroll, J. (2001). Assessing child care quality with a telephone interview. *Early Childhood Research Quarterly, 16,* 165–189.

Howes, C., James, J., & Ritchie, S. (2003). Pathways to effective teaching. *Early Childhood Research Quarterly, 18,* 104–120.

Howes, C., Whitebook, M., & Phillips, D. (1992). Teacher characteristics and effective teaching in child care: Findings from the National Child Care Staffing Study. *Child and Youth Care Forum, 21*(6), 399–414.

Kontos, S., Howes, C., Shinn, M., & Galinsky, E. (1995). *Quality in family child care and relative care.* New York: Teachers College Press.

La Paro, K.M., Sexton, D., & Snyder, P. (1998). Program quality characteristics in segregated and inclusive early childhood settings. *Early Childhood Research Quarterly, 13,* 151–167.

National Institute of Child Health and Human Development Early Child Care Research Network. (2000). Characteristics and quality of child care for toddlers and preschoolers. *Applied Developmental Science, 4,* 116–135.

Paulsell, D., Nogales, R., & Cohen, J. (2003). *Quality child care for infants and toddlers: Case studies of three community strategies.* Washington, DC: Mathematica Policy Research, Inc., and ZERO TO THREE.

Phillips, D.A., Mekos, D., Scarr, S., McCartney, K., & Abbott-Shim, M. (2000). Within and beyond the classroom door: Assessing quality in child care centers. *Early Childhood Research Quarterly, 15,* 475–496.

Phillipsen, L.C., Burchinal, M., Howes, C., & Cryer, D. (1997). The prediction of process quality from structural features of child care. *Early Childhood Research Quarterly, 12,* 281–303.

Porter, T., Habeeb, S., Mabon, S., Robertson, A., Kreader, L., & Collins, A. (2002). *Assessing Child Care and Development Fund (Ccdf) investments in child care quality: A study of selected initiatives.* New York: Bank Street College of Education.

Raikes, H.A., Raikes, H.H., & Wilcox, B. (in press). Regulation, subsidy receipt and provider characteristics: What predicts quality in child care homes? *Early Childhood Research Quarterly.*

Raikes, H.H., Wilcox, B., Peterson, C., Hegland, S., Atwater, J., Summers, J. Thornburg, K., Torquati, J., Edwards, C., & Raikes, H.A. (2003). *Child care quality and workforce characteristics in four Midwestern states.* Lincoln: The Gallup Organization and the University of Nebraska.

Ramey, S. (2005, March 8–11). *Ramey Immersion Training and Evaluation (RITE).* Annual Meeting of the Child Care Policy Research Consortium.

Sachs, J. (2000). Inequities in early care and education: What is America buying? *Journal of Education for Students Placed at Risk, 5,* 383–395.

Scales, P.C. (1998). Asset building and risk reduction: Complementary strategies for youth development. *Pregnancy Prevention for Youth: An Interdisciplinary Newsletter, 1*(2), 1–2.

U.S. Department of Health and Human Services. (1994). *The statement of the Advisory Committee on Services for Families with Infants and Toddlers.* Washington, DC: Author.

Whitebook, M. (1996). NAEYC accreditation as an indicator of program quality: What research tells us. In S. Bredekamp & B.A. Willer (Eds.), *NAEYC accreditation: A decade of learning and the years ahead* (pp. 31–46). Washington, DC: National Association for the Education of Young Children.

Whitebook, M., Howes, C., & Phillips, D.A. (1990). *Who cares? Child care teachers and the quality of care in America* (Final report of the National Child Care Staffing Study). Oakland, CA: Child Care Employee Project.

Wisconsin Child Care Research Partnership. (2003a, March). *Improving child care quality* (Public Policy Series on Alternative Policy Options, Report No. 2). Retrieved from http://www.uwex.edu/ces/flp/ece/wccrp.html

Wisconsin Child Care Research Partnership. (2003b, March). *Trends over time: Wisconsin's child care workforce.* Madison, WI: University of Wisconsin–Extension.

# Completing the Model

## Connecting Early Child Care Worker Professional Development with Child Outcomes

KYLE L. SNOW

$\mathbf{A}$s detailed in other chapters of this book, there are two assumptions that appear to be consistent for professional development in the early childhood workforce, regardless of the specific definitions provided. First, professional development is a critical aspect of the career development of the workforce. Indeed, the National Association for the Education of Young Children (NAEYC; 1993) position statement on professional development specified that the range of activities captured under the banner "professional development" is necessary not only to advance individual training, but also to compensate for the extreme variability in backgrounds of the workforce. The second assumption is that professional development improves the quality of care provided. For example, in its highly regarded yearbook on state pre-kindergarten programs, the National Institute for Early Education Research (NIEER; Barnett, Hustedt, Robin, & Schulman, 2004) included professional development programs as part of its quality index. Implicit in this second assumption is yet another: that quality of care is related to better early childhood outcomes. However, this constitutes an incomplete logic model in that professional development is linked with improvements in quality, and quality is linked to child outcomes. Yet, seldom is the third link, that between professional development and childhood outcomes, articulated and empirically tested.[1] Indeed, in its position statement, NAEYC (1993) provided a set of nine principles of effective professional development, but none indicated a need to consider the results of professional development experiences on child development. In this regard, the conceptualization of the importance of professional development reflects a further incomplete logic model whereby the professional development experience(s) is posited to influence the recipient of

---

The opinions and assertions contained herein are the private opinions of the author and should not be construed as official or as representing the views of the National Institute of Child Health and Human Development or the National Institutes of Health.

[1]The idea of an incomplete logic model was first suggested by Martha Zaslow during several sessions at the 2004 National Head Start Research Conference.

the training in some ways without considering the impact on children served by the recipients of the training.

The lack of a complete conceptual model is not limited to studies of professional development of the early childhood workforce, but is evident in numerous areas and professions, including K–12 education, despite the publication of Guskey's (2000) handbook on the evaluation of professional development and the establishment of the National Staff Development Council (NSDC) and its collection of resources (see http://www.nsdc.org). One field in which professional development has been linked to outcomes for program participants is out-of-school time. From this field, Bouffard and Little (2004) drew a series of recommendations for how best to conduct studies on professional development when the impact of training on child outcomes is important. Several of these are particularly timely for studies of professional development in the early childhood workforce. First is the need to design studies of professional development to extend beyond the immediate impression professional development makes on its participants (e.g., Mizell, 2003) to focus on the benefits to be derived by those that should ultimately benefit from more capable early childhood workers—the children. Guskey (2001) called such an approach "backward planning," but in this context, it represents the missing link in the incomplete logic model surrounding professional development. Second, the child outcomes examined should be consistent with the intent of the program. Hence, at the very least, studies of professional development around childhood literacy should plan to assess key literacy outcomes for the children. Third, outcomes must be conceptualized as both short-term outcomes (e.g., changes in early childhood workers) and long-term outcomes for children (see Gusky, 2001). Finally, when the goal of professional development is to improve the lives of children, the activities included in professional development and the evaluation plan should be guided by extant theory and research.

The chapters that follow are somewhat unique in the field in that they provide complete models for the effect of professional development on children and carry to fruition the challenges laid out by Bouffard and Little (2004). These chapters are based on professional development experiences delivered with differing duration, intensity, and targeted domain of child functioning. Despite these differences in approach, these chapters each provide a complete conceptualization of professional development in the service of improving child competency in early literacy, early mathematics, and self-regulation. All are important domains of school readiness as defined at the national and state levels, so attention is increasingly being paid to child competence in these areas for accountability and program development. Also, attention has fallen on how the early childhood workforce approaches improving child functioning in these areas.

Consistent with the attention given to literacy in recent years, much has been written about what early childhood workers can or should do to promote early literacy. Chapter 6 provides a brief overview of how the early childhood field has brought literacy activities to children and preparation to the workforce. Still, outside of their own work, few of these activities have connected professional development with important early literacy outcomes in children. The authors provide a detailed accounting of the lessons they have learned from more than 10 years of research on professional development targeted at improving young children's literacy skills.

Despite the National Research Council's (2001) report *Adding It Up: Helping Children Learn Mathematics,* early mathematics has been and continues to be largely absent from early childhood programs. Indeed, the NAEYC and the National Council of Teachers of Mathematics issued a joint position statement in 2002 attempting to bring mathematics into the critical discourse about early childhood that had previously focused much more intensely on early literacy and the promotion of social and emotional health and well-being (see http://www.naeyc.org/resources/position_statements/psmath.htm). Chapter 7 illustrates both the need for better early mathematics preparation in the early childhood workforce and provides a coherent, brief overview of what mathematics looks like in early childhood settings. As this chapter indicates, the first critical challenge faced in bringing mathematics professional development to early childhood workers is overcoming their poor to nonexistent training in and understanding of mathematics. In constructing professional development within this context, the authors provide a detailed plan for the initial and continuous training of early childhood workers. An important and challenging component in this system is ongoing assessment of childhood mathematical outcomes.

Finally, Chapter 8 tackles professional development intended to promote child self-regulation, which is a relatively new area of concern and attention (e.g., Raver & Knitzer, 2002). It appears to be a fundamental component of child functioning that permeates much of the other activities that engage children in early childhood programs. However, this same set of skills can be difficult to identify and can potentially prove to be challenging to providers of professional development. As the authors indicate, in practice, teachers epitomize a range of theoretical orientations about child development, and these can sometimes lead to conflicting expectations regarding both the young child's capacity to self-regulate as well as the importance of self-regulation not only as a valuable socio-emotional skill but also as a skill that includes valuable cognitive components. By applying a Vygotskian framework to early childhood development, the authors provide a coherent set of expectations for children and their self-regulation. Most important, this chapter shows that adopting a Vygotskian perspective and allowing it to guide interactions with young children enables early childhood workers to affect child self-regulation in important and identifiable ways.

The chapters in Section II provide three excellent models for studies of professional development. Each incorporates theory and research in the design of the professional development as well as the empirical assessment of the impact of these activities on both early childhood workers and children. In doing so, they potentially raise the bar to which other studies of professional development must be compared. Until the consideration of professional development moves beyond the concern that participants enjoyed training or believed it was valuable and in the direction of being concerned about how these experiences affect children, the field cannot hope to design the most effective professional development experiences to support the critical work of the diverse early childhood workforce.

## REFERENCES

Barnett, W.S., Hustedt, J.T., Robin, K.B., & Schulman, K.L. (2004). *The state of preschool: 2004 state preschool yearbook.* Retrieved April 20, 2005, from http://nieer. org/yearbook

Bouffard, S., & Little, P.M.D. (2004). *Promoting quality through professional development: A framework for evaluation.* Cambridge, MA: Harvard Family Research Project.

Guskey, T.R. (2000). *Evaluating professional development.* Thousand Oaks, CA: Corwin Press.

Guskey, T.R. (2001). JSD forum: The backward approach. *Journal of Staff Development, 22*(3), 60.

Mizell, H. (2003). Facilitator: 10, refreshments: 8; evaluation: 0. *Journal of Staff Development, 24*(4), 10–13.

National Association for the Education of Young Children (NAEYC). (1993). *A conceptual framework for early childhood professional development.* Washington, DC: Author. Available online at http://www.naeyc.org

National Research Council. (2001). *Adding it up: Helping children learn mathematics.* J. Kilpatrick, J. Swafford, & B. Findell (Eds.), Mathematics Learning Study Committee, Center for Education, Division of Behavioral and Social Sciences and Education. Washington, DC: National Academy Press.

Raver, C.C., & Knitzer, J. (2002). *Ready to enter: What research tells policy-makers about strategies to promote social and emotional school readiness among three- and four-year-old children.* New York: Columbia University, National Center for Children in Poverty.

CHAPTER 6

# Toward Effective Support for Language and Literacy Through Professional Development

DAVID K. DICKINSON AND JOANNE P. BRADY

This chapter describes the creation of professional development approaches designed to enhance the capacity of early childhood programs to support the language and literacy development of children from low-income backgrounds. After outlining the policy terrain and reviewing the need for enhanced literacy support, the chapter describes varied professional development models and research reflecting their effectiveness. It concludes with a discussion of lessons learned in the course of a 10-year search for effective ways to deliver professional development.

## THE CHALLENGES OF PROVIDING PROFESSIONAL DEVELOPMENT

There is widespread frustration with the lack of a coherent, well-supported system to enhance the knowledge and skills of early childhood practitioners. Despite literature documenting its problems, much of what counts as professional development continues to be characterized by the workshop approach: awareness-building, interactive sessions that are superficial and require little preparation and follow-through by participants. Lack of movement toward more promising in-depth approaches has less to do with a deficiency of knowledge about past inadequacies than the absence of an adequately funded and well-articulated plan that reconciles the goals of professional development

This chapter reports results of work carried out by a team of researchers and professional development specialists at Education Development Center (EDC)'s Center for Children & Families, who are continuing to refine, deliver, and examine the Literacy Environment Enrichment Program (LEEP). Development was initially supported by the Spencer Foundation, with major grants to David K. Dickinson at EDC in 1995 and 1999. EDC, with Dr. Dickinson serving as Principal Investigator, also received grants from Office of Education Research and Improvement (Grant No. R305T990312-00), the Interagency Education Research Initiative (Grant No. REC-9979948), and the Agency for Children and Families (Grant No. 90YD0094). Work done with the State of Connecticut was supported by Early Childhood Educator Professional Development grants, 2001–2005, and state contracts through the Bureau of Early Childhood, Career and Adult Education. The Program-Delivered Literacy In-service Training (PD-LIT) intervention research is sponsored by a 5-year grant (2001–2006) from the U.S. Department of Health and Human Services, Administration for Children and Families (Award No. 90YD0094) to EDC as part of the national Quality Research Consortium on Head Start, with Nancy Clark-Chiarelli now serving as Principal Investigator. All of this work was carried out at EDC's Center for Children & Families in Newton, Massachusetts with the realities of diverse early childhood programs and the capacities of existing delivery systems. There have been laudable efforts. States have attempted to improve the early education workforce through professional development programs linked to college credit, on-the-job mentoring, and systems for enhancing career and compensation (Morgan et al., 1993; Park-Jadotte, Golin, & Gault, 2002; Wheelock College Institute for Leadership and Career Initiatives, 2002). Although these initiatives hold promise, too many can flash brightly but briefly, vanishing due to lack of funding or support (National Association of Child Advocates, 2000; Park-Jadotte et al., 2002; U.S. General Accounting Office, 2002).

There are growing pressures that may result in significant changes in approaches to provision of professional development in the coming decades. With new federal requirements, early childhood programs and states are being compelled to take significant steps to improve the skills of the early childhood workforce, especially with respect to support for literacy. Since the 1990s, the K–12 system has used standards to clarify its educational objectives, and early learning standards are being embraced by early childhood policy makers (Scott-Little, Kagan, & Frelow, 2003; White House, 2002). Driven by the No Child Left Behind (NCLB) Act of 2001 (PL 107-110), states and local programs are focusing on indicators of what young children should be learning and striving to ensure alignment with federal guidelines.

Similarly, since the early 1990s, shifts in early childhood policies have increased pressure to provide staff high-quality professional development. With the Head Start Reauthorization Act of 1994 (PL 103-252), Congress required the Head Start Bureau to develop performance measures to ensure that children were making progress in content areas such as early literacy and scientific and mathematical thinking. This effort is being expanded with the National Reporting System that Head Start is implementing to track child outcomes.

As the early childhood community confronts a multitude of challenges in this new era of accountability, it still grapples with the economic reality that the United States does not provide adequate funding for the early care and education system. Early childhood programs contend with average annual teacher turnover rates of 30% as opposed to a 6.6% annual turnover rate for K–12 teachers (Bellm, Burton, Whitebook, Broatch, & Young, 2002; National Center for Education Statistics, 1997; Whitebook, Sakai, Gerber, & Howes, 2001). Even in Connecticut, with its well-developed set of expectations and generous state support for quality improvement, turnover rates range from 25%–60%, with a state average of 47% (Gruendel, Oliveira, & Geballe, 2003). These rates are fueled by many factors, including low compensation, poor career mobility, lack of supervisory support, and burnout (Cost, Quality, and Child Outcomes Study Team, 1995; Kagan & Cohen, 1997; Park-Jadotte et al., 2002; Whitebook et al., 2001). High turnover rates drive up costs of providing professional development and seriously undermine efforts to achieve coherence in programmatic initiatives.

For many years, staff at Education Development Center (EDC) have been providing professional development to Head Start programs throughout New England. In our work at EDC, we have found that preschool teachers are open to learning and committed to the children they teach. However, they are also steeped in a culture of workshops that value "training techniques"—quick "fun" activities that are neither linked to theoretical understandings of child development nor support teachers in applying those understandings in their classrooms. Also, even committed teachers sometimes have poor prior education, have limited literacy skills, and struggle with self-doubts about their own capacity to learn postsecondary material. Furthermore, many work full time, bear responsibility for their families, hold a second job, and struggle with personal stressors related to low-income status.

Community colleges are the most accessible and affordable institutions of higher education for the early childhood workforce. As of 2003, private and public community colleges served nearly half of all U.S. undergraduates and more than half of ethnic and racial minorities (American Association of Community Colleges, 2003). These institutions are key to educating early childhood staff, but they face their own challenges. Chronically underfunded, they have small education departments in which a few full-time faculty must juggle responsibilities associated with academic institutions, oversee the work of many adjuncts, and teach courses in multiple content areas. Furthermore, in a survey of early childhood programs, Early and Winton (2001) found comparatively few early childhood faculty in community colleges; rather, community colleges have adjuncts and part-time staff. Not surprisingly, relatively few faculty have up-to-date knowledge of early literacy, and even those who do have relevant knowledge have minimal time to plan courses that draw on the rich knowledge now available.

## The Need For Professional Development Related to Language and Literacy

The importance of language and literacy development during the preschool years has been highlighted by broad-ranging literature reviews compiled by expert panels (Bowman, Donovan, & Burns, 2001; Shonkoff & Phillips, 2000; Snow, Burns, & Griffin, 1998). These reports make strong arguments regarding the critical importance of the preschool years, as they summarize studies showing long-term linkages between the literacy abilities of children at the beginning of school and later in school (e.g., Whitehurst & Lonigan, 2001). Cunningham and Stanovich (1997) found that first-grade reading ability was a strong predictor of a variety of eleventh-grade measures of reading ability, even when controlling for measures of cognitive ability. Similarly, the Home–School Study reported first order correlations between kindergarten measures of receptive vocabulary, decoding, and print knowledge and seventh-grade reading comprehension and decoding in the range of .5–.71 (Snow, Tabors, &

Dickinson, 2001). This stability is particularly troubling because it means that schools are failing to narrow the large gaps in the level of achievement between children from different racial, economic, and linguistic backgrounds (National Assessment of Educational Progress, 1999). Furthermore, the trajectory of children's school-age success has been traced downward into the preschool years (McCardle, Scarborough, & Catts, 2001; Scarborough, 2001).

Although there is ample evidence that preschool classrooms have the capacity to bolster children's development (Barnett, S., 2001; Barnett, W.S., 1995; Dickinson & Tabors, 2001; National Institute of Child Health and Human Development Early Child Care Research Network, 2000; Peisner-Feinberg et al., 2001), there also is considerable reason to believe that current levels of support often are far from optimal (Dickinson, McCabe, & Clark-Chiarelli, 2004; Dickinson, St. Pierre, & Pettengill, 2004; Dickinson & Tabors, 2001). In order to create optimally effective classrooms, there is need for support for the full range of skills and abilities that undergird early literacy. Increasingly it is becoming evident that such support must include attention to print, phonemic awareness, and oral language (Dickinson, McCabe, Anastasopoulos, Peisner-Feinberg, & Poe, 2003; Storch & Whitehurst, 2002). Language may be the most challenging capacity to bolster because the needs of children from low-income backgrounds are so great (Hart & Risley, 1995) and current levels of interaction in many early care and education settings fall well below optimal levels (Dickinson et al., 2004).

This chapter now turns to describe how the EDC staff has attacked these complex issues. Our evaluations of successive professional development models have convinced us that specific research-based approaches can be effective when they take the form of sustained initiatives that build pedagogical knowledge by helping teachers understand how to link theory to practical classroom strategies. These initiatives must include accountability procedures so that teachers are motivated to engage in the difficult work of reflecting and implementing new practices. Furthermore, in order to be sustained, professional development needs to include strategies that include supervisory staff and teaching assistants. The chapter concludes by noting that much remains to be learned about how to fashion effective systems for delivering needed professional development—systems that include institutions of higher learning and nonprofit agencies.

## FOSTERING PROFESSIONAL
## GROWTH: SUCCESSIVE APPROXIMATIONS

The work described in this chapter was initiated against this backdrop of recognition of the need for effective professional development that would support early literacy development. In the early 1990s, the first chapter author began to develop a model of professional development designed to build the literacy expertise of preschool teachers. As this effort evolved, other projects based in the Center for Children & Families at EDC extended this work and continue to develop and refine new approaches. This chapter describes the varied approaches developed at EDC's Center for Children & Families, reports data on their effectiveness, and considers the implications of our work. The projects to be described are

- Teacher–Researcher Model: Spencer Foundation-funded pilot project

- Credit-Bearing Model: Literacy Environment Enrichment Program (LEEP)

- Distributed Learning Model: Technology-Enhanced LEEP (T-LEEP)

- Systems Reform Model: Striving to Achieve Reading Success (STARS)

- Whole-School Model: Program-Delivered Literacy In-service Training (PD-LIT)

EDC is continuing to deliver and study the effectiveness of STARS and PD-LIT and is seeking funding to extend work along the lines of T-LEEP. At each phase of development, EDC's professional development models have been linked to evaluation research; therefore, this chapter shares data on the impact of these intervention models collected since 1994.

## Teacher–Researcher Model: Spencer Foundation-Funded Pilot Project

Beginning in the late 1980s, work on emergent literacy matured as researchers documented the developmental trajectories of young children's reading and writing (e.g., Sulzby & Teale, 1991). Environmental supports for development were beginning to be identified (e.g., Neuman & Roskos, 1993; Roskos & Neuman, 2001), but few teachers were aware of this work. Initial results from the Home–School Study of Language and Literacy Development (e.g., Dickinson & Smith, 1994; Dickinson & Tabors, 1991, 2001) convinced the first author of the need to find ways to enable preschool teachers to greatly enhance the quality of support they provide for language and early literacy.

*Core Features*    In the early 1990s, there was considerable interest in supporting professional development by helping teachers become researchers in their own classrooms (Cochran-Smith & Lytle, 1990). In year one of the decade-long search, the first chapter author developed a prototype for the approach, adopting the teacher–researcher model. He observed a teaching team, discussed observations and made suggestions for the coming weeks. In these interactions, he discussed the details of teacher conversations with children and encouraged the teachers to note and record their language interactions. To assist in this reflection, he provided teachers with readings, which were discussed when he met with the teachers. In year two, researchers from

EDC worked closely with a teaching team—a lead teacher and an assistant teacher—in a local Head Start center. Again they observed in the classroom, focusing on issues they had previously discussed with the teaching team. Following the observations, they supported the team in reflecting on their practice. Together, this team worked with all three teaching teams in the same Head Start center as in year one.

The teacher–researcher model was based in the Head Start center, with on-site visits and meetings of individual teams and, in year two, occasional gatherings of all involved teaching teams. Teachers were paid for participating and were expected to engage in the collaborative venture by keeping logs, reflecting on and discussing their practice, and participating in team meetings. The researchers attempted to create an atmosphere of joint problem solving, acting as coaches, observing interactions with a focus that emerged from prior observations, and then discussing what they saw. They also were resource providers, supplying teachers with readings to help them think more deeply about issues of interest.

**Lessons Learned**    Some teachers made improvements in how they worked with children. An experienced teacher became more aware of the nature of her conversations with children. A beginning teacher learned to move around the room less and began engaging children in more productive conversations instead of constantly worrying about management. The researchers learned even more than the teachers. Major lessons included the following:

- The need to be didactic: The teachers wanted a more focused, didactic approach. They saw us as resources and wanted much more clear-cut guidance.

- The need to embed strategies in curriculum: The researchers' desire to focus on teacher–child interactions was viewed as overly narrow and disembodied; teachers wanted to link interactions to broader curriculum planning and day-to-day classroom organization concerns.

- The desire for credits, not money: Financial rewards were not an effective way to bolster motivation. Within this small group, one teacher was perceived by others as being involved only for the money whereas the others were primarily interested in professional growth. The monetary rewards were not central to motivating the high-involvement teachers and undermined their enthusiasm because of the resentment they felt toward the teacher who was only "along for the ride."

- The drawbacks of on-site meetings: Meeting in the Head Start center often was not productive because the research work was not clearly enough differentiated from the life of the classrooms. Last-minute changes in meeting times at the center conflicted with the small group's meeting times, as did other schedule conflicts (e.g., coffee breaks, end-of-day hassles with buses) and crises (e.g., a flooded classroom). Also, the everyday issues of life in a busy program tended to intrude into conversations, detracting from the researchers' ability to focus on literacy and language.

- The need for leadership support: The lack of full support and involvement of the program's director undermined the effectiveness of the intervention. This made it difficult to have predictable meeting times, and the director failed to understand and support the changes that teachers were attempting to implement.

The researchers' ultimate goal was to develop an approach to professional development that could reach far more teachers than could be supported through a teacher–researcher model. Thus, this approach was discontinued as the researchers moved toward development of an academic course, adopting the approach that came to be known as LEEP.

## Credit-Bearing Model: Literacy Environment Enrichment Program (LEEP)

After 2 years of piloting the teacher–researcher model, the EDC team began developing the Literacy Environment Enrichment Program (LEEP). Building on the lessons learned from our work with teachers, we fashioned a course that carried college credits. A traditional academic graduate school model, meeting for 10 extended evening sessions at EDC, was initially adopted. The course was successful, but EDC could not sustain it because it is not a university, and the foundation funding that had supported the previous work had ended.

Fortunately, at that point the New England Resource Center for Head Start had negotiated credit arrangements with 12 colleges and universities throughout the New England region to accept LEEP as a four-credit course. EDC staff developed two intensive 3-day sessions that were separated by 3 months. Each highly interactive session blended discussion, demonstrations and lectures, and hands-on activities. Between sessions, participants applied and practiced course content by completing a carefully sequenced series of assignments. Also, a supervisor track was created, establishing the requirement that teachers and supervisors attend as a team and thereby ensuring onsite support for teachers as they implemented practices and assistance if they encountered difficulties with the academic demands of the experience.

High goals were set for participants. Assignments included texts used in strong college programs (e.g., Schickedanz, 1999) and required students to try new strategies and reflect on their practice. Because teachers need considerable support in developing their analytical capacities,[1] support for reflection was

---

[1]From 1994 to 1998, an EDC team developed the early Childhood Generalist Assessment and its scoring for the National Board for Professional Teaching Standards (NBPTS). This assessment is designed for accomplished teachers and emphasizes teachers' ability to meet high and rigorous standards with respect to children's learning.

woven into assignments and the activities and discussions during class sessions (Adger, Hoyle, & Dickinson, 2004; Brady & Chalufour, 2004). Researchers drew on their past experience with the National Board for Professional Teaching Standards (NBPTS) to fashion assignments that helped guide teachers' mastery of key concepts and strategies and assisted course instructors in evaluating the impact of teaching and learning events. Assignments were carefully sequenced to build a bridge between instructional sessions and teachers' classrooms. Each assignment required LEEP participants to carry out application activities, set goals to improve their practice, and analyze the effectiveness of their teaching in terms of children's literacy learning. Also, some assignments were completed with supervisors, thereby creating settings within which analytic conversations could occur. For example, supervisors were given checklists of desired behaviors that they used as they observed a teacher reading to children. The meeting that followed this observation was structured by the content of the checklist and the guiding questions that were to be addressed during the conference. A culminating project required teachers to plan, deliver, and evaluate the success of an integrated project that provided activities specifically designed to foster children's language and literacy development.

**Core Features**    LEEP was designed to help teachers acquire strong pedagogical content knowledge related to literacy (Shulman, 1987). Central to LEEP were the following elements:

- Knowledge of literacy and language development: The course provided a solid introduction to early literacy development and aspects of oral language that are related to literacy.

- Informal assessment: Knowledge of literacy and language development was deepened and applied as it was employed to carry out informal assessments of children.

- Pedagogical knowledge: Emphasis was placed on knowledge of pedagogical strategies that can be employed to foster literacy. Such strategies included classroom organization, strategies for reading and discussing books, and ways to support writing and plan an integrated curriculum.

- Reflection: Teachers were encouraged to reflect on instruction during class sessions and as they carried out assignments such as audiotaping, transcribing, and then analyzing transcripts of conversations they had with children.

**Evidence of Effectiveness**    Evidence of LEEP's success has come from informal reports from programs, a large comparison group study, and a longitudinal examination of program impact. Several programs reported that when they underwent a review by Head Start or, in one case, the military, they received special commendation for the strength of their literacy program. These comments often were occasioned by visits to the classrooms of teachers who had participated in LEEP. Another interesting by-product was that several teachers were motivated to enroll or re-enroll in higher education programs in their communities.

The most potent evidence of success comes from a pre-post comparison group research study that examined the impact of the course on teachers and supervisors and assessed the impact on children during the year when the teachers participated in LEEP.[2] From 1998 to 2000, LEEP was delivered to more than 300 Head Start teachers and supervisors across six states. Its impact showed promising changes in teachers' practices.

EDC employed a quasi-experimental design and a sample of 72 preschool teachers (LEEP $n = 39$; comparison $n = 33$) and 522 preschool children from North Carolina and New England. Classrooms of intervention and comparison group teachers were visited in the fall prior to the first session of LEEP, and observations were conducted using a battery of classroom observation tools. The same observational tools were employed again in the spring after all coursework was completed. Children in the classrooms of teachers in the comparison group and of those taking LEEP were assessed in the fall and again in the spring. It was found that LEEP has a powerful impact on classroom practices that are likely to foster children's language and literacy development. Controlling for teacher background factors and preintervention scores of classroom quality, LEEP participation predicted higher spring scores on all portions of the Early Language and Literacy Classroom Observation (ELLCO) Toolkit (Smith & Dickinson, 2002) when compared with the comparison group. The ELLCO Toolkit includes a subscale that evaluates the general classroom environment (e.g., climate, classroom organization, behavior management, materials) and a subscale that evaluates support for language, literacy, and curriculum (e.g., book reading, support for language, writing, engaging families effectively). The toolkit also includes an environmental checklist and a rating of literacy-related activity. Effects for the impact of participation in LEEP on spring scores were large for the classroom Language, Literacy, and Curriculum subscale. For example, in a regression model predicting spring scores on this subscale, participation in LEEP was added as the final variable, and the power of the model nearly doubled (from .37 to .73). Large to moderate effects were also found for checklist data and ratings of literacy activities. (Dickinson, Caswell, & Chalufour, 2005). Analyses also indicate that having a teacher with LEEP training is a predic-

[2]Funding for this study was provided to EDC by the Office of Educational Research and Improvement, Grant No. R305T990312-00, and the Spencer Foundation.

tor of both receptive vocabulary and phonemic awareness. Children in class-rooms of teachers with LEEP training scored higher on average on spring measures of both receptive vocabulary and phonemic awareness than children in classrooms with teachers who did not have LEEP training (Dickinson, Miller, & Anastasopoulos, 2001).

Evidence of the lasting nature of LEEP's impact comes from a qualitative study in which Kloosterman and Dickinson (2001) tracked 10 teachers and 7 supervisors who attended LEEP. Follow-up visits to classrooms that included observations and interviews with the full teaching team revealed changes in classroom practices and in the nature of the teacher–supervisor relationship. Two teacher–supervisor teams were followed for 3 years after LEEP, and eight teacher–supervisor teams were followed for 2 years (Dickinson & Kloosterman, 2003; Kloosterman & Dickinson, 2001). Enduring changes were seen in how books were read, in how often books were read, in the types of material read, and in teachers' use of thematic approaches to instruction. Supervisors' new practices also were retained, with improvements in the nature of communication representing an area of marked progress. Changes also included efforts to provide positive feedback, to listen to teachers, and to encourage teachers' efforts.

**Challenges**     Despite mounting evidence pointing to the success of LEEP in bringing about substantial and sustained changes in classroom practices, there were several obstacles:

- On-site support: It was difficult and costly to provide on-site support to teacher–supervisor teams because the participant pool was drawn from a six-state region.

- Density of content: The amount of content that could be covered using the extended session approach was limited by the need to intersperse activities with content because effective learning required application. Thus, the number and depth of discussions on discrete topics covered was limited by the available time.

- Impact on interactions: Given time constraints and limited on-site coaching, there was concern that teachers might change surface features (e.g., the quality of the books in classroom, the frequency of book readings) but make few changes in how they interacted with children (e.g., engaging in extended conversations, using explicit strategies to scaffold children's writing).

- Focused talk about practice: Toward the end of LEEP's implementation, researchers from the Center for Applied Linguistics noted limitations in the depth of discussion about details of classroom practice.

- Need for exemplars of practice: As researchers evaluated assignments, they became convinced of the need for videotapes that could provide exemplars of practice and focus for conversations.

LEEP represented our first concerted effort to develop an approach to professional development that could be taken to scale and would be likely to result in significant changes in practice. LEEP provided the model that was used as the starting point for subsequent models.

## Distributed Learning Model: Technology-Enhanced LEEP (T-LEEP)

With support from the Interagency Educational Research Initiative (IERI),[3] several concerns about LEEP were addressed. EDC developed Technology-enhanced LEEP (T-LEEP), which used distance learning technologies. This model combined face-to-face delivery with interactive television (ITV) and web-based resources and discussions, distributing the learning opportunities over three delivery methods.

T-LEEP began and ended with day-long, face-to-face sessions. During the first session, participants established relationships, were oriented to the ITV, learned to use computers to access and navigate Literacy Village (T-LEEP's web site), and began the process of building a community of learners. The last session wove together course themes and allowed participants to share their learning and connect it to early learning standards. Each of the eight intervening sessions had three segments: Professional Conversations (45 minutes); ITV sessions linking an originating site with three remote sites (2 hours); and Professional Collaborations (45 minutes).

Professional Conversations occurred prior to the ITV portion of the class and were led by trained facilitators who were based at remote sites and guided activities designed to explore topics related to the session and discuss the homework just completed. During the ITV component, EDC instructors at the originating site presented content and strategies and engaged participants at all sites in analysis and discussions, using a range of stimulus material (e.g., videotaped vignettes, work samples, case material) and taking advantage of the fact that ITV makes possible live discussions to which participants in all sites can listen and contribute. Instructors closed each ITV session by summarizing the material covered and referencing the assignment on the topic

---

[3]The IERI work was supported by the National Science Foundation, National Institute of Child Health and Human Development, and the Institute for Education Sciences (formerly the Office of Educational Research and Improvement). This 3-year grant was awarded to EDC in 1999, with partners at the FPG Child Development Institute and the Center for Applied Linguistics.

addressed during that session. During the concluding face-to-face segment, teams of supervisors and teachers met to plan how they would implement their joint assignments at their programs.

The Literacy Village web site included profiles of exemplary teachers with interviews and videotapes of their classroom work. It also contained resources (e.g., children's literature, activities to support phonological awareness), and a bulletin board for discussion. Teachers used this site to gain access to resources that they used to carry out assignments and for strategies to extend their efforts related to particular topics.

**Core Features of T-LEEP**   Using technology brought a mix of new challenges and clear opportunities to develop increasingly effective instruction. Important design features included the following:

- Pacing and delivery: Over a span of 6 months, T-LEEP teachers and supervisors participated in 10 sessions, spaced 2–3 weeks apart, thereby allowing more occasions for instructor–teacher interaction than the intensive delivery approach used for LEEP.

- Explicit content: EDC refined the content and elaborated on the conceptual underpinnings of early language and literacy development. In particular, more time was devoted to oral language, emergent writing, and phonological awareness. Earlier, in each of these areas, teachers had misconceptions or acquired only partial understanding of key concepts.

- Pictures of practice: Videotapes help demystify concepts, and pictures of exemplary practice leave lasting images of the interactions teachers are striving to achieve. EDC collected videotape footage from exemplary classrooms that were aligned with course content. Vignettes allowed illustration of key points; increased teacher capacity to analyze strategies; and consideration of the interplay among instruction, assessment, and learning (Brady & Chalufour, 2004).

- Representations of learning: EDC collected children's work samples that illustrate a range of understanding and a diversity of modes of expression. These were used to help teachers move from abstract discussion of children's development to authentic analysis of children's learning.

**Evidence of Effectiveness**   To examine the effectiveness of T-LEEP, EDC researchers collected classroom- and child-level data in Connecticut, Massachusetts, and North Carolina, collaborating with researchers from the FPG Child Development Institute at The University of North Carolina–Chapel Hill. The researchers used a quasi-experimental design and a sample of 65 preschool teachers (T-LEEP $n$ = 28; comparison

$n = 37$) and 455 preschool children from North Carolina and New England. Intervention and comparison group classrooms were observed prior to and after T-LEEP participation, and children in these classrooms were assessed using a battery of tests of language and literacy development. Controlling for all teacher background factors and preintervention scores, T-LEEP predicted higher postintervention scores on all portions of the ELLCO when compared with the comparison group (Clark-Chiarelli & Buteau, 2003; Clark-Chiarelli et al., 2003). Even more impressive was the finding that T-LEEP had substantial effects on children. Program effects were analyzed using hierarchical linear modeling, a sophisticated analytic technique that allows researchers to obtain a more accurate estimate of variance in outcomes among children in a classroom. After accounting for all child and teacher background variables and child preintervention scores, participation in T-LEEP predicted 42% of the between-class variation in children's receptive vocabulary. T-LEEP participation was also associated with higher scores in both phonemic awareness and emergent literacy outcomes at a level of statistical significance, accounting for 16% of the between-class variation in spring phonemic awareness scores and 15% of the between-class variation of spring emergent literacy scores (Clark-Chiarelli & Buteau, 2003).

**Challenges**    Although equipment failures brought an element of anxiety to carefully orchestrated T-LEEP sessions, technical aspects of delivery proceeded more smoothly than anticipated. Instead, recruitment and attrition were the main obstacles. In addition to the rigors of the course, potential participants might have been apprehensive about the use of technology. Even those who completed the course had a rudimentary understanding of computers and the Internet. Despite the availability of technical support, this could account for some of the attrition problems.

Attrition data for T-LEEP were sobering. Although LEEP—and the Striving to Achieve Reading Success (STARS) model, which is described next—had 10% and 13.5% attrition rates respectively, T-LEEP's rate was 45%. Perhaps 10 sessions extending over nearly 6 months proved to be too many, especially because most were held after a full day's work. The pacing may also have been a factor. Having just 2 weeks between sessions may have added a level of stress that made it difficult for participants to handle the workload. EDC may have also misjudged the difference between Head Start and child care regarding the level of program support that teachers and supervisors receive. Many Head Start programs have time set aside for professional development and are accountable for child outcomes; they also are accustomed to having supervisors who are freed up from direct service responsibilities. Child care programs on average have fewer resources to support professional development and many small agencies have directors or site managers who also teach, making it difficult to meet and sustain T-LEEP's teacher–supervisor team requirement.

## Systems Reform Model:
## Striving to Achieve Reading Success (STARS)

Working with the Connecticut State Department of Education (CSDE) in 2001 the second author began exploring ways to integrate credit-bearing professional development into a statewide system. Together, an EDC team and the Connecticut State Department of Education developed an approach that was funded through the Early Childhood Educator Professional Development Initiative of the U.S. Department of Education. Striving to Achieve Reading Success (STARS) was designed to use LEEP as the centerpiece to improve teacher practices and child outcomes in Connecticut's high educational need communities. Drawing on lessons from LEEP and T-LEEP, EDC attempted to situate professional development in the existing systems supporting early childhood staff by involving higher education and building a professional development lattice by collaborating with Connecticut Charts-A-Course (CCAC). Responsible for Child Development Associate (CDA) credential, CCAC wanted to align its literacy modules with LEEP for entry-level staff.

STARS is delivered to a range of Connecticut's early childhood programs that serve children from low-income backgrounds in child care, Head Start, and pre-K programs. For several reasons, it was decided that training for the STARS version of LEEP (also called "STARS-LEEP") would be delivered in three 2-day sessions—most often Fridays and Saturdays. First, this training schedule increased access for staff in early childhood programs that do not have resources for substitutes or professional development days. Spanning a weekend limited the burden on such programs. Second, this arrangement helped ensure the personal commitment of the participants. Willingness to give up personal time indicated an understanding of the nature of the commitment needed to complete this credit-bearing professional development experience. Because of Connecticut's increased emphasis on college credit, teachers and supervisors have been motivated to participate, especially because the STARS grant supports all of the tuition expenses.

Although the supervisor component characteristic of earlier versions of LEEP was retained, a new approach was designed to help supervisors work with the teachers in their programs. Prior to STARS, EDC instructors had not shared with supervisors our growing insight into the challenges teachers face as they strive to support children's literacy and language development. Therefore, the supervisor component was altered specifically to build supervisors' capacity to recognize misconceptions and intervene. STARS moved away from providing generic information about ways of engaging in clinical supervision and toward an approach in which literacy content was infused. STARS also incorporated more videotaping into supervisors' assignments, asking them to videotape teachers and analyze those tapes and to videotape themselves as they engaged in supervisory sessions with teachers. These supervisory interactions were discussed with EDC instructors.

STARS courses are co-taught with faculty from higher education institutions in Connecticut. Each year faculty are recruited and oriented to the LEEP model, the instructional design, and its rationale. As co-instructors, higher education faculty deliver part of the course content, make on-site visits to STARS participants, and use the rubrics developed to grade the performance-based assignments. In its third year as of 2004, STARS is striving to bring about systemic changes as it works with the Connecticut State Department of Education and its partners to address articulation agreements among colleges and to have the STARS-LEEP accepted by more institutions as a part of their core curriculum.

***Core Features of STARS***    STARS drew on much of the pedagogy and materials developed in prior iterations of the basic LEEP model while introducing several important new elements:

- State supported delivery: STARS is a collaborative venture between the state of Connecticut and EDC. The state plays a key role in recruitment, pays for staff to attend sessions, and is the ultimate force in determining whether programs are in compliance with state-mandated education levels.

- Linkage to community colleges: STARS is seeking to build the capacity of community colleges, the institutions of higher education that are training new teachers and need to work with the state to continue efforts to raise performance levels of teachers across the state.

- Refined use of videotapes to support supervisors: STARS has developed and refined a cost-effective model designed to help supervisors better support teachers and become more aware of their own supervisory practices.

***Evidence of Effectiveness***    Data on the effectiveness of STARS come from anecdotal channels and from ongoing evaluation conducted by a third party, the Center for Community and School Action Research (CCSAR). Feedback from STARS participants has been uniformly positive. Although participants report that the work is challenging, they also can see the results of their immediate application of the strategies learned. These reports are bolstered by results that come from qualitative data being collected by CCSAR. Focus groups conducted with participants in 2002 and 2003 indicated that participants consider STARS-LEEP significantly different from their other professional development experiences. Teachers and supervisors believe the intensity (2-day sessions) and pacing (spaced 5 weeks apart) are a plus. The intensity is appealing to participants because it allows full-time staff to allocate the time needed to complete the course without consuming weekends for an extended period. Moreover, the pacing of the sessions allows participants ample time to apply what they are learning (CCSAR, 2003).

Focus group results also suggest that STARS-LEEP is distinguished by providing early childhood staff new frameworks for structuring their classrooms—from the simple to the more involved (CCSAR, 2003). Participants noted the changes that they have made range from supporting writing around the room to learning about the value and ways to initiate and extend rich conversations with children. Many also pointed to the fact that they already noticed children's positive responses, which motivates participants to continue to try out new practices and ideas. These qualitative findings are supported by classroom observations conducted in the spring and fall by CSSAR researchers. Analyses indicate that classrooms with STARS teachers have significantly higher post-intervention scores than comparison group classrooms, as measured by the ELLCO (Center for Community and School Action Research, 2003).

**Challenges and Future Directions**    Despite refinements to the supervisor track, the extent to which supervisors could provide needed ongoing support to teachers was still questionable at the end of the second year. The project evaluation of CSSAR found data supporting these concerns. Although supervisors and teachers appreciate the new professional relationship established during the professional development, supervisors' responsibilities prevent them from continuing the close content-rich discussions activated by the course (CCSAR, 2003). In addition, Connecticut's early child programs vary in size. Even under the best circumstances, the ratio of teachers to supervisors is high. As the STARS project began to involve more teachers within each program, it could no longer require supervisors to take the course with teachers. After all, supervisors are only motivated to take this credit-bearing professional development once. Therefore, EDC designed and is piloting a content-focused mentoring program devised for teams and potentially with teachers whose supervisors are already STARS graduates. Mentors work with their protégés for 6 months after the completion of the course to support the further refinement of participants' understanding and skill in application. Recruited from successful LEEP graduates, STARS mentors are experienced in adult education and have recent teaching experience with preschoolers. Mentors receive specialized training and ongoing support from EDC's STARS staff. The mentoring component was launched in January 2004, and initial reports indicate that mentors and protégés are working together on the application of specific literacy practices.

Despite the active participation of nearly 300 participants in STARS-LEEP professional development, programwide adoption of the concepts and practices embodied in STARS continues to be elusive. When program directors participate in the training, they are more likely to support their staff in doing so. Furthermore, they are in a better position to implement programwide changes. However, this type of support is seen in programs where leadership staff are already committed to the reforms being encouraged by STARS. What remains to be seen is whether systemic efforts could occur in programs where commitment prior to the course is not as strong.

The higher education component has its own continuing challenges. Adoption of STARS-LEEP as an approved early childhood literacy course is slow and cumbersome in most institutions. Also, the STARS course is a significant departure from traditional college courses in its mode of delivery and the value put on classroom application. Instructors with whom EDC staff work are provided a well-developed set of materials that includes PowerPoint slides with key points, suggested topics of conversation, and videotape segments and work samples with guidance for engaging teachers in analytic discussions. Not all faculty are comfortable with these instructional methods. A few question the comprehensive nature of the materials, interpreting the defined scope and sequence as a limit to their professionalism. Far from a script, EDC views the materials as a sound structure in which able instructors can liberate their content knowledge and professional expertise. Conversely, others tend to use the materials rigidly, appearing not to be in full command of the concepts to be covered during the class session. This range of experiences suggest that in order to hand off the model, EDC needs to devise new strategies to secure the buy-in of instructors and provide some form of ongoing support to ensure fidelity of implementation.

## Whole Program Model: Program-Delivered Literacy In-service Training (PD-LIT)

In LEEP, T-LEEP, and STARS-LEEP, professional development was delivered to supervisor and teacher teams. The goal was that supervisors would provide teachers with continued encouragement to implement changes and begin to institutionalize key literacy approaches in their programs. Although it appears that LEEP teachers were supported in sustaining new practices, these approaches did not spread to other classrooms (Dickinson & Kloosterman, 2003). Given the high levels of turnover in preschool classrooms, this means that the long-term impact of LEEP will fade. In an effort to obtain full buy-in and complete institutionalization of valued practices, EDC developed Program-Delivered Literacy In-service Training (PD-LIT).

A 5-year Head Start Quality Research Center grant to EDC enabled the design and study of the effectiveness of PD-LIT. This program is a systemic intervention created to build the capacity of local programs to deliver training, ensure implementation of recommended practices, and then sustain these practices. PD-LIT sought to communicate the same basic information about development and pedagogy and employed some of the videotape materials used in the other earlier models. Unlike the other models, PD-LIT is given during in-service workshop times to all classroom staff in a program. The incentive to adopt new practices, is thus tied to a teacher's desire to do a better job and receive a better job performance evaluation. To help ensure the incorporation of specific practices, EDC worked with the program to develop a set of explicit statements of practices that should be implemented in classrooms (e.g., read books every day, create a well-provisioned writing center).

PD-LIT training materials are packaged in a relatively low-tech format designed for use in preschool programs. Training materials are on overhead transparencies that are organized for ease of use, and videotape segments are on VHS cassettes. In order to create materials that were amenable to such delivery, EDC worked closely with staff from the Head Start program administered by Communities United, Incorporated (CUI). Development teams comprised of CUI and EDC staff developed the eight 4-hour modules, and CUI staff pilot tested these materials in their program.

PD-LIT has been delivered in two programs under different circumstances. In the pilot, EDC staff and program staff shared delivery of the workshops. In order to reach all of the program staff, each module was delivered three times. The first time, an EDC staff member took the lead and was assisted by the CUI staff member who would later assume responsibility. In the second session, the CUI trainer was responsible, supported by the EDC trainer when needed. During the third session, the CUI trainer delivered the workshop on her own. In the second year, EDC began work with Action for Boston Community Development (ABCD), which runs multiple Head Start delegate programs around Boston. EDC began its partnership with ABCD by working closely with administrators to hammer out the myriad details essential for successful implementation: the release time of staff, including the in-house trainer; the pacing and scheduling of the PD-LIT modules; and systems for monitoring follow-through in classrooms. Because the goal was an in-service model to reach staff and children in two different program sites, each with its own local director, on-site meetings were held to work out the site-specific issues. Also, in the year prior to implementation in ABCD-run centers, leaders in the two programs who were selected for inclusion took T-LEEP to ensure they had the knowledge required for effective support of literacy in their programs.

In the first year of delivery, PD-LIT modules were presented by a high-level trainer who was oriented to the materials by EDC staff. He delivered on-site training to all staff in each of the two participating centers. This approach proved to be cumbersome and was replaced by delivery of the workshop to both programs in one central location. Centralized delivery proved to be more effective, as it was less stressful for the trainer and provided staff with opportunities to interact with those from other centers.

**Core Features**    PD-LIT was characterized by two distinctive features that set it apart from the other models:

- Systemic training: All teaching staff and supervisory staff are trained at the same time and expectations for what constitutes appropriate support for language and literacy are articulated and provide shared reference points for conversations about practice.

- Program "ownership" of training: The training is delivered by staff from the program. Teachers receive the training from leadership in their own program, eliminating issues that arise from "outsiders" imposing new procedures and enabling programs to repeat the trainings in subsequent years if necessary. This approach increases the likelihood of full institutionalization of valued practices.

**Evidence of Effectiveness**    PD-LIT addresses recruitment problems because staff are expected to attend as part of their job responsibilities. Evaluation responses indicate widespread satisfaction among participants. Another feature of the model is that recruitment of participants shifted from efforts to recruit many individual teaching teams to conversations with program leaders who decide whether the program would participate in PD-LIT. This creates a shift from the highly personal issues that individual teachers had to consider when deciding to enroll to broader programwide considerations (e.g., Do we need to focus on literacy? Can we commit this much time?). Thus, the community, state, and federal policy-related factors play a much larger role in determining participation patterns.

The impact of the training on program practices has varied by program. In the program where the intervention was delivered by staff who helped develop the training materials, there was considerable buy-in, and supervisors made energetic efforts to help teachers adopt recommended practices. The changes in practice were most noteworthy in the area of writing. EDC staff visited the classrooms in the fall and again in the spring and coded classroom practices using ELLCO. The findings included significant changes in practices related to writing (Dickinson, Howard, Caswell, & Sprague, 2002). EDC staff have been unable to collect long-term follow-up data but know that the year after EDC's involvement ended, the program ran the workshops again, with special effort to ensure that staff who were second-language learners received additional time to understand the concepts and related classroom practices. Program leaders report that the entire program has begun to fully incorporate recommended practices and has reached a much higher level of understanding of practices that support language and early literacy.

Data are being collected on the impact of PD-LIT in ABCD centers by using the same basic methods as for prior evaluations of LEEP, with the exception that comparison group teachers and children are from a randomly selected delegate program from within ABCD. In ABCD centers, the delivery was slowed down so that it took 2 years to deliver the full set of workshops. Analyses that used Hierarchical Linear Modeling to examine data collected after the first of these 2 years compared intervention and comparison group classrooms and controlled for fall scores. EDC found that PD-LIT classrooms received higher scores on the ELLCO classroom observation tool (Clark-Chiarelli et al., 2004). The size of effects is smaller than what has been found for LEEP, but the intervention was not fully implemented when these data were collected. That said, there is reason to believe that the training may not have an immediate effect equivalent to LEEP (see the "Challenges and Future Directions" section for more information). The real strength of PD-LIT lies in its potential to be fully institutionalized, with the result being that the impact could persist and even increase over time.

**Challenges and Future Directions**    The pilot provided important insights about the pacing of modules. Feedback from the pilot test indicated a need for more time between modules to allow teachers to implement the practices presented. In the new program, this more spread-out approach to delivery raised some issues of its own because the long time period between sessions resulted in a loss of energy and commitment to the initiative.

EDC staff are still learning how to effectively "hand off" the training to a program. In the first year, EDC's partner (CUI) worked closely with EDC, reducing the complexity of the endeavor. With ABCD, EDC staff found that they were able to arrange only limited time for orienting the trainer. As a result, not all training sessions were as successful as they were when delivered by those who helped develop the sessions. Also, because of limited meeting time with ABCD leadership staff, EDC staff were not able to arrive at mutually agreed-on expectations for performance subsequent to the in-service session.

EDC visits to classrooms to track fidelity of implementation showed that the level of on-site support was not sufficient to support teachers in making major changes in practice. As a result, there is now an on-site visit to meet with the supervisors to discuss successes and challenges. EDC chose to work with supervisors rather than directly with teachers because of its commitment to an approach that builds and works through the program's supervisory systems.

PD-LIT is designed to include all staff in the program whereas other versions of LEEP include early childhood practitioners who are prepared to take on credit-bearing professional development. As a result of the shift in target audience, some staff struggle to understand the concepts and material presented. Furthermore, the fact that the intervention does not carry credit lessens the requirement for reflection and evidence of the adoption of specific practices. Therefore, in a whole–school change approach such as PD-LIT, success is highly dependent 1) on teachers' desire to learn and to adopt new practices and 2) on their supervisors' ability to assess teachers' attempts at implementation and provide needed support for adoption.

## CONCLUSIONS AND RECOMMENDATIONS

This concluding section provides our current, tentative thoughts related to challenges we have encountered in our efforts to address the complex issues that the nation and the early childhood community face in enhancing the language and literacy skills of large numbers of children from low-income backgrounds. First, we consider factors that contribute to the effectiveness of the intervention—delivery mechanisms and instructional design. Next, we briefly discuss challenges and strategies related to taking interventions to scale and to institutionalizing and sustaining change.

### Delivery Considerations for Intervention Effectiveness

For a professional development initiative to be effective, it must result in substantial improvements in classroom practices and evidence that the changes in practice translate into improvements in children's development. Efforts to enroll programs and staff must not require excessive effort, and attrition must be low. Also, for sustained impact to occur, the intervention cannot be simply delivered to teachers working in isolation; systems must be in place to encourage institutionalizing effective practices. One set of factors that plays a role in determining the effectiveness of professional development interventions relates to how the intervention is organized and delivered.

*Timing and Duration*    EDC's interventions have lasted from 5 months to 2 years. There are no data on very brief interventions because they are expected to have a decreased likelihood of success. Available data clearly indicate that the 5- to 6-month interventions can be effective in changing classroom practices and bolstering children's learning. At present, it is unclear whether the extended time for delivering PD-LIT will prove to be an asset or will undermine the energy and completeness of adoption.

The pacing of the intervention is determined by the following related variables: length of each session, the frequency of sessions, and the intervals between sessions. Delivery of training in intensive, extended sessions (e.g., 2- or 3-day sessions) typically means that there will be relatively few such events. When there are only a few extended sessions, as is the case with LEEP, these sessions tend to take place several months apart. The length and number of sessions provided are related to the conceptual density of the material that is presented during the professional development experience. Staff for intensive 2- to 3-day workshops cannot teach the same amount of conceptually sophisticated materials as they can teach when several shorter sessions are spread over time. Participants need time to link conceptual material to practices. In intensive workshop approaches, considerable workshop time must be spent helping participants make these linkages. In shorter sessions, some application time also is needed, but teachers can return to their classrooms, try out methods, and then return the next session to discuss their insights. Therefore, the overall conceptual load of class time can be heavier than that of extended sessions. At this point, EDC's results indicate that either format results in sizable effects on classroom practices. Data from T-LEEP analyses provide clear evidence of sizable effects on children's learning.

***On-Site Support***    Many professional development efforts involve considerable amounts of coaching of teachers by mentors. EDC's models have attempted to help teachers by working with the supervisory staff charged with supporting teachers' professional development. Although EDC obtained gratifying evidence of success with LEEP and T-LEEP, there is a need for even stronger on-site support for teachers to ensure full adoption of recommended practices. Thus, the STARS model increased coaching of supervisors by using analysis of videotapes of conferences. PD-LIT moved toward providing more on-site support to supervisors. There is much to learn about the most effective ways to engage supervisory personnel in helping teachers and about the impact of these efforts on teacher's efforts and children's learning. Also, much work needs to be done to devise research tools that can track the impact of interventions on supervisors and mentors and to begin to investigate relationships between the quality of supervision and the ability of teachers to adopt new, effective practices.

## Instructional Design Issues for Intervention Effectiveness

As EDC struggled to determine the right "packages" for its training materials, it also worked to develop approaches to designing the content of sessions and of assignments in ways that help teachers fully integrate concepts with classroom practices.

***Foundational Knowledge***    Teachers must be provided conceptual knowledge about the nature of language and literacy development. As noted previously, many early childhood teachers lack even the most basic education about child development, and most have limited knowledge of language and early literacy development. Many issues addressed in this concluding section are fundamentally related to creating conditions that enable teachers to acquire the needed pedagogical content knowledge. This lack of foundational knowledge is particularly problematic in preschool classrooms, where most of the programming is left to the teacher because there is often only limited specific guidance from a curriculum. Therefore, among teachers who lack conceptual grounding in how to think about literacy, the instructional approach employed is a mix of their program's standing patterns of practice, folk theories, and personal beliefs about how children learn to read and write. The end product is often a program that falls far short of the ideal (Dickinson, McCabe, & Clark-Chiarelli, 2004; Dickinson, St. Pierre & Pettengill, 2004).

***Problem-Solving and Supported Analysis***    Another primary objective of EDC's instructional design has been to devise methods to help teachers gain skill in reflecting on their practice. With help from its partners at the Center for Applied Linguistics, EDC came to realize that its most effective interactions during classes occurred when there was a problem-solving atmosphere (Adger et al., 2004). To create such a climate, EDC staff often introduced concepts through lecture-discussions, then provided work samples or videotapes of classrooms and guided teachers toward use of the new concepts. Often during these discussions teachers also drew on experiences from their own classrooms. When work samples were used, the same general structure was employed except that teachers worked in small groups as they examined and talked about the samples.

The most potent means to help teachers acquire skill reflecting on practice was in the assignments given as part of the credit-bearing versions of LEEP. These assignments are grounded in teacher's classroom work and guide teachers toward application of course content through a structured sequence of activities that moves from doing (e.g., trying out a new instructional strategy, collecting information about a child), to talking about the activity with a supervisor, to writing about it in a manner that encourages reflection but does not place a premium on formal written English. One of the drawbacks of PD-LIT has been that it is not bolstered by the academic structure; thus, it does not have a strong personal accountability system to ensure that teachers engage in activities designed to support reflection.

***Adoption of Strategies***    In-service education holds a powerful advantage over preservice training—there is no gap between the methods one learns in school and those one actually employs in the real world. During class sessions and in readings, teachers see and learn about classroom strategies related to instruction and assessment. For assignments, they must try some of these strategies and reflect on the experience. The result is that teachers strive to link theory to practice in their own classroom and to reflect on their efforts.

***Summary Comments***    Analyses of multiple waves of data collection on different versions of LEEP have convinced EDC that its approach has led to beneficial changes in practice in hundreds of classrooms. EDC has not conducted studies that systematically disentangle the web of activities employed to determine the key ingredients. In the coming years, systematic examination of the factors discussed might lead to greater understanding of which instructional design features are of primary importance.

The other dimension of effectiveness—minimizing attrition—is a nettlesome problem. Many factors contribute to patterns of attrition. Potentially important factors include the academic preparation of teachers, teachers' expectations of the experience, on-site support for academic challenges, the nature of extrinsic motivators and the teacher's intrinsic motivation, life circumstances, and program support. Issues related to attrition are closely linked to questions about ways to effectively engage child care providers who have limited educational background, with teachers in community child care and family child care settings being particularly challenging to reach.

Information exists about another factor that might affect attrition: the time element. Attrition among T-LEEP participants was far greater than for LEEP or STARS. T-LEEP required attendance at the most sessions (10) and allowed the least time between sessions (2 weeks). These observations suggest possible features of intervention that may contribute to attrition. However, caution must be used in drawing conclusions because the prototype for LEEP took a form similar to T-LEEP and had a much lower level of attrition (about 15%). Unlike T-LEEP, the early version academic course was given in one location, people did not have to travel far for each session, and novel uses of technology were not involved. Clearly much remains to be learned about the complex factors that lead to attrition and about effective ways to address these issues.

## Institutionalizing Effective Approaches

The ability to bring about a reform is only of passing interest if the changes disappear soon after the intervention ends. In each approach, EDC has attempted to create structures that will ensure some degree of continuity that is not totally dependent on the classroom teacher. EDC's work with supervisors has been directed toward the goal of providing ongoing support and encouragement to individual teachers. As of 2004, there were indications that this approach can result in lasting changes in the dynamics between a given teacher and supervisor, but there may not be dramatic changes in overall supervisory practices or in literacy programs in other classrooms (Education Development Center, 2003). There are many powerful forces at work within programs that lead to the status quo; it may take more than the knowledge and effort of a single supervisor and teacher to substantially alter the dynamics.

PD-LIT is attempting to create programwide adoption of strategies and expectations for performance. In addition, it is attempting to build the capacity for programs to cope with turnover problems by training new staff using high-quality materials with which they are familiar. PD-LIT offers the hope of systemic institutionalization of practices. For this to occur, however, the initial delivery of the intervention must be strong enough to bring about initial changes in practices, which are sufficiently large to result in observable changes in classroom practice. Although it would be ideal to see immediate measurable changes in children's learning, this may be asking for too much. Programs need to realize that adoption of practices that result in sizable changes in children's growth likely will require efforts that are sustained over several years.

STARS is seeking to institutionalize changes at yet another level—that of the institutions of higher education that provide in-service training. This initiative involves a very different set of challenges. Faculty in community colleges and state universities are often overwhelmed and have scant time for working to effect the institutional changes required to get new courses adopted and set in place new systems for working with in-service teachers. University bureaucracy moves slowly, and universities need to see changes as being in their interest. They also face multiple financial challenges.

## Taking Professional Development Efforts to Scale

The magnitude of the challenges faced makes eminently clear the need to devise interventions that can be delivered efficiently to large numbers of programs and teachers in a manner that is cost-effective and retains the effectiveness of the intervention. EDC has attempted to achieve this goal in different ways. In all interventions except for PD-LIT, course material was delivered by EDC staff. The use of core staff to deliver well-specified training sessions reflects EDC's belief that effective instruction requires a complex mix of conceptual and pedagogical knowledge, high-quality materials rich with pictures of practice, and familiarity with the training materials. This basic approach has served EDC well. The T-LEEP showed that distance need not limit the ability of skilled trainers to engage groups of teachers effectively. LEEP showed that regional institutes offered as courses can be effective.

Retaining a cadre of qualified, EDC-based trainers who are equipped with course materials and course-related materials is an effective approach as long as there is an appropriate balance between the need for training staff and available trainers. However, fluctuations in demand for professional development mean that it could be difficult to ensure the availability of enough well-trained staff. If this model is employed in more distant locations, there is the possibility that it will be hard for trainers to make needed adjustments to local circumstances. Also, staff in the programs might be less receptive to training sessions when they are provided by relative strangers.

PD-LIT represents an alternative approach to scaling up. EDC's goal is to equip programs with training materials, skill in using these materials, and systems for clarifying the practices that should be found in all classrooms. This approach avoids the possible pitfalls associated with having trainers external to programs doing the training, but it leaves open the possibility that the professional development will not be delivered in a manner that is accurate or effective. Issues associated with ensuring that teachers receive strong on-site support also become increasingly more pressing as responsibility for delivery of the intervention shifts to the program.

The ability of interventions to go to scale successfully is linked to development of broad policies that create incentives for change and provide funds to help programs engage in the kind of comprehensive, sustained professional development initiatives most likely to result in substantial changes. Both programs and colleges are complex institutions, but the systems and political dynamics in many universities and colleges are such that it will take focused efforts to create incentives that make substantial change attractive.

## Concluding Thoughts

Although many daunting organizational challenges must be confronted, the field is beginning to learn how to provide professional development that changes practice. Unfortunately, relatively little is known about strategies for instituting and institutionalizing new practices. Even more important, there is only the faintest understanding of the nature and magnitude of changes in classroom practice that are needed to substantially enhance children's learning. The efforts we have described resulted in demonstrated improvements in learning, but the field knows far too little about exactly what was changed in classrooms that resulted in improved learning and what aspects of the training experiences brought about the critical changes in practice. Also, the field has not even attempted to take on the daunting challenges associated with providing professional development support to those who work in family child care settings.

In the coming decades, responses to these myriad challenges will likely require collaborative efforts of many groups. Federal and state policy makers must continue to uphold high standards that encourage programs and individuals who engage in effective professional development, create supports that enable them to participate, and put in place reward structures that make participation worth their while. Publishers must provide curricula and professional development materials that draw on current knowledge and support teachers as they seek to respond to the new expectations for practice. EDC's efforts have focused on providing high-quality professional development that enables teachers to be more effective with any curriculum; it is anticipated that pairing high-quality professional development with a strong curriculum would result in even more dramatic improvements in child outcomes. Finally, universities and nonprofit organizations are key to helping programs better support children's language and literacy by devising professional development approaches and systems for delivering them to program staff. A well-articulated network of resources must be devised—with states, local programs, universities, nonprofit organizations, and publishers as key partners—to provide high-quality professional development to all sectors of the early childhood community.

## REFERENCES

Adger, C.T., Hoyle, S.M., & Dickinson, D.K. (2004). Locating learning in in-service education for preschool teachers. *American Educational Research Journal, 41*(4), 867.

American Association of Community Colleges. (2003). *Community colleges past to present.* Retrieved April 11, 2005, from http://www.aacc.nche.edu/Content/Navigation Menu/AboutCommunityColleges/HistoricalInformation/PasttoPresent/Past_to_Present.htm

Anastasopoulos, L., Dickinson, D.K., & Peisner-Feinberg, E. (2002, April). *Changes in classroom practices and associated impacts on children.* Paper presented at the Annual Conference of the American Education Research Association, New Orleans, LA.

Barnett, S. (2001). Preschool education for economically disadvantaged children: Effects on reading achievement and related outcomes. In S. Neuman & D.K. Dickinson (Eds.), *Handbook of early literacy research* (pp. 421–443). New York: The Guilford Press.

Barnett, W.S. (1995). Long-term effects of early childhood programs on cognitive and school outcomes. *The Future of Children: Long-Term Outcomes of Early Childhood Programs, 5*(3), 25–50.

Bellm, D., Burton, A., Whitebook, M., Broatch, L., & Young, M. (2002). *Inside the Pre-K classroom: A study of staffing and stability in state-funded prekindergarten programs.* Washington, DC: Center for the Child Care Workforce.

Bowman, B., Donovan, M.S., & Burns, M.S. (2001). *Eager to learn: Educating our preschoolers.* Washington, DC: National Academies Press.

Brady, J., & Chalufour, I. (2004, June). *Performance assessment through assignments in credit-bearing professional development.* Paper presented at the annual meeting of the National Association for the Education of Young Children Institute for Early Childhood Professional Development, Baltimore, MD.

Center for Community and School Action Research. (2003). *Striving to achieve reading success.* New Haven: Southern Connecticut State University.

Clark-Chiarelli, N., & Buteau, E. (2003). *Using technology to support preschool teachers' professional development* (Final Report submitted to the Interagency Education Research Initiative [IERI] for Award #9979948). Newton, MA: Education Development Center.

Clark-Chiarelli, N., Dickinson, D.K., Bolte, G., & Buteau, E. (2004, June). *The impact of Program-Delivered Literacy Inservice Training (PD-LIT) on teacher practice and present children's achievement.* Paper presented at the Head Start Research Conference, Washington, DC.

Clark-Chiarelli, N., Dickinson, D.K., Peisner-Feinberg, E., Anastasopoulos, L. Caswell, L., Spragne, K., Kraemer-Cook, B., & Sayer, A. (2003, November). Presentation at the Interagency Educational Research Initiative project meeting, Washington, DC.

Cochran-Smith, M., & Lytle, S.L. (1990). Research on teaching and teacher research: The issues that divide. *Educational Researcher, 19*(2), 2–11.

Cost, Quality, and Child Outcomes Study Team. (1995). *Cost, quality, and child outcomes in child care centers: Public report.* Denver: University of Colorado at Denver.

Cunningham, A.E., & Stanovich, K.E. (1997). Early reading acquisition and its relation to reading experience and ability 10 years later. *Developmental Psychology, 33*(6), 934–945.

Dickinson, D.K., Anastasopoulos, L., Miller, C., Caswell, L., Peisner-Feinberg, E.S., & Poe, M. (2002, April). *Enhancing preschool children's language, literacy and social development through an in-service professional development approach.* Paper presented at the American Education Research Association, New Orleans, LA.

Dickinson, D.K., Caswell, L., & Chalufour, I. (2005). *Building support for language and early literacy in preschool classrooms through in-service professional development.* Unpublished manuscript.

Dickinson, D.K., Howard, C., Caswell, L., & Sprague, K. (2002). Supporting literacy development through a systemic program-delivered intervention. In L.B. Tarullo (Ed.), *The Head Start Quality Research Centers.* Symposium presented at the National Head Start Research Conference, Washington, DC.

Dickinson, D.K., & Kloosterman, V.I. (2003). *An examination of factors that affect the capacity of preschool programs to support children's early literacy development* (Final Report). Newton, MA: Education Development Center.

Dickinson, D.K., McCabe, A., Anastasopoulos, L., Peisner-Feinberg, E.S., & Poe, M.D. (2003). The comprehensive language approach to early literacy: The interrelationships among vocabulary, phonological sensitivity, and print knowledge among preschool-aged children. *Journal of Educational Psychology, 95*(3), 465–481.

Dickinson, D.K., McCabe, A., & Clark-Chiarelli, N. (2004). Preschool-based prevention of reading disability: Realities vs. possibilities. In A. Stone, E. Silliman, B.J. Ehren & K. Apel (Eds.), *Handbook of language and literacy: Development and disorders* (pp. 209–227). Mahwah, NJ: Lawrence Erlbaum Associates.

Dickinson, D.K., Miller, C.M., & Anastasopoulos, L. (2001, April). *The impact of an in-service intervention with Head Start teachers and supervisors on children's language, literacy and social development.* Paper presented at the Annual Conference of the Society for Research in Child Development, Minneapolis, MN.

Dickinson, D.K., & Smith, M.W. (1994). Long-term effects of preschool teachers' book readings on low-income children's vocabulary and story comprehension. *Reading Research Quarterly, 29*(2), 104–122.

Dickinson, D.K., St. Pierre, R., & Pettengill, J. (2004). High-quality classrooms: A key ingredient to family literacy programs. In B. Wasik (Ed.), *Handbook of family literacy* (pp. 137–154). New York: The Guilford Press.

Dickinson, D.K., & Tabors, P.O. (1991). Early literacy: Linkages between home, school, and literacy achievement at age five. *Journal of Research in Childhood Education, 6,* 30–46.

Dickinson, D.K., & Tabors, P.O. (Eds.). (2001). *Beginning literacy with language: Young children learning at home and school.* Baltimore: Paul H. Brookes Publishing Co.

Early, D.M., & Winton, P.J. (2001). Preparing the workforce: Early childhood teacher preparation at 2- and 4-year institutions of higher education. *Early Childhood Research Quarterly, 16,* 285–306.

Education Development Center. (2003). *Using technology to support preschool teachers' professional development* (Final report). Newton, MA: Author.

Gruendel, J.M., Oliveira, M., & Geballe, S. (2003). *All children ready for school: The case for early care and education.* Retrieved April 11, 2005, from http://info.med.yale. edu/chldstdy/CTvoices/kidslink/kidslink2/reports/PDFs/ResourceChallenges.PDF

Hart, B., & Risley, T.R. (1995). *Meaningful differences in the everyday experience of young American children.* Baltimore: Paul H. Brookes Publishing Co.

Head Start Reauthorization Act of 1994, PL 103-252, 42 U.S.C. §§ 9831 *et seq.*

Kagan, S.L., & Cohen, N.E. (1997). *Not by chance: Creating an early care and education system for American's children.* New Haven, CT: Yale University, Bush Center in Child Development and Social Policy.

Kloosterman, V., & Dickinson, D.K. (2001). *A qualitative study of enduring effects on teachers and supervisors.* Presentation at the Annual Conference of the American Educational Research Association, Seattle, WA.

McCardle, P., Scarborough, H.S., & Catts, H.W. (2001). Predicting, explaining, and preventing children's reading difficulties. *Learning Disabilities Research and Practice, 16*(4), 230–239.

Morgan, G., Azer, S.L., Costley, J.B., Genser, A., Goodman, I.F., & Lombardi, J. (1993). *Making a career of it: The state of the states report on career development in early care and education.* Boston: Wheelock College, The Center for Career Development in Early Care and Education.

National Assessment of Educational Progress. (1999). *Trends in academic progress: Three decades of student performance.* Washington, DC: U.S. Department of Education, Office of Educational Research and Improvement.

National Association of Child Advocates. (2000). *Making investments in young children: What the research on early care and education tells us.* Washington, DC: Author.

National Center for Education Statistics. (1997). *Characteristics of stayers, movers, and leavers: Results from the teacher follow-up survey: 1994–1995.* Washington, DC: Author.

National Institute of Child Health and Human Development Early Child Care Research Network. (2000). The relation of child care to cognitive and language development. *Child Development, 71*(4), 960–980.

Neuman, S.B., & Roskos, K. (1993). *Language and literacy learning in the early years: An integrated approach.* Orlando, FL: Harcourt.

No Child Left Behind (NCLB) Act of 2001, PL 107-110, 20 U.S.C. §6301 *et seq.*

Park-Jadotte, J., Golin, S.C., & Gault, B. (2002). *Building a stronger child care workforce: A review of studies of the effectiveness of public compensation initiatives.* Washington, DC: Institute for Women's Policy Research.

Peisner-Feinberg, E.S., Burchinal, M.R., Clifford, R.M., Culkin, M.L., Howes, C., Kagan, S.L., & Yazejian, N. (2001). The relation of preschool child-care quality to children's cognitive and social developmental trajectories through second grade. *Child Development, 72*(5), 1534–1553.

Roskos, K., & Neuman, S.B. (2001). Environment and its influences for early literacy teaching and learning. In S.B. Neuman & D.K. Dickinson (Eds.), *Handbook of early literacy research* (pp. 281–292). New York: The Guilford Press.

Scarborough, H.S. (2001). Connecting early language and literacy to later reading (dis)abilities: Evidence, theory, and practice. In S.B. Neuman & D.K. Dickinson (Eds.), *Handbook of early literacy research* (pp. 97–110). New York: The Guilford Press.

Schickedanz, J.A. (1999). *Much more than the ABC's: The early stages of reading and writing.* Washington, DC: National Association for the Education of Young Children.

Scott-Little, C., Kagan, S.L., & Frelow, V.S. (2003). *Standards for preschool children's learning and development: Who has standards, how were they developed, and how are they used?* (Research report). Greensboro: SERVE, The University of North Carolina. Retrieved April 11, 2005, from http://www.serve.org/_downloads/REL/ELO/Standards2003.pdf

Shonkoff, J.P., & Phillips, D.A. (Eds.). (2000). *From neurons to neighborhoods: The science of early childhood development.* Washington, DC: National Academies Press.

Shulman, L.S. (1987). Knowledge and teaching: Foundations for the new reform. *Harvard Educational Review, 57,* 1–22.

Smith, M.W., & Dickinson, D.K. (with Sangeorge, A., & Anastasopoulos, L.). (2002). *Early Language and Literacy Classroom Observation (ELLCO) Toolkit.* Baltimore: Paul H. Brookes Publishing Co.

Snow, C.E., Burns, S.M., & Griffin, P. (1998). *Preventing reading difficulties in young children.* Washington, DC: National Academies Press.

Snow, C.E., Tabors, P.O., & Dickinson, D.K. (2001). Language development in the preschool years. In D.K. Dickinson & P.O. Tabors (Eds.), *Beginning literacy with language: Young children learning at home and school* (pp. 1–26). Baltimore: Paul H. Brookes Publishing Co.

Storch, S.A., & Whitehurst, G.J. (2002). Oral language and code-related precursors to reading: Evidence from a longitudinal structural model. *Developmental Psychology, 38*(6), 934–947.

Sulzby, E., & Teale, W. (1991). Emergent literacy. In R.B. Barr, M. Kamill, P.B. Mosenthal & D.B. Pearson (Eds.), *Handbook of reading research* (Vol. 2, pp. 727–758). New York: Longman Publishers.

U.S. General Accounting Office. (2002). *Child care: States have undertaken a variety of quality improvement initiatives, but more evaluations of effectiveness are needed* (GAO-02-897). Washington, DC: Author.

Wheelock College Institute for Leadership and Career Initiatives. (2002). *Report on 2001 early childhood/school-age career development survey.* Boston: Author.

White House. (2002). *Good Start, Grow Smart: The Bush administration's early childhood initiative–executive summary.* Retrieved February 28, 2003, from http://www.whitehouse.gov/infocus/earlychildhood/earlychildhood.pdf

Whitebook, M., Sakai, L., Gerber, E., & Howes, C. (2001). *Then and now: Changes in child care staffing, 1994–2000.* Washington, DC: Center for the Child Care Workforce and the Institute of Industrial Relations.

Whitehurst, G.J., & Lonigan, C. (2001). *Get ready to read! An early literacy manual: Screening tool, activities, & resources.* Upper Saddle River, NJ: Pearson.

CHAPTER 7

# Helping Early Childhood
# Educators to Teach Mathematics

HERBERT P. GINSBURG, ROCHELLE GOLDBERG KAPLAN,
JOANNA CANNON, MARIA I. CORDERO, JANET G. EISENBAND,
MICHELLE GALANTER, AND MELISSA MORGENLANDER

This chapter is about helping prospective and current child care providers, teachers, and other early childhood education professionals teach mathematics effectively to young children at the preschool and kindergarten levels. Many education agencies across the country are faced with a mandate to implement programs of early childhood mathematics education (ECME). Teaching mathematics to 3-, 4-, and 5-year-olds is a challenge requiring considerable knowledge and skill. Yet few early childhood professionals have had the benefit of sound preparation in ECME. The United States therefore faces a pressing need to develop programs that train prospective and practicing early childhood professionals to teach mathematics effectively. This chapter describes two such programs: one involving a set of higher education courses in ECME and the other using in-service workshops that revolve around a specific mathematics curriculum. Drawing on observations of how an early mathematics program was implemented in inner-city settings, the chapter concludes by describing some ways in which the educational system can be structured to support teachers' professional development.

## THE NEED FOR PREPARATION IN
## EARLY MATHEMATICS EDUCATION

American children's mathematics performance is weaker than it should be. Children from China, Japan, and Korea outperform their American counterparts in mathematics achievement, perhaps as early as kindergarten (Stevenson, Lee, & Stigler, 1986), and certainly during the early school years (Mullis et al., 1997) and beyond (Mullis et al., 2000). Within the United States, children from low-income backgrounds—a group comprised of a disproportionate number of African Americans and Latinos (National Center for Children in Poverty, 1996)—show lower average levels of academic achievement than do their peers from middle- and upper-income backgrounds (Denton & West, 2002).

Although there is no single remedy for this unfortunate situation, a strong foundation in preschool education, including mathematics, can help to promote learning in the later years (Bowman, Donovan, & Burns, 2001;

Peisner-Feinberg et al., 2001). However, ECME is not only preparation for schooling. Learning mathematics is developmentally appropriate and can be enjoyable for 3-, 4-, and 5-year-olds: They already possess a surprisingly competent informal mathematics (Ginsburg, Klein, & Starkey, 1998), they spontaneously engage in everyday mathematical activities (Seo & Ginsburg, 2004), and they are ready to learn complex mathematical ideas (Greenes, 1999).

In response to the educational need and opportunity, many states and education agencies have decided to introduce programs of early childhood education. By the beginning of the new century, Texas and Illinois began to expand preschool programs, particularly for children considered at risk. Georgia, New York, and Oklahoma adopted a policy of universal preschool education. Furthermore, educators have come to recognize that mathematics needs to occupy a central place in early childhood education. Thus, in New Jersey, many preschools and child care centers serving children from low-income backgrounds are faced with a mandate to teach mathematics as well as literacy.

This explicit emphasis on education places a heavy burden on early childhood professionals. In addition to fulfilling all of their other responsibilities, they must now become proficient in teaching new programs, both in literacy as well as mathematics, and all for very low pay. Yet through no fault of their own, few early childhood professionals have had the benefit of sound preparation for ECME. One reason is that child care providers typically receive minimal college education, let alone a course in ECME. A second reason is that although most teacher training institutions offer their students many courses in literacy, most require only one course in mathematics education. Moreover, this "math methods" course typically does not focus on ECME, perhaps because few, if any, mathematics programs for which preschool teachers needed to be trained previously existed.

The nation's laudable efforts to introduce programs of early education on a wide scale, particularly for children from low-income backgrounds, will not succeed unless child care providers and preschool educators receive sound training in ECME. To do this, however, the widespread confusion about what ECME entails must be clarified.

## WHAT IS MATHEMATICS EDUCATION FOR YOUNG CHILDREN?

Since the early part of this century, early childhood professionals have been rethinking their approach to ECME (Clements, Sarama, & DiBiase, 2004). The current view, echoing a position that was influential in earlier periods of our history (Balfanz, 1999), proposes that teaching mathematics to young children is both developmentally appropriate and desirable. The joint position statement of the National Association for the Education of Young Children

(NAEYC) and the National Council of Teachers of Mathematics (NCTM) asserts that "high-quality, challenging, and accessible mathematics education for 3- to 6-year-old children is a vital foundation for future mathematics learning" (2002, p. 1). High-quality ECME has several basic characteristics.

## Early Mathematics Is Both Broad and Deep

The content of ECME encompasses a wide variety of topics, including number, shape, measurement, pattern, logic, operations, and spatial relations. In turn, each entails several interesting subtopics. The topic *number* is sometimes unfortunately called "numeracy." Number covers matters such as the counting words (e.g., "One, two, three . . ."), the ordinal positions (e.g., "First, second, third . . ."), and the idea of cardinal value (e.g., "How many are there?"). *Shape* includes not only simple plane figures (e.g., circle, triangle) but also hexagons and octagons (if young children can say and understand "brontosaurus," they can do the same for "octagon"), solids (e.g., cubes, cylinders), and symmetries in two and three dimensions. *Spatial relations* includes ideas such as position (e.g., in front of, behind), navigation (e.g., "First go three steps to the left"), and mapping (e.g., creating a schematic representing the location of objects in the classroom). Early mathematics is broad in scope and must deal with more than the topic of number and simple shapes.

Early mathematics is also deep. Consider for example the topic of enumeration—that is, counting a set to determine its number. A child sees on his or her right a haphazard arrangement including a red block, a small stuffed dog, and a penny. How many items are in this set? To answer correctly, the child must appreciate several basic ideas. The first is that different objects can all be counted as part of one set. One can count blocks, dogs, and pennies or big things and small things. One can even count fantastical images like five red unicorns. A second idea is that the number words (i.e., "One, two, three . . .") must be associated once and only once with each object in the set. The red block is "one," the dog is "two"; it is impossible to say both "one" and "two" when referring to the red block. The third idea is that the final number in the sequence (i.e., "three") does not refer to the penny alone. Even though one might say "three" while pointing to the penny, this number word describes not that solitary object but instead the cardinal value of the group as a whole. One could have started the count with the penny, in which case it would have been "one," not "three." Therefore, any object in the group could have been "one," "two," or "three," but the group as a whole has three objects—regardless of the order in which they are counted.

The breadth and depth of early mathematics represents a challenge and an opportunity for those who teach it. One aspect of the challenge is that the teacher must have a deep understanding of the fundamental ideas of number, shape, pattern, logic, and so forth (Ma, 1999; Shulman, 1987). Teaching early mathematics is more than imparting a few rote skills or trivial ideas. There is an opportunity to build on children's deep interest in these ideas.

## Children Have an Interest in and Knowledge of Early Mathematics

For many years, early childhood educators' views were heavily influenced by an interpretation of Piaget's (1952) theory suggesting that young children's cognitive immaturity prevents them from learning mathematics. As a result, it was decided that there is no point in attempting to "push development" by providing specific instruction in abstract mathematics concepts. Rather, because Piaget emphasized that children learn from their own actions, developmentally appropriate practice was seen as giving young children the opportunity to play and freely explore their surroundings. This general approach was adapted by NAEYC's 1986 standards (Bredekamp, 1987) and still seems to dominate the thinking of many early childhood professionals.

The NAEYC has since changed its position (Bredekamp & Copple, 1997), partly on the basis of new psychological research showing that young children develop an "everyday" or "informal" mathematics with several important characteristics. One is that young children have a spontaneous interest in mathematical ideas. Naturalistic research has shown, for example, that young children enjoy saying the counting words up to relatively large numbers, such as 100 (Irwin & Burgham, 1992), and even want to know what the "largest number" is (Gelman, 1980). Also, during free play, young children spend a good deal of time determining which tower is higher than another, creating and extending interesting patterns with blocks, exploring shapes, creating symmetries, and so forth (Seo & Ginsburg, 2004). Much of this activity is spontaneous, occurring without adult guidance. Indeed, adults are often unaware of the mathematics involved when children do these things.

The second point is that young children are competent in a wider range of mathematical abilities (Ginsburg, Klein, & Starkey, 1998) than Piaget's (1952) theory might lead one to believe. From an early age, children seem to understand basic ideas of addition and subtraction (Brush, 1978), ratios (Hunting, 1999), and spatial relations (Clements, 1999). They can spontaneously develop various methods of calculation (Groen & Resnick, 1977), such as counting on from the larger number (Baroody & Wilkins, 1999).

A third point is that when given instruction, young children are ready to learn some rather complex mathematics. Thus, children can be taught—and enjoy learning—interesting aspects of addition (Zur & Gelman, 2004) and symmetry (Zvonkin, 1992), among other topics (Greenes, 1999).

In brief, young children are eager mathematicians. Although their thought is in some respects limited and different from that of adults, young children deal with mathematical ideas in everyday play, are curious about the subject, know something about it, and can learn complex mathematics when it is taught.

## Adult Guidance

Free play is not enough to promote early mathematical thinking. Children do indeed learn some mathematics from free play, but it does not afford the extensive and explicit examination of mathematical ideas that only adult guidance can provide. Free play can provide a useful foundation for learning, but a foundation is only an opportunity for building a structure. Of course, young children should engage in a great deal of free play: In addition to being enjoyable, it promotes learning. At the same time, adult guidance is necessary to build a structure on the foundation of children's everyday mathematics. As Dewey (1976, p. 281) put it, "Guidance is not external imposition. It is freeing the life-process for its own most adequate fulfillment."

The question is not whether adults should guide the children but how. The NAEYC/NCTM (2002) position statement suggests that adults should deliberately introduce mathematical concepts, methods, and language and should help children examine mathematical concepts in depth. All of this must be done in ways that are developmentally appropriate—for example, by building on children's spontaneous mathematical interests and informal knowledge. Clearly, developmentally appropriate teaching should not involve extensive use of written materials or other methods used at higher grades, should not entail a "push-down" curriculum (i.e., a curriculum originally designed for older children), and should not continually engage the children in instruction. At the same time, the adult needs to play an active role in teaching early mathematics to individuals, small groups, and even entire classrooms.

## A Systematic Curriculum

The NAEYC/NCTM (2002) joint position statement also proposed that the "early childhood curriculum needs to go beyond sporadic, hit-or-miss mathematics . . . [and should provide] carefully planned experiences that focus children's attention on a particular mathematical idea or set of related ideas." It is no longer enough for teachers to introduce a few activities or projects, exciting as they may be, in an unplanned way. Instead, teaching ECME requires a curriculum—obviously not a textbook, but a series of organized activities designed to introduce mathematical ideas in a systematic manner.

The idea of an organized curriculum is not a new concept for at least some early childhood educators. Early childhood curricula such as High/Scope (Hohmann & Weikart, 2002) have provided a structured sequence of activities for young children. However, such curricula offer only minimal coverage of mathematics, usually based mainly on the Piaget stages. Curricula taking a wider and deeper approach to mathematics are now available. Among the notable examples, one program relies heavily on children's literature (Casey, Anderson, & Schiro, 2002); a second, designed primarily for children from low-income backgrounds, offers a comprehensive approach involving both activities and literature (Balfanz, Ginsburg, & Greenes, 2003); and a third makes extensive use of computers (Clements & Sarama, 2003).

## THE CHALLENGE FOR TEACHER PREPARATION

The attempt to develop high-quality ECME involving strong adult guidance places heavy demands on teachers and child care providers and requires them to do much more than they are now accustomed to doing. At a minimum, teachers and child care providers should be able to do the following:

- Understand basic mathematical ideas in a deep way
- Appreciate children's learning and thinking, particularly their everyday mathematics
- Assess children's learning and thinking
- Develop appropriate pedagogy for young children
- Master a mathematics curriculum, and actively teach it nearly every day

   Given these requirements, the challenge is to prepare a new generation of teachers and child care providers to appreciate ECME and to teach it well. In addition, it requires an older generation to think differently about ECME—in particular, to understand that it involves more than free play or a push-down curriculum and to change the way they teach it. Two methods to achieve these goals are described next: a set of higher education courses and in-service workshops.

## Higher Education

We are developing three courses designed to support professionals at different points in their careers. The first is a complete ECME course for graduate students who are already teachers and are pursuing professional development in either early childhood education or in early mathematics education. The intended students for this course are advanced practitioners preparing to become early mathematics curriculum leaders and staff developers. Second, from this comprehensive course, we are developing shorter ECME modules that can be used as portions of curriculum methods courses for undergraduate or graduate students in teacher certification programs. Third, we are creating another set of ECME modules for community or junior college students preparing to become aides or assistants in early childhood settings. The basic features common to the three courses are described next.

## Course Goals

### Awareness of Young Children's Capabilities

The first goal is to develop students' awareness of young children's capacities and potential for learning mathematics in a variety of contexts, including play, family life, and purposefully structured school-learning activities. Such awareness requires that students

- Uncover and examine their personal theories of children's mathematical capabilities and educating young children in mathematics
- Enrich these theories by learning how current psychological and educational research portray the conceptual and procedural underpinnings of young children's mathematics
- Use their new understanding to guide observations and analyses of children's mathematical knowledge during free play and more structured school activities

### Analysis of Mathematics Concepts and Appropriate Learning Activities

The second goal is for students to use their increased awareness of children's mathematical thinking to select and skillfully implement appropriate activities for extending children's spontaneous knowledge of mathematics to the larger concepts and procedures of conventional school mathematics. This goal is supported by several elements, which require students to

- Analyze the mathematics that children already know in relation to the mathematics that needs to be learned (Baroody & Wilkins, 1999; Ginsburg, 1989)—of course, this means that the students need to understand deeply the mathematics taught to the children (Ma, 1999)
- Develop a deeper understanding of how to organize instruction in the context of specific mathematics concepts and procedures (Carpenter, Fennema, Peterson, Chiang, & Loef, 1989) and how teachers can serve as guides for this journey (Vygotsky, 1978)
- Develop plans for integrating mathematics instruction with existing activities such as those related to language, science, and art

### Assessing Knowledge and Development of Mathematical Thinking

The third goal requires students to master procedures for assessing the effects of their guided instruction in mathematics (Copley, 1999; No Child Left Behind Act of 2001 [PL 107-110]). They need to understand and administer both quantitative evaluations and informal assessments, particularly individual and small group observations and clinical interviews (Ginsburg, Jacobs, & Lopez, 1998).

**Mathematics Content**    Each course focuses on the main areas of mathematics knowledge and mathematics content that teachers of young children need to address, as outlined in the joint NAEYC/NCTM (2002) position statement and by the NCTM (2000) standards for pre-K through second grade. These areas include but are not necessarily limited to number and operations; geometry, spatial relations, and measurement; patterns and logical reasoning; and making sense of data.

Each area is examined from three perspectives. First, students will consider young children's spontaneous use of the content in everyday school situations or at home; students will explore both the strengths and limitations of individual children's understanding of the content. Second, students will examine ways in which children's mathematical knowledge and applications of that knowledge can be expanded through appropriately structured classroom practices and experiences. Third, students will develop ways of assessing the growth of children's mathematical understanding in the context of planned classroom experiences.

**Course Experiences**    Each course incorporates several instructional components. One involves direct preschool classroom observations and interpretive reports communicated through on-line and in-class discussions. These activities will help students to develop awareness of their own theories of mathematics learning and their beliefs about young children's mathematical capabilities.

A second component involves individual and collective analysis of videotape vignettes of young children engaged in mathematical behaviors in their everyday lives, in their conversations with other children and adults, and during structured classroom activities. This activity provides students with a clear picture of how mathematical thinking develops from birth through the preschool period and until approximately age 6 or 7. The videotape vignettes will be available on DVD and can be viewed by students at home and then viewed again in class. In addition, the videotape clips may be incorporated into a university on-line course delivery system so that initial viewing, individual reflective analysis, and collective group discussions about the material can take place on line (Ginsburg, Jang, Preston, Appel, & VanEsselstyn, 2004).

A third key element of each course is an examination of the important theoretical and research literature (Ginsburg, Klein, & Starkey, 1998) that has become a motivating force behind mathematics education reform. Prior to coming to class, students will respond to on-line discussions about the content of the readings, which are expected to help students place their observations and personal interpretations in a broader context and relate them to a body of established knowledge about young children's mathematics thinking. This combination of reflective analysis and relevant evidence will then provide a context for understanding how formal mathematics instruction can be incorporated into developmentally appropriate curricular activities.

Toward this end, a fourth course component is the engagement of students in the development, implementation, and assessment of appropriate curricular activities. This element also begins with viewing of videotape materials. Some activities include planned mathematics learning experiences designed to serve as models for developing new instructional strategies and as sources for critical analysis of how lessons can be improved. Students will also analyze other videotapes that involve clinical interviews with children who participated in the lesson. These interviews will model a powerful way to assess young children's learning in the classroom setting. Students will also read relevant literature describing mathematics activities that have been used successfully with young children (e.g., Copley, 1999). Following the observational analysis and examination of the relevant literature, the students will design, implement, and assess mathematics lessons appropriate for classroom use. These lessons will be videotaped, shared, and peer critiqued in class.

*An Example*    This section describes a distinctive element of this course: the use of observation and analysis of carefully selected videotape segments to stimulate students' understanding of ECME. The broad yet basic topics of counting and enumeration have been selected to illustrate how observation and analysis reveal the complexity of young children's abilities and to suggest productive directions for developmentally appropriate instruction.

Obviously, children need to learn the counting words; no one is born knowing "one, two, three . . ." (or "un, deux, trois . . ."). At the same time, learning the number words involves more than rote memory; children have to learn rules and ideas as well (Ginsburg, 1989). To illustrate these points and to enable students to construct an understanding of counting, this course component begins with a short videotape clip showing a 3-year-old being asked to count aloud. He counts spontaneously from 1 to 12 without error and then says that is all he knows. An adult interviewer then models counting for him, but along the way deliberately makes a few mistakes. One time the adult counts, "1, 2 3, 4, red . . . ," and before he can go any further, the boy smiles and says, "No, you made a mistake. Red is a color not a number." The interviewer goes on and this time counts, "1, 2, 3, 4, 5, 6, 7, 8, 9, 10, 9. . . ." Once again, the child quickly corrects the adult: "No, you can't say that. You already said 9." Next the interviewer begins to count by continuing from where he left off, saying, "9, 10, 11. . . ." The child, filled with glee, tells the adult that he is wrong again: "You have to start with 1." Finally, the interviewer counts correctly to 15, then continues by saying, "18, 26, 38, 100, 240." This time the boy thinks and then says, "That's good!"

At this point, the students have an opportunity to talk about what they have seen in order to develop conclusions about young children's knowledge about the conventional number word list. They can infer from the videotape segment that young children are capable of an abstract distinction between number words and color words; that they seem to learn the initial counting words (probably up to 12 or so) by memorizing a string of sounds that must be said in the same way all of the time, always starting from 1; and that young children may have a general sense of big and small number words, perhaps recognizing that big number words are said later in the list. Students are also able to infer that young children know that there are rules for counting numbers, such as that you have to start from 1 and you cannot repeat the same number twice. They can see that at a certain point in the segment, the child's knowledge of the number list breaks down so that he can accept as accurate the sequence "18, 26, 38, 100, 240."

This segment does not, however, illustrate how young children apply counting words to sets of objects. Therefore, another segment is viewed in which a 3-year-old girl demonstrates how young children enumerate sets, both accurately and inaccurately. When shown a group of two chips, the girl points to one at a time and says the count words "1, 2," saying the "2" in a raised voice and with emphasis. Then, shown a vertical row of four chips, she enumerates them in a similar way, "1, 2, 3, 4," pointing to each chip as she says a number and again raising her pitch on the number "4." Next she is asked to count the two sets together. For this task, she pushes the chips together so that they are now randomly arranged. She proceeds to point to the chips as she sings the numbers to a popular tune, "1, 2, 3, 4, 5, 6, 7, 8, 9, 10." This time her voice rises on the "9" to keep in tune with the melody, and her pointing includes some chips more than once and other chips not at all.

The ensuing discussion should lead to some important conclusions about young children's enumeration. For example, enumeration is accurate as long as set size is small (approximately five items) and arranged in an orderly way; enumeration may break down when the elements are haphazardly arranged. Most important, the question arises whether a child's raised voice at the end of a count really means that the child knows how many items are in a set or whether it means something else (e.g., "This is the end of the song").

Past practice (Ginsburg, Kaplan, & Baroody, 1992) has shown that this kind of collective videotape viewing, group analysis, and generation of conclusions based on evidence can lead to helpful questions for planning further instruction. The questions, though, need to hone in on the observed abilities that can then be used to expand children's knowledge in a particular domain—in this case, enumeration. Instructors might want students to think about the following questions before selecting activities for increasing young children's ability to count objects in a quantitatively meaningful way:

- What kind of set sizes should be used? How should countable objects be arranged? Should teachers guide children to make any kinds of arrangements before counting?

- What should children be taught about the number list? Which rules should be emphasized? How can teachers help children break down the string of number words into discrete number names?

- What functions do number words and number lists serve for children? When are numbers used in spontaneous play? How can teachers set up centers to stimulate and reinforce the use of number words in play?

- What kind of attention-focusing questions should teachers use to enable children to focus on certain important elements of counting? What should teachers do when children make counting mistakes in the use of number words or of one-to-one correspondence to attach number words to objects?

- How can teachers build on children's raised voices at the end of a count to help them appreciate cardinality? How can teachers help link number words to quantitative values? What changes in the appearance of sets should teachers model to highlight the unchanging values of set sizes?

*Evaluation of Student Beliefs*    Two of the chapter authors have already taught courses similar to those described. An evaluation of one of these courses shows its success in promoting deeper understanding of ECME and in changing students' conceptions of ECME. To measure the impact of each course, we developed a pre- and postcourse questionnaire assessing students' beliefs about ECME. In particular, we were interested in determining whether we met our goal of helping students understand preschoolers' thinking about mathematics and how it might be supported.

The most noticeable change from the pre- to the postcourse questionnaire was that students seemed to develop a broader understanding of appropriate mathematical content for young children and its importance in ECME. After taking the course, students increased the number of mathematical concepts and skills that they believed are very important for young children to learn. Students also increased their estimate of the amount of time that they believed teachers should spend on mathematics instruction.

After taking the course, students also appeared to be more cognizant of the fact that young children are capable of understanding and learning complex mathematical concepts. For example, students were more likely at the end than at the outset of the course to endorse the ideas that ECME should provide children with challenging problems, that young children are spontaneously interested in spatial relations, and that virtually all children are capable of doing well in mathematics. There was less change in students' beliefs about ECME pedagogy; they continued to maintain a "constructivist" position toward learning, believing that it involves active learning rather than a process of memorizing information provided by others.

These findings suggest that the course was most beneficial for teaching students about young children's cognition—what they like to learn, what they can learn, and what they should learn. These findings are not surprising, given that the most vivid feature of the course—the videotape clips—centered on these issues. More frequent use of videotape clips illustrating pedagogy might result in greater change in students' beliefs in this area, too.

Future evaluation work should examine several other issues. How do students learn from videotape segments? How robust and long lasting are the concepts and skills that students acquire in the course? Most important, do the teachers use this learning in their classroom teaching to improve young children's learning?

## In-Service Workshops

Professional development in ECME is as important and valuable for practicing teachers[1] as it is for college and graduate students. Because they are unfamiliar with early mathematics, many practicing teachers can benefit from ongoing professional development. They have a great deal to learn (and sometimes to unlearn). They need to understand basic mathematical ideas, gain insight into children's mathematical thinking and learning, develop appropriate pedagogy, and master a curriculum.

Our working hypothesis is that in-service professional development should include—but not be limited to—a series of workshops revolving around a specific curriculum. Teachers can best learn about the mathematical content, the psychology of the children, and the pedagogy in the context of a set of activities that they plan to implement in their classrooms. We therefore developed a series of workshops revolving around the Big Math for Little Kids (BMLK) curriculum (Ginsburg, Greenes, & Balfanz, 2003), which is specifically developed to promote the learning of children from low-income backgrounds. We chose to focus on BMLK for several reasons. The most immediate was that having developed the curriculum, we wanted to help teachers use it effectively. More important, the curriculum's focus on children from low-income backgrounds is of vital concern to ECME. Finally, because the BMLK curriculum is comprehensive, workshops revolving around the topics it covers and the issues it raises can be valuable for other programs as well.

***Principles Underlying the Workshops***     The workshops were based on several major principles. One is that like their students, teachers should learn actively in real contexts (Bransford, Brown, & Cocking, 1998); hence, the workshops encouraged teacher participation and sometimes involved teachers in learning the same activities that they would later teach their students.

A second principle is that because the teachers have a great deal to learn, particularly when they are beginning to master a curriculum, learning opportunities need to be extensive, taking place over the course of an academic year.

---

[1]In this section, *teachers* refers to all those providing direct instruction in classrooms or child care centers—aides, child care providers, and other early childhood education professionals.

One-shot workshops, all too frequently the norm, are of little lasting value (Sarama, 2004).

A third principle stresses the effectiveness of a case-based approach that engages teachers in the close analysis of specific teaching episodes, dilemmas of instruction, and problems of student learning. Case-based learning—which is very popular in business, legal, and medical education—has been encouraged for teacher professional development as well (Gragg, 1994; Rand, 2000). Cases stimulate learning in a context where theory and practice are genuinely and meaningfully intertwined (Kinzer & Risko, 1998). Cases enable teachers to discuss issues, problems, and classroom concerns and to brainstorm ways to resolve them. Often presented through videotape segments or vivid narratives, cases bring to life the main features of the activities in the curriculum and present a forum in which teachers can discuss divergent perspectives.

A fourth principle is that use of videotape materials is particularly effective in providing the basis for the intensive study of activities and lessons (Beck, King, & Marshall, 2002; Flake, 2002; Lampert & Ball, 1998). Videotape examples can bring to life the reality of teaching young children mathematics, showing how a teacher introduces an activity and how the children react. Videotapes stimulate discussion and analysis of children's thinking, pedagogy, curriculum activities, and the mathematics involved in a lesson. Because they can be played and replayed, videotapes provide opportunities for careful review and examination of the "evidence"—that is, the important but not always obvious events taking place in the course of the activity. Analysis of videotapes is as important for teachers as it is for college and graduate students.

### General Features of the Workshops    Using the previously described principles, we developed a series of seven workshops to introduce the BMLK curriculum (Ginsburg, Galanter, & Morgenlander, 2004). This section describes features of the workshops that may be of general interest because they can inform development of similar workshops for other curricula.

The first workshop introduced teachers to broad principles of ECME as well as to general features of the BMLK program. The workshop began by presenting recent psychological research on children's everyday mathematics. The teachers examined a series of videotapes (similar to those used in the course on mathematical thinking described in the previous section) that illustrated this research by showing both naturalistic observations of young children playing with blocks and interviews exploring young children's knowledge of addition and subtraction. The teachers engaged in a discussion of what the videotapes show about young children's everyday mathematics. The explicit message was that ECME should be based on up-to-date research showing that young children from all backgrounds are capable of and enjoy learning higher levels of mathematics than often assumed.

The introductory workshop then presented three alternative approaches to ECME: play, instruction (push-down curriculum), and "artful guidance." The goals were to bring to the surface conflicts that often characterize discussions of ECME and to help the teachers understand that the play and instruction positions represent extremes on a continuum, that neither is fully appropriate for young children's education, and that a balanced approach involving sensitive adult intervention—which we call "artful guidance"—is necessary to promote early mathematics learning. Our goal was to initiate—not conclude—discussion of these emotionally charged issues: They cannot be deeply understood apart from experience with implementation of specific curricular activities.

The introductory workshop concluded with specific details of the BMLK program. It presented a videotape example of an activity involving pattern, then described the overall structure of the program—the mathematical topics, the planning chart, the teachers' guide, the approach to assessment, the take home materials, and so forth.

Throughout the year, at appropriate times, teachers attended workshops devoted specifically to introducing each of the six BMLK units. Thus, toward the end of September, after children are comfortable in the classroom, teachers participated in a workshop on the first unit about numbers. In mid-November, teachers participated in the next workshop on shape, and so forth.

Although each workshop was unique, all involved a similar format that included 1) children's everyday mathematics and learning, 2) the relevant mathematical content, 3) methods of assessment, 4) the specific activities comprising the unit, and 5) issues of pedagogy, including pacing. The workshops were also intended to promote the establishment of small communities of teachers working together on the common goal of improving their implementation of the program. The hope was that discussions of the issues raised in the workshops would carry over to the schools and centers where the teachers worked. The following sections describe each major feature of the workshops.

*Children's Everyday Mathematics and Learning*    Workshops often began with what the psychological research teaches about children's everyday mathematics and learning. Being able to take and understand the learner's perspective is a crucial component of sensitive teaching (Clements, 2004). Most often, teachers were asked to analyze videotapes of children's everyday behavior (e.g., children engaged in a rhythmically complex clapping game) or videotapes of clinical interviews (e.g., on concepts of addition). Analysis of such videotapes helped teachers to understand where the children are coming from when they attempt to learn any mathematical topic.

Sometimes we tried to help the teachers experience the child's learning process. One example involved learning to count by specifically memorizing the first 10 or so counting numbers, a series of essentially arbitrary syllables, and then discovering the rules—the base-10 pattern—that underlie larger numbers. After watching a videotape of a woman saying the counting numbers from 1 to 20 several times in Tagalog (a language used in the Philippines), workshop participants were asked to repeat her counting. As the adults laughed in the struggle to make out where one word starts and another ends and to say the correct sequence, they were reminded how difficult it must be for children to learn the initial counting numbers. After a few repetitions, they began to notice a pattern emerging in the numbers after 10—namely that the word for 10 seems to be repeated each time along with another number word that resembles the numbers from 1 to 9. Then teachers eventually came to understand that after 10 comes the Tagalog equivalent of 10-1, then 10-2, and so on until 10-9. In this way, teachers not only experienced the discovery of the relevant pattern but also discussed its mathematical meaning.

*Relevant Mathematical Content*    Workshops always explicitly introduced mathematical content. As noted previously, ECME involves deep mathematical issues, and teachers need to review them or even learn about them for the first time. For example, the workshop called "What Are Numbers?" covers important issues such as the structure of the counting numbers and the nature of cardinal numbers. Some teachers gain important insights when encouraged to consider that the number 34 can be conceptualized as "3 ten 4" or that the cardinal value 5 refers not to the last number counted but to the set as a whole. The importance of promoting teachers' mathematical understanding, even at the preschool level, cannot be emphasized enough. Young children ask difficult mathematical questions and deal with deep mathematical content.

*Methods of Assessment*    To extend teachers' ability to understand children's thinking, each workshop introduced methods of assessment, particularly observation and clinical interviewing. Teachers were shown how to observe carefully in the context of particular activities and how to ask questions designed to illuminate children's understanding of key concepts underlying the activities. It was hoped that these methods would enable teachers to learn about children's thinking—their insights as well as their misconceptions, their correct strategies as well as their incorrect strategies—and then to use this information to inform everyday teaching.

*Specific Activities Comprising the Unit*    The workshops mainly focused on the specific activities for each mathematical topic. Thus, in the case of number (a large unit), the workshop covered basic activities on counting numbers, cardinality, and ordinality. Matters introduced included preparation of the necessary materials, the optimal size of the group, teaching techniques that might be useful, and difficulties that might arise. Because the idea of a systematic curriculum was new for many teachers, the workshops included a discussion of pacing and planning. Emphasis was given to how various activities build on children's understanding of ideas presented in earlier activities, how repetition of activities is often desirable, and how setting clear goals can help the teacher progress through the curriculum.

Discussions highlighted the essential role of language in children's mathematical work. The goal was for teachers to become aware of the mathematical vocabulary that children must learn and of the ways in which children need to use language to communicate mathematical ideas and their thinking about mathematics. Discussion also covered the ways in which teachers could introduce mathematical concepts and language through reading storybooks and in other ways.

To help teachers become familiar with the activities and to raise important issues, the workshops incorporated several techniques that we hoped would inspire interest, provide food for thought, and involve fun. These included role playing, analysis of videotape examples or cases of teaching, and stimulated discussion.

In the role-playing scenario, teachers were asked to take on the roles of either teacher or student for a given activity. For example, one teacher was asked to teach three others how to create a pattern of sounds by using kazoos. Although teachers were sometimes reluctant to try something new in front of their colleagues, eventually they joined in and seemed to enjoy it. This specific, active experience helped teachers to take the perspective of the student and understand the learning involved.

Analysis of videotaped examples of other teachers doing the activity also led to fruitful discussions. As in college courses, such case-based learning was especially fruitful in raising very specific issues about how to implement the activities and about the kinds of learning that these activities seem to promote.

Workshop components also stimulated discussion about the activities and curriculum. Often, open-ended questions were posed to explore key issues. Asking questions such as, "Why is it important for young children to learn about measurement?" or "What are some different ways to use the materials in this activity?" would get participants actively thinking and discussing basic issues of ECME.

*Issues of Pedagogy*    Finally, specific activities—role playing, analysis of videotapes, and discussion—were used to introduce questions of pedagogy. Thus, in the discussion of the counting numbers, it became evident that the only way to learn the first 10 numbers is through rote memory. Manipulatives are of no value in this instance. In considering activities designed to teach cardinal numbers, however, teachers quickly concluded that children must have experience in working with real objects to create meaningful notions of cardinal value. When teachers focused on implementation of specific activities, discussions of abstract pedagogical issues such as the roles of instruction, play, constructivism, and manipulatives became meaningfully grounded in everyday experience.

***How Successful Were the Workshops?***    We have only begun to evaluate the workshops; most of our effort was devoted to creating them. To guide development, we engaged in a process of "formative evaluation." Workshops were tested with different groups of teachers, and we took careful field notes about what was done and how the teachers reacted. In one district, the mathematics supervisor offered feedback on a regular basis after each workshop. We attempted to determine whether teachers were receptive to workshops, paid attention, participated, and seemed to assimilate the material. Often the negative aspects of teachers' reactions were abundantly clear: Sometimes most of the participants tuned out, clearly did not understand the topics discussed, and did not engage in useful discussions. Yet other times, the teachers seemed to be deeply engaged, made insightful comments, and displayed clear motivation to introduce the activities into their classrooms.

The formative evaluation results were then used to revise and improve the workshops. Some activities were retained, and others were eliminated or modified as seemed necessary. For example, after the first few workshops, it became apparent that giving the teachers an opportunity to work in small groups sometimes led to more interesting discussions and active participation. The workshop format was changed to make additional small group discussion possible. In a continual effort to improve the workshops, the process was repeated with another group of teachers. The result after a year was the revised version of the workshops, which require further evaluation and modification.

Clearly more rigorous research is needed to determine the immediate effects of the various workshops. Did the teachers gain insight into children's everyday mathematics? Did teachers come to understand the purpose of the various activities? Did they change their beliefs about ECME? Of course the ultimate test is whether the workshops improve teaching and, in turn, mathematics achievement.

Despite the need for further research, our informal observations made one point abundantly clear: What works for one group does not necessarily work for the next. The success of the workshops depends on factors such as group size (smaller groups obviously promote more interaction and discussion than larger groups), attendance (sometimes many teachers did not show up for the workshops), and the available materials and equipment (schools and districts vary in the extent to which they can provide functioning videotape equipment and necessary materials). Perhaps most important, teachers' education level and previous experience are key factors: Teachers who have never engaged in any substantial teaching at the preschool level and are in fact initially opposed to the idea of ECME clearly need a different kind of workshop than teachers with previous experience at the elementary level who are excited by the prospect of teaching mathematics to young children. Trainers will have to modify workshops to accommodate local conditions and meet local needs.

## THE LARGER CONTEXT OF EARLY CHILDHOOD EDUCATION

As a part of the larger movement to improve early childhood education, the BMLK initiative illustrates many of the problems likely to be encountered by other reform efforts. Hence, in addition to designing, conducting, and evaluating workshops for in-service teachers, we chose to observe what happens as teachers attempted to implement the BMLK curriculum. We considered that this look at the real world of ECME could help inform the design and implementation of professional development programs.

### The Methods of Research

We decided to conduct observations over a long period of time in the classrooms of teachers who attended the workshops and to interview the teachers about their work and their beliefs concerning ECME. Mathematics teaching was observed in 11 preschool and kindergarten classrooms in two different inner-city settings where the BMLK curriculum was being implemented for the first time. Some of the preschool and kindergarten classrooms were part of the publicly supported child care system and others were part of the public school system. In both settings, our observations began when the program was first implemented; the observations lasted from October to June in one setting and from January to July in the other.

Our approach was exploratory. Research assistants observed each classroom weekly during the time BMLK was taught on that day and interviewed the teachers to elicit their perspectives on the implementation. Observers wrote detailed field notes about each visit, following a predetermined format that involved four topics: 1) external administrative, personal, or structural factors (e.g., district curriculum requirements, relations between supervisors and teachers, time available for mathematics teaching) that seemed to affect the implementation; 2) how the teacher actually implemented the curriculum and assessment methods in the classroom; 3) the teacher's thoughts about the curriculum and its implementation; and 4) the observers' reflections on that day's visit. Beyond these guidelines, the observers were free to discuss whatever prominent issues emerged in the course of their visits.

To provide insight into teacher beliefs, frequent focus groups were conducted with the teachers and others (e.g., supervisors) involved in implementing the BMLK curriculum. In addition, some teachers were asked to complete detailed questionnaires about specific curricular activities that they taught and their beliefs about ECME.

Although analysis of these data is incomplete, the following sections present an initial account of what was learned about personal, structural, and administrative barriers; teacher beliefs; teacher knowledge of mathematics; and pedagogical and assessment practices that teachers actually used in the classroom, regardless of what they said they did or should be done. The sections highlight what the observations revealed about problems in implementing effective programs of early mathematics and opportunities for growth.

**Barriers**    The call to act on visionary goals such as free, universal, and high-quality early childhood education has created a good deal of turmoil, as well as opportunity, for local and state education authorities. Many systemic barriers—such as lack of space, insufficient funding, low pay for teachers and especially child care providers—stand in the way of implementing virtually all early childhood education programs (Gallagher, Clayton, & Heinemeier, 2001; Sarama, DiBiase, Clements, & Spitler, 2004). Our observations focused on everyday obstacles to successful program implementation such as teacher attitudes, problems in communication between teachers and supervisors, and lack of administrative support.

One of the biggest problems encountered was that a significant group of the teachers (because of the small sample, percentages cannot be estimated) simply did not want to be involved in the project but were forced by the administration to participate. The issue was not a question of nuanced differences in educational philosophy or approach (these are described in the "Teacher Beliefs" section); it was an outright rejection of ECME. For example, several teachers conveyed palpable hostility toward using the curriculum and attending any workshops. One lead teacher displayed a striking avoidance strategy when she completely withdrew contact from the curriculum and gave full teaching responsibility to an aide who was not receiving any training in ECME. At the same time, many teachers who had never before taught early mathematics were enthusiastic about learning to do so.

In one setting, the attitudes of rejectionist teachers were probably influenced, and certainly not helped, by lapses in communication with the administration and with lack of administrative support for the effort. Several of the teachers were told to use up to three separate mathematics curricula but received no direction from the administration in how to balance them in a meaningful way. Other teachers were given little guidance in how they could coordinate the teaching of mathematics with another new mandate—teaching literacy. Some overworked supervisors, many of whom were poorly trained in ECME, failed to attend most workshops and did not make planned classroom visits; as a result, they could do little to help classroom teachers.

Sometimes it appeared that the administration lacked a coherent educational plan. The administration often waited until the last moment to inform classroom teachers about upcoming workshops, with an inevitable increase in teacher absence. In general, although requiring teachers to implement early mathematics, the administration did not provide adequate supports—particularly from supervisors—for doing so. We can only speculate about the reasons. Perhaps the administration was unfamiliar with the new emphases on ECME and lacked good models for implementing it. In any event, some administrations have as much to learn about ECME as do teachers.

Although barriers were both abundant and striking, many teachers, supervisors, and administrators made heroic efforts to implement what were for them new, untried, and risky programs of ECME. Despite being buffeted by various pressures from the state and federal governments—for example, to administer (inappropriate) high-stakes tests to young children—these early childhood educators succeeded more often than one might expect.

**Teacher Beliefs**    Numerous reform efforts have documented that teachers must "buy into" an educational innovation for it to succeed (Berends, 2000; Schwartzbeck, 2002; Wagner, 2001). Therefore, we decided to obtain information on teachers' beliefs. In particular, we wanted to learn if teachers shared our vision that sound ECME involves a strong but sensitive adult role, introduction of challenging mathematics, and development of young children's natural interest in mathematics.

The findings were unsettling. There was a marked polarity in teachers' beliefs, and both extremes initially opposed the curriculum. Some teachers held the laissez-faire belief that they should have limited involvement in helping children learn. They saw their role as providing children with stimulating materials and nurturing their interest in learning, but they did not want to engage in active teaching. For instance, one teacher attempted to implement an activity designed to help students draw the specific number of objects indicated by a numeral at the bottom of the page. Instead of encouraging students to draw the correct number of objects, this teacher let children draw whatever they wanted while praising their work (whether they drew distinct objects, let alone the number corresponding to the given numeral). This suggests a "deep-seated skepticism about the value of rigorous instruction of any sort" (Damon, 1997, p. 296).

Other teachers believed that they should have a dominating, indeed domineering, role in teaching mathematics. These teachers appeared uncomfortable with the unpredictability of letting children play an important role in their own learning. Several teachers stated that they would not let their students work with manipulatives because these objects overexcited the children and made activities go in unanticipated directions.

There was also a large division between teachers on the matter of beliefs concerning children's interest in and ability to learn various mathematical ideas. At one end were teachers who believed that children could not and would not want to do much of the mathematics covered in the curriculum. In their view, children were not cognitively "ready" to learn mathematical ideas; teaching them this content would confuse and frustrate them. Several teachers were absolutely convinced that young children could not learn abstractions—for example, almost anything involving written representation—and must be limited to the most concrete forms of learning.

In contrast to these teachers, others overestimated children's abilities and understanding. A number of teachers said that they did not need to teach the curriculum because their children already knew and would be bored by much of the content (e.g., counting from 1 to 50). These teachers did not seem to consider that children's understandings might not be fully formed and could be expanded on (e.g., even if able to say the counting numbers in order, children might fail to recognize or understand the repeating decade pattern).

Not all teachers expressed these beliefs as strongly as they are illustrated here, but the ideas were still prevalent. Consequently, our vision of mathematics instruction is likely to face opposition from both extremes. Some teachers believe in play and others in instruction. Some believe that children can learn almost nothing, and others believe that they already know almost everything. The challenge is to help teachers develop the skills and knowledge that will allow them to achieve a balanced approach to ECME.

***Teacher Knowledge of Mathematics***     As we observed teachers implementing BMLK, a critical issue became apparent: Some teachers displayed serious misunderstandings of the mathematical content itself. Elementary school teachers often fail to understand the mathematics they attempt to teach (Post, Harel, Behr, & Lesh, 1991; Shulman, 1987). For example, Ma (1999) found that American elementary teachers understand the procedural steps required to solve mathematics problems but unlike Chinese teachers, they lack a deeper understanding of the underlying ideas. Our observations suggest that these difficulties appear at the preschool level as well. For example, one of the first activities in the BMLK preschool unit on patterns involves encouraging the children to create simple alternating patterns (e.g., ABABAB) with color connecting cubes. Of the seven teachers observed doing this activity, four demonstrated through their teaching an understanding of the mathematical idea of a pattern: They taught their students that a pattern involved a repetition of key attributes; that the pattern could go on and on, that there are different kinds of repetition patterns (e.g., AABAAB) as well as other patterns (e.g., ascending or descending patterns), and that a pattern can be generated by a "rule." The classroom practices of the other three teachers seemed to indicate a lack of understanding of the basic concept. One teacher began the lesson by presenting the children with three different color cubes that were connected, (blue, green, yellow) and then asking, "What comes next?" In this case, it is impossible to tell what comes next. The children had every right to be confused, as the teacher had not yet constructed a pattern. When the children floundered, the teacher had no effective way of helping them. The other two teachers also seemed to confuse a design with a pattern.

These preliminary findings suggest that professional development should emphasize the teaching of mathematical content. Although they attempted to cover many of the basic mathematical principles, the workshops obviously were not fully successful in this regard and need to be improved.

**Pedagogical Practices**    A major goal of any program of professional development is the improvement of classroom teaching. Hence, we were eager to observe teachers' implementation of the curriculum in the classroom. Did they engage in rigid instruction, let the children play in an unsupervised manner, or attempt to teach with the sensitivity and balance that characterizes "artful guidance"? Because there is almost no empirical research that analyzes early pedagogy in detail (perhaps because so little of it is actually done), we took an exploratory approach, attempting to learn more about the methods used to teach mathematics to young children.

Two striking phenomena were observed. One is that effective early childhood pedagogy is complex and intellectually challenging. The second is that many teachers are capable of learning it.

Consider first an example of preschool mathematics teaching. One day, Belinda, a preschool teacher, read a BMLK storybook designed to help children learn the defining features and names of different shapes. An excerpt from the observer's field notes regarding this activity follows:

> When they reached a page with circles on trees, Belinda took out circular disks and had children count how many circles she put out. She also had them compare little circles and big circles, colors, and so forth. She involved each child with an instruction at one time or another. They only got approximately 5 pages into the book before they started to get restless. Belinda had them all stand up and do a counting activity involving physical movements such as jumping while saying the numbers from 10 to 19 and hopping while saying the numbers from 20 to 29. If they could name the next decade—for example, saying that after 29 comes 30—then they were allowed to go into the center of the circle and lead everyone else in a new physical movement. Finally, it was time for a brief snack. Belinda passed out cookies, noting that they were shaped like circles. As the children munched on them, they started to make new shapes.

Belinda utilized a number of pedagogical techniques in this episode. For instance, she chose to incorporate the use of manipulatives into the reading of her storybook. She also encouraged her students to utilize their prior counting knowledge as well as their verbal skills to count and describe key features of the manipulatives. At various points during the activity, Belinda attempted to ensure that individual children were participating by asking each child a question and letting children lead the counting activity. Later, Belinda changed activities when children became restless; she introduced a physical activity that would be likely to reenergize her students. However, Belinda did not abandon her shape instruction; instead she encouraged her students to continue thinking about the features of shapes during their snack time.

Something as basic as teaching children about shapes is not a simple matter; it requires a series of careful and informed decisions about practice. Like Belinda, teachers need to be sensitive to a variety of mathematical, psychological, and pedagogical considerations, including concrete representations that can be used to teach mathematical concepts; children's prior mathematical knowledge that is relevant to the content being learned; the status of students' engagement, attention, and thinking; mathematical and nonmathematical (e.g., verbal expression and literacy) learning goals; everyday activities that can be used to teach mathematical lessons; and opportunities for students to construct their own understandings of content. Keeping all of these factors in mind, teachers need to skillfully blend them into a series of activities that promote the learning of specific content. This type of teaching is not easy and seems similar to good mathematics instruction at older age levels (Ball, 2000; Schoenfeld, 1999).

Unfortunately, not all early childhood education teachers have the skills or knowledge to teach in this way. Nonetheless, many teachers observed—both in child care and public school settings—were able to engage in this kind of "artful guidance" or at least seemed to have the potential to learn to do so. Some of the teachers struggled throughout the year to develop even the most basic pedagogy, but others were truly exceptional or improved significantly over time, despite the fact that they were initially opposed to doing ECME and encountered many administrative obstacles to their work.

Although teaching preschool mathematics is not easy—and in fact may be at least as demanding as teaching algebra—many poorly prepared and supported teachers can do it well or learn to do it well. Making this happen on a wide scale, however, requires major effort.

*Assessment Practices*    Classroom assessment is an essential component of teaching; to provide appropriate instruction, teachers must constantly evaluate and reevaluate student understanding (Bowman et al., 2001). Although teachers in higher grades often base evaluations of student progress on written work and tests, early childhood teachers must rely on informal methods of assessment (Shepard, 2001). Yet some evidence suggests that early childhood teachers seldom systematically evaluate and document student progress (Bowman et al., 2001). One reason may be their lack of experience with sequential, comprehensive curricula.

In any event, we were interested in the extent to which teachers employed informal assessment methods in their classrooms. They had received considerable instruction in doing so. The BMLK curriculum provided teachers with guides to using several assessment methods, including observation and clinical interview, linked to particular classroom activities. As discussed previously, the workshops devoted a good deal of time to examination of assessment techniques. In fact, two entire workshops focused on assessment.

Observations of and conversations with teachers revealed several interesting phenomena. One was that the teachers almost never used the BMLK evaluation materials or the observation and interview techniques presented in the workshops. A second is that teachers were very concerned about assessment. Even preschool and kindergarten teachers felt that they were overburdened with testing requirements of various sorts. For example, in the spring, children were required to take state-required standardized tests, including a mathematics test. Some teachers were clearly threatened by those tests and were very concerned with teaching the skills the children needed in order to pass. Some teachers said that they could not teach the BMLK curriculum for a period of time because they had to prepare their children for the tests. High-stakes testing clearly has major effects on ECME.

A third phenomenon was that although they resented the frequent testing that children had to endure and did not do the assessments suggested by the BMLK curriculum, teachers nevertheless used their own informal methods for classroom assessment. Indeed, the assessments were so thoroughly built into their everyday teaching that many teachers were probably unaware that what they were doing involved assessment.

Teachers used some fascinating techniques. To assess student understanding, teachers often complemented the curriculum activities with their own tasks that were analogous to test items. Some of these tasks were quite creative. For example, one teacher took the opportunity to evaluate counting skills when she had a student report to an inquiring cook how many children were present that day (and therefore how many lunches were needed). Some teachers followed up on classroom activities with new tasks and questions. They provided hints for children having difficulty, more challenging tasks for those who were successful, or questions that served both to stimulate thinking and elicit in-depth information about understanding. The questions often appeared in the form of "How did you do it?", probing for underlying strategies and concepts, but more imaginative examples were also observed. In one such instance, students were choosing between a narrow and a wide cylinder on which to balance a larger rectangular block, and their teacher asked, "Which cylinder do you think builders would use?"

We also noticed organized systems of attending to and keeping track of student learning. One teacher focused on three or four students at a time at a math center (small work station) so that she could monitor individual understanding. She circulated children through the center, varying each student's time spent there depending on mastery of the task. In some cases, she asked a student to revisit the task the next day: This was a way of keeping track of children who needed extra help. Other teachers said they tracked student progress with written records. Although these documents were unavailable for review, the classrooms that reportedly used this formal evaluation method were those in which aides and assistant teachers played an active role in mathematics instruction, therefore necessitating communication among the adults.

Admittedly, not all of the teachers used such formal assessment practices, and those who did were not methodical about administering them. Furthermore, teachers who found difficulty carrying out the curriculum's activities in the first place tended not to assess children's learning. Despite this variability, it is encouraging to learn that the extra sensitivity early childhood teachers must have toward ongoing student learning (because they cannot depend on written work) is sometimes displayed in assessment techniques that they bring into a new academic program, even if they are not aware of doing so. In order to improve classroom assessment, professional development workshops may need to be altered to elaborate on the methods that teachers already use or to adapt the curriculum's assessment methods to better fit into teachers' everyday ways of learning about children.

**Summary**    Long-term observations of ordinary classrooms show that implementation of ECME programs must overcome many obstacles, including lack of administrative support for the innovation, excessive testing requirements, teachers who believe that ECME is inappropriate, and teachers who lack the content knowledge necessary for teaching early mathematics. At the same time, there are reasons for optimism. Despite limited support, many teachers teach early mathematics effectively, and others can learn to do so. Furthermore, many teachers incorporate useful informal assessment procedures into their everyday teaching. Given these findings, the next section describes how professional development efforts should be structured to foster the potential existing in the system and to overcome barriers standing in the way of successful implementation.

## STRUCTURING ECME
## IN-SERVICE PROFESSIONAL DEVELOPMENT

After designing and testing our workshops, and after observing classroom implementation of BMLK over the course of almost a year, we reviewed what we had learned and attempted to improve our approach to professional development. Several conditions are necessary for success in this area.

First, a school district (or other agency implementing the program) should have a well-articulated and coherent set of goals, with a long-term plan for implementing them. The district needs to be clear about what it wants to accomplish and committed to providing the support necessary to achieve its goals. Second, supervisory personnel—math supervisors, center directors, lead teachers, and early childhood education specialists—need to be deeply involved in the professional development and implementation efforts. They need to provide leadership and support; the demand for ECME is unlikely to bubble up from the ranks of teachers. Third, professional development needs to be intensive, long-term, and responsive to local needs and desires. Workshops for Head Start classrooms are likely to differ from those for public school teachers or child care providers. Fourth, teachers implementing the program need support of many types: time to learn the program, to plan, to explore, and to develop skills; opportunities to put their own stamp on the program and share experiences with other teachers; sufficient curriculum materials and supplies; and nurturance (not pressure) from competent, trained supervisors.

Guided by these principles, we have developed what appears to be a promising collaboration between the New York City Administration for Children's Services (ACS) and Teachers College at Columbia University. The collaboration aims to provide effective structures and methods for ECME professional development within the context of a large group of publicly supported child care centers entrusted with the care of children from low-income backgrounds. The centers, all serving preschool children, receive support from several sources, including Head Start, ACS, and the city board of education.

Given our previous experiences, we designed a year-long professional development plan that focused on preparing center directors and education supervisors to conduct BMLK professional development at their child care sites and to support and monitor their teachers' implementation of the program. First, ACS agreed to implement the plan on a trial basis for a year, thus providing the necessary administrative support for the effort. Then, we created a 2-day summer institute designed to introduce the directors and supervisors to issues related to ECME and to the BMLK program. The institute was designed to review the material from the previously described workshops to introduce participants to general ideas of ECME and to the specifics of the BMLK program. Directors and supervisors from around the city were invited to attend the institute on a voluntary basis and, if they agreed, to serve as trainers and supervisors for implementation of the program in the fall. Representatives of 15 programs attended the summer institute, which was favorably received.

As of June 2005, participants have been attending monthly train-the-trainer workshops designed to provide detailed training in the BMLK workshops that participants will conduct with teachers in their own centers. Participants not only learn the program but also discuss the need to observe teachers carefully in classrooms and to help teachers develop "communities of learners" as they engage in learning how to implement the program. In addition, the monthly meetings serve as a forum for discussion and for sharing of experiences and concerns as trainers and supervisors in ECME. The workshops thus provide education supervisors with a challenging and continuing opportunity for professional development. The goal is to develop a pool of experts who will contribute to disseminating knowledge of ECME and serve as trainers and mentors to new education directors/supervisors. As of June 2005, 11 program supervisors are participating in the training program and are engaged in implementing the BMLK program in approximately 50 classrooms for 4-year-olds. Many of the supervisors have proved so competent and enthusiastic that we have asked them to play a major role in conducting the next summer institute. The plan is eventually to evaluate the implementation process in some detail, paying particular attention to the role of supervisors in promoting the effectiveness of ECME.

In summary, the previously described formative experiences can be translated into the following recommendations for comprehensive in-service training in ECME:

- Start small: Pilot studies provide the groundwork for adapting the program to specific contexts.

- Think big: Implementation projects must be viewed as long-term and comprehensive. Plans should be made for implementation, continuation, and evaluation.

- Conduct a summer institute for supervisors: This event provides participants with the time to understand the program and to plan and envision the implementation process in their respective programs.

- Provide supervisors with a sense of ownership: Train-the-trainer workshops get supervisors involved in the training of their staff and helps develop a community of learners among supervisors.

- Help supervisors to conduct frequent classroom observations: Provide teachers with constructive feedback and opportunities for discussion.

- Help supervisors to create an atmosphere that is conducive to teacher learning: Teachers need ample opportunities to observe each other as they engage in BMLK activities and to discuss their findings.

- Be patient: Understanding new ideas about early childhood mathematics is not easy, and teachers will need time to learn the program, explore it, and reflect on their practices and observations. Teachers need to construct an understanding of ECME.

## CONCLUSIONS AND RECOMMENDATIONS

There is an urgent need to prepare prospective and current child care providers, teachers, and other early childhood education professionals to implement effective ECME. This chapter has described a three-pronged approach involving use of higher education courses, in-service workshops, and a comprehensive plan for structuring the in-service preparation of teachers. Although many obstacles stand in the way of success, there are reasons for optimism, particularly the fact that some professionals can learn to teach early mathematics very effectively.

A program of research and development is needed to investigate many factors affecting preparation for ECME. One set of issues involves the effectiveness of various higher education courses, workshops, and plans for structuring in-service education in ECME. Research is needed to clarify matters such as what students learn from courses in ECME and how it affects their later teaching; what teachers learn from workshops and how it affects their classroom behavior; and how well different in-service structures work in different early childhood settings. Particular attention should be paid to the role of supervisors in promoting effective teaching. The ultimate test for courses, workshops, and in-service structures is success in improving children's mathematics achievement.

A second set of issues refers to basic phenomena related to teachers and teaching. Further insight is needed about fundamental issues such as teacher views of ECME, the obstacles impeding reform in ECME, and the nature of pedagogy appropriate for ECME.

A third set of issues relates to the different settings in which ECME is implemented. Unlike education at the higher grade levels, ECME takes place in a multitude of settings—during all-day and half-day education schedules, during academic-calendar and all-year education schedules, in Head Start programs and home child care environments, in parochial schools and public schools. It is important to investigate how variations in professional preparation can meet the special needs of various settings in which ECME takes place. Thus, an urgent topic for development and research is the possibility that effective preparation in ECME can also be created for home child care providers, who are responsible for a large proportion of preschoolers.

Clearly the challenges are great. Yet, research and development can contribute to implementation of effective ECME and, thus, to the well-being of preschoolers in the United States and around the world.

## REFERENCES

Balfanz, R. (1999). Why do we teach children so little mathematics? Some historical considerations. In J.V. Copley (Ed.), *Mathematics in the early years* (pp. 3–10). Reston, VA: National Council of Teachers of Mathematics.

Balfanz, R., Ginsburg, H.P., & Greenes, C. (2003). The Big Math for Little Kids early childhood mathematics program. *Teaching Children Mathematics, 9*(5), 264–268.

Ball, D.L. (2000). Bridging practices: Intertwining content and pedagogy in teaching and learning to teach. *Journal of Teacher Education, 51*(3), 241–247.

Baroody, A.J., & Wilkins, J.L.M. (1999). The development of informal counting, number, and arithmetic skills and concepts. In J.V. Copley (Ed.), *Mathematics in the early years* (pp. 48–65). Reston, VA: National Council of Teachers of Mathematics.

Beck, R.J., King, A., & Marshall, S.K. (2002). Effects of video case construction on preservice teachers' observations of teaching. *Journal of Experimental Education, 70*(4), 345–361.

Berends, M. (2000). Teacher-reported effects of new American school designs: Exploring relationships to teacher background and school context. *Educational Evaluation and Policy Analysis, 22*(1), 65–82.

Bowman, B.T., Donovan, M.S., & Burns, M.S. (Eds.). (2001). *Eager to learn: Educating our preschoolers.* Washington, DC: National Academies Press.

Bransford, J.D., Brown, A.L., & Cocking, R.R. (Eds.). (1998). *How people learn: Brain, mind, experience, and school.* Washington, DC: National Academies Press.

Bredekamp, S. (Ed.). (1987). *Developmentally appropriate practice in early childhood programs serving children from birth through age 8.* Washington, DC: National Association for the Education of Young Children.

Bredekamp, S., & Copple, C. (Eds.). (1997). *Developmentally appropriate practice in early childhood programs* (Rev. ed.). Washington, DC: National Association for the Education of Young Children.

Brush, L.R. (1978). Preschool children's knowledge of addition and subtraction. *Journal for Research in Mathematics Education, 9,* 44–54.

Carpenter, T.P., Fennema, E., Peterson, P.L., Chiang, C.-P., & Loef, M. (1989). Using knowledge of children's mathematics thinking in classroom teaching: An experimental study. *American Educational Research Journal, 26,* 499–531.

Casey, B., Anderson, K.L., & Schiro, M. (2002). *Layla discovers secret patterns.* Chicago: Wright Group/McGraw-Hill.

Clements, D.H. (1999). Geometric and spatial thinking in young children. In J.V. Copley (Ed.), *Mathematics in the early years* (pp. 66–79). Reston, VA: National Council of Teachers of Mathematics.

Clements, D.H. (2004). Major themes and recommendations. In D.H. Clements & J. Sarama (Eds.), *Engaging young children in mathematics* (pp. 7–72). Mahwah, NJ: Lawrence Erlbaum Associates.

Clements, D.H., & Sarama, J. (2003). *DLM Express math resource package.* Columbus, OH: SRA/McGraw-Hill.

Clements, D.H., Sarama, J., & DiBiase, A.-M. (Eds.). (2004). *Engaging young children in mathematics: Standards for early childhood mathematics education.* Mahwah, NJ: Lawrence Erlbaum Associates.

Copley, J.V. (Ed.). (1999). *Mathematics in the early years.* Reston, VA: National Council of Teachers of Mathematics.

Damon, W. (1997). Learning and resistance: When developmental theory meets educational practice. In E. Amsel & K.A. Renninger (Eds.), *Change and development: Issues of theory, method, and application* (pp. 287–310). Mahwah, NJ: Lawrence Erlbaum Associates.

Denton, K., & West, J. (2002). *Children's reading and mathematics achievement in kindergarten and first grade.* Washington, DC: National Center for Education Statistics, U.S. Department of Education.

Dewey, J. (1976). The child and the curriculum. In J.A. Boydston (Ed.), *John Dewey: The middle works, 1899–1924. Vol. 2: 1902–1903* (pp. 273–291). Carbondale: Southern Illinois University Press. (Original work published 1902)

Flake, J. (2002). Using web videos and virtual learning environments to help prospective teachers construct meaning about children's mathematical thinking. *Journal of Computers in Mathematics and Science Teaching, 21*(1), 33–51.

Gallagher, J.J., Clayton, J.R., & Heinemeier, S.E. (2001). *Education for four-year-olds: State initiatives. Executive summary.* Chapel Hill: The University of North Carolina, FPG Child Development Center, National Center for Early Development & Learning.

Gelman, R. (1980). What young children know about numbers. *Educational Psychologist, 15,* 54–68.

Ginsburg, H.P. (1989). *Children's arithmetic: How they learn it and how you teach it* (2nd ed.). Austin, TX: PRO-ED.

Ginsburg, H.P., Galanter, M., & Morgenlander, M. (2004). *Big Math for Little Kids workshops.* New York: Teachers College Innovations.

Ginsburg, H.P., Greenes, C., & Balfanz, R. (2003). *Big Math for Little Kids (BMLK).* Parsippany, NJ: Dale Seymour Publications.

Ginsburg, H.P., Jacobs, S.G., & Lopez, L.S. (1998). *The teacher's guide to flexible interviewing in the classroom: Learning what children know about math.* Boston: Allyn & Bacon.

Ginsburg, H.P., Jang, S., Preston, M., Appel, A., & VanEsselstyn, D. (2004). Learning to think about early childhood mathematics education: A course. In C. Greenes & J. Tsankova (Eds.), *Challenging young children mathematically* (pp. 40–56). Boston: Houghton Mifflin.

Ginsburg, H.P., Kaplan, R.G., & Baroody, A.J. (1992). *Children's mathematical thinking: Videotape workshops for educators.* Evanston, IL: Everyday Learning Corporation.

Ginsburg, H.P., Klein, A., & Starkey, P. (1998). The development of children's mathematical thinking: Connecting research with practice. In I. Sigel & A. Renninger (Eds.), *Handbook of child psychology: Vol. 4. Child psychology and practice* (5th ed., pp. 401–476). New York: John Wiley & Sons.

Gragg, C.I. (1994). Teachers also must learn. In L.B. Barnes, C.R. Christensen & A.J. Handsen (Eds.), *Teaching and the case method: Text, cases, and readings* (3rd ed., pp. 15–22).Watertown, MA: Harvard Business School Press.

Greenes, C. (1999). Ready to learn: Developing young children's mathematical powers. In J. Copley (Ed.), *Mathematics in the early years* (pp. 39–47). Reston, VA: National Council of Teachers of Mathematics.

Groen, G., & Resnick, L.B. (1977). Can preschool children invent addition algorithms? *Journal of Educational Psychology, 69,* 645–652.

Hohmann, M., & Weikart, D.P. (2002). *Educating young children: Active learning practices for preschool and child care* (2nd ed.). Ypsilanti, MI: High/Scope Press.

Hunting, R. (1999). Rational number learning in the early years: What is possible? In J. Copley (Ed.), *Mathematics in the early years* (pp. 80–87). Reston, VA: National Council of Teachers of Mathematics.

Irwin, K., & Burgham, D. (1992). Big numbers and small children. *The New Zealand Mathematics Magazine, 29*(1), 9–19.

Kinzer, C., & Risko, V. (1998). Multimedia and enhanced learning: Transforming preservice education. In D. Reinking, M. McKenna, L. Labbo, & R. Kieffer (Eds.),

*Handbook of technology and literacy: Transformations in a post-typographic world* (pp. 185–202). Mahwah, NJ: Lawrence Erlbaum Associates.

Lampert, M., & Ball, D.L. (1998). *Teaching, multimedia, and mathematics: Investigations of real practice.* New York: Teachers College Press.

Ma, L. (1999). *Knowing and teaching elementary mathematics.* Mahwah, NJ: Lawrence Erlbaum Associates.

Mullis, I.V.S., Martin, M.O., Beaton, E.J., Gonzalez, D.L., Kelly, D.L., & Smith, T.A. (1997). *Mathematics achievement in the primary school years: IEA's Third International Mathematics and Science Study (TIMSS).* Chestnut Hill, MA: Boston College, Center for the Study of Testing, Evaluation, and Educational Policy.

Mullis, I.V.S., Martin, M.O., Gonzalez, D.L., Gregory, K.D., Garden, R.A., & O'Connor, K.M. (2000). *TIMSS 1999 international mathematics report: Findings from IEA's repeat of the Third International Mathematics and Science Study at the eighth grade.* Chesnut Hill, MA: Boston College, International Study Center.

National Association for the Education of Young Children & National Council of Teachers of Mathematics. (2002). *Early childhood mathematics: Promoting good beginnings.* Retrieved September 7, 2004, from www.naeyc.org/resources/position_statements/psmath.htm

National Center for Children in Poverty. (1996). *One in four: America's youngest poor (Abridged version).* New York: Author.

National Council of Teachers of Mathematics. (2000). *Principles and standards for school mathematics.* Reston, VA: Author.

No Child Left Behind (NCLB) Act of 2001, PL 107-110, 20 U.S.C. §6301 et seq.

Peisner-Feinberg, E.S., Burchinal, M.R., Clifford, R.M., Culkin, M.L., Howes, C., Kagan, S.L., & Yazejian, N. (2001). The relation of preschool child-care quality to children's cognitive and social developmental trajectories through second grade. *Child Development, 72*(5), 1534–1553.

Piaget, J. (1952). *The child's conception of number* (C. Gattegno & F.M. Hodgson, Trans.). London: Routledge & Kegan Paul Ltd.

Post, T.R., Harel, G., Behr, M.J., & Lesh, R. (1991). Intermediate teachers' knowledge of rational number concepts. In E. Fennema, T.P. Carpenter & S.J. Lamon (Eds.), *Integrating research on teaching and learning mathematics* (pp. 177–198). Albany: State University of New York Press.

Rand, M.K. (2000). *Giving it some thought: Cases for early childhood practice.* Washington, DC: National Association for the Education of Young Children.

Sarama, J. (2004). Technology in early childhood mathematics: Building Blocks as an innovative technology-based curriculum. In D.H. Clements, J. Sarama & A.-M. DiBiase (Eds.), *Engaging young children in mathematics: Standards for early childhood mathematics education* (pp. 361–375). Mahwah, NJ: Lawrence Erlbaum Associates.

Sarama, J., DiBiase, A.-M., Clements, D.H., & Spitler, M.E. (2004). The professional development challenge in preschool mathematics. In D.H. Clements, J. Sarama & A.-M. DiBiase (Eds.), *Engaging young children in mathematics: Standards for early childhood mathematics education* (pp. 415–446). Mahwah, NJ: Lawrence Erlbaum Associates.

Schoenfeld, A.H. (1999). Models of the teaching process. *Journal of Mathematical Behavior, 18*(3), 243–261.

Schwartzbeck, T.D. (2002). *Choosing a model and types of models: How to find what works for your school.* Washington, DC: National Clearinghouse for Comprehensive School Reform.

Seo, K.-H., & Ginsburg, H.P. (2004). What is developmentally appropriate in early childhood mathematics education? Lessons from new research. In D.H. Clements, J. Sarama, & A.-M. DiBiase (Eds.), *Engaging young children in mathematics: Standards for early childhood mathematics education* (pp. 91–104). Mahwah, NJ: Lawrence Erlbaum Associates.

Shepard, L.A. (2001). The role of classroom assessment in teaching and learning. In V. Richardson (Ed.), *The handbook of research on reaching* (4th ed.). Washington, DC: American Educational Research Association.

Shulman, L.S. (1987). Knowledge and teaching: Foundations of a new reform. *Harvard Educational Review, 57*(1), 1–22.

Stevenson, H., Lee, S.S., & Stigler, J. (1986). The mathematics achievement of Chinese, Japanese, and American children. *Science, 56,* 693–699.

Vygotsky, L.S. (1978). *Mind in society: The development of higher psychological processes.* Cambridge, MA: Harvard University Press.

Wagner, T. (2001). Leadership for learning: An action theory of social change. *Phi Delta Kappan, 82*(5), 378–383.

Zur, O., & Gelman, R. (2004). Young children can add and subtract by predicting and checking. *Early Childhood Research Quarterly, 19*(1), 121–137.

Zvonkin, A. (1992). Mathematics for little ones. *Journal of Mathematical Behavior, 11*(2), 207–219.

# CHAPTER 8

# Self-Regulation as a Key to School Readiness

*How Early Childhood Teachers*
*Can Promote this Critical Competency*

ELENA BODROVA AND DEBORAH J. LEONG

This chapter focuses on self-regulation and its contribution to school readiness as promoted by early childhood teachers. The chapter makes the case for self-regulation as a key component of school readiness and reviews current views of self-regulation and interventions designed to improve the self-regulatory abilities of young children. Self-regulation has traditionally been a part of the social-emotional realm, but in this chapter, we broaden that perspective to include cognitive abilities, as we define *self-regulation* as the ability to regulate emotions and thinking. The chapter ends with an overview of the Vygotskian approach that brings unique perspective on self-regulation. For Vygotskians, many aspects of self-regulation are learned, and preschool is considered an important time period for its development. We suggest that when early childhood educators understand these and other methods, they can help children enter school with higher levels of self-regulation.

## SELF-REGULATION AND SCHOOL READINESS

Kindergarten teachers have known for years that one of the reasons young children are not ready for school is that they lack self-regulation. In fact, in one study after another, kindergarten teachers rank the level of self-regulation as one of the most important indicators of child school readiness. Indeed, it often outweighs other factors such as chronological age, overall background knowledge, or the child's mastery of specific academic skills such as counting or letter recognition. In their description of a self-regulated kindergartner, teachers in one study described such a child as being able to 1) sustain attention and be enthusiastic and curious in new activities, 2) inhibit impulsivity and follow directions, and 3) take turns and be sensitive to other children's feelings (Lewit & Baker, 1995).

These responses, however inconsistent they may seem with the emphasis on "academic" school readiness, come as no surprise if one is to reflect on the demands of an elementary classroom (e.g., Huffman et al., 1998; Levine et al., 1997). In fact, children are required to control their attention in school by blocking out the distractions and focusing on the specific elements of the classroom environment that are not the most obvious or engaging. For instance, paying more attention to a teacher when a playmate is whispering is not easy. Young students are required to conform to a routine, which often means that they have to switch from something they are enjoying to something of less interest. They are also expected to be able to follow directions that sometimes have multiple interrelated steps so that skipping any one of them affects the ultimate outcome. The essential lessons often involve forming associations between seemingly unrelated pieces of information, such as the association between a letter symbol and the name of a letter. Such lessons require that children control their memory. To meet these and other demands of the elementary school classroom, children need to develop self-regulatory abilities.

The observations of kindergarten teachers about the relationship between self-regulation and school readiness have been confirmed by new research data. Researchers have found links between self-regulation at early ages and children's functioning in school far beyond kindergarten and first grade. Reviews of research, such as *From Neurons to Neighborhoods* (Schonkoff & Phillips, 2000), *Eager to Learn* (Bowman, Donovan, & Burns, 2001), and *Ready to Enter* (Ravner & Knitzer, 2002), all discuss the importance of self-regulation for later school achievement. In these reports, self-regulation is thought to be a core ability that cuts across the regulation of emotions, physical behavior, and social interactions and includes the ability to monitor and control cognitive processes, such as attention.

Lack of social-emotional regulation is associated with aggression and lack of social skills, emotional outbursts, and inattention and feelings of being overwhelmed (Saarni, Mumme, & Campos, 1998). Children who have not learned self-regulation in preschool can develop aggressive habits of interaction that are difficult to break in later years (Broidy et al., 2003; Nagin & Tremblay, 1999). Children lacking emotional self-regulation are at higher risk for disciplinary problems (Huffman, Mehlinger, & Kerivan, 2000) because they are less capable of cooperating or resolving conflicts successfully. Children who lack self-regulation do not participate as productively in classroom activities—including learning activities (Ladd, Birch, & Buhs, 1999). This lack of social-emotional self-regulation can stand in the way of a child's ability to have positive teacher–child interactions in kindergarten, which, in turn, predicts poor academic performance as well as behavior problems in later years (e.g., Hamre & Pianta, 2001; Ravner & Knitzer, 2002).

Cognitive self-regulation, as a component of executive functioning and attentional processes, is directly linked with students' achievement in school (Lyon & Krasnegor, 1996). However, the effects of cognitive self-regulation on young children's readiness for academic learning have not yet received the same amount of attention as the effects of social-emotional self-regulation. Although the link between various manifestations of cognitive self-regulation and academic achievement is well documented for middle school and high school students (Zimmerman, 2002), much less is known about how self-regulation precursors developed in preschool contribute to the later development of executive functions (Schonkoff & Phillips, 2000). Early studies focusing on young children's use of executive processes involving planning ahead, focusing attention, and remembering past experiences in order to bring them to bear on the problem at hand were primarily conducted with children with special needs. Those children, it can be argued, represent extreme cases of the lack of self-regulation. New studies of the development of executive function propose that self-regulation may play a key role in its development and provide more definitive evidence of a link with problem solving (e.g., Diamond & Taylor, 1996; Zelazo, Muller, Frye, & Marcovich, 2003).

From these studies and other research, it seems that self-regulation affects children's ability to successfully function in a school setting in two ways: first, *social-emotional* self-regulation makes it possible for children to conform to classroom rules and to benefit from learning in various social contexts (e.g., in large and small groups, in cooperative dyads, individually) and second, *cognitive* self-regulation allows children to use and further develop cognitive processes necessary for academic learning and problem solving. Although, in most studies, researchers have focused on specific effects of either cognitive or social-emotional self-regulation, there is some evidence that these two facets of self-regulatory ability are connected—children lacking emotional self-control are likely to have problems with the regulation of cognitive processes, such as attention (Derryberry & Reed, 1996; LeDoux, 1996). This is probably due to the commonality of the neurological mechanisms governing both emotional and cognitive self-regulation. Moreover, earlier patterns in the development of emotional control have been shown to be predictive of children's later ability to exercise control over their cognitive functioning (Blair, 2002).

Collectively, research seems to point to the importance of children developing self-regulation at an early age. But how well do preschools prepare children for becoming self-regulated learners? The preschool years are seen as the primary period for acquiring self-regulation in all its forms. However, there is evidence that young children are not acquiring the requisite levels of self-regulation to assure that they will do well in school (Bronson, 2000; Thompson, 2001).

There is a growing chorus of concern that young children are not entering school with the self-regulatory skills that they need (e.g., Hyson, Copple, & Jones, in press; Ravner & Knitzer, 2002). In a nationally representative survey of kindergarten teachers, 46% reported that more than half of their children do not have sufficient levels of self-regulation (Rimm-Kaufman, Pianta, & Cox, 2000). In a study of Head Start classrooms, teachers reported that problem behaviors related to lack of social-emotional self-regulation, such as kicking or threatening others, occurred once a day for 40% of the children.

There were six or more instances of problem behaviors for 10% of the children (Kupersmidt, Bryant, & Willoughby, 2000; Willoughby, Kupersmidt, & Bryant, 2001). An observational study found that preschool children in one classroom engaged in 32 instances of misbehavior within a 10-minute period of time (Goldstein, Arnold, Rosenberg, Stowe, & Ortiz, 2001).

Yet, it has been demonstrated that teachers can have a positive effect on children's self-regulatory capacities (e.g., Burchinal, Peisner-Feinberg, Bryant, & Clifford, 2000). And, unfortunately, when preschool teachers fail to handle social-emotional problems well, they perpetuate unregulated behaviors in their young pupils (Arnold, McWilliams, & Arnold, 1998).

Although there seems to be agreement among researchers as well as among practitioners as to the general importance of self-regulation for successful functioning in school, no such agreement exists on what mechanisms are responsible for the development of self-regulation. Nor is there general understanding of the role early childhood teachers play in promoting self-regulation in their students. The next part of the chapter reviews some of the most common views on the development of self-regulation and discusses their relevance in the context of preparing early childhood teachers. Then it describes some of the interventions that have been developed either to explicitly target self-regulation or have self-regulation gains as a by-product of the intervention. Finally, the chapter presents our view on the development of self-regulation that stems from Vygotsky's cultural-historical theory and discusses the implications of this approach for the professional development of preschool and kindergarten teachers.

## CONTRASTING PERSPECTIVES ON SELF-REGULATION

### Self-Regulation as a Personality Trait

There are a number of approaches to understanding self-regulation in existing research. One perspective views differences in children's self-regulatory abilities as resulting from underlying differences in their psycho-physiological characteristics, such as temperament. This approach seems to evolve from an earlier one that focused on such personality traits as "impulsivity" and "reflectivity." These terms have changed, and children are more often described as being "underregulated" or "overregulated" (e.g., Hart, Atkins, & Fegley, 2003), although these characteristics are still being considered as largely innate rather than acquired. In this perspective, the child's ability to purposefully engage in or refrain from certain behaviors—physical as well as social—is linked to this child's level of effortful control—the temperament trait that emerges at the end of the first year of life and regulates the reactive aspects of temperament (e.g., Murray & Kochanska, 2002).

This approach helps identify the early signs of self-regulation or the extremes of the trait but gives little insight about how these characteristics are tempered or can be modified by teacher guidance and intervention. Over-emphasizing the link between individual personality characteristics and self-regulation may lead some teachers to lower their expectations for the children who possess an "impulsive" temperament. Because a personality trait is less amenable to intervention, teachers are less likely to intervene. We believe that it is more helpful for teachers to recognize that there is a large spectrum of personality characteristics in children that make it easier for some or more difficult for others to develop self-regulation. At the same time, *all* children should be viewed as having the potential to become "self-regulated," although their individual trajectories in achieving this, as well as the support they need, may differ.

## Self-Regulation as a Function of Classroom Contexts

Several studies have found that the classroom environment can suppress or encourage the self-regulatory behaviors of children. Even in "self-regulated" children, manifestations of self-regulated behaviors have been found to be highly subject to contextual cues. For example, elementary-age children do not act in a self-regulatory manner if the classroom does not emphasize such things as choice of activities, reflection on learning, corrective feedback, and focus on mastery rather than performance (e.g., Perry, 1998). Although most of the findings of this and similar studies with elementary-age children cannot be directly applied to early childhood settings because the settings differ so much, some of the findings provide insights applicable to young children. For example, although the choice of activities and process of reflection on learning may not look the same in preschool and in elementary school classrooms, both can still be seen as appropriate in the organization of young children's classroom experiences. The evidence suggests that classrooms that support activity choice and reflection do produce more self-regulatory behaviors in children (Stright & Supplee, 2002). When teacher–child interactions involve a variety of strategies beneficial for the development of self-regulatory behaviors, even children with initially low levels of metacognition demonstrate the ability to engage in self-appraising and self-monitoring behaviors. They are, thus, essentially showing increases in their cognitive self-regulation (Cox, Daniel, & Boston, 1985).

## Lack of Self-Regulation as a Learning Disability

A further approach focuses on the extreme cases of the lack of self-regulation in children who are not developing typically and warrant a clinical diagnosis such as attention-deficit/hyperactivity disorder (ADHD) with the subsequent need for clinical interventions such as therapy or medication. The validity of such diagnoses in young children based solely on their "unregulated" behaviors can be complicated by the fact that many of the behaviors are typical for children of this age (Rutter & Sroufe, 2000). We leave it for the reader to judge whether the item on a teacher-rating ADHD scale "When in trouble blames someone else" describes the behavior of a seriously troubled child or of a typical 4-year-old!

We have found that an emphasis on clinical diagnoses sometimes encourages teachers to mistake the lack of self-regulation that is within normal boundaries for the indication of a neurological disorder. Clearly, children whose lack of self-regulation can be attributed to the imbalance of their brain chemistry do exist, but they account for only a small portion of children who are "out of control." Lack of self-regulation can be exacerbated by factors such as negative experiences and parenting styles (Schonkoff & Phillips, 2000), so even children with extremely low levels of self-regulation cannot be automatically assumed to have ADHD or a similar condition.

## Self-Regulation as a Function of Brain Development

With the advent of new and more sophisticated methods of brain research it has become possible to establish relationships between the development of self-regulation and the maturation of particular areas of the brain. It was found, for example, that relatively low levels of self-regulation in preschool-age children are associated with the children not yet utilizing the areas of the brain responsible for planning and reflection (Bronson, 2000). Research on the brain seems to indicate that self-regulation is tied to the development of the prefrontal cortex, which is not only important for the development of control over emotions, but also that of focused attention as well as planning and monitoring of cognitive behaviors. There is evidence that positive emotionality and negative emotionality induce different patterns of activation of the prefrontal cortex (Davidson, Jackson, & Kalin, 2000) and that this can affect levels of attention (Davidson, 1999). The fact that the same area of the brain is responsible for emotional control and for the metacognitive functions further supports the idea of the interconnection between social-emotional self-regulation and cognitive self-regulation (Blair, 2002).

It may seem that this neurodevelopmental perspective on self-regulation is very similar to the maturational one. However, unlike researchers of the past, those who study brain development today recognize the complex nature of the relationship between physiological processes, environmental influences, and the child's own experiences in shaping developing psychological processes. From this perspective, teachers need to be aware of the fact that by creating experiences that support self-regulation, they actually contribute to the formation of children's developing brains.

## Self-Regulation as a Characteristic of an Advanced Level of Mental Functioning

Some studies have examined self-regulation as a highly developed process and identified the components of self-regulation as it looks when fully developed. Many of the studies within this approach focus on cognitive self-regulation and view it in the context of such processes as metacognition, metamemory, and reflective thinking. In other studies, self-regulation is studied in the context of motivational processes, such as self-efficacy (e.g., Zimmerman, 2002). In both cases, it is implied that children have to have already developed a substantial base of cognitive and motivational processes—something that typically does not occur until middle childhood—to develop self-regulation. In their mature state, self-regulatory processes were found to be influenced by many variables, including factors present in the classroom. For example, by varying format of assignments, type of feedback, or by explicitly teaching various strategies, teachers were able to significantly increase the levels of self-regulatory behavior in their students (Kitsantas, Zimmerman, & Cleary, 2000; Zimmerman, 2002; Zimmerman & Kitsantas, 1997).

Research on metacognition and self-regulated learning in older children provides a "bigger picture," demonstrating the outcomes of the development of self-regulation and justifying its importance for advanced academic learning. However, emphasis on the "maturational" aspect of self-regulation might lead some early childhood teachers to believe that there is nothing they can do to promote self-regulation until children reach the "right" age.

## Self-Regulation as a Gradually Developing Cognitive Competency

Although few studies have looked at the precursors of cognitive self-regulation abilities in preschool-age children, there is some evidence that children do not need to be in middle or high school to exhibit self-regulatory behaviors or some forms of metacognition. It has been found, for example, that preschool-age children can engage in primitive forms of metacognition and reflection when the content of the task is familiar to them (e.g., Brown & DeLoach, 1978). Furthermore, there is evidence that kindergartners are not only able to engage in planning and self-monitoring behaviors themselves, but can also detect these behaviors in their peers (Hwang & Gorrell, 2001).

Another view of self-regulation in cognition can be found in the Cognitive Complexity Control (CCC) Theory (Zelazo et al., 2003), which examines how executive function develops in young children. *Executive function* is a term used to describe the regulation of cognitive processes. CCC theory examines goal-directed problem solving, how children accomplish this through the use of self-directed speech, and the relationship between intentionality and strategy choice. The child's ability to handle more and more complex rules with age is determined in part by the child's ability to monitor and reflect on strategy choice, which leads to the activation of appropriate strategies and the inhibition of inappropriate ones. These skills grow during the preschool period. Intentionality, activation, and inhibition, as well as reflection, are all processes that form part of cognitive self-regulation.

This review of the research on the development of self-regulation shows that this field is so varied that there are differing definitions of self-regulation. These disparities make it difficult to determine how a classroom teacher can promote self-regulation in young children. Another source of information comes from existing interventions, some of which have resulted in increased levels of self-regulation even when it had not been the primary target of the particular intervention. The next section provides a brief review of several interventions and attempts to identify the aspects of self-regulation that were affected.

## SELF-REGULATION INTERVENTIONS: INCREASING THE LEVELS OF SELF-REGULATION IN THE EARLY CHILDHOOD CLASSROOM

Early childhood teachers are struggling with growing numbers of children who need specific support to develop self-regulation at the same time that they feel themselves under pressure to meet national standards in purely academic areas (Yoshikawa & Knitzer, 1997). Teachers report that they feel overwhelmed and do not know what to do to support their young students. In an increasing number of cases, children with behavioral problems are simply being expelled from classrooms (Knitzer, 2002). Although there have been many calls for incorporating self-regulation into teacher training, this has been difficult to accomplish.

This section discusses interventions that have been designed to target self-regulation broadly, along with inventions aimed at specific aspects of self-regulation. The theoretical approaches underlying these interventions differ as widely as the approaches described in the previous section. For many interventions, the data on their effects on self-regulation are primarily anecdotal or are inferred from other data. The lack of commonly used reliable instruments to measure self-regulation in young children makes it difficult to evaluate the efficacy of individual interventions and compare them to each other. For the purposes of this chapter, we only describe interventions that were specifically designed to be implemented in real-life settings outside of research labs.

Most interventions have been designed for elementary-age children or junior high and high school students. The interventions in elementary school and beyond focus either on changing the classroom context by providing more choices (Perry, Phillips, & Dowler, 2004) or individual coaching for children who have self-regulation problems that they exhibit in the classroom. A majority of the interventions deal with social-emotional self-regulation, emphasizing children who are at risk and display problem behaviors (Joseph & Strain, 2003). The few interventions designed specifically for young children focus on the family as well as the preschool classroom context.

## Family Interventions

Family interventions focus on helping parents discover what they can do to support self-regulation. For example, the Supports for Early Learning Foundation program (SELF) works with individual children from infancy to early childhood and their families (Harrison, Du Rivage, & Clarke, 1999). Using a broad definition of self-regulation, which includes physiological, behavioral, social-communicative, and emotional self-regulation, the SELF instrument is used to assess the children as well as to provide intervention strategies to the family. There is an extensive effort to provide training in the SELF process, and once members of a group are trained, they can provide training and technical assistance to those working in early childhood settings. However, the intervention has not yet been formally evaluated.

## In-Classroom Interventions

Some programs implemented in an entire classroom emphasize social-emotional development and self-regulation. For example, the Promoting Alternative Thinking Strategies program (PATH) provides classroom interventions for the development of social-emotional self-regulation through activities aimed at learning to identify emotions in others and to develop social problem-solving skills (Kusche & Greenberg, 1994). Comparing children in classrooms where PATH was implemented with children in control classrooms, children who participated in the PATH program tended to have higher levels of social skills and were less likely to misread social cues. No specific measures of self-regulation were used in these studies because social-emotional self-regulation was considered by the authors to be an integral part of social-emotional competency targeted by this program.

Some programs that work on social-emotional development and classroom behavioral problems advocate better classroom management strategies combined with classroom problem solving. One such program is the training model developed at the Center on the Social-Emotional Foundations for Early Learning (CSEFEL; http://www.csefel.uiuc.edu). The CSEFEL model provides teachers with training in general classroom management skills and classroom interventions for specific children as a means of promoting prosocial behavior. At this point, evaluations have only been conducted relative to the teacher training program. Several programs train teachers to make finer distinctions in "problem behavior," provide alternative ways of guiding children, and use conflict management techniques including class meetings where children discuss classroom problems (Gartrell, 2004; Harris & Fuqua, 2000).

There are some interventions aimed at elements of cognitive self-regulation. In ScienceSmart (French, 2004), children learn about science in a way that gives them practice in managing attention, planning, and problem solving. It, therefore, emphasizes development in a content area, and self-regulation is a by-product of the program.

What emerges from these interventions is a list of techniques that seem to be used in a number of programs:

• Visual reminders, such as social interaction rules posted in the classroom; lists of tasks to be done; or the tracking of strategies used to solve problems

• Providing choices in activities so that children regulate where they want to go and what they want to do

• Modeling social-emotional problem solving using either videos or stories and pictures and providing practice in using the strategies in a variety of settings, such as class meetings

• Exploiting naturally occurring disagreements to teach about social problem solving and to model self-regulation

• Creating activities that help children learn academic content that incorporate elements of self-regulation

• Using reinforcement and carefully planned classroom management strategies

## THE VYGOTSKIAN APPROACH TO
## THE DEVELOPMENT OF SELF-REGULATION

Vygotsky's view on self-regulation presents an alternative to the theoretical approaches discussed previously and, at the same time, provides clear directions for promoting self-regulation in young children. Because he did not divide self-regulation into cognitive and social-emotional components, Vygotsky instead viewed it as an integral competency, one of the major characteristic of uniquely human "higher mental functions." Although the term *self-regulation* is used widely by Vygotsky's students, it did not appear in Vygotsky's own writings (he used the words *volitional, voluntary,* and *willful* behavior). For Vygotskians, self-regulation is the use of deliberate behavior and plays a prominent role in the preschool years, constituting one of the most critical advances in child development that happens at this time. Vygotsky explicitly linked school readiness to the development of self-regulation, noting that it allows a preschool child to make the necessary transition from learning that "follows the child's own agenda" to the learning that "follows the school agenda" (Vygotsky, 1956).

According to Vygotsky, children's self-regulatory abilities originate in social interactions and only later become internalized and independently used by children (Vygotsky, 1977). This means that self-regulation is not something that emerges spontaneously as a function of the classroom environment or evolves as the child matures. Instead, Vygotskians propose that self-regulation is taught formally or informally within the social context—the classroom being one of the possible contexts—but families and peer groups provide alternative contexts for learning self-regulation. When none of the social contexts support the development of self-regulatory behaviors, children continue to operate as "slaves to the environment," being guided by ever-changing external stimulation and being incapable of intentional actions.

Children can learn self-regulating abilities when they engage in informal interactions with adults or peers. For example, long before children are able to self-regulate their behaviors, they participate in "other-regulation," or interactions in which their behavior is guided by others (e.g., Wertsch, 1979). When this "other-regulation" occurs with a more competent person, usually a parent or a teacher, this adult not only guides the child's behavior in the ways the child is not yet capable, but also arms this child with specific "mental tools" that will allow the child to eventually use self-regulatory skills independently (Bodrova & Leong, 1996). One of these tools is "private speech," or speech that children address to themselves. When children engage in private speech, the same words that adults once used to regulate children's behaviors are now used by children themselves for the purposes of self-regulation. Studies of private speech have found a direct link between children's use of private speech and their self-regulatory abilities (Berk & Landeau, 1993; Berk & Spuhl, 1995; Winsler, Diaz, Atencio, McCarthy, & Chabay, 2000).

Vygotskians argue that if the only type of "other-regulation" that the child engages in is when all regulation is done by an adult, then true *self-*regulation will not develop. Although children might be able to internalize some rules and expectations, they will still lack the ability to self-initiate desired behaviors or to refrain from the undesired ones. Every teacher might remember some of these "pseudo-regulated" children who stayed in control only as long as the adult was watching them.

To develop self-regulation, children need to engage in "other-regulation" in which they are the ones regulating the behavior of peers and are practicing acting intentionally in the situations where they regulate themselves. Consequently, activities such as make-believe play, in which a preschool child practices regulating his or her peers, being regulated by them, and regulating his or her own behavior, are important to self-regulation development. Make-believe play provides a unique context that supports the use of self-regulation through a system of roles and corresponding rules (Vygotsky, 1977). A young child can withstand the impulse to play with an interesting-looking toy held by one of the "passengers" if he is the "bus driver" and is supposed to pretend to drive the bus. Without the role of "bus driver," the child would not be able to resist the intriguing toy. Children regulate themselves (as does the child staying in the role of bus driver), but they also regulate each other. The children "riding" the pretend bus would tell a "passenger" that she cannot pretend to drive because she is not the bus driver. Children thus monitor other children's behavior, noting when someone is playing inappropriately for the role.

Make-believe play also enables preschoolers to self-regulate by providing a way to forgo their immediate wishes for gratification by allowing them to fulfill their desires in a symbolic form. Instead of eating the cake that is going to be given out at the birthday party at the end of the day, children can pretend to have that party and eat the cake now. Several studies show a strong connection between highly developed forms of make-believe play and various self-regulatory behaviors (Elias & Berk, 2002; Elkonin, 1978).

Because Vygotskians believe the acquisition of self-regulation depends on the nature of social interactions, the social context in which a child spends most of his or her time prior to coming to school is very important for developing self-regulation. Most preschool-age children spend some time in early childhood programs, therefore, the degree to which the classroom focuses on self-regulation has the potential to influence its development. Furthermore, the preschool as a context to support self-regulation is even more critical today for those young children whose families or peer groups do not seem to provide necessary supports.

The Vygotskian approach implies that *all* preschool children should engage in activities that provide support for their self-regulation instead of focusing an intervention on the individual children who are most at risk for not developing self-regulation or that targets isolated components of self-regulation. Given the importance of self-regulation for school readiness and for later social and academic success, the Vygotskian approach suggests that it should become a primary focus of the preschool experience.

## CLASSROOM APPLICATIONS OF THE VYGOTSKIAN APPROACH TO THE DEVELOPMENT OF SELF-REGULATION

Two examples of Vygotskian-based intervention are the Metropolitan State College of Denver's *Tools of the Mind Research Project,* in which self-regulation practice is embedded in all classroom activities and make-believe play is at the center of the curriculum, and Mid-continent Research for Education and Learning (McREL)'s *Scaffolding Early Literacy* project, in which Vygotskian techniques are applied to the area of literacy. These two interventions share the same philosophy and implement similar instructional strategies and differ mainly in their primary focus (self-regulation versus literacy) and the methods of teacher preparation.

*Tools of the Mind* focuses on the development of cognitive and social-emotional self-regulation. Self-regulation practice is embedded into all activities from the moment the children walk into the room, through their literacy and math activities, to snack and outdoor play. The content of training for the teachers is geared toward the self-regulatory levels of the children, with content presented at multiple points during the year to be responsive to the current levels of children's development. The classroom demands and difficulty level of the content are increased as children are able to attend and remember deliberately. There is a strong emphasis on teachers' ability to observe and assess children's level of self-regulation and to individualize activities to help children progress.

Training involves an initial 3-day workshop at the beginning of the year and half-day workshops in October, January, and March/April. The training includes teachers, teaching assistants, those providing special services (e.g., special education, English as a second language, literacy specialists), school district master teachers, and administrative staff so that support for self-regulation is provided consistently by all staff members providing and supporting instruction. Between 15 and 30 staff members participate in a workshop at any one time. The initial 3-day workshop begins with a day focusing on the Vygotskian approach in general and how it views and attempts to support self-regulation in children. The second day of the initial workshop turns to make-believe play as a context in which self-regulation develops. Teachers are instructed in how to diagnose different levels of play and how to support play so that it becomes more elaborate and self-sustaining. They are taught how to observe the facets of play that support self-regulation, such as intentional assumption of roles and turn-taking in playing out the pretend story. The third day focuses on practical changes that can be made in classroom scheduling and physical arrangements of the room to support the kinds of play activities that will foster the development of self-regulation. In *Tools of the Mind,* materials for a manual are provided initially and then in sections at each of the follow-up workshops because it was found that teachers may want to push too fast through the developmental sequences identified rather than allow children ample time to consolidate their skills at each level. Providing materials and further information at each of the brief follow-ups helps maintain the pacing.

The follow-up workshops focus on: 1) observing self-regulation in individual children and providing supports tailored to individual children's needs; 2) supporting self-regulation in contexts apart from play, such as in center activities and organized large- and small-group activities; 3) focusing specifically on self-regulation in activities focusing on academic content, such as reading and early mathematical skills; and 4) supporting children who are not doing well in the development of self-regulation. Training is conducted by the developer with the help of three trainers who have had extensive *Tools of the Mind* experience and who provide on-site support for the school personnel. In addition to workshops, the trainers visit classrooms at least once a month, depending on the size of the preschool program. During these monthly visits, master teachers in the buildings are given feedback about which teachers need more support and on which specific activities. Master teachers and trainers monitor fidelity to the program.

Currently, seven programs have fully implemented *Tools of the Mind*—six school districts and one Head Start program—all serving children who are at risk. There are approximately 150 classroom teachers and more than 2,500 children participating in the program. Twenty of the classrooms are inclusive, and 51% of the children are English language learners. Data are being collected on child outcomes and teacher–child interaction by the National Institute for Early Education Research in a double randomized design study of a subsample of the current programs. The teacher–child interaction measures being collected on a subsample of the programs include the Supports for Early Literacy Assessment (SELA; Smith, Davidson, Weinsenfeld, & Katasaros, 2001), The Preschool Classroom Implementation Rating Scale (PCI; Frede, 1989), and the Classroom Assessment Scoring System (CLASS; La Paro, Pianta, & Stuhlman, 2004).

Children in the study are tested in both English and Spanish when appropriate. Child measures collected included the literacy and math measures from the Woodcock-Johnson Tests of Achievement, Applied Problems Test and Letter–Word Identification Test (Woodcock & Mather, 1989); the Get Ready to Read Screening Tool (Whitehurst & Lonigan, 2001); the Peabody Picture Vocabulary Test, Third Edition (PPVT-III; Dunn & Dunn, 1997); the Expressive One-Word Picture Vocabulary Test (EOWPVT; Brownell, 2000); the IDEA Oral Language Proficiency Test (Williams, Ballard, Tighe, Dalton, & Amori, 1991); and the Social Skills Rating System (Gresham & Elliot, 1990). In conjunction with this study, data on inhibitory control were collected on a subsample of children in the National Institute for Early Education Research (NIEER) study (see http://nieer.org/docs/index. php?DocID=19).

The *Scaffolding Early Literacy* program focuses primarily on the development of early literacy skills in preschool- and kindergarten-age children. Self-regulation and early literacy are viewed as supporting each other in the course of development—as children develop the ability to regulate their attention and memory, they are better able to acquire literacy skills. Yet, once children learn to write, they use written language to further regulate their behaviors. The program has been piloted in school and district sites, area education agencies, and Head Start and Even Start programs in urban, suburban, and rural areas with several hundred teachers participating at varying levels of implementation. The format for the professional development has been refined since

2003 in collaboration with several sites, which demonstrates long-term commitment to the implementation of the program (Bodrova, Leong, Norford, & Paynter, 2003).

Professional development for the teachers participating in the *Scaffolding Early Literacy* program is conducted in several phases. In Phase 1, several teachers are selected for in-depth training and implementation of the program. At this time, the developer of the program trains these "model teachers" as well as on-site trainers (typically, reading specialists or district early childhood education specialists). In Phase 2, classrooms of model teachers become the demonstration sites where other teachers can observe the implementation of the instructional strategies. In this phase, the developer continues to provide support to the Phase 1 teachers by observing their implementation, demonstrating and modeling in their classrooms, and holding debriefings and planning sessions. In addition, in Phase 2, general training is provided to Phase 2 teachers, who get their on-going support primarily from Phase 1 teachers and from on-site trainers. This model ensures that sites are able to sustain the implementation of the program without direct participation of the developer. The two-phase training differs from the approach taken in *Tools of the Mind* and provides an alternative model.

The aim of training in *Scaffolding Early Literacy* is to work with rather than replace the early literacy approaches already in place in particular schools and school districts. The aim is to instruct teachers in processes for introducing the early literacy content that support rather than undermine self-regulation. Some of the direct drill and instruction approaches that are used in early literacy instruction can fail to support or unintentionally hinder children's emerging self-regulation. Alternative approaches can take the same content and incorporate it into activities that are supportive of self-regulation. Conventional early literacy instruction may involve a long sequence of children individually demonstrating or reciting while others wait and watch. For example, children may be asked to bring in an object from home that starts with a particular letter. The classroom activity will involve a long sequence of presentations during which children waiting for their turn may become disengaged. Although the intent of this activity is to have children practice speaking and listening skills, in many classrooms, teachers never use this opportunity to introduce more sophisticated vocabulary because they are too busy disciplining these disengaged listeners. In *Scaffolding Early Literacy,* teachers have children work in pairs and ask them to carry out "show and play" rather than "show and tell." The children are asked to incorporate the objects brought from home into a play theme and then engage in play with each other. This provides a context for active engagement, rather than waiting and watching, and role taking and coordinating roles can be practiced while the early literacy content is incorporated. The intent throughout the training is to plan for activities that are highly engaging to the children, incorporate opportunities to practice oral language and early literacy skills, and provide opportunities to practice self-regulation.

Data on the effectiveness of the *Scaffolding Early Literacy* program are now being collected on four sites—recipients of the Early Reading First grants. The instruments used to assess child outcomes vary from site to site and include PPVT, Phonological Awareness Literacy Screening: Pre-kindergarten (PALS-preK; Invernizzi, Sullivan, & Meier, 2001), Get it-Got it-Go (Missall & McConnell, 2004), and Get Ready to Read (http://www.getready-toread.org). Teacher interactions with children and the classroom environment are assessed using the Early Language and Literacy Classroom Observation (ELLCO; Smith & Dickinson, 2002).

The focus on self-regulation means three things for these Vygotskian-based interventions. First, teachers use specifically designed activities to help children practice self-regulation. Second, teachers are also taught how to design contexts that encourage children to engage in "other-regulation," thus, practicing the precursors to self-regulation even without direct adult guidance. One example of a specific activity is the use of "Buddy Reading." Children read to each other in pairs. Children are given cards with pictures on them to help them remember to either "read" (a picture of lips) or "listen" (a picture of an ear). These cards help children to enact the correct behavior and to inhibit inappropriate behavior. Thus, the "listening card" reminds the child who listens that he or she is not supposed to talk. The children practice both book-handling skills and concepts of print at the same time that they are practicing self-regulation. Third, teachers are taught to analyze and then redesign the activity settings where children are less likely to practice self-regulatory behaviors (e.g., the circle time that is too long, the "choice time" in which all choices are determined by the teacher).

For Vygotskians, *play* is the context that best supports self-regulation at the highest level. Teachers are taught how to use this context to encourage self-regulation by extending the natural properties of play. Because dramatic play is child initiated, more instances of self-regulation occur spontaneously. When themes are engaging, they can provide the context for mature play— play with well-defined roles, elaborate scenarios, and imaginative use of props—thus increasing the opportunities for self-regulation. Teachers learn how to help children create rich themes for dramatic play and to pretend without realistic props. Teachers learn how to turn field trips, books, and many other experiences into fodder for play themes. Children learn to think about play and to talk about it before it happens. This planning of the scenario, the roles, and the actions provides the basis for the private speech that helps children internalize and regulate their behaviors. By discussing and planning, children engage in high levels of both "self-" and "other-regulation."

Teachers are taught techniques to help children sustain a high level of make-believe play over longer and longer periods of time in both *Tools of the*

*Mind* and *Scaffolding Early Literacy*. For example, teachers learn how to scaffold interventions—being less and less intrusive as children plan and execute play on their own. A teacher would assume a temporary role in play if children had trouble deciding who is going to play the mommy and the baby in housekeeping. The teacher might only ask a group of children to clarify what they are playing and what they will be doing when she finds that they have begun to run out of ideas to expand their spaceship. When a child is having trouble figuring out who to be in the restaurant play, the teacher may simply make a suggestion of a role and action that child could do to join the others.

## WHAT HAS BEEN LEARNED FROM TRAINING TEACHERS IN THE VYGOTSKIAN APPROACH TO SELF-REGULATION

Classroom teachers tend to have an eclectic approach to teaching, borrowing practices from many theoretical perspectives, even though in many cases these theoretical perspectives are in conflict with each other (e.g., combining a constructivist approach to teaching [in which children are expected to make many choices on their own] with a token economy approach to behavioral management of the classroom [in which teachers keep a tight rein on children's choices by handing out or withholding rewards]). This leads to conflicting expectations for children and practices that lack the consistency needed for children to learn.

The following trends are manifested in a number of practices about self-regulation that teachers subscribe to all at the same time:

- Do nothing, just wait until children become more mature.

- Identify, diagnose, and medicate.

- Institute the "three strikes and you are out" rule in early childhood education classrooms.

- Attempt to change the parenting practices, and if all else fails, blame the parents.

The problem with these practices is that they neither lead to a pro-active stance on the part of the teacher nor do they lead to changes in classroom activities that would actually teach self-regulation. Reconceptualizing self-regulation as something that emerges in all children with different degrees of teacher scaffolding helps teachers to see what they can do to help children develop this critical competency.

To summarize the contribution of the Vygotskian approach to self-regulation, teachers should receive training on:

- The integrated nature of cognitive and social-emotional self-regulation

- How self-regulation develops in young children: "other-regulation" precedes self-regulation

- An understanding of what the teacher's role is in promoting the development of self-regulation

- How to support the development of make-believe play as a vehicle for the development of self-regulation

- How to create cooperative–interactive activities in which children engage in "other-regulation"

- How to model and provide the conditions in which children can use private speech to support their own self-regulation

## CONCLUSIONS AND RECOMMENDATIONS

Both teachers and the community at large are beginning to realize the essential role that self-regulation plays in a child's readiness for school. As programs have upgraded their instruction in early literacy and numeracy, there is a dawning recognition that many children who are having problems learning to read and write have been exposed to the knowledge and skills they need to know but have failed to learn them. This failure to learn often occurs despite the teacher's best efforts to provide appropriate experiences. The cause of such failures to learn academic skills may in fact be due to the children's lack of self-regulation—they cannot pay attention nor remember on purpose. When this is the case, the children cannot take advantage of the learning opportunities that the classroom affords them. Gaps in knowledge and skills cannot be addressed in isolation; it is also critical to address the development of self-regulation as the underlying skill that makes learning possible.

Although the previously described Vygotskian-based approaches were developed for formal preschool settings such as prekindergarten and Head Start, we are beginning to consider the application of these approaches to other settings. The approaches described should certainly work in child care classrooms, but to date, there have been very limited attempts to explore this possibility. Many of the ideas could also be adapted for home-based child care settings as the mixed-age nature of many of these programs would easily encourage the development of play. In such programs, the opportunities to infuse self-regulation activities exist but are different than those developed for larger groups of children. At present, rather than focusing on the range of early care and education settings, attempts to adapt the Vygotskian approach are occurring in the kindergarten age group, with an emphasis on developing specific activities and techniques for helping children transition to the formal school setting of the elementary school.

We argue that addressing self-regulation at the preschool level is critical. Without self-regulation, many children will fall farther and farther behind in their learning of content. Teachers must be trained in methods to support self-regulation to the same degree that they are shown how to teach literacy. Self-regulation, in fact, is one key to future learning.

## REFERENCES

Arnold, D.H., McWilliams, L., & Arnold, E.H. (1998). Teacher discipline and child misbehavior in day care: Untangling causality with correlational data. *Developmental Psychology, 34,* 276–278.

Berk, L.E., & Landeau, S. (1993). Private speech of learning disabled and normally achieving children in classroom academic and laboratory contexts. *Child Development, 64,* 556–571.

Berk, L.E., & Spuhl, S.T. (1995). Maternal interaction, private speech, and task performance in preschool children. *Early Childhood Research Quarterly, 10,* 145–169.

Blair, C. (2002). School readiness: Integrating cognition and emotion in a neurobiological conceptualization of children's functioning at school entry. *American Psychologist, 57*(2), 111–127.

Bodrova, E., & Leong, D.J. (1996). *Tools of the mind: The Vygotskian approach to early childhood education.* New York: Merrill/Prentice Hall.

Bodrova, E., Leong, D.J., Norford, J.S., & Paynter, D.E. (2003). It only looks like child's play. *Journal of Staff Development, 24*(2), 47–51.

Bowman, B.T., Donovan, M.S., & Burns, M.S. (Eds.). (2001). *Eager to learn: Educating our preschoolers.* Washington, DC: National Academy Press.

Broidy, L.M., Nagin, D.S., Tremblay, R.E., Brame, B., Dodge, K.A., Fergusson, D., et al. (2003). Developmental trajectories of childhood disruptive behaviors and adolescent delinquency: A six-site, cross-national study. *Developmental Psychology, 30*(2), 222–245.

Bronson, M.B. (2000). *Self-regulation in early childhood.* New York: Guilford Press.

Brown, A.L., & DeLoach, J.S. (1978). Skills, plans, and self-regulation. In R.S. Sigler (Ed.), *Children's thinking: What develops* (pp. 3–35). Mahwah, NJ: Lawrence Erlbaum Associates.

Brownell, R. (2001). *Expressive One-Word Picture Vocabulary Test (EOWPVT).* Minneapolis, MN: Pearson Assessments.

Burchinal, M.R., Peisner-Feinberg, E.S., Bryant, D.M., & Clifford, R.M. (2000). Children's social and cognitive development and child care quality: Testing for differential associations related to poverty, gender, or ethnicity. *Applied Developmental Science, 4*(3), 149–165.

Cox, J., Daniel, N., & Boston, B. (1985). *Educating able learners: Programs and promising practices.* Austin: University of Texas Press.

Davidson, R.J. (1999). In perspectives on affective styles and their cognitive consequences. In T. Dalgleish & M. Power (Eds.), *Handbook of cognition and emotion* (pp. 103–123). Chichester, England: Wiley.

Davidson, R.J., Jackson, D.C., & Kalin, N.H. (2000). Emotion, plasticity, context, and regulation: Perspectives from affective neuroscience. *Psychological Bulletin, 126,* 890–909.

Derryberry, D., & Reed, M. (1996). Regulatory processes and the development of cognitive representations. *Development and Psychopathology, 8*(1), 215–234.

Diamond, A., & Taylor, C. (1996). Development of an aspect of executive control: Development of the abilities to remember what I said and to "Do as I say, not as I do." *Developmental Psychobiology, 29,* 315–334.

Dunn, L.M., & Dunn, L.M. (1997). *The Peabody Picture Vocabulary Test, Third Edition (PPVT-III).* Circle Pines, MN: AGS Publishing.

Elias, C.L., & Berk, L.E. (2002). Self-regulation in young children: Is there a role for sociodramatic play? *Early Childhood Research Quarterly, 17*(2), 216–238.

Elkonin, D.B. (1978). *Psychologija igry {The psychology of play}.* Moscow: Pedagogika.

Frede, E. (1989). *Preschool Classroom Implementation Rating Scale (PCI).* Ewing, NJ: The College of New Jersey.

French, L. (2004). Science as the center of a coherent, integrated early childhood curriculum. *Early Childhood Research Quarterly, 19*(1), 138–149.

Gartrell, D. (2004). *The power of guidance: Teaching social emotional skills in early childhood classrooms.* Clifton Park, NY: Thompson Delmar Learning.

Goldstein, N.E., Arnold, D.H., Rosenberg, J.L., Stowe, R.M., & Ortiz, C. (2001). Contagion of aggression in day care classrooms as a function of peer and teacher response. *Journal of Educational Psychology, 93*(4), 708–719.

Gresham, F.M., & Elliot, S.N. (1990). *Social Skills Rating System.* Circle Pines, MN: AGS Publishing.

Hamre, B.K., & Pianta, R.C. (2001). Early teacher–child relationships and the trajectory of children's school outcomes through eighth grade. *Child Development, 72*(2), 625–638.

Harris, T.T., & Fuqua, J.D. (2000). What goes around comes around: Building a community of learners through circle times. *Young Children, 55*(1), 44–47.

Harrison, H., Du Rivage, J., & Clarke, J. (1999). *Infants and toddlers self-regulation: An approach for assessment and intervention.* Albuquerque: University of New Mexico.

Hart, D., Atkins, R., & Fegley, S. (2003). Personality development in childhood: A person centered approach. *Monographs of the Society for Research in Child Development, 68*(Serial No. 272, No. 1).

Huffman, L.C., Brian, Y., Del Carment, R., Pedersen, F., Doussard-Roosevelt, J., & Porges, S. (1998). Infant temperament and cardiac vagal tone: Assessments at twelve months of age. *Child Development, 69,* 624–635.

Huffman, L.C., Mehlinger, S.L., & Kerivan, A.S. (2000). *Risk factors for academic and behavioral problems in the beginning of school.* Chapel Hill: University of North Carolina, FPG Child Development Center.

Hwang, Y.S., & Gorrell, J. (2001). *Young children's awareness of self-regulated learning (SRL)* (ERIC Clearinghouse Report No. PS029405). San Bernardino: California State University.

Hyson, M., Copple, C., & Jones, J. (in press). Bringing developmental theory and research into the early childhood classroom: Thinking, emotions, and assessment. In K.A. Renninger & I.E. Sigel (Eds.), *Handbook of child psychology: Child psychology in practice* (Vol. 4). New York: John Wiley & Sons.

Invernizzi, M., Sullivan, A., & Meier, J.D. (2001). *Phonological Awareness Literacy Screening: Pre-kindergarten.* Charlottesville: University of Virginia.

Joseph, G.E., & Strain, P.S. (2003). Comprehensive evidence-based social-emotional curricula for young children: An analysis of efficacious adoption potential. *Topics in Early Childhood Special Education, 23*(2), 65–76.

Kitsantas, A., Zimmerman, B.J., & Cleary, T. (2000). The role of observation and emulation in the development of athletic self-regulation. *Journal of Educational Psychology, 92*(4), 811–817.

Knitzer, J. (2002). *Promoting social and emotional readiness for school: Toward a policy agenda.* Paper presented conference of Set for Success: Building a Strong Foundation for School Readiness Based on the Social-Emotional Development of Young Children, Kansas City, MO.

Kupersmidt, J.B., Bryant, D., & Willoughby, M. (2000). Prevalence of aggressive behaviors among preschoolers in head start and community child care programs. *Behavioral Disorders, 26*(1), 42–52.

Kusche, C.A., & Greenberg, M.T. (1994). *The paths curriculum.* Seattle, WA: Developmental Research and Programs.

Ladd, G., Birch, S., & Buhs, E. (1999). Children's social and scholastic lives in kindergarten: Related spheres of influence? *Child Development, 70,* 1373–1400.

LeDoux, J. (1996). *The emotional brain.* New York: Simon & Schuster.

Levine, M.D., Swartz, C., Reed, M., Hill, M., Wakely, M., Lind, S., et al. (1997). *"Schools attuned" syllabus.* Chapel Hill: University of North Carolina School of Medicine.

Lewit, E., & Baker, L.S. (1995). School readiness. *The Future of Children, 5,* 128–139.

Lyon, G.R., & Krasnegor, N.A. (1996). *Attention, memory, and executive function.* Baltimore: Paul H. Brookes Publishing Co.

Missal, K.N., & McConnell, S.R. (2004). *Technical report: Psychometric characteristics of individual growth and development indicators—picture naming, rhyming, & alliteration.* Minneapolis, MN: Center for Early Education and Development.

Murray, K.T., & Kochanska, G. (2002). Effortful control: Factor structure and relation to externalizing and internalizing behaviors. *Journal of Abnormal Child Psychology, 30*(5), 503–514.

Nagin, D.S., & Tremblay, R.E. (1999). Trajectories of boys' physical aggression, opposition and hyperactivity on the path to physically violent and nonviolent juvenile delinquency. *Child Development, 70*(5), 1181–1196.

Perry, N.E. (1998). Young children's self-regulated learning and contexts that support it. *Journal of Educational Psychology, 90*(4), 715–729.

Perry, N.E., Phillips, D.A., & Dowler, J. (2004). Examining features of tasks and their potential to promote self-regulated learning. *Teachers College Record, 106*(9), 1854–1878.

La Paro, K., Pianta, R., & Stuhlman, M. (2003). Classroom Assessment Scoring System (CLASS): Findings from the pre-k year. *The Elementary School Journal, 104,* 409–426.

Ravner, C.C., & Knitzer, J. (2002). *Ready to enter: What research tells policymakers about strategies to promote social and emotional school readiness among three- and four-year-old children.* New York: National Center for Children in Poverty, Mailman School of Public Health, Columbia University.

Rimm-Kaufman, S., Pianta, R.C., & Cox, M. (2000). Teachers' judgments of problems in the transition to school. *Early Childhood Research Quarterly, 15,* 147–166.

Rutter, M., & Sroufe, L. (2000). Developmental psychopathology: Concepts and challenges. *Development & Psychopathology, 12*(3), 265–296.

Saarni, C., Mumme, D.L., & Campos, J.J. (1998). Emotional development: Action, communication and understanding. In W. Damon (Series Ed.) & N. Eisenberg (Vol. Ed.), *Handbook of child psychology (5th ed.). Vol. 3: Social, emotional and personality development* (pp. 237–309). Hoboken, NJ: John Wiley & Sons.

Schonkoff, J.P., & Phillips, D.A. (Eds.). (2000). *From neurons to neighborhoods: The science of early childhood development.* Washington, DC: National Academy Press.

Smith, M.W., & Dickinson, D.K. (with Sangeorge, A., & Anastasopoulos, L.) (2002). *Early Language and Literacy Classroom Observation (ELLCO) Toolkit, Research Edition.* Baltimore: Paul H. Brookes Publishing Co.

Smith, S., Davidson, S., Weinsenfeld, G., & Katasaros, S. (2001). *Supports for Early Literacy Assessment (SELA).* New York: New York University.

Stright, A.D., & Supplee, L.H. (2002). Children's self-regulatory behaviors during teacher-directed, seat-work, and small-group instructional contexts. *Journal of Educational Research, 95*(4), 235–244.

Thompson, R.A. (2001, November). *The roots of school readiness in social-emotional development.* Paper presented at the conference of Set for Success: Building a Strong Foundation for School Readiness Based on the Social-Emotional Development of Young Children, Kansas City, MO.

Vygotsky, L.S. (1956). Obuchenije i razvitije v doshkol'nom vozraste [Learning and development in preschool children]. In *Izbrannye psychologicheskije trudy {Selected psychological studies}* (pp. 426–452). Moscow: RSFSR Academy of Pedagogical Sciences.

Vygotsky, L.S. (1977). Play and its role in the mental development of the child. In M. Cole (Ed.), *Soviet developmental psychology* (pp.76–98). White Plains, NY: M.E. Sharpe.

Wertsch, J.V. (1979). The regulation of human action and the give-new organization of private speech. In G. Ziven (Ed.), *The development of self-regulation through private speech* (pp. 79–98). New York: John Wiley & Sons.

Whitehurst, G.J., & Lonigan, C. (2001). *Get Ready to Read screening tool.* Lebanon, IN: Pearson Early Learning Group.

Williams, C.O., Ballard, W.S., Tighe, P.L., Dalton, E.F., & Amori, B.A. (1991). *IDEA Oral Language Proficiency Test.* Brea, CA: Ballard & Tighe Publishers.

Willoughby, M., Kupersmidt, J.B., & Bryant, D. (2001). Overt and covert dimensions of antisocial behavior in early childhood. *Journal of Abnormal Child Psychology, 29*(3), 177–187.

Winsler, A., Diaz, R.M., Atencio, D.J., McCarthy, E.M., & Chabay, L.A. (2000). Verbal self-regulation over time in preschool children at risk for attention and behavior problems. *Journal of Child Psychology and Psychiatry, 7,* 875–886.

Woodcock, R.W., & Mather, N. (1989). *WJ-R Tests of Cognitive Ability—standard and supplemental batteries: Examiner's manual.* In R.W. Woodcock & M.B. Johnson, *Woodcock-Johnson Pscyho-Educational Battery–Revised.* Allen, TX: DLM Teaching Resources.

Yoshikawa, H., & Knitzer, J. (1997). *Lessons from the field: Head start mental health strategies to meet changing needs.* New York: National Center for Children in Poverty, Columbia University, Mailman School of Public Health.

Zelazo, P.D., Muller, U., Frye, D., & Marcovich, S. (2003). The development of executive function in early childhood. *Monographs of the Society for Research in Child Development, 68*(Serial 274, No 3).

Zimmerman, B.J. (2002). Achieving academic excellence: A self-regulatory perspective. In M. Ferrar (Ed.), *The pursuit of excellence through education* (pp. 85–110). Mahwah, NJ: Lawrence Erlbaum Associates.

Zimmerman, B.J., & Kitsantas, A. (1997). Developmental phases in self-regulation shifting from process goals to outcome goals. *Journal of Educational Psychology, 89*(1), 29–36.

# Designing Models for Professional Development at the Local, State, and National Levels

NAOMI KARP

J ohn Wooden, the legendary basketball coach at the University of California, Los Angeles, led his teams to an astounding 10 national collegiate basketball championships. He was an expert motivator, and when he deemed effort at practices to be inadequate, it is reported that Wooden would remind his teams that failing to prepare is preparing to fail. That phrase rings all too true for what is happening in the United States, both in early childhood education and early childhood professional development.

As of 2005, policy makers and educators expect young children to come to kindergarten having mastered many competencies and concepts that they used to have to know when they entered first grade. Unfortunately, too many young children lack access to high-quality early learning experiences, opportunities, and programs that will adequately prepare them to be successful in kindergarten and beyond. Thus, by not ensuring that *all* young children have access to high-quality programs, we, as a society, are preparing these children to fail.

According to the National Research Council (2001), young children from families with limited resources or with multiple challenges are much more likely to be successful in school if they attend *high-quality* early learning programs. Unfortunately, many children from families with low incomes participate in early care and education settings of such low quality that their learning and development may be put in jeopardy.

It is known that the achievement gap begins long before many children reach the front doors of their schools. However, research indicates that early childhood care and education settings that provide young children with enriched curricula and well-trained teachers help to improve the chances that children from families with low incomes will succeed in school (American Association of Colleges for Teacher Education [AACTE], 2004; National Research Council, 2001). The National Research Council (2001) report also found that teacher education and preparation are central to the quality of an early childhood program, and this quality predicts young children's learning and development outcomes. The report further showed that "responsive interpersonal relationships with teachers nurture young children's dispositions to learn" (p. 6) and that there is a consistent relationship between a teacher's appropriate, positive behaviors and the amount of formal education and training that a teacher has received.

Unfortunately, early childhood teachers in the United States are not receiving high-quality educations. Spodek and Saracho (1990) concluded that early childhood teachers as a whole are less educated and not as prepared for teaching tasks than any other group; yet, early childhood teachers may have more influence on children than teachers at any other age level. Progress since that publication has been painfully slow.

If we, as a society, are ever going to close the achievement gap, we have to develop early childhood professional development curricula and models that prepare teachers who in turn can prepare children to succeed. For a variety of reasons, however, U.S. early childhood professional development programs still face enormous hurdles and are not on a par with programs in other countries (Committee for Economic Development, 2002; Organization for Economic Cooperation and Development, 2001).

The U.S. Department of Education identified five "essentials for excellence" in early childhood programs (2000, p. 7):

1. Interdisciplinary preparation for diverse early childhood settings

2. A system that balances specialized preparation with realism and accessibility

3. Faculty with resources needed to prepare tomorrow's professionals

4. Structures and processes that will support and sustain innovation

5. Tools to define, recognize, and assess high-quality early childhood teacher preparation

In addition, the U.S. Department of Education (2000) identified four other challenges facing the field:

1. Early childhood professional preparation covers a range of education settings, including community-based program classes, 2-year programs, 4-year programs, and graduate-level studies.

2. The fact that early childhood professional development programs are dispersed across multiple higher education settings results in a workforce that receives different levels of information about school reform, assessments, and standards. Thus, too many teachers may be poorly prepared to understand and analyze new standards, curricula, and assessment practices as they relate to and impact on developmentally appropriate practices.

3. New methods of assessing performance in early childhood teacher preparation will result in programs developing new standards for measuring teachers' competencies, knowledge, and practice.

4.  Early childhood teachers' knowledge of subject matter and content needs to be strengthened, especially in language and reading. Traditionally, early childhood education as a field has shied away from curriculum and content. However, this is a critical area if young children and their teachers are to be successful.

The National Center for Early Development and Learning (NCEDL, 2002) and Gwen Morgan (2003) identified some of the policy factors that impede progress toward improving early childhood professional development. For example, all 50 states have different rules and regulations affecting the training qualifications and requirements of the adults who spend their days with our youngest children. There are also vast discrepancies among the states in funding policies, teacher salaries, licensing, child–adult ratios, and other factors that impact program quality, all of which affect child outcomes (NCEDL, 2002).

In addition, in 2000, NCEDL staff conducted the National Survey of Early Childhood Teacher Preparation Programs in Institutions of Higher Education. The purpose of the survey was to establish baseline information regarding the number of programs that offered early childhood education degrees, characteristics of the faculty, and the actual courses and training experiences the students received. The data from this survey run counter to what the research tells us about high quality. Some key findings from the survey include the following:

1.  There are more than 1,200 programs across the country, and almost one third of all institutions of higher education offer some type of early childhood education professional development program. However, it is difficult to identify the programs because they are spread across different colleges and departments and have different names.

2.  Most institutions offer an associate's degree or lower-level certificates, and less than half award a bachelor's degree in early childhood education.

3.  The faculty tends to be highly Caucasian and non-Hispanic, not reflecting the diversity of today's children. When comparing early childhood faculty with the faculty within the larger institution, the data show that early childhood teacher preparation programs have a small number of faculty (average 3.4), and they serve a larger number of students The typical student to full-time faculty ratio of 61 to 1 is 60% higher than the 38.7 to 1 ratio of higher education institutions as a whole.

4.  Fifty-four percent of the faculty members in early childhood programs work part-time, whereas 45% work part-time at the institutions in which these programs are housed.

5.  Early childhood programs based in 2-year institutions have less than half the number of full-time faculty members. When compared with 4-year institutions, 2-year institutions have twice as many part-time faculty.

6.  Several key weaknesses in course work were revealed by the survey:

    •  Close to 80% of bachelor's degree programs indicate that preparing students to work with young children with disabilities was part of their mission, yet only 60% offer one or more courses in the area.

    •  Ninety-five percent of the associate's degree programs indicate that their programs include a focus on infants and toddlers, yet only 60% require one or more courses, and 63% require practicum experience.

    •  Less than 50% of programs require a course in working with racially and ethnically diverse children, and very small numbers of programs require any courses focusing on children whose families do not speak English.

7.  A major, ongoing problem is access to university-level courses by those who have attained an associate's degree.

The findings from this survey again illustrate how U.S. society is preparing early childhood teachers—and, ultimately, the children with whom they spend their days—to fail.

Another major policy issue is the fact that vast areas in the United States are rural, poor, and lacking well-prepared early childhood teachers who are able to prepare young children to succeed. It is necessary to develop research-based strategies for educating adults in these geographic areas who can then provide young children in the Mississippi Delta; on reservations; in isolated, rural towns; and in other areas lacking both fiscal and educational resources with the opportunities and experiences needed to achieve to high standards.

Section III of this book discusses some of the hurdles and some of the creative, evidenced-based, ongoing efforts underway to improve early childhood professional development. The author of Chapter 8 says that the United States currently bases professional development on the three "C's": courses, credentials, and curriculum (or materials). Because there are such wide discrepancies in the quality of early childhood settings, the author theorizes that professional development should be structured so that there is an emphasis and focus on the quality of interactions between teachers and children rather than on the three "C's." This new model calls for new measures that assess classroom practices and give teachers feedback on how to improve those practices.

Chapter 9 discusses the challenges facing states: aligning early childhood learning objectives with specific content standards used in elementary schools and making sure that teacher education courses align with children's learning standards. The authors focus on how Ohio is addressing this thorny problem, specifically in the area of early literacy development. Looking at Child Development Associate (CDA) credential, associate's degree, and bachelor's degree professional development programs, they point out where there is congruence and where there is misalignment. They also call for the development of new, easy-to-use measures to examine alignment.

Chapter 10 provides an historical perspective of how National Association for the Education of Young Children (NAEYC) standards for early childhood professional development have evolved since the 1980s. The standards influence teacher preparation at associate's, initial-licensure, and advanced levels. Because these standards are used in institutions of higher education, they also are used to evaluate higher education programs and to determine if programs meet standards for recognition by NAEYC and the National Council for the Accreditation of Teacher Education (NCATE). The new standards not only call for raising the bar in actual teacher preparation requirements but also require practitioners, researchers, and policy makers to work together to analyze the impact that this new level of rigor requires to implement and what the outcomes will be on both teachers and children.

It is time that policy makers, educators, and society as a whole address in depth the policy and implementation issues related to early childhood professional development. It is critical to create a seamless system of both high-quality early childhood care and education and high-quality early childhood professional development programs. As former president Clinton noted in an April 15, 2000, speech, "Pearl Buck once said, 'If our American way of life fails the child, it fails us all.'" The American way of life must include redoubled efforts to close the achievement gap so that its most vulnerable citizens can be successful in school and beyond. Failing our children cannot be an acceptable option.

## REFERENCES

American Association of Colleges for Teacher Education. (June 2004). *The early childhood challenge: Preparing high quality teachers for a changing society.* Washington, DC: Author.

Clinton, W.J. (2000, April 15). *Presidential radio address on preventing youth violence.* Retrieved April 15, 2005, from http://www.clintonfoundation.org/legacy/041500-presidential-radio-address-on-preventing-youth-violence.htm

Committee for Economic Development. (2002). *Preschool for all: Investing in a productive and just society. A statement by the research committee of the Committee for Economic Development.* New York: Author.

Morgan, G. (2003). Regulatory policy. In D. Cryer & R.M. Clifford (Eds.), *Early childhood education and care in the U.S.A.* (pp. 87–105). Baltimore: Paul H. Brookes Publishing Co.

National Center for Early Development and Learning. (2000a, May). *Spotlight #22: Directory of teacher-prep institutions.* Chapel Hill, NC: Author.

National Center for Early Development and Learning. (2000b, November). *Spotlight #28: Teacher prep and diversity.* Chapel Hill, NC: Author.

National Center for Early Development and Learning. (2002, Winter). *Regulation of child care: Early childhood research and policy briefs.* Chapel Hill: Frank Porter Graham Child Development Institute, University of North Carolina.

National Research Council. (2000). *Eager to learn: Educating our preschoolers.* Washington, DC: National Academy Press.

National Research Council. (2001). *Eager to learn: Educating our preschoolers.* Washington, DC: National Academy Press.

Organization for Economic Cooperation and Development. (2001). *Starting strong: Early childhood education and care.* Paris, France: Author.

Spodek, B., & Saracho, O. (1990) Introduction. In B. Spodek & O. Saracho (Eds.), *Yearbook in early childhood education: Early childhood teacher preparation* (Vol. 1, p. viii). New York: Teachers College Press.

U.S. Department of Education. (2000). *New teachers for a new century: The future of early childhood education.* Washington, DC: Author.

# CHAPTER 9

# Standardized Observation and Professional Development

## A Focus on Individualized Implementation and Practices

ROBERT C. PIANTA

Widespread and systematic use of standardized observation in early education and care settings from toddlerhood through the early elementary grades has the potential to reshape professional development and address major shortcomings in education and care provided to young children. Well-validated methods to observe teachers' and caregivers' actual interactions and practices with children have been used in numerous large-scale research studies and in state-supported efforts to improve program quality such that these instruments capture aspects of interaction and practice that promote children's developmental growth and competence. As a result, it is possible to envision a system of professional development in which caregivers and teachers of young children draw on systematic, objective observations of their practices and interactions with children to engage in a range of instructional, informational, and experiential professional development activities that are directly aimed at improving these teachers' own individual practices and interactions with children. In this way, the focus of professional development is improvement and growth in teachers' own implementation practices rather than an emphasis on coursework, generic practices, and curricula (Hamre, Bridges, & Fuller, 2003). The end result of an observationally based system is a redefining of professional development and in-service training from a coursework/generic approach to a teacher-focused approach, which concentrates on aspects of classroom practice and quality and has direct and demonstrated links to child outcomes and teacher well-being. This chapter presents the rationale for using classroom observation as the linchpin of professional development in early education and care and the ways in which such a system addresses major shortcomings in the delivery of education and care services to young children.

## THE POLICY CONTEXT FOR CENTERING PROFESSIONAL DEVELOPMENT ON OBSERVATION

Several realities focus attention on professional development in early care and education as a mechanism for addressing shortcomings observed in the larger K–12 educational system. For example, as in K–12, there is increasing emphasis on accountability, especially for publicly funded early care and education programs to show desired results in terms of increased school readiness. Furthermore, there are serious concerns about equity and access to high-quality programming, such as when many children from less advantaged backgrounds—even when enrolled in early care and education programs—receive lower-quality experiences than their peers with more advantages (Bryant, Clifford, Early, et al., 2002; Pianta, 2003a). Inconsistency in findings regarding associations between professional development and training and the quality of early care and education settings (see Chapter 4 of this book) raises concerns about whether current models of professional development are adequate. Together, these issues are serious challenges for policy makers attempting to formulate mechanisms for implementing early education and care programs that positively affect child outcomes at scale.

## Accountability

There is little doubt that public attention to the education and care of young children is at record levels. Child care for infants and toddlers remains one of the single most discussed issues in American society. Such discussions involve debates about the merits and liabilities associated with nonparental care, ways to improve and ensure high quality in care settings, and the financial costs associated with care and its improvement (National Institute of Child Health and Human Development [NICHD] Early Child Care Research Network, 1993, 1998). Regardless of one's stance on the issues reflected in these debates, the evidence is clear that exposure to nonparental care is the norm in the United States and the public's investment in such care (whether through taxpayer-based government expenditure or private financing of care) is considerable.

Moving up the age range, investment in preschool education and care programs—whether through public, state-supported prekindergartens, community-based preschool, or private center-based child care—has soared (Blank, Shulman, & Ewen, 1999). Since the mid-1990s, a movement has emerged to support public funding of prekindergarten programs for 4-year-olds, largely to address the educational needs of children who live in poverty or face related social disadvantages. Increasingly, the worlds of early childhood and elementary education are merging. For example, national surveys of kindergarten teachers and state directors of early childhood education programs indicate that nearly half of public elementary schools house a program for children younger than age 5 (Clifford, Early, & Hills, 1999). By the mid-1990s, nearly a million children younger than age 5 were enrolled in programs in some way tied to schools, including those related to the Individuals with Disabilities Education Act (IDEA) and its amendments, Head Start, Title 1, and local and state initiatives (Clifford et al., 1999).

The unprecedented level of investment in and attention to early care and education has taken place in a policy climate that emphasizes accountability. In particular, this context expects that when public funds are spent for education and care, those settings should be held responsible for their contribution to desired outcomes (e.g., positive caregiving and developmental stimulation, readiness for school). Regardless of one's position on the broader issue of accountability per se as practiced and implemented, accountability assessments even for early education and care settings rest on direct assessment of children. This is exemplified by the adoption of child outcome accountability assessments in Head Start, the use of standardized assessments and benchmarks for child performance in prekindergartens, and a growing parental interest in knowing what contributions center-based child care experiences make to their children's school readiness.

Adopting policies and practices that view direct assessment of children as the only means for ensuring accountability of early education and care settings is markedly limited for young children for a number of reasons. The technical adequacy (reliability, validity) of direct assessments for young children is widely recognized as being lower than that of older children, in large part because children's competences are fairly unstable and situationally dependent (La Paro & Pianta, 2000). Furthermore, because the competencies of children are greatly dependent on the quality of their experiences in education and care settings, it makes sense to assess, for accountability purposes, the quality of those settings (Pianta, 2003b). From this perspective, accountability assessments directly target the resources for development in education and care settings, not the emerging, unstable, and difficult-to-assess competencies of children who may or may not be exposed to high-quality resources.

Programs of research establish that the kind of instruction and interactions with adults that occur in early education and care settings have reliable and detectable effects on young children's achievement and social competence (e.g., Barnett, Young, & Schweinhart, 1998; Howes, Phillipsen, & Peisner-Feinberg, 2000; Meyer, Waldrop, Hastings, & Linn, 1993; Morrison, 1999; NICHD Early Child Care Research Network, 1996, 2002b; Peisner-Feinberg & Burchinal, 1997; Ripple, Gilliam, Chanana, & Zigler, 1999). These findings strongly support the view that for young children, experiences in classrooms matter and that interactions between children and teachers are a primary mechanism through which classroom experiences affect development. In fact, some states' systems for rating or monitoring child care settings include direct observations of the environment, and making such information available on line appears to have a small but detectable effect on the quality of care (Witte & Queralt, 2004).

Given these realities about classroom experiences and standardized assessments of child functioning, one way to address the mandate for accountability is to assess the nature and quality of early education and care settings, rather than children—in a sense, to move from assessment of "product" or "output" to an assessment of "input" or "process." This focus transforms questions of accountability such as "Are early education and care programs working?" to "Are early education and care programs providing children with experiences of the sort that are known to relate to positive outcomes?" and thereby acknowledges that development is influenced not only by education and care settings but even more so by experiences in the family (NICHD Early Child Care Research Network, 1998). Yet as of 2004, there are very few systems of accountability focused on classroom or setting quality in early education and care.

## Access

It is widely recognized that access to high-quality early education and care programming is a key component of improving child outcomes (e.g., school readiness) at scale and that access to high-quality programming should be a primary concern of policy. Most state legislation that supports the implementation and expansion of prekindergarten programs for 4-year-olds emphasizes that such programs should or must be of high quality (Bryant, Clifford, Early, et al., 2002). Similarly, state and federal legislation on child care, particularly concerning subsidies, also emphasizes quality as a key criterion (Hamre et al., 2003). In the elementary grades, federal legislation, such as the No Child Left Behind (NCLB) Act of 2001 (PL 107-110), also emphasizes the importance of high-quality instruction. In fact, it would be difficult to find any policy document pertaining to the education and care of young children that did not link high-quality programming, access, and equity. Conversely, the embrace of high quality as a standard for programming is marginally supported by extant findings that show only small associations between quality and child outcomes in child care (NICHD Early Child Care Research Network, 2002b) and in early elementary (NICHD Early Child Care Research Network, 2002a) settings. The debate often has a "glass half empty/half full" tone because the large number of careful studies that do provide evidence for quality–outcome associations are often small in terms of increments in explained variance. It should also be noted that the quality–outcome associations detected in most natural history studies, such as the NICHD Study of Early Child Care and Youth Development (NICHD Early Child Care Research Network, 2002b), reflect the range and level of quality currently available in communities, not what the range and level of quality could be under different circumstances.

Despite universal recognition of the importance of quality, systematic information is lacking at state, local, or federal levels to gauge whether children are attending high-quality programs or to determine ways of improving program quality that focus on the actual interactions between children and teachers in classrooms—the form of quality that matters most for child development. This lack of focus in policy and professional development may be in part responsible for doubts expressed concerning further investments in quality or training, given the small associations detected between quality and child outcomes (see Chapter 4 and Hamre et al., 2003, for more detailed discussions). For example, although state legislation may mandate high quality, regulations typically codify the legislative mandate in terms of structural quality indicators such as teacher credentialing or class size (Hamre et al., 2003; Ripple et al., 1999). It is critical to understand that these distal or structural indicators of quality are by no means strongly related or equivalent to quality as observed in actual classrooms (NICHD Early Child Care Research Network, 1999, 2002a, 2004; Hamre et al., 2003). In short, even if every single teacher or classroom was in compliance with state regulations or mandates for high quality (e.g., have bachelors' degrees in early childhood education; use a state-supported curriculum), there would be considerable variation in the actual experiences offered to children in the early education and care settings staffed by those teachers, and equity or access to high quality would by no means be ensured (Pianta et al., in press). In short, the quality metrics used to address the policy concerns of access and equity are disconnected from children's and adults' interactions in early education and care settings.

## Professional Development

A primary mechanism to improve access to high-quality early education and care and equity in the distribution of quality is professional development—systematic attention to training the workforce in these settings (Chapter 4; Hamre et al., 2003). Few members of the education and care communities doubt that professional development for the early education workforce is of paramount importance for the delivery of high-quality services (Caspary, 2002). The combination of a shortage of teachers and skilled care providers, the expansion of educational programming slots for prekindergarten children and the demand for child care, and an increased emphasis on instruction (particularly in literacy and language development) combine to make preservice and in-service professional development a linchpin in the development of high-quality programming for children younger than age 6. Yet the vast majority of professional development for quality improvement does not directly link to or focus on actual interactions between children and adults in real settings, particularly for teachers who are already trained and certified (Caspary, 2002; Hamre et al., 2003).

Reviews of professional development in early education and care (Hamre et al., 2003) and empirical reports demonstrating links between child care teachers' practices and child outcomes  suggest that in contrast with teachers who have less formal education or no specific training in early childhood education, teachers with bachelor's degrees, specifically in early childhood education, provide somewhat higher quality learning experiences for children in their care (e.g., Burchinal, Peisner-Feinberg, Pianta, & Howes, 2002; NICHD Early Child Care Research Network, 1999). It has also been demonstrated that receiving training and professional development related to early childhood curricula or practices is related to teachers' increased sensitivity and stimulation (for language) in interactions with young children in child care homes (Clarke-Stewart, Vandell, Burchinal, O'Brien, & McCartney, 2002) and centers (Burchinal et al., 2002; NICHD Early Child Care Research Network, 1999). However, it is quite clear that these links between training or education and quality are by no means consistent or strong—instead, the literature is filled with a mixture of null associations between training and quality and small, albeit significant, associations (Chapter 4; Hamre et al., 2003). This state of the literature leads to conclusions that the approaches to professional development (e.g., general education, training in general methods) as well as research on professional development (e.g., using global indicators of quality, relying on teacher self-report) are simply too general to provide useful information (for policy or for practice) regarding training that provides teachers with the knowledge and skill to alter their interactions with children in ways that improve child outcomes (Hamre et al., 2003; Pianta et al., in press). In short, the fairly mixed and weak linkages of professional development and training with quality may be a function of a very diffuse and generalized approach.

Studies assessing teachers' knowledge and attributes reveal that these factors are key aspects of producing high-quality interactions. For example, child care providers' psychological characteristics are significantly associated with child care quality in terms of their behavior and interactions with children; caregivers' nonauthoritarian attitudes about child rearing predict more positive parenting behavior in home-based care (Clarke-Stewart et al., 2002) and in centers (NICHD Early Child Care Research Network, 1999). In addition, caregivers' depression is associated with more intense negative caregiver–child interactions, including those involving harshness and withdrawal (Hamre & Pianta, 2004a, 2004b). These psychological attributes have received virtually no attention in the literature on classroom quality. In one conceptualization of teacher attributes related to quality, Howes, James, and Ritchie (2003) emphasized that teachers' perceptions of relationships with children under their care is itself an indicator of the quality of children's experiences in that setting, and the researchers demonstrated that closeness and conflict in teachers' experiences with children predict a range of child outcomes. This literature on teacher attitudes and relational experiences suggests that psychological processes involved in interactions with children play a key role in the actual quality of those interactions, yet such processes are by and large not the focus of most professional development activities (Hamre et al., 2003).

As is summarized in comprehensive reviews of the role of professional preparation in the quality of early education and care (Chapter 4; Hamre et al.,

2003), the policy and practice question has always been "How much is enough?" in terms of formal training, coursework, or degrees. When framed in these terms, the assessed outcome of most professional development is whether teachers attended the activity, took the course, or completed the degree program—not whether the practices and quality of care offered to children in their classrooms were improved. Again, the metric used to evaluate the success of policy—in this case policies aimed at improving quality programming for young children through professional development—is not a direct reflection of children's experiences of such programming and is at best a fairly distal indicator. It is not surprising that several of the conclusions and future directions mentioned in the comprehensive Policy Analysis for California Education (PACE) review (Hamre et al., 2003) pertained to the need to focus more directly on the experiences offered to children in early education and care and the specific knowledge and experiences acquired by adults (e.g., teachers, care providers) that can be causally linked to improvement in the classroom.

## WHAT IS KNOWN ABOUT CHILDREN'S EXPERIENCES IN EARLY EDUCATION AND CARE SETTINGS?

Since the mid-1990s, several large-scale observational research efforts related to early education and care have reported results pertaining to the quality of experiences offered to children from toddlerhood through the early grades. In addition, some states have embarked on programs of observation in which state-representative samples of preschool settings have been observed (Marshall et al., 2002). This work is relevant to this discussion for two reasons. First, naturalistic observations of programs in action, particularly those that have been implementing services for some time, offer a window on the products of the professional development systems in place. That is, given that teachers and care providers are required to participate in training and professional development activities, observations of a large number of classroom and care settings can function as a sort of "temperature taking" in relation to what the current professional development system is producing. Second, investigators using both research- and evaluation-focused efforts have had to address successfully the challenges posed by observing many classrooms in many locations under very diverse circumstances—conditions that reflect the challenges of observing at scale. Thus, a by-product of the rigorous training and reliability regimens necessary to conduct objective, standardized observation studies has been a set of extensively field-tested procedures for measurement, psychometrics, and validation that is a tremendous resource for applications of observational technology at scale. The success of these programs in meeting these challenges also indicates the fairly mature state of the infrastructure for observation at scale—in hundreds and even thousands of early education and care settings.

Large-scale observation work relies on extensive research and development conducted over the course of decades, albeit at a smaller scale, regarding the nature and aspects of experiences in early education and care settings that produce gains for children (e.g., Ramey et al., 2000) and studies on ways to best measure those setting characteristics. This work is foundational to a body of knowledge on how to define and measure quality informing large-scale research on thousands of early education and care settings. Large-scale observational studies have included the observations of approximately 1,000 children in child care settings at 24, 36, and 54 months of age and in first-grade classrooms (study conducted by the NICHD Study of Early Child Care and Youth Development [NICHD Early Child Care Research Network, 1996, 1999, 2002a]); more than 240 prekindergarten classrooms in six states (Bryant, Clifford, Early, et al., 2002), 223 kindergarten classrooms in three states (Pianta, La Paro, Payne, Cox, & Bradley, 2002); and global quality in Head Start settings (Head Start Bureau, 1998). As a set, these results capture the best estimate to date of the state of American early education and care in terms of the actual experiences offered to children, and as previously noted, provide a window on the products of the professional development system in its current form.

Two main conclusions can be drawn from this work. First, despite variation from study to study, the quality of early education and care settings is, on average, mediocre regarding the kind of interactions and stimulation known to produce developmental gains for children. Second, there is tremendous variation in quality offered to children from time to time or setting to setting; sometimes this variation is systematically related to factors such as family income or teacher characteristics, and other times there is little or no relation between quality and the parameters used to regulate or influence it (see NICHD Early Child Care Research Network, 2002a; Hamre et al., 2003; Pianta et al., 2002).

The National Center for Early Development and Learning (NCEDL)'s six-state study of prekindergarten (Bryant, Clifford, Pianta, Howes, & Burchinal, 2002) offers the best information on prekindergarten quality and child outcomes. Supporting the need for continued capacity building focused on quality, the NCEDL study reported marked variation in the nature and quality of educational experiences offered to children in prekindergarten programs, and that on average, there is considerable room for improvement. It is important to note that the six states participating in the NCEDL study were chosen because they had all been implementing prekindergarten programs for at least 5 years and thus had a somewhat mature infrastructure. More specifically, across the 250 classrooms sampled in the six states, overall average classroom quality was rather mediocre (below the 5 level on the Early Childhood Environment Rating Scale–Revised Edition [ECERS-R], Harms, Clifford, & Cryer, 1998), with the full range of quality represented. Ratings of classroom productivity and emotional quality were below the mid-point on a seven-point scale despite teachers being fully credentialed and experienced and using an organized curriculum (Pianta, Howes, et al., 2003). Individual children in some classrooms were exposed to few, if any, instances of any form of literacy-focused activities, whereas in other classrooms children received up to almost an hour of literacy-related activities, including narrative storytelling, practice with letters, participation in rhyming games, and listening activities. In terms of social processes, nearly all teachers reported fairly high levels of relational conflict with at least one student, and observations showed wide variation in the emotional and instructional quality of teachers' interactions with individual children. On average, these classrooms were rated as moderately low on the use of effective management practices and on teacher sensitivity, indicating that the social interactions between children and adults were ineffective in regulating children's experience.

In kindergarten and first grade, the pattern of mediocrity and variation is the same (NICHD Early Child Care Research Network, 2002a; Pianta et al., 2002). For example, children typically received instruction in whole-group experiences, but in some classrooms children were never taught in a whole group and in others this was the mode of instruction all day. Although literacy instruction was the predominant activity offered to children, children in a substantial number of classrooms were offered no literacy activities at all. In some kindergarten or first-grade classrooms, 100% of the activity observed in a morning-long block was organized as teacher-directed instruction. In others, none of the activities observed could be coded as this form of instruction. In some of these classrooms, children were engaged in center activities for the entire observation; in others, center activities never occurred. How teachers interacted with a target child was also highly variable.

While acknowledging the wide variation across classrooms, mean scores suggest a picture of the typical early education classroom for prekindergarten through third grade: whole-group instruction, a positive social environment, and low levels of productivity and engagement in learning-related activities. These environments can be characterized as socially positive but instructionally passive: children listen and watch, much time is spent on routines or management of materials, and children have few interactions with teachers that have an explicit instructional dimension or that provide feedback on child performance. Despite being generally well-organized and busy places, classrooms appear low in *intentionality,* a term that refers to directed, designed interactions between children and teachers in which teachers purposefully challenge, scaffold, and extend children's skills.

To summarize, the high levels of between-setting variability and fairly low levels of observed quality (variously defined), even in samples in which all the teachers are credentialed (e.g., NICHD Early Child Care Research Network, 2002a; Pianta et al., 2002; Pianta et al., in press), can be interpreted to suggest that the current system of training and professional development does not en-sure equal access to high-quality early education and care experiences. Further-more, another major finding across all of these studies and age ranges (a finding consistent with the PACE review of professional development) is that variation in factors such as teacher education, credentialing, or training, as well as the use of any or specific curricula, do not bear consistent or strong relations to observed quality or to child outcomes (Hamre et al., 2003; Pianta et al., in press). This lack of consistent or strong association between training and quality suggests the current system of professional development is simply not up to the task of ensuring high-quality experiences for children.

## LINKING POLICY, PROFESSIONAL DEVELOPMENT, AND OUTCOMES: FOCUSING ON CLASSROOM PROCESS AND INTERACTIONS

Children whose families have low incomes or who attend high-poverty or low-resource settings (Pianta, Howes, et al., 2003) may be particularly unlikely to experience high-quality child care environment. However, Head Start settings may provide higher quality than the typical setting for children living in poverty who do not attend Head Start programs (Head Start Bureau, 1998). The set of classroom, program, or teacher parameters used to regulate class-room/setting quality does not appear to ensure high quality, nor does profes-sional development as currently implemented. However, observations of class-room quality are not used as a source of feedback in a system in which this finding is associated with policy parameters, professional development, and child and teacher outcomes. In short, most policy and professional develop-ment discussions and initiatives lack information on the quality of classroom and care setting experiences offered to children.

A mechanism that links early education and care policies (e.g., class size, financial resources) or professional development (e.g., in-service training, pre-service training) with the actual classroom experiences of young children would help address the diffuse and overgeneralized approach to professional development and quality (Chapter 4; Hamre et al., 2003; Howes, 1997). Systems of professional development aimed at improving the quality of care and child outcomes have been evaluated by using the ECERS-R (Harms et al., 1998; Howes, 1997; Rhodes & Hennessy, 2000) and related instruments. States have occasionally relied on ECERS-R observations to track levels and access to quality child care or have linked the ECERS-R assessments to pro-fessional development opportunities for child care providers (e.g., Howes, 1997; see Hamre et al., 2003; Rhodes & Hennessy, 2000). The result has been demonstrable gains in quality, particularly when training of providers has focused directly on the practices and dimensions related to quality (e.g., Howes, 1997). Thus, there is some suggestion—albeit neither widespread in terms of consistency across samples, nor powerful in terms of effect size—that tight, direct, and well-mapped linkages between provider/teacher training and an observational tool with validated links to child outcomes gives teachers a means of tracking and possibly improving the quality of child–teacher interactions that contribute to social or academic growth (Howes, 1997; Rhodes & Hennessy, 2000). Despite these suggestions in the child care literature, this system for improving quality centered on observational assessments has rarely been used in the more formalized environments of prekindergarten or the elementary grades, its use in child care is not at all widespread, and there is no indication that observational and professional development systems have been designed to address the need for coherence across the toddlerhood and early school years (Pianta & Cox, 1999).

Figure 9.1 depicts linking policy and professional development with child and teacher outcomes as a function of observational assessment of classroom or setting processes and interactions. In this model, factors relevant to educational policy and professional development experiences are linked with educational outcomes for children and for teachers as a function of the social and instructional qualities of the environment. The model hypothesizes that decisions about policy factors such as class size, curriculum, or the nature and quality of professional development affect children's social and academic performance or teachers' outcomes (e.g., leaving or staying in the profession) as a function of changes in the classroom environment. In this model, the use of a standardized metric for the classroom environment allows evaluation on a systematic basis of the extent to which manipulations and variations in policy or professional development result in the expected changes in classroom process and child and teacher outcomes.

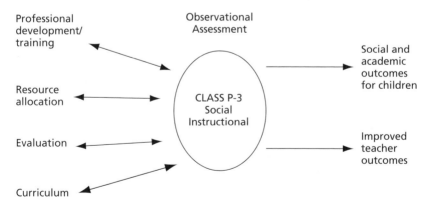

**Figure 9.1.**   Linking policy and professional development with teacher and child outcomes through standardized observations of classroom processes. (*Key:* CLASS = Classroom Assessment Scoring System; Pianta, La Paro, & Hamre, 2004).

What is critical from a reform or policy standpoint is the way that class-room process measurement has potential to assist in professional development initiatives that *systematically* produce gains for children and teachers. In fact, classroom observation allows for more direct feedback about the quality and effectiveness of professional development. For example, by using observations to assess classroom processes, policy makers and trainers can gauge the need for alterations in training, curriculum implementation, or resource allocation that in turn can produce better classroom quality. This feedback loop between classroom quality and policy is underutilized and underexamined, largely because standardized measurement is lacking for actual classroom processes being implemented in schools and care settings. In short, states, trainers, and school divisions have operated without tools to link policy and training to children's and teachers' experiences in classrooms; hence, they have little infor-mation regarding how policies or training may or may not work and whether these work to produce change in classrooms. As was noted previously, obser-vations of experiences offered to children in early education and care settings suggest that the current system of professional development is not effective.

## ASSESSING CLASSROOM QUALITY

Several observational instruments have been developed to capture aspects of class-room quality related to child outcomes in early education and care environments:

- ECERS-R (Harms et al., 1998)
- Assessment Profile for Early Childhood Programs (Assessment Profile; Abbott-Shim, Sibley, & Neel, 1992)
- Arnett Scale of Caregiver Behavior (Arnett Scale; Arnett, 1989)
- Adult Involvement Scale (Howes & Stewart, 1987)
- Classroom Practices Inventory (CPI; Hyson, Hirsch-Pasek, & Rescorla, 1990)
- Observational Record of the Caregiving Environment (ORCE; NICHD Early Child Care Research Network, 1999)
- Classroom Observation System-1 (COS-1; NICHD Early Child Care Research Network, 2002a)
- Classroom Assessment Scoring System (CLASS; Pianta, La Paro, & Hamre, 2004)

Each instrument has to some extent been validated as measuring teacher–child interactions and classroom attributes that contribute to positive outcomes for children. In discussing the potential for these instruments to function at scale in a system of professional development, policy, and quality improvement for early education and care settings (as suggested in Figure 9.1), three issues are central: definition of quality, links to child outcomes, and consistency in measurement and definition across ages.

# Defining Quality: Processes and the Physical Environment

A key distinction between the CLASS or ORCE and the ECERS-R or other rating-based tools, such as the Early Language and Literacy Classroom Observation (ELLCO) Toolkit by Smith and Dickinson (2002), is that the CLASS and ORCE scales are based entirely on interactions of teachers and children in the classroom. In the CLASS and ORCE, scoring for any scale is not determined by the presence of materials, the physical environment or safety, or the adoption of a specific curriculum (Hamre et al., 2003). When higher scores can only be obtained as a function of high-quality interactions in the setting, then the estimate of quality provided by the instrument is less dependent on the variation in physical infrastructure that tends to be fairly well-established in many child care, prekindergarten, and elementary settings.

This distinction between observed interactions and physical materials or reported use of curriculum is important because in many early education and care settings, materials and curriculum are fairly well established and organized; usually an assortment of curricula and materials is available. Yet it is critical not to overestimate quality because of a focus on materials or curricula when the *use and implementation* of curriculum and materials through interactions with children determines the value of the classroom for developmental progress (Greenberg, Domitrovich, & Baumgardner, 2001; Morrison & Connor, 2002; Rutter & Maughan, 2002; Pianta, 2003b). This distinction is clearly emphasized in the CLASS and ORCE, which focus on what teachers do with the materials they have and on the interactions teachers have with children.

*Dimensions of Quality and Child Outcomes*    At the broadest level, classroom process can be described in terms of the social-emotional climate of the classroom or child care setting, the nature and quality of teacher–child interactions, and the quality of instruction. In terms of the social-emotional climate and quality of teacher–child interactions, the capacity to maintain caring and supportive relationships with children is crucial for all teachers of young children (Pianta, 1999). Sensitive teacher–child interactions form the basis for the development of these supportive relationships (Kontos & Wilcox-Herzog, 1997). Pianta (1999) described the teacher–child relationship as a system that regulates the child's experience in the classroom and is a conduit of resources for the child's development. The emotional climate of an early education and care setting is reflected in several dimensions shown to be related to child outcomes:

- Positive climate: reflects the enthusiasm, enjoyment and emotional connection that the teacher has with the children as well as the nature of peer interactions

- Negative climate: includes evidence of anger, hostility, or aggression exhibited by the teacher and/or children in the classroom

- Sensitivity: reflects how responsive the teacher is to children's academic and emotional needs and the degree to which the teacher can be viewed as a secure base for children

These constructs collectively and separately predict 1) children's performance on standardized tests of literacy skills in prekindergarten and first grade (NICHD Early Child Care Research Network, 2003; Pianta, 2003b), 2) lower levels of maternal reports of internalizing behaviors in kindergarten and first grade (NICHD Early Child Care Research Network, 2003), and 3) children's engagement in the classroom across all grade levels (Bryant, Clifford, Early, et al., 2002; NICHD Early Child Care Research Network, 2002b, 2003). These studies demonstrate an important fact: These aspects of classroom experience uniquely predict child outcomes, adjusting for selection effects and prior child functioning.

The ways that teachers and care providers create structures and limits for interactions and social behaviors in the setting are key features of the degree to which the setting is psychologically and physically safe, predictable, and consistent—all features that contribute to positive child functioning (Morrow, Tracey, Woo, & Pressley, 1999; Yates & Yates; 1990). Relevant dimensions of quality related to management include the following (Pianta et al., 2004):

- Overcontrol: the flexibility that teachers display related to children's interests and classroom schedules and the degree to which autonomous behavior in children is fostered

- Behavior management: how well teachers monitor behavior, as well as prevent and redirect challenging behavior

- Productivity: how well the classroom runs with respect to routines—how well children understand the routine and the degree to which teachers provide activities and directions so that maximum time can be spent in productive learning activities

Studies using the CLASS or ORCE indicate that ratings of productivity uniquely predict children's performance on academic achievement tests in prekindergarten and elementary grades, that behavior management is a significant predictor of child engagement and peer competence, and that overcontrol is related to higher levels of internalizing behavior (Bryant, Clifford, Early, et al., 2002; NICHD Early Child Care Research Network, 2005; Pianta, 2003b).

With respect to instructional support, observational data indicate that highly skilled teachers monitor their students' performance and provide additional explanation and ideas (Meyer et al., 1993). In this way, teachers provide feedback to students through scaffolding and support (Yates & Yates, 1990). National Association for the Education of Young Children (NAEYC) guidelines include instructional strategies to promote children's development, interaction, and participation in the classroom through teaching to enhance children's learning (Bredekamp & Copple, 1997). Drawing on earlier work using the ORCE, the CLASS has three scales that focus on instructional support provided in the classroom:

1.  Concept development: the degree to which teachers promote higher-order thinking and problem solving, going beyond fact and recall activities for children

2.  Instructional learning formats: how teachers engage children in activities and facilitate engagement so that learning opportunities are maximized

3.  Quality of feedback: how teachers extend children's learning through their responses and participation in activities

Together, these constructs—quality of feedback in particular—form an index of the instructional value of the classroom that predicts a child's academic functioning in literacy and general knowledge; there are indications that this association is due to increased child engagement in the activity (NICHD Early Child Care Research Network, 2003). These scales tend to be less strongly associated with social functioning than do the assessments of emotional quality (NICHD Early Child Care Research Network, 2003).

It is important to note that these constructs, individually and collectively in composite form, predict positive changes in children's literacy scores from 54 months of age to first grade (NICHD Early Child Care Research Network, 2003). It should also be noted that the previously described dimensions of quality are also relevant for most early education and care settings (home or center based) for children as young as 24 months of age (Hamre et al., 2003; NICHD Early Child Care Research Network, 1999).

*Coherence, Consistency, and Dimensional Assessment*    A third issue in the use of observational systems for early education and care settings' policy and improvement is whether quality is conceptualized and assessed, to the extent possible, using a consistent or coherent definition and metric across ages. Observations of quality in classroom-like settings with young children most often involve ratings of the environment on a variety of clearly articulated dimensions that are purported to index quality. Similar observational methods can be used in home-like settings as well (NICHD Early Child Care Research Network, 1996). Standardized procedures to evaluate the classroom environment, such as the ECERS-R (Harms et al., 1998), have received extensive validation in the field. Related instruments such as Stipek's Early Childhood Classroom Observation Measure (ECCOM; 1996) designed to assess instruction, management, social climate, cultural sensitivity, and resources of preschool and kindergarten classrooms are similar in the use of rating scales to index quality. Research instruments such as the ORCE and the COS-1 and COS-3, which were developed for the large-scale NICHD Study of Early Child Care (see NICHD Early Child Care Research Network, 1996, 2002a, 2003), employ both a time-sampling coding system for indexing the occurrence of discrete practices or activities (e.g., caregivers talking to children) as well as global ratings of the qualities of the environment (e.g., teacher sensitivity, positive emotional climate).

Clearly, there are considerable differences in the specific activities and behaviors in which a caregiver or teacher may engage a 3-year-old or a 6-year-old. In fact, sensitivity to such differences may itself be a hallmark of quality (NICHD Early Child Care Research Network, 1999). Notwithstanding these differences at the level of discrete behaviors and activities, ample evidence suggests that at a dimensional or global level, the desirable or beneficial qualities of adult–child interactions and classroom climate are quite consistent across the age span of the 3–6 years (NICHD Early Child Care Research Network, 2002a, 2002b) and across care/educational settings. For example, in the NICHD child care study (1999, 2002a, 2002b), teacher sensitivity, captured using ratings on a seven-point scale, consistently figures as a prominent contributor to global quality indicators (in home, center-based, or classroom settings) and as a predictor of child outcomes, even though the discrete behaviors reflecting sensitivity may differ somewhat between 3-year-olds and 6-year-olds. In fact, the results from the NICHD study are so robust with respect to this issue—relying on the same set of global dimensions (e.g., teacher sensitivity) to assess quality while allowing for differences in concrete, grade-specific anchor points—that the CLASS was developed as an across-grade/age observational system using dimensional conceptualization and definitions of quality for preschool through third grade (Pianta et al., 2004). By using these common dimensions across grades, the CLASS focuses attention on classroom quality in a consistent manner across the first 4 years of schooling, thus strategically contributing to increased consistency and coherence in children's experiences over time.

In sum, considerable work has already been accomplished with regard to the conceptualization, development, and validation of tools to assess multiple dimensions of quality in early education and care settings. It appears that the instruments of greatest potential value for professional development and quality improvement focus on the quality of interactions between teachers and children (and, to a lesser extent, among peers and with materials) and on the use of dimensional ratings that are strategically designed to remain coherent and consistent across the preschool–elementary years (Pianta et al., 2004). In some ways, centering professional development and accountability assessment on indicators of the classroom/care environment reflects an acknowledgement that the curriculum in early education and care is the nature and quality of child–teacher interaction (NAEYC, 2001; Pianta, 2003b).

## ACCESS, EQUITY, AND PROFESSIONAL
## DEVELOPMENT FOR THE PREKINDERGARTEN WORKFORCE

By focusing on teacher–child interactions as the core curriculum in early education and care (NAEYC, 2001; Pianta 2004), professional development initiatives and research can focus on how the nature and form of information and support provided for teacher–child interactions promote interactions that have greater developmental value for children. This conceptualization of professional development is supported in naturalistic studies of child care settings (NICHD Early Child Care Research Network, 2002b) and is being tested in an evaluation of planned variation in teacher support provided via direct observation and Internet-mediated feedback to a large sample of prekindergarten teachers (Pianta, Kinzie, et al., 2003). In this project, which is called MyTeachingPartner (MTP; Pianta, Kinzie, et al., 2003) and described at http://www.myteachingpartner.net, teachers videotape their implementation of lessons/activities every 2 weeks, then send the tape to a consultant who edits the tape for positive examples and constructive comments/feedback to improve quality. The consultant then posts the edited videotape on the teacher's private MTP web page with written comments for the teacher to review. Once the teacher reviews the edited videotape and comments and provides his or her own responses, the consultant and teacher meet via a video-based, one-to-one, on-line interaction to discuss the feedback. This process, called the MTP Consultancy Cycle, repeats every 2 weeks. In addition, all teachers (in the Consultancy Cycle condition and in the comparison condition) have access to the MTP web site, which has videotape clips of teaching tips and high-quality implementation examples selected by using the CLASS. The planned variations in training/implementation support are tested in the context of teachers implementing a common package of learning activities in literacy, language development, and building positive relationships with children; thus, differences in outcomes (for children and for teachers) can be attributed to the training/implementation conditions rather than to curriculum variation.

Because states have quickly moved to provide early education services for young children, the demand for graduates of preservice programs is very high, with many states relying on teachers who have elementary-grade certifications and teachers with 2-year degrees who have received certification as part of a grandfather clause (Clifford et al., 1999). Several states have begun to address the staffing and qualification crisis. Some have created professional development initiatives to encourage providers to seek additional training or education or a credential and range from voluntary (Colorado), to free training and coursework (Connecticut, Massachusetts). However, to meet this demand for high-quality professional development and to do so at scale,  mechanisms must be developed and tested for delivering ongoing, high-quality training to large samples of teachers/classrooms (Pianta, Kinzie, et al., 2003). As noted previously, one promising mechanism for reaching large numbers of teachers/ classrooms is the use of the Internet, both as a conduit for two-way communication and feedback and for more passive one-way interactions with materials and resources (Pianta, Kinzie, et al., 2003).

Professional development conducted while teachers are in service can range from site-based, after-school workshops to year-long coursework with built-in practicum assignments conducted within the classroom. A combination of a primary training method (e.g., knowledge-based workshop) and follow-up support is the most common form of in-service training, with variation in the mechanisms of delivery and intensity of the source and follow-up. Almost no empirical evidence is available to help decide which variant of primary source and follow-up is best-suited for teachers' training and skill-development needs. This absence of evidence for the effectiveness of delivery mechanisms renders it nearly impossible to base training decisions on scientific grounds (Bryant, Clifford, Early, et al., 2002). Most in-service training and support programs use a classroom-focused model in which an instructor provides generalized knowledge and information to groups of teachers. Follow-up tends to be limited to advice on applying specific techniques (Bryant, Clifford, Early, et al., 2002). These approaches tend not to provide ongoing, individualized feedback on teachers' observed practices. In sum, in-service training as practiced is at best only loosely linked to an individual teachers' work in his or her classroom. This is particularly problematic for teachers requiring support, knowledge, and skills in addressing children's social and relational needs (Pianta, 1999).

However, teachers do actively seek outside assistance from experts, particularly for challenging practice problems. For example, the University of Virginia's web-based Office of Special Education (http://curry.edschool. virginia.edu/go/specialed) attracts considerable traffic and frequent requests for consultation. An analysis of 244 e-mail messages to the site suggests that teacher requests total 20% of the inquiries made, with inquiries requesting help with their own teaching and intervention situations figuring prominently (J.W. Lloyd, personal communication, September 2003).

As introduced earlier, MTP has designed and will evaluate a training/ implementation support model that directly addresses teachers' needs for ongoing, individualized feedback on their own practices. Figure 9.2 depicts how this program of professional development is designed. Because this approach uses the Internet as the basis for delivering knowledge and support, it has the potential to reach large numbers of teachers at scale individually and to do so without costs related to travel and time lost to travel. As part of the evaluation, teachers will initially be trained in a workshop format to use a common set of learning and social/relational activities for a preset amount of time per week. In the context of this common experience, planned variations in follow-

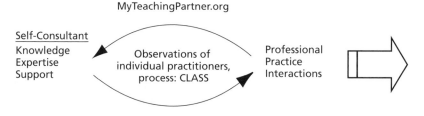

**Figure 9.2.** Regular, individualized, feedback and professional development. (*Key:* CLASS = Classroom Assessment Scoring System; Pianta & La Paro, 2003.)

up using the Internet will be evaluated. Two models of training will be implemented by prekindergarten teachers for 2 years in this longitudinal study: 1) web training, in which teachers will receive workshop training in the curriculum and access a web site with written suggestions; lessons; and video-taped demonstration clips, additional material, and examples and 2) web training plus consultancy, in which teachers will receive the same workshop and training as the other condition but also receive biweekly, live, Internet-mediated consultation focused on their practices in implementing the curriculum. The previously described MTP Consultancy Cycle was designed after reviewing extant research, interviewing experts, and working closely with focus groups of preschool teachers. The MTP Consultancy Cycle solution addresses several professional development needs identified by prekinder-garten teachers and program administrators, including: 1) establishing a collaborative partnership between users and consultants which enables teachers to seek support for their teaching practice; 2) providing access to knowledge and practice through consultation and guided review of teaching strategies; 3) offering opportunities for feedback on teaching practice, as teachers learn to implement the curricular strategies; and 4) consultants who are engaged, knowledgeable and experienced, and fully versed in the strategies and curriculum being implemented. Consultants are specifically selected for their ability to assist novice teachers as well as seasoned professionals. The MTP Consultancy Cycle provides teachers with direct feedback on lessons they implement and with consultation about how to improve quality of implementation. Biweekly consultation includes review of videotaped observations of the teachers' lessons, review of incidental interactions with children, coaching by the consultant in implementation, and support through  regular contact with the same consultant.

## CONCLUSIONS AND RECOMMENDATIONS

From reviews of basic research to large-scale initiatives on curriculum reform and quality improvement, there is ample evidence that the knowledge base exists to design at-scale efforts to improve the quality of experiences for children in most early education and care settings, particularly those that are supported by public funds and operate in elementary schools or community-based settings. Generic approaches to professional development and static metrics (e.g., courses, degrees, quantity of training) as well as reliance on structural or very global indicators of program quality do not produce the consistent and strong evidence expected of an association between education and training and program quality or child outcomes.

Large-scale observational research studies have helped create a measurement and training infrastructure that can support large-scale observations of early education and care settings that are focused on settings that are known to contribute to child outcomes. Thus, the final step in the process of creating pathways toward improved quality is professional development that emphasizes the dimensions of quality observed in these settings. Relying on this infrastructure, it is possible to foresee a not-too-distant future in which teachers have their own individualized portfolio of quality assessments and improvement standards, measured against validated exemplars. Professional development activities can be tailored to teachers' own practices as assessed using these observational metrics, and the resulting assessment portfolios can be used to track quality improvement at classroom, program, and state levels. Such a system of professional development and policy making, centered on observations of actual quality in classrooms, provides an alternative to the present system, which appears to produce weak associations between quality and policy/professional development indicators and highly variable and often mediocre experiences for young children. Clearly, one issue that needs to be resolved is the costs of this alternative system, including an evaluation of its costs and benefits relative to the costs and benefits of the current system (see Chapter 12). This issue notwithstanding, the current system needs improvement to ensure high-quality programming and improved outcomes for young children.

## REFERENCES

Abbott-Shim, M., Sibley, A., & Neel, J. (1992). *Assessment profile for early childhood programs: Preschool, infant, school-age.* Atlanta, GA: Quality Assist.

Arnett, J. (1989). Caregivers in day-care centers: Does training matter? *Journal of Applied Developmental Psychology, 10,* 541–552.

Barnett, W.S., Young, J.W., & Schweinhart, L.J. (1998). How preschool education influences long-term cognitive development and school success: A causal model. In S. Barnett & S. Boocock (Eds.), *Early care and education for children in poverty: Promises, programs and long-terms results* (pp. 167–184). New York: State University of New York Press.

Blank, H., Schulman, K., & Ewen, D. (1999). *Seeds of success: State prekindergarten initiative, 1998–1999.* Washington, DC: Children's Defense Fund.

Bredekamp, S., & Copple, C. (Eds.). (1997). *Developmentally appropriate practice in early childhood programs* (Rev. ed). Washington, DC: National Association for the Education of Young Children.

Bryant, D., Clifford, R., Early, D., Pianta, R., Howes, C., Barbarin, O., & Burchinal, M. (2002, November). *Findings from the NCEDL Multi-State Pre-Kindergarten Study.* Annual meeting of the National Association for the Education of Young Children, New York.

Burchinal, M., Peisner-Feinberg, E., Pianta, R., & Howes, C. (2002). Development of academic skills from preschool through second grade: Family and classroom predictors of developmental trajectories. *Journal of School Psychology, 40*(5), 415–436.

Caspary, K. (2002). *California's pioneering training and retention initiatives for early childhood educators.* Berkeley, CA: Policy Analysis for California Education.

Clarke-Stewart, K.A., Vandell, D.L., Burchinal, M., O'Brien, M., & McCartney, K. (2002). Do regulable features of child-care homes affect children's development? *Early Childhood Research Quarterly, 17*(1), 52–86.

Clifford, R.M., Early, D.M., & Hills, T.W. (1999). Almost a million children in school before kindergarten: Who is responsible for early childhood services? *Young Children, 54*(5), 48–51.

Greenberg, M.T., Domitrovich, C., & Bumbarger, B. (2001). The prevention of mental disorders in school-aged children: Current state of the field. *Prevention and Treatment, 4,* 1–48.

Hamre, B., Bridges, M., & Fuller, B. (2003). *Early care and education staff preparation, quality, and child development.* Unpublished manuscript, University of California, Berkeley.

Hamre, B.K., & Pianta, R.C. (2004a). *Can instructional and emotional support in the first grade classroom make a difference for children at risk of school failure?* Manuscript submitted for publication.

Hamre, B.K., & Pianta, R.C. (2004b). Self-reported depression in nonfamilial caregivers: Prevalence and associations with caregiver behavior in child care settings. *Early Childhood Research Quarterly, 19*(2), 297–318.

Harms, T., Clifford, R.M., & Cryer, D. (1998). *Early Childhood Environment Rating Scale–Revised Edition (ECERS-R).* New York: Teachers College Press.

Head Start Bureau. (1998). *Head Start Family and Child Experiences Survey (FACES).* Washington, DC: U.S. Department of Health and Human Services

Howes, C. (1997). Children's experiences in center-based child care as a function of teacher background and adult:child ratio. *Merrill Palmer Quarterly, 43*(3), 404–425.

Howes, C., James, J., & Ritchie, S. (2003). Pathways to effective teaching. *Early Childhood Research Quarterly, 18*(1), 104–120.

Howes, C., Phillipsen, L., & Peisner-Feinberg, C. (2000). The consistency and predictability of teacher-child relationships during the transition to kindergarten. *Journal of School Psychology, 38*(2), 113–132.

Howes, C., & Stewart, P. (1987). Child's play with adults, toys, and peers: An examination of family and child care influences. *Developmental Psychology, 23,* 423–430.

Hyson, M.C., Hirsh-Pasek, K., & Rescorla, L. (1990). The Classroom practices inventory: An observation instrument based on NAYEC's guidelines for developmentally appropriate practices for 4- and 5-year-old children. *Early Childhood Research Quarterly, 5,* 475–494.

Kontos, S., & Wilcox-Herzog, A. (1997). Teachers' interactions with children: Why are they so important? *Young Children, 52*(2), 4–13.

La Paro, K.M., & Pianta, R.C. (2000). Predicting children's competence in the early school years: A meta-analytic review. *Review of Educational Research, 70*(4), 443–484.

Marshall, N.L., Creps, C.L., Burstein, N.R., Glantz, F.B., Robeson, W.W., Barnett, S., Schimmenti, J., & Keefe, N. (2002). *Early care and education in Massachusetts public school preschool classrooms.* Cambridge, MA: Abt Associates.

Meyer, L.A., Wardrop, J.L., Hastings, C.N., & Linn, R.L. (1993). Effects of ability and settings on kindergarteners' reading performance. *Journal of Educational Research, 86*(3), 142–160.

Morrison, F.J. (1999, August). *Improving literacy in America: The role of school transition.* Symposium conducted at the 107th annual meeting of the American Psychological Association, Boston, MA.

Morrison, F.J., & Connor, C.M. (2002). Understanding schooling effects on early literacy: A working research strategy. *Journal of School Psychology, 40*(6), 493–500.

Morrow, L.M., Tracey, D.H., Woo, D.G., & Pressley, M. (1999). Characteristics of exemplary first-grade literacy instruction. *Reading Teacher, 52*(5), 462–476.

National Association for the Education of Young Children. (2001). *Recommended practices for early childhood educators.* Washington, DC: Author.

National Institute of Child Health and Human Development Early Child Care Research Network. (1993). Child-care debate: Transformed or distorted? *American Psychologist, 48,* 692–693.

National Institute of Child Health and Human Development Early Child Care Research Network. (1996). Characteristics of infant child care: Factors contributing to positive caregiving. *Early Childhood Research Quarterly, 11*(3), 269–306.

National Institute of Child Health and Human Development Early Child Care Research Network. (1998). Relations between family predictors and child outcomes: Are they weaker for children in child care? *Developmental Psychology, 34,* 1119–1128.

National Institute of Child Health and Human Development Early Child Care Research Network. (1999). Child outcomes when child care center classes meet recommended standards for quality. *American Journal of Public Health, 89,* 1072–1077.

National Institute of Child Health and Human Development Early Child Care Research Network. (2002a). The relation of global first-grade classroom environment to structural classroom features and teacher and student behaviors. *The Elementary School Journal, 102*(5), 367–387.

National Institute of Child Health and Human Development Early Child Care Research Network. (2002b). Structure>process>outcome: Direct and indirect effects of caregiving quality on young children's development. *Psychological Science, 13,* 199–206.

National Institute of Child Health and Human Development Early Child Care Research Network. (2003). Social functioning in first grade: Associations with earlier home and child care predictors and with current classroom experiences. *Child Development, 74*(6), 1639–1662.

National Institute of Child Health and Human Development Early Child Care Research Network. (2004). Does class size in first grade relate to changes in child academic and social performance or observed classroom processes? *Developmental Psychology, 40*(5), 651–664.

National Institute of Child Health and Human Development Early Child Care Research Network. (2005). A day in third grade: A large-scale study of classroom quality and teacher and student behavior. *The Elementary School Journal, 105,* 305–323.

No Child Left Behind (NCLB) Act of 2001, PL 107-110, 20 U.S.C. §6301 *et seq.*

Peisner-Feinberg, E.S., & Burchinal, M.R. (1997). Relations between preschool children's child-care experiences and concurrent development: The Cost, Quality, and Outcomes Study. *Merrill-Palmer Quarterly, 43*(3), 451–477.

Pianta, R.C. (1999). *Enhancing relationships between children and teachers.* Washington DC: American Psychological Association.

Pianta, R.C. (2003a, March). *Professional development and observations of classroom process.* Paper presented at the SEED Symposium on Early Childhood Professional Development, Washington, DC.

Pianta, R.C. (2003b). *Standardized classroom observations from pre-k to third grade: A mechanism for improving quality classroom experiences during the p–3 years.* New York: Foundation for Child Development.

Pianta, R.C. (2004). *The MTP philosophy statement on teacher-child interactions.* Unpublished manuscript, University of Virginia, Charlottesville.

Pianta, R.C., & Cox, M.J. (Eds.). (1999). *The transition to kindergarten.* Baltimore: Paul H. Brookes Publishing Co.

Pianta, R.C., Howes, C., Burchinal, M., Bryant, D., Clifford, R., Early, D., & Barbarin, O. (in press). Features of pre-kindergarten programs, classrooms, and teachers: Do they predict observed classroom quality and child–teacher interactions? *Applied Developmental Science.*

Pianta, R.C., Howes, C., Early, D., Clifford, R., Bryant, D., & Burchinal, M. (2003, April). *Observations of quality and practices in pre-k classrooms: Associations with child outcomes and teacher attributes.* Paper presented at the Biennial Meeting of the Society for Research in Child Development, Tampa, FL.

Pianta, R.,C., Kinzie, M., Pullen, P., Justice, L., Lloyd, J., & Fan, X. (2003). *Web training: Pre-k teachers, literacy, and relationships* (Grant #1 R01 HD046061-01). Washington, DC: National Institute of Child Health and Human Development.

Pianta, R.C., La Paro, K.M., & Hamre, B. (2004). *Classroom Assessment Scoring System (CLASS).* Unpublished measure, University of Virginia, Charlottesville.

Pianta, R.C., La Paro, K.M., Payne, C., Cox, M.J., & Bradley, R. (2002). The relation of kindergarten classroom environment to teacher, family, and school characteristics and child outcomes. *The Elementary School Journal, 102*(3), 225–238.

Pianta, R.C, & Walsh, D.J. (1996). *High-risk children in schools: Constructing sustaining relationships.* New York: Routledge.

Ramey, C.T., Campbell, F.A., Burchinal, M., Skinner, M.L., Gardner, D.M., & Ramey, S.L. (2000). Persistent effects of early childhood education on high-risk children and their mothers. *Applied Developmental Science, 4,* 2–14.

Rhodes, S., & Hennessy, E. (2000). The effects of specialized training on caregivers and children in the early-years settings: An evaluation of the foundation course in playgroup practice. *Early Childhood Research Quarterly, 15,* 559–576.

Ripple, C.H., Gilliam, W.S., Chanana, N., & Zigler, E. (1999). Will fifty cooks spoil the broth? The debate over entrusting Head Start to the states. *American Psychologist, 54,* 327–343.

Rutter, M., & Maughan, B. (2002). School effectiveness findings, 1979–2002. *Journal of School Psychology, 40*(6), 451–475.

Smith, M.,W. & Dickinson, D.K. (with Sangeorge, A., & Anastasopoulos, L.) (2002). *Early Language and Literacy Classroom Observation (ELLCO) Toolkit.* Baltimore: Paul H. Brookes Publishing Co.

Stipek, D.J. (1996). Motivation and instruction. In D.C. Berliner & R.C. Calfee (Eds.), *Handbook of educational psychology* (pp. 85–113). New York: Macmillan.

Witte, A.D., & Queralt, M. (2004). *What happens when child care inspections and complaints are made available on the Internet?* (National Bureau of Economic Research Working Paper 10227). Cambridge, MA: National Bureau of Economic Research.

Yates, G.C.R., & Yates, S.M. (1990). Teacher effectiveness research: Towards describing user-friendly classroom instruction. *Educational Psychology, 10*(3), 225–238.

CHAPTER 10

# Alignment in Educator Preparation for Early and Beginning Literacy Instruction

## A State-Level Case Example

KATHLEEN ROSKOS, CATHERINE A. ROSEMARY, AND M. HEIDI VARNER

The International Reading Association and the National Association for the Education of Young Children (IRA/NAEYC, 1998) published a joint position statement titled *Learning to Read and Write* out of concern for opportunity and appropriate practice in early literacy during the preschool years. The statement summarized current issues in early literacy education (e.g., the growing diversity of the preschool population) and reviewed research on children's literacy development. It devoted one paragraph, consisting of three sentences, to the role of the early educator in children's literacy development:

> Early childhood teachers need to understand the developmental continuum of reading and writing and be skilled in a variety of strategies to assess and support individual children's development and learning across the continuum. At that same time teachers must set developmentally appropriate goals for young children and then adapt instructional strategies for children whose learning and development are advanced or lag behind those goals. Good teachers make instructional decisions based on their knowledge of reading and writing, current research, appropriate expectations, and their knowledge of individual children's strengths and needs. (p. 15)

These three sentences lay out a daunting set of professional responsibilities for the early childhood teacher that have only grown more urgent in the recent policy environment.

It is often stated that the early educator is key to ensuring the positive outcomes for young children's cognitive and social competencies so crucial for school readiness and future achievements (Bowman, Donovan, & Burns, 2001; Cost, Quality & Child Outcome Study Team, 1995; Espinosa, 2002; Frede, 1998; Howes, 1997; National Institute of Child Health and Human Development [NICHD], 2001; Schumacher, Irish, & Lombardi, 2003; Snow, Burns, & Griffin, 1998). The adults who take care of, converse with, read to, and play with children can have a profound influence on their lives, ushering them into the language, materials, symbols, and ways of the world. U.S. society underestimates the potential influence of these "other adults" on the cognitive and socioemotional development of young children, leaving to chance that their knowledge and skills will invigorate children's learning potential. Research confirms that it is often the least educated who teach young children—our most eager of learners (Early & Winton, 2001).

This chapter is a discussion of preparation—not of young children for school but of adults for their role as early educators of young children and, in particular, their responsibilities as early literacy teachers. At a fundamental level, early literacy teaching is a shared responsibility in a literate society and includes adults in many roles, such as reading to young children; helping them learn new words; teaching them the alphabet and how to spell simple words; and joining them in rhyming games, chants, and songs. The early educator has a higher level of responsibility of helping children develop school readiness skills, thus entailing preparation or professional education. It is not enough to tell or show children; they must be helped to understand if they are to acquire the knowledge and skills they need for strong language and literacy skills that undergird future learning achievements.

The chapter begins with a brief description of two powerful influences pressing for change in early educator preparation—standards and science. The need to align programs to scientifically based reading research, professional standards of preparation, and goals for child outcomes in reading and writing is a consistent theme emerging from these influences, and such alignment is a key feature of high quality in professional education across training levels. It examines alignment as a quality feature through a state-level lens, summarizing case examples of the degree of alignment in early and beginning literacy pedagogy across a sample of one state's early childhood credentialing programs. The results of this analysis, preliminary at this point, shed light on alignment as a quality feature of early educator professional education. The chapter's closing comments address the implications of this state-level case example on alignment in relation to broader topics of educator preparation in literacy, such as 1) improving professional education program design and integrity, 2) developing a continuum of teacher learning across entry points into the profession, 3) strengthening professional preparation standards, and 4) conducting more fine-grained research on the actual impact of coursework on teaching quality and its relation to child outcomes.

## INFLUENCE OF STANDARDS

With tidal wave force, the standards movement swept into the early education field at the start of the 21st century with the promise of a seamless P–12 continuum of cognitive development and learning linked to academic achievement. The movement has rallied considerable support. Two key early childhood professional organizations endorsed early learning standards as integral to a comprehensive system of education and care for young children (NAEYC and the National Association of Early Childhood Specialists in State Departments of Education [NAECS/SDE], 2002). Current federal initiatives, such as *Good Start, Grow Smart* (2002; see Chapter 1), call for "voluntary" guidelines or standards in an effort to promote school readiness, especially in language and early literacy. The newly revised Head Start Child Outcomes Framework (2003) articulates standards as five elements of language development and literacy and 31 performance indicators in these learning domains (e.g., "uses an increasingly complex and varied spoken vocabulary"). The report *At the Starting Line* (American Federation of Teachers, 2002) made the recommendation that states, in taking steps toward high-quality, universal early childhood education "require and enforce standards for all programs" (p. 6). Increasingly, states are adopting child outcome standards in language, literacy, and mathematics at the preschool level (27 states as of 2003; Scott-Little, Kagan & Frelow, 2003).

Thus, content standards—what young children (four-year-olds) and increasingly very young children (three-year-olds) should know and be able to do—are rapidly becoming a critical part of states' educational architecture in developing systems of service delivery for young children. As a structural element, content standards frame curricula, professional development, and assessments aimed at improving children's school readiness skills. They are increasingly seen as the most powerful option for improving prekindergarten instruction.

Content standards, however, do not stop at the door of expectations for children. They are also the harbingers of change in what is expected of educators if children are to achieve the benchmarks of standards set for them. If young children need to develop *print awareness and concepts* (Head Start Domain Element 4), for example, then early educators should understand literacy development and its early precursors or "emergent processes," should know how to assess for these linguistic abilities and use assessment data to create conditions for early literacy learning, and should know how to teach concepts about print and comprehension strategies and strive to meet the established expectations for all children.

These expectations for early childhood educators have implications for early educator preparation from entry level to advanced degrees. This is reflected in the new NAEYC *Standards for Early Childhood Professional Preparation* at the initial licensure level (2001; see Chapter 11). The Teaching and Learning Standard (Standard 4), for instance, includes the key element of *understanding content knowledge in early education* that describes the "extensive, research-based knowledge and skill" required of candidates in language and literacy. This NAEYC program standard establishes a framework for aligning the content to be taught to professionals with what children must learn to become effective speakers, listeners, readers, and writers by the end of third grade.

Still, even as this structure promotes alignment, it does not flesh out the specifics that ensure that the educator's pedagogy will be well-matched to desired child outcomes. For this, preparation programs will need to adjust instruction in order to address learning needs of individuals at different entry points into the profession yet maintain sufficient integrity of content for good alignment to rigorous learning standards. The press of child learning standards on what educators should know and be able to do is hard because it demands a new kind of attention to the details of educator learning, which cannot go every which way but must "get in line" with expected learning outcomes for children. New expectations (content standards) for children's learning, in sum, set in motion new expectations for teachers' learning (also content standards) and for the clear alignment between them.

## Influence of Science

The impetus for standards continues to gather strength and power from the science of learning, of early education, and of early literacy acquisition. Brain development research, for example, documents the developmental benefits of early exposure to language for building neural connections and early forming concepts and skills, such as pretense and narrative sense, from infancy (Eliot, 1999; Gopnick, Meltzoff & Kuhl, 1999). Research in early education converges on findings indicating that high-quality early education positively affects all children's success in school and the quality of their future with special benefits for children who are at risk (Espinosa, 2002; Howes, Phillips, & Whitebrook, 1992). Highly rated process aspects of quality in early care and education (e.g., adult–child interaction) coupled with good structural features of quality (e.g., qualified teachers) help to produce more robust learning environments for children that support their language and literacy skills as well as social skills (Espinosa, 2002).

Two decades of research on early literacy acquisition reveals the early predictors of school reading success, including oral language comprehension, phonological awareness, alphabet letter knowledge, concepts about print, and print motivation (Bus & van IJzendoorn, 1999; Hart & Risley, 1995; Lonigan, 2004; Neuman & Dickinson, 2001; Senechal, LeFevre, Smith-Dechant, & Colton, 2001; Snow, Burns, & Griffin, 1998). Effective strategies for promoting early language and literacy learning are also identified by the research (i.e., elaborated discussions including rare words, print-rich settings, phonological awareness activities, interactive storybook reading, literacy-enriched play settings, emergent writing activities; Bodrova, Leong, Gregory, & Edgerton, 1999; Dickinson & Tabors, 2001; Elley, 1989; Morrow, 1990; Neuman & Roskos, 1998; Roskos & Christie, 2000; Whitehurst et al., 1988).

Rapid growth in the scientific knowledge base of early learning, especially in early language and literacy, has deepened understanding of children's language and literacy capabilities and also raised expectations of their learning in these domains. It has been only since the 1970s that studies have shown that literacy development starts in children before they enter school. It is now clear that even very young children are capable of forming nascent concepts about print that are growth producing (Bowman, Donovan, & Burns, 2001; Olson & Gayan, 2001). Yet, even as a wealth of scientific knowledge exists, access to it has been largely limited to the academic community and high-level professionals (e.g., professors, researchers, psychologists, curriculum specialists). With the spotlight on the importance of early literacy for 3- to 5-year-olds, however, the demand for the widespread distribution of scientific knowledge grows ever more acute, thus placing tremendous pressure on educator preparation and training. Developing the educators' *scientific* knowledge along with the skills to apply it accurately and well, though, is not the same as disseminating information to them. It requires preparation programs that are well-aligned along different dimensions.

## WHAT IS ALIGNMENT?

The term *alignment* literally means *formation of a line; also, the line so formed.* Applied to education, the term is a "modern descendent of the efficiency movement in curriculum of the early 20th century" (Marsh & Willis, 1995, p. 238). Adopted in the push for "effective schools" in the 1980s and 1990s, *alignment* meant achieving congruency between the planned and enacted curriculum through extensive testing; the degree of alignment served as a rather strict indicator of fidelity of use in curriculum implementation.

In the current standards-based environment, *alignment* is generically used by educators and policy makers to mean "being in agreement; a condition of close cooperation." It frequently refers to "how well all policy elements in a system work together to guide instruction and ultimately student learning" (Webb, 1997, cited in Rothman, Slattery, Vranek, & Resnick, 2002, p. 5). Both historical and present-day uses of the term may apply when considering the concept in the professional preparation context. Its inherent themes of congruency, agreement, and cooperation lay at the core of program design represented in at least three different forms of alignment that can be examined at the program and course level. The basic source of alignment is at the course level, which in combination with other courses creates alignment at the program level. The program level provides a macro-view of alignment, whereas the course level offers a narrower view, and each level contains alignment features reflective of the other.

One of the more obvious types of alignment for educator preparation in the area of early literacy is the *external alignment* between a course of study for early educators and the scientific knowledge base in language and early literacy. This can be measured in terms of the direct *correspondence* between program descriptions, course descriptions, and syllabi and the professional body of knowledge (principles, facts, processes, techniques, strategies). Although challenging with respect to identifying, sorting, and presenting key concepts in clear language, this surface level of alignment is rather easily accomplished at both program and course levels. A program, for example, may include an early literacy course, the content of which can be easily mapped to the early literacy knowledge base.

More difficult to achieve is *horizontal alignment,* which is characterized by markers of consistency, balance, and integration of knowledge, skills, and dispositions in the scope or range of instruction. This, too, originates at the course level to create an overall *comprehensive* course of study that ensures 1) balanced coverage of the essential content and skills to be learned; 2) integration of knowledge, skills, and dispositions for later practice; and 3) consistency of coverage in knowledge, skills, and dispositions over time. Horizontal alignment helps to develop educator expertise through consistent exposure to essential understandings of the domain in integrative ways that support the transfer of learning. It focuses instructional attention on integrating essential content-skill-disposition constellations across a set of learning experiences, albeit flexibly given the uncertainties inherent in educators' learning. This form of alignment can be quite challenging to "bring into line" and to monitor in the realities of program implementation at the course level due to variations in instructor quality and retention.

Equally difficult to achieve is *vertical alignment,* identifiable in the *developmental progression* built into the learning experiences of a single course, which, in turn, contribute to learning as a result of the total program. The professional education program and its related coursework should advance the educators' conceptual understanding of the knowledge base, skill mastery, and professional dispositions (e.g., reflection) through more challenging experiences that are sensitive to adult needs. Features such as the amount of content, how much time is allocated to learning in the domain, and the complexity or depth of understanding are broad indicators of vertical alignment in coursework and between program levels. These show the degree to which scientific concepts, representing the knowledge base, are carried forward to become functional in educator practice and the broader professional field. Vertical alignment involves "lining up" essential concepts, skills, and dispositions to be learned and developing learning trajectories that will "pull forward" the educator's capabilities—a goal also difficult to achieve and manage in the realities of professional education.

## EXAMINING ALIGNMENT

Standards and science are powerful influences on an emerging early literacy learning domain in early childhood education, giving it shape and meaning that have deep implications for the professional preparation of early educators at different entry points into the field. Both influences compel us to confront the complexities of alignment in preparing early educators for their role as early literacy teachers. To what degree do programs align with state-adopted or endorsed prekindergarten learning standards, and how well do they prepare educators to help children meet early learning standards in language and literacy? Are programs and courses aligned with the scientific knowledge base, and how well do they develop the early educator's capabilities for effective early literacy teaching grounded in research?

These are challenging questions that pose new problems but also new possibilities for improving the professional education of early childhood teachers. The study that follows is an initial attempt to examine alignment as an important design feature in creating and improving educator preparation and professional development programs in early literacy pedagogy. It presents a state-level case study of alignment at three early childhood credentialing levels in professional education: Child Development Associate (CDA), 2-year associate's degree, and 4-year baccalaureate degree. As a "case in point," the study describes features of alignment in early literacy-related coursework at and across these different credentialing levels in Ohio. Three research questions framed the case study.

1.  To what degree do course(s) in teacher preparation programs align with the professional knowledge base of early and beginning reading pedagogy? These data provide evidence of *external alignment* between program/ course content and the scientific knowledge base as the basis for desired child outcomes in early literacy.

2.  To what degree are courses comprehensive, including curricular components that emphasize the four different perspectives on early literacy pedagogy of knowing, assessing, planning, and teaching? In addition, to what extent is there a balance of elements involving mastery of information and application of the knowledge through skills in practice? These data provide information about the extent to which learning experiences are well-balanced (a good mix of theory and practice), consistently presented (over the life of a course or a series of courses), and integrated (opportunity to practice using new concepts and skills), thus indicating *horizontal alignment.*

3.  To what degree does coursework build teachers' capacity to develop expertise in early literacy pedagogy within a professional program? Also, to what degree does an early entry professional program prepare teachers for more advanced professional education in early literacy? Data along these lines provide evidence of the developmental progression built into a teacher education curriculum, indicated by the amount of content presented (e.g., number of concepts and skills), how much time is allocated to learning concepts and skills in early literacy pedagogy, and the complexity of the information in deepening understandings and skills. These data yield information about the *vertical alignment* within a program and between programs that prepare early educators for their role as literacy teachers.

These research questions provide an opportunity to explore alignment both as a structural and a process variable in professional education program design at different entry levels along a continuum of teacher development in early literacy pedagogy. As a structural variable, alignment is a connecting element that links systems (e.g., child and educator standards) and concepts (e.g., content to the scientific knowledge base) reflected in features of correspondence and comprehensiveness. As a process variable, alignment is a means (as in *to align*) for acting on those structures indicated by features of developmental progression that help "bring elements into line" for a stated purpose, namely preparing a high-quality teacher. Baseline information related to both of these functions can begin to shed light on alignment as an influential element of curriculum design in teacher education and professional development.

## The State Context in Brief

Since the 1990s, two landmark education reform initiatives have given shape and direction to early educator preparation in Ohio. Sweeping changes in teacher licensure in 1998 introduced an Early Childhood License that required teacher education programs to prepare individuals for teaching children ages 3–8 and prekindergarten through third grade. In December 2001, the state adopted P–12 Academic Content Standards in the English Language Arts and Mathematics. At the prekindergarten level, 10 standards in the English Language Arts are delineated in a total of 60 indicators, and five standards in Mathematics are specified in 34 indicators that identify expected levels of student performance. Although many hoped that the convergence of these two initiatives might strengthen and unify preschool and primary grade teacher preparation, this vision is yet to be realized. Vast differences remain in teacher requirements for positions in different early childhood settings. Chartered and nonpublic schools, for example, require only a high school diploma to teach prekindergarten, whereas public preschools require a Pre-Kindergarten Associate license at a minimum.

Elsewhere in Ohio, improvements in early educator preparation were uneven during all of the changes taking place in the 1990s. Although Head Start made significant advancements in requirements for roles stemming from federal legislation (e.g., associate's degrees by 2003; per re-authorization, bachelor's degrees by 2008), requirements for roles in child care systems (e.g., center-based, home-based) remained virtually unchanged. As a result, Ohio's system of early educator preparation is a fragmented one in which different "neighborhoods" of professional groups (e.g., Head Start, child care) maintain their own standards and requirements for entry (Kantor, Fernie, Scott, & Verzaro-O'Brien, 2000). Moreover, credentials earned in one program do not readily transfer to another, which inhibits individual career development and, on a larger scale, systemic improvements in early educator preparation.

A broad-based Early Childhood Professional Development Work Group, formed in 1994, accepted the challenge of developing a career pathway system that would interlink professional "neighborhoods" with a standards-based approach to credentialing and licensure. The group proposed pathways for different roles, including center-based teaching and directing, school-age child care, and family child care, conceptualizing a continuum of professional development with "milestones" as markers of advancement. The teacher role, for example, would consist of four career pathways—assistant teacher, associate teacher, teacher, and lead teacher—applicable to all early childhood settings. The Work Group also strongly encouraged articulation agreements across institutions of higher education to ease transitions along a career pathway or between them. The Work Group agenda continues, and elements of the career pathway system have been incorporated into state-led initiatives and legislation, although a comprehensive system is not yet in place (Kantor et al., 2000). Thus, although recent initiatives provide a supporting framework for alignment, it is not clear whether alignment is present in actuality. The present study provides an initial exploration of this issue.

## Selecting the Sample

In Ohio, a total of 71 higher education institutions offer postsecondary degrees in early childhood education, including 5 CDA certificate programs, 21 associate's degree programs, 47 bachelor's degree programs, and 13 early childhood master's degree programs. Utilizing the Ohio Department of Education teacher preparation web site, individual institution web sites, and telephone and/or e-mail contacts, basic information was gathered for each program (e.g., location, program size, most recent number of graduates, number of required program hours). Early educator preparation programs were identified by type, and a sample was randomly selected for inclusion in the present research, which totaled three CDA, four associate's degree, and five bachelor's degree programs. Selected institutions were contacted to gain consent for participation, to set up a telephone interview with the program coordinator, and to request syllabi for any and all early literacy-related coursework within an early childhood program. Eight institutions agreed to participate, with one of the institutions offering both associate's and bachelor's degrees in early childhood. The final sample consisted of nine case examples—three CDA case examples, three associate's degree case examples, and three bachelor's degree case examples.

## Data Collection

Data were gathered from three sources to identify alignment characteristics relevant to early literacy pedagogy in each program: 1) course descriptions,

2) syllabi and related documents (e.g., field work assignments), and 3) interviews with program heads. Course descriptions represent the official description of a course per institutional policies and, thus, indicate the most salient concepts and skills to be taught. They offer a "quick" look at what educators are expected to learn. A course syllabus and companion documents offer a more complete picture of what will be taught, when, how, and expected learning outcomes. Course timetables in particular indicate critical topics to be covered. Telephone interviews, averaging 30 minutes in length, were conducted with program heads to learn more about the early literacy coursework in the program, to corroborate items indicated in the course descriptions and syllabi, and to probe for perceived strengths and weaknesses in the early literacy training provided. These data sources were organized for analysis into case examples for each institution, consisting of all early literacy-related course descriptions and syllabi in a specific program and interview transcripts.

**Data Analysis**    Our analytic purpose was to examine the case examples for their alignment features, specifically 1) evidence of correspondence to external, research-based standards that is indicative of *external alignment;* 2) evidence of comprehensiveness, shown by a balance of theoretical and practical topics, and repeated exposure to essential topics in early literacy through coursework taking the differing perspectives of knowing, assessing, planning, and teaching and integration of knowledge and skill in content, thus indicative of *horizontal alignment;* and 3) developmental progression, inferred from the amount of time allocated for instruction and the amount of content available as a proxy for complexity or depth of information, thus indicating *vertical alignment.*[1] According to curriculum experts, alignment features such as correspondence to external standards, comprehensiveness in the scope of the curriculum, and sequential levels of content over time, are critical attributes of quality in curriculum design (Marsh & Willis, 1995; Wiggins & McTighe, 1998; Zais, 1976).

We selected the *Teaching Early Language and Literacy: A Core Curriculum for Educators (Preschool)* (2003) and *Teaching Reading and Writing: A Core Curriculum for Educators (Grades K–3), Second Edition* (2003), both state-sponsored professional education curricula in reading pedagogy, as the standards against which to compare alignment features of the case examples (see Tables 10.1 and 10.2, respectively). These curricula, the former geared to preschool early lit-

---

[1]Although, ideally, vertical alignment would be examined by direct assessment of the complexity of the content in the case records along with time allocated for instruction, the information in the case records was not sufficient for the direct evaluation of complexity. As a result, the amount of content available was assessed for vertical alignment in the same way as for external alignment: the percent of standards-based components present. External alignment looks within program levels at extent of standards-based components covered, whereas vertical alignment looks across learning activities within a program or across program levels at the developmental progression.

**Table 10.1**  Learning domains and core components of *Teaching Early Language and Literacy: A Core Curriculum for Educators (Preschool)* (2003)

| Domain | Component |
|---|---|
| I. Knowing Early Literacy Content | Knowing about language and literacy development |
| | Knowing about phonological awareness and alphabetics |
| | Knowing about early reading and writing |
| | Knowing about children's literature |
| | Knowing about print motivation |
| | Knowing about cultural and linguistic relevance |
| | Knowing about family literacy |
| II. Assessing Early Literacy | Knowing and applying basic principles |
| | Analyzing assessment results |
| | Being ethical |
| III. Planning for Early Literacy Instruction | Acknowledging literacy expectations (guidelines and standards |
| | Preparing the literacy environment |
| | Selecting instructional approaches and/or programs |
| | Selecting materials and high-quality children's literature |
| | Providing interventions |
| | Fostering home–school partnerships |
| | Encouraging reflection |
| IV. Teaching Early Literacy | Teaching oral language |
| | Teaching awareness of sounds, letters, and words |
| | Teaching concepts about print and comprehension strategies |
| | Teaching text structure |
| | Teaching writing |
| | Integrating instructional activities |
| | Using technology |

From *Teaching early language and literacy: A core curriculum for educators (preschool)* (pp. 11–14). (2003). Columbus: Ohio Department of Education; adapted by permission.

eracy education and the latter to primary grade reading instruction, provide frameworks for the state's large-scale professional development program in reading instruction for prekindergarten through third-grade teachers. Each curriculum includes research-based content foundational in teaching children

**Table 10.2** Learning domains and core components of *Teaching Reading and Writing: A Core Curriculum for Educators, Second Edition* (2003)

| Domain | Component |
| --- | --- |
| I. Knowing the Content of Literacy Education | Knowing about literacy development |
| | Knowing about the English language |
| | Knowing about literacy processes |
| | Knowing about literacy education models and methods |
| II. Planning for Literacy Instruction | Acknowledging literacy curriculum expectations |
| | Organizing instruction |
| | Preparing the literacy environment |
| | Bridging home and school |
| III. Teaching Literacy (The following concepts are common to the Teaching Literacy domain: teaching protocol, instructional talk, scaffolding) | Teaching oral language |
| | Teaching about words |
| | Teaching reading comprehension |
| | Teaching writing |
| IV. Assessing Literacy Achievement | Assessing reading and writing behaviors |
| | Translating assessment results |
| | Reflecting on literacy assessment goals and uses |

From *Teaching Teaching Reading and Writing: A Core Curriculum for Educators, Second Edition* (pp. 10–11). (2003). Columbus: Ohio Department of Education; adapted by permission.

to read and write and is cross-referenced with the state's prekindergarten through third grade English Language Arts Standards. Each is organized into four learning domains (knowing, assessing, planning, teaching) that provide comprehensive coverage of early reading pedagogy content (see curriculum components in Tables 10.1 and 10.2). Each includes a challenging content that requires adequate time to learn and practice and also lends itself to increasingly more complex treatment (e.g., assessing early literacy), thus affording opportunities to deepen the teacher's knowledge base and improve skill mastery of effective techniques for teaching reading. Each curriculum, in sum, includes credible features of external, horizontal, and vertical alignment demonstrated in correspondence to external professional standards, comprehensive coverage of the learning domain, and developmental progression in the content to be learned. These curricula, therefore, offer a "gold standard" against which other literacy pedagogy curricula at the course and program level might be compared.

We applied a two-phase coding technique to each of the data sources (interview, course description, syllabus) comprising a case. In Phase 1, the team read each source document (i.e., interview transcript, course description, syllabus) and coded each document for any explicit reference to one or more of the curricular components cited in the relevant core curriculum. The curricular components are categorized based on their main focus (i.e., knowing, assessing, planning, teaching). Coursework at the CDA and associate's degree credential levels was coded for curriculum components found in the *Teaching Early Language and Literacy: A Core Curriculum for Educators* (*n* = 24 components) because this curriculum served as the "standard" of what teachers should know and be able to do in preschool literacy instruction. Coursework at the bachelor's degree level was coded for curriculum components in *Teaching Reading and Writing: A Core Curriculum for Educators, Second Edition* (*n* = 15 components) because this curriculum served as the "standard" of what teachers should know and be able to do in primary grade reading instruction. Tables 10.1 and 10.2 list the components in each curriculum and identify each component's emphasis: early literacy content, assessing early literacy, planning for early literacy instruction, and teaching early literacy. The initial time a curriculum component (e.g., knowing about children's literature) was noted in a source document, it was marked and numbered; repetitions of the component were not marked. This approach allowed an unduplicated count of each curriculum component per source document. It also allowed an unduplicated count of proportion of curriculum components covered that focused on knowing early literacy content, assessing early literacy, planning for early literacy instruction, and teaching early literacy.

In Phase 2, each marked reference that described a curriculum component was analyzed and coded *K* to indicate a primary emphasis on knowledge (what educators should *know* as in *knowing about the basic research that supports phonological awareness as predictor of reading achievement*), *S* to indicate a focus on skill (what educators should be *able to do* as in *use critical skills for analyzing assessment results*), or *B* to indicate a dual emphasis on *both* knowledge and skill (as in *know methods for selecting effective reading programs and apply a method in practice situations*). Following a discussion of initial coding discrepancies, we recoded data sources, achieving an average intercoder reliability of 95% for the set of case examples (see a coding example in the appendix at the end of this chapter).

In addition to identifying and analyzing the curriculum components located in each source document, we estimated the amount of instructional time allocated to early and beginning literacy pedagogy in the total professional education programs of the case examples. Here we calculated the number of hours based on course credit, either on a semester or quarter basis, and then determined the percent of instructional time allocated to literacy pedagogy (i.e., instruction provided directly by the course instructor). We did not include assigned field or clinical hours in this calculation because instruction in these activities may or may not be delivered by faculty.

Coded source documents per case were then analyzed to describe the curricular components covered; the extent to which the curricular components covered focused on the domains of knowing, assessing, planning, and teaching; and the emphasis of each curriculum component covered primarily on knowledge (K), skill (S), or both (B). CDA and associate's degree case examples were compared with the *Preschool Early Literacy Core Curriculum*, which consists of 24 curriculum components (see Table 10.1). Bachelor's degree case examples were compared with *Teaching Beginning Reading and Writing: A Core Curriculum for Educators–Revised*, which includes 15 curriculum components (see Table 10.2). Three calculations were made for each case example: 1) the total percent of standards-based curriculum components represented in a case example as evidence of correspondence to the knowledge base; 2) the percent of standards-based curriculum components by domain—knowing, assessing, planning, and teaching—as evidence of repeated exposure to the concepts and skills in different ways; and 3) the percent of standards-based components that addressed knowledge and/or skill indicating the balance of theory and practice as well as integration of knowledge and skill. In addition, the percent of time allocated to instruction in literacy pedagogy was estimated in each case as evidence of opportunity to learn. These calculations are summarized in Tables 10.3 and 10.4.

Despite the small number of case examples, this kind of qualitative analysis is useful because it helps to show the potential strength of a professional education curriculum in preparing teachers for their role as literacy teachers and also permits comparison between major program types (CDA, associate's degree, bachelor's degree), thus shedding light on continuities and discontinuities in a continuum of early literacy pedagogy in the early childhood field (preschool through third grade).

To analyze the degree or quality of alignment by case and between program types, we established a four-interval scale using the percent of standards-based curriculum components as the metric to describe alignment as weak (1%–24% of standards-based curriculum components), minimal (25%–49%), moderate (50%–74%), or strong (75%–100%). Data from the previous analyses were distributed according to these intervals to yield descriptive profiles of the degree of external, horizontal, and vertical alignment by case example and by program type. The total percent of standards-based components located in the case documents was used to assess both external and vertical alignment. Because complexity, a direct measure of vertical alignment, could not be directly assessed from the case records, it was inferred from percent of standards-based components in the case documents. Although external alignment examines percent of standards-based components within a program type as an indicator of correspondence to the professional knowledge base, vertical alignment considers this statistic from the perspective of progression across learning activities within a program or across program levels. Evidence of standards-

Table 10.3  Descriptive information of standards-based components by case example

| Program type | Case | Percent standards-based (SB) components | Percent SB components by learning domain | | | | Percent SB components emphasizing knowledge (K), skill (S), or both (B) | | |
|---|---|---|---|---|---|---|---|---|---|
| | | | Know | Assess | Plan | Teach | K | S | B |
| Child Development Associate | 1 | 7% | 0% | 0% | 14% | 14% | 0% | 8% | 0% |
| | 2 | 44% | 29% | 33% | 71% | 43% | 21% | 21% | 4% |
| | 3 | 0% | 0% | 0% | 0% | 0% | 0% | 0% | 0% |
| Associate's degree | 4 | 54% | 71% | 0% | 57% | 86% | 17% | 25% | 29% |
| | 5 | 44% | 71% | 33% | 29% | 43% | 21% | 21% | 4% |
| | 6 | 42% | 29% | 67% | 43% | 29% | 13% | 13% | 4% |
| Bachelor's degree | 7 | 88% | 75% | 100% | 75% | 100% | 7% | 20% | 67% |
| | 8 | 94% | 100% | 100% | 75% | 100% | 7% | 40% | 67% |
| | 9 | 88% | 100% | 100% | 100% | 50% | 20% | 27% | 40% |

**Table 10.4**    Estimated percent of time allocated to literacy coursework by program type

| Program type | Case | Estimated percent of time |
|---|---|---|
| Child Development Associate | 1 | <1% |
|  | 2 | 5% |
|  | 3 | <1% |
| Associate's degree | 4 | 7% |
|  | 5 | 4% |
|  | 6 | 4% |
| Bachelor's degree | 7 | 16% |
|  | 8 | 16% |
|  | 9 | 14% |

based components suggests learning opportunities that are more likely to be both sensitive to teacher development and representative of pedagogic knowledge that is of sufficient coherence and depth.

The mean percent of standards-based curriculum components by learning domain (knowing, assessing, planning, and teaching) and knowledge and/or skill content emphases was used to estimate horizontal alignment. In addition, the mean percent of standards-based components in cases by program type was calculated and compared to further explore developmental progression as a feature of vertical integration between professional education programs.

## Results

Our exploratory effort provided us with several informative results, and the degree of *external alignment* found in this set of nine cases is shown in Table 10.5. Two observations are notable. First, all the cases at the bachelor's degree level show strong external alignment to the scientific research base in reading. This is understandable given the rigorous program accreditation requirements pertaining to curriculum content at the baccalaureate level (e.g., the National Council for the Accreditation of Teacher Education [NCATE]). Teacher education coursework in reading pedagogy, for example, must be grounded in the content standards established by the International Reading Association (e.g., Assessment, Diagnosis, and Evaluation Standard: Candidates use a variety of assessment tools and practices to plan effective instruction). Second, case examples at the associate's degree level tend to show better external alignment than those at the CDA level, although CDA case 2 is on par with most associate's degree cases, and associate's degree case 4 shows moderate alignment to the professional knowledge base in reading. Thus, although the trend here

**Table 10.5** External alignment by case example and program type

| Program type | Case example | Weak | Minimal | Moderate | Strong |
|---|---|---|---|---|---|
| Child Development Associate | 1 | ● | | | |
| | 2 | | ● | | |
| | 3 | ● | | | |
| Associate's degree | 4 | | | ● | |
| | 5 | | ● | | |
| | 6 | | ● | | |
| Bachelor's degree | 7 | | | | ● |
| | 8 | | | | ● |
| | 9 | | | | ● |

shows more attention to external alignment of the professional education curriculum as the credential level advances, the two contrary cases suggest that it may be an emerging concern at earlier levels of professional preparation with respect to early literacy pedagogy. This make sense as syntheses of scientifically based reading research in early literacy are relatively recent (e.g., National Reading Council, 1998, 2001; Shonkoff & Phillips, 2000). Institutions are only beginning to re-examine their preparation programs in light of this body of knowledge, and some may be further along in this work than others.

Table 10.6 shows the degree of *horizontal alignment* or to what extent a curriculum offers a comprehensive treatment of early literacy pedagogy through coverage of curricular components that emphasize all four domains

**Table 10.6** Horizontal alignment by case example and program type

| Program type | Case example | Weak | Minimal | Moderate | Strong |
|---|---|---|---|---|---|
| Child Development Associate | 1 | ● | | | |
| | 2 | | ● | | |
| | 3 | ● | | | |
| Associate's degree | 4 | | ● | | |
| | 5 | | ● | | |
| | 6 | | ● | | |
| Bachelor's degree | 7 | | | ● | |
| | 8 | | | ● | |
| | 9 | | | ● | |

(knowing, assessing, planning, and teaching) and content that emphasizes both knowledge and direct application of skills.

An observation worthy of mention is that teacher education curricula do not demonstrate strong horizontal alignment based on the evidence reviewed. In addition, their design elements are only partially successful in delivering a comprehensive set of learning-to-teach reading experiences that reflects strong features of balance across knowing, assessing, planning, and teaching as well as across knowledge and application of skills. What does this look like?

When horizontal alignment is weak, as in cases 1 and 3, the curriculum over-relies either on theoretical topics (e.g., Vygotsky's zone of proximal development) or practical techniques; does not allow for a topic to be presented from the multiple perspectives of knowing, assessing, planning, and teaching; and fails to show how knowledge (e.g., of how writing develops) informs pedagogic skill (e.g., how to scaffold the young child's writing to higher levels of performance). When horizontal alignment is minimal to moderate, curricula present a more balanced view of theory and practice, although still tending to dwell on one over the other (often on practice without grounding in theory). They allow for more redundancy in coverage of topics by emphasizing the different perspectives of learning, assessing, planning, and teaching, and they provide more opportunities for integrating knowledge (i.e., of assessment principles) with skills (i.e., implementing an assessment cycle).

Two examples may help to clarify this "middle ground" between weak and strong horizontal alignment further. In case 2, the curriculum demonstrated the feature of integrating knowledge and skill in the standards-based component of *knowing about children's literature* in the Knowing the Content of Literacy Education domain (see Table 10.1). Students are required to complete a "Book in a Box" project that included explicit links to research-based criteria for literature selection. The students, in short, needed to use new knowledge they were learning to complete an authentic task that applied to real classrooms. In the case 7 curriculum, the feature of repeated exposure is evident in several components, among them *preparing the literacy environment* in the Planning for Literacy Instruction domain (see Table 10.2). Topics such as *supportive classroom environments to teach phonics, structuring reading opportunities,* and *creating an environment for student learning* coupled with specific assignments (e.g., establishing transitions and routines) occur regularly across a four-course sequence in literacy pedagogy.

These data show another observation, however, that is troubling—namely that the cases at the bachelor's degree level reflect only a moderate degree of horizontal alignment. Granted, the case documents offer but a small window on each curriculum, yet the foundational data analyzed here do suggest that these curricula may not be strong enough to prepare high-quality teachers for the demands of research-based kindergarten through third-grade reading instruction as called for in the No Child Left Behind (NCLB) Act of

2001 (PL 107-110). In all three cases, the standards-based component of *organizing for instruction*, for example, stresses effective instruction at first through third grades but offers little guidance in how to plan and deliver effective early literacy instruction at the kindergarten and preschool levels, even though the teaching license applies to prekindergarten through third-grade practice. Standards-based components, such as *knowing about the English language, bridging home and school, teaching oral language*, and *teaching writing*, were often only lightly addressed in the professional education curricula of these cases.

The degree of *vertical alignment* in the cases and by program type is based on the total percent of standards-based curriculum components found in course and/or program descriptions (see Table 10.7). For purposes of this analysis, the proportion of standards-based components present also served as a proxy for complexity. Standards-based components, we infer, introduce challenging content and also induce more complex treatment of essential concepts and skills. The data suggest a trend, once again, toward stronger vertical alignment as the level of professional education progresses also seen in both external and horizontal alignment of curricula in these cases. It is heartening to note the consistently strong degree of vertical alignment in the cases at the bachelor's degree level, indicating that these curricula adequately support candidates' development of reading pedagogy concepts and skills. Likewise, the minimal to moderate vertical alignment in cases at both CDA and associate's degree credentialing levels shows the inclusion of challenging early literacy pedagogy content in these teacher preparation curricula, thus pointing to potentially more rigorous preparation at these levels.

Shifting our attention from results that describe curriculum alignment features at the individual case level, we also explored curriculum alignment at the program level, focusing in particular on information about the curric-

**Table 10.7**   Vertical alignment by case example and program type

| Program type | Case example | Weak | Minimal | Moderate | Strong |
|---|---|---|---|---|---|
| Child Development Associate | 1 | ● | | | |
| | 2 | | ● | | |
| | 3 | ● | | | |
| Associate's degree | 4 | | | ● | |
| | 5 | | ● | | |
| | 6 | ● | | | |
| Bachelor's degree | 7 | | | | ● |
| | 8 | | | | ● |
| | 9 | | | | ● |

ular vertical alignment between program types. This permits at least a pre-liminary look at the degree to which curricula at one level might build capac-ity for the next program tier and contribute to developmental progression (vertical alignment) across professional education learning experiences. Figure 10.1 illustrates these results and offers a bird's eye view of vertical alignment across curricula. From this information, we make two preliminary observations. One is the apparent steep climb from curricular experiences at the CDA level to those at the associate's degree level and then to the bache-lor's degree level. What this implies is a very challenging "course to be run" for individuals who seek to advance their careers toward licensure as an early childhood teacher.

There were no curricula by program type that fully met the "gold stan-dard" of state-sponsored professional education curriculum in preschool and primary grade literacy pedagogy. Although the "gold standard" is arbitrary, it may represent professional education curricula in literacy pedagogy as too demanding, too unrealistic, and too ambitious even though firmly rooted in the scientific knowledge base on early literacy development and beginning reading instruction. Moreover, all of these programs are already fully accred-ited to prepare teachers for their role as literacy teachers. Still, when held to

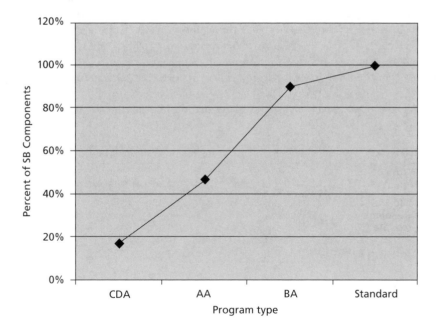

**Figure 10.1.** Vertical alignment to the standard by program type. (*Key:* SB = standards based, CDA = Child Development Associate, AA = associate's degree, BA = bachelor's degree)

what might be a "stiff" standard, the aggregated case data for each program type did not meet the criteria at 100%, suggesting there is room for improvement in their respective curricula.

Instructional time allocated to literacy pedagogy sheds further light on the vertical alignment between program tiers. At the bachelor's degree level, the amount of time spent on literacy methods is mandated at 12 semester credit hours in Ohio, although institutions may allocate the number of credits differently and require more literacy-related coursework. For all practical purposes, the 12 semester credit hour requirement establishes 180 hours of instruction at a minimum. Without further research, it is not possible to say if this amount of time is sufficient or not, but given the myriad of requirements for early childhood licensure, it probably represents a substantial proportion of total program time devoted to teaching kindergarten through third-grade reading pedagogy.

All three associate's degree case examples devoted one course to early literacy pedagogy, representing a larger proportion of the total program for some institutions than others. Given the significance of language and literacy in the preschool years for school readiness, however, the amount of time may be insufficient. Candidates may need more time to learn basic concepts of early literacy teaching and assessment and to integrate abstract concepts into their everyday teaching actions and routines.

At the CDA level, only case 2 allocated a specific course or set of sessions to early literacy. Although concepts of early literacy pedagogy may be integrated into existing coursework and workshop sessions, this is neither enough exposure nor does it afford sufficient practice with basic early literacy techniques (e.g., interactive storybook reading).

## CONCLUSIONS AND RECOMMENDATIONS

This is our initial attempt to examine *alignment*—a widely used term in education that seems simple but lacks technical definition. When applied to program or curriculum, alignment generally refers to how well all elements work together to guide instruction and ultimately learning (i.e., goals, content, learning activities, assessments). In a standards-based environment, curriculum alignment also expands to include the larger contexts of the professional knowledge base, student outcomes, and expectations of educators. For exploratory purposes, we assembled nine case examples of professional education curricula in CDA, associate's degree, and bachelor's degree programs and analyzed the literacy-related coursework within and between them for features of external, horizontal, and vertical alignment. Useful points for further consideration can be derived from this information.

One area for further consideration is paying closer attention to the *external alignment* of program curricula to scientifically based reading research and the early literacy knowledge base, especially at prebaccalaureate levels in which such alignment may be persistently weak or minimal. As early learning content standards take hold in states followed by pressure for higher teaching quality in language and literacy, the need for external alignment in curricula becomes critical to ensure adequate preparation for effective, appropriate early reading instruction.

Another area for consideration is achieving *horizontal alignment* in teacher education curricula, the source of which is in coursework in which the set of learning experiences is comprehensive in design and delivery. To achieve a balance of theoretical and practical topics, repeated exposure to essential concepts and skill, and the integration of knowledge and skill in practice—the curricular stuff of comprehensiveness—is a challenging and difficult enterprise. But without it, the educator's conceptual understandings may not be in sync with technical skills to produce high-quality teaching and expert performance. Tendencies are strong across these cases toward "doing" at the expense of "knowing" and shortchanging scientific thinking in practical activity. As Dewey (1964) warned, such tendencies unchecked can easily slip into a tyranny of technique over the critical reflection so necessary for intelligent action in teaching. Lacking theoretical knowledge, practitioners are limited in their ability to exercise judgment because they tend to over-rely on firsthand experiences and gut reactions in making instructional decisions. In the Ohio context, the Early Childhood Professional Development Subcommittee forewarned of this problem, concluding early on in their work that "training is not coordinated around core knowledge and competencies nor is it articulated with role advancement" (Kantor et al., 2000, p. 176). The subcommittee recommended a "collective stewardship" among various agencies, organizations, and groups in creating a system of educator preparation with a unified voice on integrating competence and skill in pedagogic content.

A third observation relates to *vertical alignment* of curricula within and across program types, or the extent to which a set of learning experiences helps the educator to develop more expertise and to progress. Fundamentally, vertical alignment is about opportunity to learn and can be demonstrated in how much content is available to learn and how much time is allocated to learning it. It is, in this sense, a measure of a program's curricular capacity to prepare educators for implementing effective practices that will impact children's learning in real settings. On a per case basis, vertical alignment of curricula ranged largely from minimal to strong, thus showing the variation in their respective curricular capacity (i.e., affording opportunity to learn). More troubling, however, was a comparison of the aggregated case data by program type to the "gold standard" of the study that revealed a rather steep progression across program types that may be challenging to individuals. If this is a glimpse of what might be, then attention, equal to that focused on early learning content standards, is urgently needed to identify, agree to, and specify what educators *must* know and be able to do as literacy teachers. In order to meet strong standards in reading and writing, children still rely on the conditions afforded them to learn, including the capabilities of their teachers to teach them. Raising the bar on teacher qualifications to meet higher expectations for children's early learning must be matched with strong, well-aligned teacher education curricula that prepare them to meet these ambitious expectations.

Finally, we offer one or two observations on the analytic tools used for identifying and assessing alignment features in this study. Setting a "gold standard" proved beneficial for illuminating strengths and gaps in the curricular components of the nine case sample set as did parsing the curriculum components analysis by domain (knowing, assessing, planning, teaching) and by content goal (knowledge and skill). More work needs to be done on developing tools for assessing alignment in practical, manageable ways. Proven useful, they can help teacher educators immensely in the development and design of more effective curricula in literacy pedagogy at course and program levels.

## REFERENCES

American Federation of Teachers. (2002, December). *At the starting line.* Washington, DC: Author.

Bodrova, E., Leong, D.J., Gregory, K., & Edgerton. S. (1999). *Scaffolded writing: A successful strategy for promoting children's writing in kindergarten.* Paper presented at the NAEYC Annual Conference, New Orleans, LA.

Bowman, B.T., Donovan, M.S., & Burns, M.S. (Eds.). (2001). *Eager to learn: Educating our preschoolers.* Washington, DC: National Academy Press.

Bradley, L., & Bryant, P. (1985). Categorizing sounds and learning to read: A causal connection. *Nature, 301,* 419–421.

Brown., E., McComb, E., & Scott-Little, C. (2003, March). *Evaluations of school readiness initiatives: What are we learning?* Greensboro, NC: SERVE.

Bus, A., & van IJzendoorn, M. (1999). Phonological awareness and early reading: A meta-analysis of experimental training studies. *Journal of Educational Psychology, 91,* 403–414.

Cost, Quality & Child Outcome Study Team. (1995). *Cost, quality and child outcomes in child care centers–Public report.* Denver: Economics Department, University of Colorado.

Danielson, C. (1996). *Enhancing professional practice: A framework for teaching.* Alexandria, VA: Association for Supervision and Curriculum Development.

Dewey, J. (1964). *John Dewey: Selected writings.* New York: Modern Library.

Dickinson, D., & Tabors, P. (Eds.). (2001). *Building literacy with language.* Baltimore: Paul H. Brookes Publishing Co.

Early, D.M., & Winton, P.J. (2001). Preparing the workforce: Early childhood teacher preparation at 2- and 4-year institutions of higher education. *Early Childhood Research Quarterly, 16,* 285–306.

Eliot, L. (1999). *What's going on in there? How the brain and mind develop in the first five years of life.* New York: Bantam Books.

Elley, W.B. (1989). Vocabulary acquisition from listening to stories. *Reading Research Quarterly, 24,* 174–187.

Espinosa, L.M. (2002). *High-quality preschool: Why we need it and what it looks like.* New Brunswick, NJ: National Institute for Early Education Research.

Frede, E.C. (1998). Preschool program quality in programs for children in poverty. In W.S. Barnett & S.S. Boocock (Eds.), *Early care and education for children in poverty: Promises, programs, and long term outcomes* (pp. 77–98). Buffalo: State University of New York Press.

*Good Start Grow Smart.* (2002, April). Washington, DC: The White House.

Gopnick, A., Meltzoff, A.N., & Kuhl, P.K. (1999). *The scientist in the crib: Minds, brains, and how children learn.* New York: Morrow & Co.

Hart, B., & Risley, T. (1995). *Meaningful differences in the everyday experiences of young American children.* Baltimore: Paul H. Brookes Publishing Co.

Head Start Bureau. (2003). The Head Start child outcomes framework. *Head Start Bulletin, 76.* Retrieved April 15, 2005, from http://www.headstartinfo.org/publications/hsbulletin76/hsb76_09.htm

Howes, C. (1997). Children's experiences in center-based child care as a function of teacher background and adult-child ratio. *Merrill-Palmer Quarterly, 43*(3), 404–425.

Howes, C., Phillips, D., & Whitebrook. M. (1992). Thresholds of quality: Implications for the social development of children in center-based child care. *Child Development, 63,* 449–460.

International Reading Association (IRA) and the National Association for the Education of Young Children (NAEYC). (1998). *Learning to read and write: Developmentally appropriate practices for young children.* Newark, DE: IRA.

Kantor, R., Fernie, D., Scott, J., & Verzaro-O'Brien, M. (2000). Career pathways in Ohio's early childhood professional community: Linking systems of preparation inside and outside of higher education. In *New teachers for a new century: The future of early childhood preparation* (pp. 155–191). Washington, DC: U.S. Department of Education, National Institute on Early Childhood Development and Education.

Lonigan, C. (2004). Emergent literacy skills and family literacy. In B. Wasik (Ed.), *Handbook of family literacy* (pp. 57–82). Mahwah, NJ: Lawrence Erlbaum Associates.

Marsh, C., & Willis, G. (1995). *Curriculum: Alternative approaches and ongoing issues.* Columbus, OH: Charles E. Merrill.

Morrow, L.M. (1990). Preparing the classroom environment to promote literacy during play. *Early Childhood Research Quarterly, 5,* 537–554.

National Association for the Education of Young Children (NAEYC). (2001). *NAEYC standards for early childhood professional preparation: Initial licensure level.* Washington, DC: Author.

National Association for the Education of Young Children (NAEYC) and the National Association of Early Childhood Specialists in State Departments of Education (NAECS/SDE). (2002, September). *The place of early learning standards in young children's educational journey.* Washington, DC: NAEYC.

National Institute of Child Health and Human Development (NICHD). (2000). *Characteristics and quality of child care for toddlers and preschoolers.* Washington, DC: Author.

Neuman, S.B., & Dickinson, D. (2001). *Handbook of early literacy research.* New York: Guilford Press.

Neuman, S.B., & Roskos. K. (Eds.). (1998). *Children achieving.* Newark: DE: International Reading Association.

No Child Left Behind (NCLB) Act of 2001, PL 107-110, 20 U.S.C. §6301 *et seq.*

Olson, R.K., & Gayan, J. (2001). Brains, genes and environment in reading development. In S.B. Neuman & D. Dickinson (Eds.), *Handbook of early literacy research* (pp. 81–96). New York: Guilford Press.

Roskos, K., & Christie, J. (2000). *Play and literacy in early childhood: Research from multiple perspectives.* Mahwah, NJ: Lawrence Erlbaum Associates.

Rothman, R., Slattery, J.B., Vranek. J., & Resnick. L. (2002, May). *Benchmarking and alignment of standards and testing* (CSE Technical Report 566). Los Angeles: Center for the Study of Evaluation, University of California.

Scott-Little, C., Kagan, S., & Frelow, V. (2003, June). *Standards for preschool children's learning and development: Who has standards, how were they developed, and how are they used?* Greensboro, NC: SERVE.

Schumacher, R., Irish, K., & Lombardi, J. (2003, August). *Meeting great expectations: Integrating early education program standards in child care.* Washington, DC: Center for Law and Social Policy.

Senechal, M., LeFevre, J., Smith-Dechant, B., & Colton, K. (2001). On refining theoretical models of emergent literacy: The role of empirical evidence. *Journal of School Psychology, 39*(5), 439–460.

Shonkoff, J.P., & Phillips, D.A. (Eds.). (2000). *From neurons to neighborhoods: The science of early childhood development.* Washington, DC: National Academy Press.

Snow, C.E., Burns, M.S., & Griffin, P. (Eds.). (1998). *Preventing reading difficulties in young children.* Washington, DC: National Academy Press.

*Teaching early language and literacy: A core curriculum for educators (preschool).* (2003). Columbus: Ohio Department of Education.

*Teaching reading and writing: A core curriculum for educators (grades K–3)* (2nd ed.). (2003). Columbus: Ohio Department of Education.

Webb, N.L. (1997). *Criteria for alignment of expectations and assessments in mathematics and science education* (Research Monograph No. 6). Madison: University of Wisconsin-Madison, National Institute for Science Education.

Whitehurst, G.J., Falco, F.L., Lonigan, C.J., Fischel, J.E., DeBaryshe, B.D., Valdez-Menchaca, M.C., & Caulfield, M. (1988). Accelerating language development through picture book reading. *Developmental Psychology, 24,* 552–559.

Wiggins, G., & McTighe, J. (1998). *Understanding by design.* Alexandria, VA: Association for Supervision and Curriculum Development.

Zais, R. (1976). *Curriculum: Principles and foundations.* New York: Harper & Row.

# Coding Sample: Institution #3AA

## PROCEDURES

### Phase One

Read each text source (interview, course description, syllabus).

1. Mark each text by numbering the explicit reference to a curricular component cited in the relevant core curriculum coursework at the CDA and associate's degree levels (i.e., *Preschool Early Literacy Core Curriculum*).

2. Place an X on the coding grid (see p. 282) for each component that is referenced under its respective text source.

3. Mark the coding grid only one time for each component under its respective text source even though there may be multiple references to each component in a single text source.

### Phase Two

1. Reread each reference.

2. Decide if the emphasis is primarily knowledge (what educators should know), skill (what educators should be able to do), or both.

3. Mark *K* for knowledge, *S* for skill, and *B* for both next to each *X* (component) listed on the grid.

| Domain | Component | Interview | Course description | Syllabi |
|---|---|---|---|---|
| Knowing content | 1. Knowing about language and literacy development | | X–K | |
| | 2. Knowing about phonological awareness and alphabetics | | | |
| | 3. Knowing about early reading and writing | | | |
| | 4. Knowing about children's literature | | | |
| | 5. Knowing about print motivation | X–S | | |
| | 6. Knowing about cultural and linguistic relevance | X–K | | X–K |
| | 7. Knowing about family literacy | | | X–K |
| Assessing early literacy | 8. Knowing and applying basic principles | X–S | | X–B |
| | 9. Analyzing assessment results | | | X–S |
| | 10. Being ethical | | | |
| Planning | 11. Acknowledging literacy expectations (guidelines and standards) | | | |
| | 12. Preparing the literacy environment | X–B | X–K | X–B |
| | 13. Selecting instructional approaches and/or programs | | X–K | X–S |
| | 14. Selecting materials and high quality children's literature | X–S | X–S | X–B |
| | 15. Interventions | | | |
| | 16. Home–school partnerships | | | |
| | 17. Reflection | | | |
| Teaching | 18. Teaching oral language | | | |
| | 19. Teaching awareness of sounds, letters, and words | | | |
| | 20. Teaching concepts about print and comprehension strategies | X–S | | X–S |
| | 21. Teaching text structure | | | |
| | 22. Teaching writing | X–S | | X–K |
| | 23. Integrating instructional activities | | | |
| | 24. Using technology | | | |

From *Teaching early language and literacy: A core curriculum for educators (preschool)* (pp. 11–12). (2003). Columbus: Ohio Department of Education; adapted by permission.

# CHAPTER 11

# NAEYC's Standards for Early Childhood Professional Preparation

*Getting from Here to There*

MARILOU HYSON AND HEATHER BIGGAR

Coherent, evidence-based standards for the preparation of early childhood professionals can be a powerful tool in improving environments and outcomes for young children. It is essential that standards stem from both professional values and credible, relevant evidence. These foundations allow for action that creates significant benefits for young children's learning and development. Within this context, this chapter focuses on the standards of quality that the National Association for the Education of Young Children (NAEYC) has established and promotes for programs that prepare adults to work with children from birth through age 8. Although the standards have wider applicability, they were developed as guides for preparing early childhood professionals at associate, baccalaureate, and advanced degree levels. Because of NAEYC's role in higher education accreditation, the standards also drive the evaluation of higher education programs, with the results determining whether programs are nationally recognized by NAEYC and the National Council for Accreditation of Teacher Education (NCATE). The standards are also being used in NAEYC's accreditation of associate-degree programs.

Describing the history, current status, and future potential of NAEYC's efforts to create and implement expectations for early childhood professional preparation, this chapter addresses the sometimes-uncertain path from "here" (where the field is now) to "there" (where it may be in the future). It includes recommendations for research and policies that may create even greater effectiveness for the standards, allowing them to more powerfully influence outcomes for early childhood professionals and young children.

## DEFINING AND DEVELOPING STANDARDS

Standards, or signposts that point the way to desired goals, have been key in allowing educators to improve outcomes for young children. This apparently

Extracts in this chapter are from National Association for the Education of Young Children. (2001). *NAEYC Standards for early childhood professional preparation: Initial licensure programs.* Retrieved August 24, 2005, from http://www.naeyc.org/faculty/pdf/2001.pdf; reprinted by permission; and from National Association for the Education of Young Children. (2002). *NAEYC Standards for early childhood professional preparation: Advanced programs.* Retrieved August 24, 2005, from http://www.naeyc.org/faculty/pdf/2002.pdf; reprinted by permission.

simple concept has profound ramifications as well as considerable challenges. Some versions of the standards movement have given it a bad name, constricting the definition of desired outcomes and shaping a narrow and potentially harmful set of applications (Hamilton, 2001). Yet coherent standards present a shared vision of excellence, bringing professionals together to work toward common goals.

## Defining Standards in Early Childhood Education

As typically used in early childhood education, the term *standards* describes widely held expectations for young children, programs, teachers and future teachers, and institutions of higher education. Terminology varies, with a number of words or phases being used to define standards in the field of early education (see Bodrova, Leong, Paynter, & Semenov, 2000; Council of Chief State School Officers, 2004). For example, *early learning standards* are expectations about the learning and development of young children. *Benchmarks* are standards for what children should know and be able to do at certain points in their schooling. *Program standards* are expectations for the characteristics and quality of schools, child care centers, or other education settings for children. *Content standards* represent what students—including adult students—should know and be able to do within a particular discipline, such as math, science, language, or the arts.

## NAEYC's Involvement in Developing Standards for Early Childhood Professional Preparation

NAEYC is a 100,000-member professional association of teachers, administrators, researchers, advocates, leaders in state and federal organizations, and others who are concerned with the positive development and education of children from birth through age 8. To foster positive development and education, NAEYC aims to improve professional practice and working conditions in early childhood education and to build public support for high-quality early childhood programs. It creates opportunities and resources to meet these goals, not only by establishing and promoting standards of quality for preparing and training early childhood professionals but also by identifying and recognizing (i.e., accrediting) quality programs for young children and their families; publishing and disseminating books, videotapes, and journals; hosting conferences and workshops; and advocating at state and federal levels.

NAEYC has a long history of setting professional standards and related guidelines or expectations. One of its first publications, *Minimum Essentials for Nursery Education,* was essentially a standards document (National Association for Nursery Education, 1929). Since then, NAEYC has set forth standards for early childhood programs and established new accreditation performance criteria (NAEYC, 2005a), as well as standards for teacher education programs.

Other NAEYC activities for standards development include establishing guidelines for developmentally appropriate practices (Bredekamp & Copple, 1997) and developing position statements, including an Early Learning Standards position statement (NAEYC & National Association of Early Childhood Specialists in State Departments of Education [NAECS/SDE], 2002) and a position statement on Early Childhood Curriculum, Assessment, and Program Evaluation (NAEYC & NAECS/SDE, 2003).

**NAEYC's Role in Professional Preparation Standards**    In 1982, NAEYC first established standards for the preparation of professionals who work with children from birth through age 8. The impetus for developing these standards came from needs within the early childhood field, as well as from NAEYC's relationship with NCATE. One of 19 specialty professional associations with NCATE-approved standards, NAEYC reviews early childhood programs at 4-year colleges and universities, evaluating these programs for their compliance with NAEYC's standards. This judgment forms an important part of NCATE's overall review of an institution's professional education programs.

In 1999, NAEYC began a major revision of its professional preparation standards, using a process of expert review and consensus building. The timing and focus of that revision were influenced by three primary factors. First and most practically, NCATE had begun to revise its unit standards, which represent general expectations for professional education units (usually, departments or schools of education) at all NCATE-affiliated institutions. The revised NCATE unit standards emphasize outputs—that is, evidence of candidates'[1] competencies as assessed by performance on a variety of measures (e.g., student teaching evaluations, comprehensive examinations, curriculum project evaluations, licensure test results) rather than inputs (e.g., credit hours, lists of required courses) (NCATE, 2002). Second, research showed evidence of the critical role of high-quality teachers in providing the experiences young children require for optimal learning and development (Barnett, 2003; Bowman, Donovan, & Burns, 2001; see also Chapter 4 of this book). Third, rapidly changing demographics and a surge of new early childhood settings and contexts (e.g., Early Head Start, state prekindergarten programs) demanded new frameworks to guide professional preparation and practice (Annie E. Casey Foundation, 2003; Barnett, 2003; Lombardi, 2003). The time was ripe for renewed attention to the standards.

In 2001, NAEYC's Governing Board and NCATE approved NAEYC's revised standards for initial licensure programs (i.e., baccalaureate or master's programs that lead to a first license to teach in early childhood educa-

---

[1]*Candidates* refers to individuals enrolled in programs preparing them for professional positions serving young children and their families.

tion). NAEYC presented its new standards to the field and linked these standards to a process whereby NCATE-affiliated institutions provide a report summarizing evidence of candidates' competence in relation to the standards, including candidates' effects on children's learning. NAEYC also provided higher education programs with technical assistance to orient them to the new standards and review process. In 2002, the NAEYC Governing Board and NCATE approved the revised standards for advanced programs (i.e., master's and doctoral programs that build on prior competencies) (NAEYC, 2002).

With the collaboration of leaders from the American Associate Degree Early Childhood Educators organization (ACCESS) and others, NAEYC has also revised standards for 2-year associate degree programs. The Governing Board approved revisions to the associate degree program standards in July 2003 (NAEYC, 2003).

### Consistencies and Differences in Levels of Early Childhood Professional Preparation

In revising these standards, NAEYC constructed five core standards—each with three to five components, or "key elements"—that are identical across three levels: associate's degree, initial-licensure, and advanced. (See Table 11.1; for more in-depth information, see the section titled "Overview of Core Standards: What All Early Childhood Professionals Should Know and Be Able to Do.") This consistency was intended to underscore that professional preparation has certain essentials; core expectations for knowledge, skills, and dispositions are shared across levels and settings.

Within this framework, however, substantive differences in depth and breadth of expected competencies distinguish levels in the continuum of professional preparation (Hyson, 2003a). That is, to receive national recognition, programs are expected to show evidence of greater depth and specialization of knowledge and skills for candidates at the advanced level than at the initial licensure level. Similarly, candidates in associate degree programs are not expected to reach the same level or type of mastery as those at an initial-licensure or advanced level (i.e., in a baccalaureate program or beyond). For example, associate degree students must achieve competency in a set of supportive skills (e.g., mastering and applying concepts from general education, demonstrating abilities in self-assessment and self-advocacy), whereas advanced students must master a set of essential professional tools and become proficient in a particular area of specialization or professional role (e.g., an accomplished teacher, a program administrator, a researcher, a teacher educator). Table 11.2 provides examples, using a sample key element for each standard, of what a candidate should know and be able to do

**Table 11.1.** National Association for the Education of Young Children (NAEYC)'s standards for early childhood professional preparation

1. In the area of **promoting child development and learning,** well-prepared early childhood professionals
   - Understand what young children are like
   - Understand what influences their development
   - Use this understanding to create great environments where all children can thrive
2. In the area of **building family and community relationships,** well-prepared early childhood professionals
   - Understand and value children's families and communities
   - Create respectful, reciprocal relationships
   - Involve all families in their children's development and learning
3. In the area of **observing, documenting, and assessing,** well-prepared early childhood professionals
   - Understand the purposes of assessment
   - Use effective assessment strategies
   - Use assessment responsibly, to positively influence children's development and learning
4. In the area of **teaching and learning,** well-prepared early childhood professionals
   - Build close relationships with children and families
   - Use developmentally effective teaching and learning strategies
   - Have sound knowledge of academic disciplines or content areas
   - Combine all of these to give children experiences that promote development and learning
5. In the area of **becoming a professional,** well-prepared early childhood professionals
   - Identify themselves with the early childhood profession
   - Are guided by ethical and other professional standards
   - Are continuous, collaborative learners
   - Think reflectively and critically
   - Advocate for children, families, and the profession

From the National Association for the Education of Young Children. (2001). *Standards for professional preparation: Initial licensure programs.* Retrieved April 18, 2005, from http://www.naeyc.org/faculty/pdf/2001.pdf; adapted by permission.

at each of the three levels—associate, initial-licensure, and advanced—although these categories may be less neatly distinguishable in practice.

# OVERVIEW OF CORE STANDARDS: WHAT ALL EARLY CHILDHOOD PROFESSIONALS SHOULD KNOW AND BE ABLE TO DO

Table 11.1 summarizes the essentials of NAEYC's five core standards. This section describes the key elements of each standard and provides examples of

**Table 11.2.** What candidates should know and be able to do across levels

| Sample key element for the National Association for the Education of Young Children (NAEYC)'s core standards | Associate degree candidate | Initial licensure (bachelor's or master's degree) candidate | Advanced (master's or doctoral degree) candidate (Example: accomplished teacher[a]) |
|---|---|---|---|
| 1. **Promoting child development and learning** <br><br> *Sample element*: Knowing and understanding young children's characteristics and needs | The candidate has completed a child development course, receives positive ratings in an observation assignment, or develops a lesson plan that reflects a child's cultural background or developmental needs. | The candidate knows about and understand the multiple, interrelated areas of child development and learning, supporting theory, and current research. He or she understands how influences interact. He or she can apply this understanding. | The candidate has greater depth and specificity of knowledge. He or she can apply this knowledge of, for example, research on risk and resilience, language development, or children's use of technology. |
| 2. **Building family and community relationships** <br><br> *Sample element*: Knowing about and understanding family and community characteristics | The candidate understands and respects diversity, understands family and community influences on learning, and realizes that "race" has a socially constructed, rather than biological, basis. | The candidate has knowledge of family theory and research, and how relationships, home language, ethnicity, cultural values, family structure, and community resources and organization relate to children's lives. | The candidate has great skill in understanding family dynamics and relationships. He or she might identify specific family types (e.g., Latino families, families of children with autism) or activities (e.g., conducting family-centered assessments) for which to specialize his or her skills and insights. |
| 3. **Observing, documenting, and assessing to support young children and families** <br><br> *Sample element*: Understanding and practicing responsible assessment | Although the candidate does not have the training to administer many assessments, he or she observes children with objectivity and fairness and practices confidentiality in sharing assessment results. | The candidate demonstrates knowledge of assessment-related legal and ethical issues, current educational concerns and controversies, and appropriate practices in assessing children with diverse needs and backgrounds. | The candidate shows enhanced skills in using and analyzing assessments, as well as competence in working with colleagues and engaging families in assessment. He or she articulates the issues well and advocates for ethical, effective practices. |

| | | |
|---|---|---|
| **4. Teaching and learning**<br>*Sample element*: Knowing and understanding the importance, central concepts, inquiry tools, and structures of content areas or academic disciplines | The candidate shows the foundations of content knowledge through coursework. He or she can explain and apply this knowledge at an introductory level in designing activities. | The candidate understands the importance of each content area and can observe and describe children's interests and capacities in each. He or she knows how the curriculum supports development in each area, how to build on interests, and how to create environments that support learning. He or she also has basic research knowledge. | The candidate's advanced understanding and detailed attention to each aspect of the element is evident. He or she has at least one area of genuine expertise—for example, using technology to help children living in poverty, focus on early childhood mathematics or applying recent research findings in the classroom. |
| **5. Becoming/growing as a professional**<br>*Sample element*: Engaging in continuous, collaborative learning to inform practice | The candidate is a good team member, seeks new information even when not required to do so, and enhances classroom performance through his or her efforts. | The candidate has an attitude of inquiry, finds resources in libraries or on line, attends conferences, has essential communication skills, and collaborates with colleagues. | The candidate has a notable ability to reflect on his or her practices, articulate bases for decisions, and connect with and use colleagues from other disciplines as resources to improve practice. He or she might seek National Board certification to demonstrate his or her skills and disposition. |

---

[a]Advanced level programs identify one or more areas of specialization for candidates to refine and individualize their professional goals. These areas include early childhood accomplished teacher, administrator, public policy and advocacy specialist, and teacher educator/researcher. For the purpose of simplicity, examples from only one specialization—accomplished teacher—are provided here.

significant trends and new research that influenced revision of the standard. The full standards documents include rationales or supporting explanations for each standard, along with extensive references documenting the standards' evidence base (NAEYC, 2001, 2002, 2003).

## Standard 1: Promoting Child Development and Learning

Candidates use their understanding of young children's characteristics and needs, and of multiple interacting influences on children's development and learning, to create environments that are healthy, respectful, supportive, and challenging for all children.[2]

Knowledge about early development appears to be an especially important predictor of competence among teachers of young children (Peisner-Feinberg et al., 2000; U.S. Department of Education, 2000). This child development focus is philosophically consistent with the long history of early childhood education.

Although child development knowledge may be a starting point, it is not the end point in thinking about early childhood education. Educators frequently emphasize that early childhood programs are and should be shaped by sources other than child development knowledge (Bloch, 1992; Goffin & Wilson, 2001; Stott & Bowman, 1996), including societal values, theories and research on curriculum and pedagogy, and cultural contexts. The relative weight early childhood professionals should give to child development knowledge—and to which version of child development knowledge—remains controversial (Hyson, 1996).

In the context of this continuing dialogue, the language of the revised child development standard (along with its key elements, supporting explanation, and references) reflects current developmental and educational perspectives on the early years and the role of adults during those years (Bowman et al., 2001; Shonkoff & Phillips, 2000). The standard emphasizes a wide range of influences on early development and learning, in particular influences that are more likely to be under the control of early childhood professionals. It goes beyond a maturationist ages-and-stages perspective (Gesell, Ilg, & Ames, 1974) to convey the powerful influence of family, community, culture/ethnicity, teacher–child interactions, and educational experiences on developmental outcomes (see Shonkoff & Phillips, 2000). This standard also emphasizes the application of child development knowledge. It encourages higher education faculty and other trainers to go beyond students' mastery of theories, facts, or research findings about early development to the actual implementation of

---

[2]"All children" means *all*: children with developmental delays or disabilities, children who are gifted and talented, children whose families are culturally and linguistically diverse, children from diverse socioeconomic groups, and other children with individual learning styles, strengths, and needs.

knowledge. For example, simply knowing about Erikson's stages of psychosocial development or about milestones in language development is insufficient. Rather, future early childhood teachers must know how to use this knowledge to make sound decisions about curriculum, assessment systems, and teaching practices, with the goal of helping every child to learn and develop well.

## Standard 2: Building Family and Community Relationships

Candidates know about, understand, and value the importance and complex characteristics of children's families and communities. They use this understanding to create respectful, reciprocal relationships that support and empower families and to involve all families in their children's development and learning.

A strong emphasis on family relationships was a notable characteristic of earlier editions of the NAEYC standards, and that emphasis continues in the current version. This emphasis has been informed not only by research evidence but also by a shared set of professional values. Respect for families and reciprocal relationships with families are at the heart of early childhood values and beliefs, and these values are prominent in NAEYC's guidelines for programs and professional practices (NAEYC, 2005a).

Because of changing demographics within the United States, and because early learning is grounded in family and community contexts (Chafel, 1997; Wozniak & Fischer, 1993), the family and community standard's supporting explanation makes specific reference to the multiple dimensions of family diversity, including family structure, language, and racial identity. Work by Rogoff and others underscores the many ways in which children's development is situated within specific, culturally diverse family contexts (Lynch & Hanson, 2004; Rogoff, 2003; Rogoff, Mistry, Goncu, & Mosier, 1993). Without an understanding of this diversity, it is difficult for teachers of young children to create consistent and supportive learning environments. With understanding, teachers build on families' preferred styles of teaching and communication while socializing young children into the conventions and strategies necessary for school success (Delpit, 1996).

Since the publication of the last edition of these standards, an even more persuasive body of research documents the importance of family relationships and interactions in predicting children's later academic success and their competence in other domains (e.g., Bornstein, 2002; Cassidy & Shaver, 1999). For example, Hart and Risley's (1995) research revealed strong associations between parents' conversations with their very young children and children's vocabulary development and later reading skills. It is therefore essential that early childhood professionals have the skills to support families in promoting children's development.

The revised family and community standard also places significantly greater emphasis on the perspective of early childhood special education. This emphasis comes largely as a result of the Individuals with Disabilities Education Act (IDEA) and its amendments, particularly regarding individualized family service plan (IFSP) processes and expectations. In light of this legislation, requirements to involve families of young children with disabilities go far beyond simply informing families about daily activities. Rather, professionals must include families of young children at every step of the way in making decisions about assessment, in creating IFSPs, and so on. As part of an interdisciplinary team, early childhood professionals must identify families' individual strengths and self-expressed needs with respect to their child and incorporate these into the creation of individualized plans (Beckman, 1996; Dunst, 2001; Turnbull & Turnbull, 2000). Coupled with increased socioeconomic and cultural diversity among families of children with disabilities, these expectations raise the bar for the kind of knowledge, skills, and professional dispositions that early childhood educators need (Vacca & Fineberg, 2000).

## Standard 3: Observing, Documenting, and Assessing to Support Young Children and Families

> Candidates know about and understand the goals, benefits, and uses of assessment. They know about and use systematic observations, documentation, and other effective assessment strategies in a responsible way, in partnership with families and other professionals, to positively influence children's development and learning.

This standard places good assessment at the heart of good early childhood practice (Meisels & Atkins-Burnett, 2000). Good assessment practices are those that measure what is developmentally and educationally significant. They are culturally and linguistically responsive, supported by professional development, family centered, embedded in ongoing activities, and used for their intended purposes. The results of such practices are sound decisions about teaching and learning, identification of concerns requiring intervention for individual children, and program-level improvements that will benefit children (NAEYC & NAECS/SDE, 2003).

Do teachers who know more about assessment do a better job of teaching young children?[3] There is some evidence that training in systematic class-

---

[3]As of 2004, the National Board of Professional Teaching Standards is conducting two studies entitled "Examining Changes in Teacher's Classroom Assessment Practices," and "Investigating the Classroom Assessment Literacy of Board Certified Teachers," which examine whether National Board certification has a positive influence on teachers' assessment competence and whether this, in turn, is related to higher student performance.

room observation or participation in the National Board for Professional Teaching Standards' certification process, sharpens teachers' ability to use effective assessment practices and individualize curriculum and instruction (Black & Wiliam, 1998; Darling-Hammond, 2004; O'Sullivan et al., 2004). Evidence from K–12 education suggests that schools with a strong focus on classroom-embedded, standards-related, ongoing performance assessments have better outcomes for children—in large part because of the improvements in teaching quality that result from this ongoing, systematic assessment process (Reeves, 2002).

Because assessment is sometimes underrepresented in early childhood teacher preparation programs, NAEYC constructed this standard and its supporting explanation to send a strong message about the centrality of assessment in guiding decisions about curriculum and teaching strategies. The standard calls for higher levels of assessment literacy for future practitioners. Another feature of the revised assessment standard is its heightened emphasis on what the document calls "responsible assessment." As policy makers and educators attach higher stakes to tests and other assessments in programs serving ever-younger children (Kagan, Scott-Little, & Clifford, 2003), teacher preparation programs have a responsibility to orient future teachers to ethical issues and professional standards surrounding early childhood assessment (American Educational Research Association, American Psychological Association, & National Council on Measurement in Education, 1999; NAEYC & NAECS/SDE, 2003; National Association of School Psychologists, 2002; Shepard, Kagan, & Wurtz, 1998). This orientation is necessary so that teachers can be informed consumers, as well as advocates on behalf of children and families.

## Standard 4: Teaching and Learning

Candidates integrate their understanding of and relationships with children and families; their understanding of developmentally effective approaches to teaching and learning; and their knowledge of academic disciplines, to design, implement, and evaluate experiences that promote positive development and learning for all children.

Some readers may have wondered why teaching and learning were not mentioned earlier in the chapter, as these topics are sometimes considered the heart of teacher preparation. The fact that the topic of teaching and learning appears fourth in a sequence following child development, families and communities, and assessment does not in any way diminish the importance of this standard. Its place in the entire set of standards reflects the interconnected nature of early development and learning and, therefore, of the requirements for early childhood professional preparation. This complex and significant standard has four components, which are detailed next.

## 4a: Connecting with Children and Families

Candidates know, understand, and use positive relationships and supportive interactions as the foundation for their work with young children.

The first component of the standard (connecting with children and families) sets forth an expectation that well-prepared teachers build close relationships with young children and their families. A compelling body of research supports the primacy of relationships in early childhood teaching and learning (e.g., Hamre & Pianta, 2001; Howes & Ritchie, 2002; Hyson, 2003b; Pianta, 1999). Positive social-emotional development and academic skills can be predicted from children's early, secure relationships with teachers and other caregivers. For this reason, professional preparation programs must deliberately develop candidates' competence in relationship building rather than leaving this area of competence to chance (Bowman et al., 2001; Shonkoff & Phillips, 2000). A special concern in preparing tomorrow's teachers is that a large number of young children have early relationships that are insecure, inconsistent, or abusive (Cassidy & Shaver, 1999; National Center on Child Abuse and Neglect, 1997; Osofsky, 1999). To support these children, teachers need special skills, not only in creating secure relationships (Howes & Ritchie, 2002) but also in linking children and families to in-depth assessment and referral services.

## 4b: Using Developmentally Effective Approaches

Candidates know, understand, and use a wide array of effective approaches, strategies, and tools to positively influence children's development and learning.

The teaching and learning standard's second component (using developmentally effective approaches) focuses on an array of teaching strategies that are consistent with national reports and NAEYC position statements and publications (e.g., Bowman et al., 2001; Bredekamp & Copple, 1997; NAEYC & National Council of Teachers of Mathematics, 2002). Research and the wisdom of practice show that a range of teaching strategies, adapted to children's characteristics and educational needs through thoughtful observation and assessment, is optimal for all children, including children with disabilities (Bowman et al., 2001; Sandall, McLean, & Smith, 2000). These strategies form a continuum—from open-ended investigation, to scaffolded interactions, to direct teaching. Some have interpreted NAEYC's recommendation that teachers use developmentally effective practices to mean that teachers should do nothing but allow children to explore and play without adult guidance or support. This is not the case. Evidence suggests that play has special significance in young children's development and learning—but play can take many forms, ranging from entirely child-initiated activity to adult-scaffolded activity (Bodrova & Leong, 2003). NAEYC rejects the academics-versus-play dichotomy in favor of integrating multiple elements into a coherent system of teaching and learning (Hyson, 2003b), in which adult planning and support provide focus, depth, and conceptual foundations to children's everyday activities.

## 4c: Understanding Content Knowledge in Early Education

Candidates understand the importance of each content area in young children's learning. They know the essential concepts, inquiry tools, and structure of content areas, including academic subjects and can identify resources to deepen their understanding.

The third component of the teaching and learning standard (understanding content knowledge in early education) focuses on subject matter knowledge, or knowledge of academic content. Some view this as the primary element in preparing effective teachers, yet the situation is more complex for early childhood educators. Certainly a major difference between the current NAEYC standards and earlier versions is a more explicit focus on academic content knowledge—not in place of, but in relation to, knowledge of child development, families and communities, and other dimensions of content knowledge in early childhood education.[4] Critics of early childhood teacher education have asserted that programs' traditional focus on learning about how children develop has often attenuated an equally important focus on knowledge in language and literacy, mathematics, social studies, science, the arts, and other disciplines (Stott & Bowman, 1996). The revised standard emphasizes that all teachers of young children—whether teaching in toddler programs, preschool, kindergarten, or second grade—need to balance their child development knowledge with adequate knowledge of the various academic domains.

There is consensus that content knowledge is important in K–12 environments (Tracy & Walsh, 2004), but educators have been less clear about the need for solid content knowledge for early childhood educators. Drawing from research synthesized in *Eager to Learn: Educating Our Preschoolers* (see Bowman et al., 2001) and elsewhere (Commission on NAEYC Early Childhood

---

[4]NAEYC/NCATE definition: "Content knowledge in early childhood professional preparation includes knowledge of child development and learning (characteristics and influences); family relationships and processes; subject matter knowledge in literacy, mathematics, science, social studies, the visual and performing arts, and movement/physical education; as well as knowledge about children's learning and development in these areas" (National Council for Accreditation of Teacher Education, 2004).

Program Standards and Accreditation Criteria, 2004), NAEYC's standards emphasize the importance of knowing the foundational concepts within each subject matter area, with a strong but not exclusive emphasis on literacy and mathematics. This knowledge informs teachers' construction of child-initiated as well as teacher-guided learning opportunities, and it is essential if teachers are to assess children's progress in these curriculum areas.

### 4d: Building Meaningful Curriculum

> Candidates use their own knowledge and other resources to design, implement, and evaluate meaningful, challenging curriculum that promotes comprehensive developmental and learning outcomes for all young children.

However, subject matter knowledge alone is insufficient without integration and application. Therefore, the fourth component of the teaching and learning standard (building meaningful curriculum) emphasizes that well-prepared early childhood teachers must couple that knowledge with a rich understanding of child development and effective pedagogy. This coupling allows teachers to plan and implement educational experiences that help all children engage with and learn the content.

## Standard 5: Becoming and Growing as a Professional

> Candidates identify and conduct themselves as members of the early childhood profession. They know and use ethical guidelines and other professional standards related to early childhood practice. They are continuous, collaborative learners who demonstrate knowledgeable, reflective, and critical perspectives on their work, making informed decisions that integrate knowledge from a variety of sources. They are informed advocates for sound educational practices and policies.

Professionalism has always been important to the preparation of early childhood educators. Again influenced by values and research, this standard emphasizes several elements. Several studies suggest a link between having a commitment or sense of intentionality about being an early childhood professional and the quality of services provided to young children (Howes, James & Ritchie, 2003; Kontos, Howes, Shinn, & Galinsky, 1995). NAEYC expects future early childhood practitioners to develop a professional identity and to view their work as a valuable and necessary contribution to the field.

As reflected in these standards, the NAEYC Code of Ethical Conduct (NAEYC, 2005b), and the position statement on Curriculum, Assessment, and Program Evaluation (NAEYC & NAECS/SDE, 2003), NAEYC also expects early childhood practitioners to be ethically grounded, taking care to prevent harm to children and refusing to take part in practices that do not benefit young children. Besides being attuned to ethical standards and dilemmas that practitioners may face, preparation programs are expected to ensure that their candidates know about a range of professional standards, such as Head Start performance standards, state early learning and K–12 standards, national accreditation standards, child care licensing standards, and other standards developed by national professional associations.

Finally, this standard calls for higher education programs and other programs that prepare early childhood professionals to emphasize continuous adult learning, critical thinking, and advocacy skills. This seems like a tall order, but it is actually a sound investment given the field's rapidly expanding knowledge base and multiple sources of information. No program for professional development—whether community-based training, Child Development Associate (CDA) certification, a 2-year degree, a 4-year degree, or beyond—can give future teachers of young children everything they need. Professional preparation programs must give practitioners the ability to guide their own learning, reflect on their experiences, and make meaning of these experiences so that practitioners may expand their competencies into the future (Schon, 1996; Yelland, 2000).

## MAKING THE STANDARDS WORK

How might the standards' evidence-based expectations work most effectively to benefit future professionals and, ultimately, young children? This section describes the current status of implementation of the standards and some of the challenges to and opportunities for implementation.

## Current Status of Standards' Implementation

As of 2005, the NAEYC professional preparation standards are having their greatest impact in higher education institutions that are affiliated with NCATE. Of the 600 NCATE-accredited institutions of higher education, approximately 150 include recognized (i.e., NAEYC approved) 4-year and/or advanced early childhood programs. Many of those programs were reviewed and approved under the former NAEYC guidelines, but by the year 2010, all recognized and newly submitting early childhood programs will be reviewed for compliance with the revised, performance-based NAEYC standards.

## Opportunities and Challenges

With the revisions to the standards come revisions to practices—teacher education practices, programmatic practices, and candidate and practitioner practices with children. These systemic changes bring new opportunities, as well as new challenges.

**Interest Among Non-NCATE-Affiliated Baccalaureate and Graduate Programs** Although NAEYC's involvement with NCATE accreditation has given force to the standards, this alone is not sufficient to ensure the standards' broad impact. The number of institutions that grant degrees in early childhood education is much larger than those that are NCATE-affiliated. There are almost 1,400 institutions of higher education that prepare candidates at the baccalaureate level or below to work with young children (Early & Winton, 2001).[5] Among the institutions not affiliated with NCATE, interest in the NAEYC standards appears to be growing. For example, some 4-year higher education programs that are not NCATE affiliated have begun to apply NAEYC's early childhood standards voluntarily, because the standards represent a national consensus on quality. Several times per year, NAEYC offers workshops about the standards and program review process designed for faculty and administrators from institutions affiliated with NCATE. In 2004, approximately one quarter of attendees identified themselves as being affiliated with non-NCATE institutions; they attended the workshops to learn about the standards for use in internal program review and improvement processes. Because of this interest, NAEYC has begun to develop self-assessment tools that faculty at both NCATE and non-NCATE institutions may use to evaluate: 1) which opportunities exist for candidates to learn and practice competencies related to the standards, 2) how they assess candidates' progress, and 3) how they use this information for program improvement.

**A New Opportunity for Associate Degree Accreditation** As noted previously, NAEYC has developed standards for 2-year or associate degree early childhood programs. With NCATE support and significant foundation and state-level funding, NAEYC has launched a system to accredit associate degree early childhood education programs that demonstrate compliance with NAEYC's national standards. Beginning in 2005 with an initial cohort of colleges in six states, NAEYC will implement a system of program report submission and peer review, open to all colleges with associate degree programs in 2006. For programs that meet NAEYC's standards and related expectations, the review will result in national accreditation. With approximately 6,700 associate degree students graduating annually from early child-

---

[5]NCATE accredits bachelors and advanced, but not associate, degree programs. It is unclear how many of the programs in the Early and Winton (2001) estimate are baccalaureate versus associate degree programs, but estimates from other sources indicate there are approximately 1,100 associate degree programs that award degrees in child development or early childhood education (Hyson & Duru, 2004). Some of these institutions offer both baccalaureate and associate degrees.

hood programs (National Center for Education Statistics, M. Glander, personal communication, May 28, 2004) and increasing numbers planning to transfer to 4-year institutions, this new system may have a significant effect on program quality and on the ability of community college graduates to articulate (i.e., transfer) credits from 2- to 4-year institutions.

### Creating Incentives and Interest Beyond Higher Education

Despite these new opportunities in colleges and universities, few incentives exist outside of higher education for professional development systems to adopt and implement the NAEYC standards. Enormous numbers of early childhood professionals—those who work in licensed child care programs, Head Start and Early Head Start programs, public school kindergarten, pre-kindergarten, and primary grades—rely on community-based training for their ongoing professional development, yet these training programs have no formal link with the NAEYC standards.

Nonetheless, professionals outside higher education are becoming more aware of the standards. This is in part because the federal *Good Start, Grow Smart* initiative requires states to create comprehensive professional development plans, and states are using the standards in the resources, training, and on-site technical assistance they offer providers (National Child Care Information Center, J. Mascia, personal communication, July 13, 2004). It is also in part because 30,000 NAEYC members received a copy of *Preparing Early Childhood Professionals: NAEYC's Standards for Programs* (Hyson, 2003a), which introduced the standards to many individuals who are not part of a higher education system. With this growing awareness, NAEYC may have a growing opportunity to provide guidance to programs outside institutions of higher education.

### Links to the Child Development Associate Credential

A key component of the field's continuum of professional development is the CDA credential (Phillips, 2004). The CDA Competency Standards include eight content areas that closely align with the NAEYC standards for early childhood professional preparation (see Table 11.3). The CDA began as a noncredit, job-embedded credential, but it has increasingly been linked to college credit. Many colleges grant 12- to 18-semester hours' credit to students entering with a CDA credential. As CDA credentialing and degree programs become increasingly connected, it becomes even more important to emphasize the links between the CDA goals and the expected outcomes in the NAEYC standards for both associate and baccalaureate programs.

### Making the Standards Understandable and Achievable

All programs—whether community based or CDA related, college credit or not, NCATE affiliated or not—face the challenge of making the demanding

**Table 11.3.** Alignment of National Association for the Education of Young Children (NAEYC) standards and Child Development Associate (CDA) content areas

| NAEYC standard | CDA content area |
|---|---|
| 1. Promoting child development and learning | 1. Planning a safe, healthy learning environment |
|  | 2. Principles of child growth and development |
| 2. Building family and community relationships | 3. Strategies to establish positive relationships with families |
| 3. Observing, documenting, and assessing to support young children and families | 4. Observing and recording children's behavior |
| 4. Teaching and learning<br>  a. Connecting with children and families<br>  b. Using developmentally effective approaches<br>  c. Understanding content knowledge in early education<br>  d. Building meaningful curriculum | 5. Steps to advance children's physical and intellectual development<br>6. Positive ways to support children's social and emotional development |
| 5. Becoming a professional | 7. Strategies to manage an effective program operation |
|  | 8. Maintaining a commitment to professionalism |

*Note:* The interconnected nature of elements within both the NAEYC standards and the CDA content areas precludes a simple one-to-one relationship. For example, although CDA Content Areas 1 and 2 map most directly onto NAEYC Standard 1, they also relate to Standard 4. Alignment as depicted here represents the most salient relationships between the standards and content areas.

and complex NAEYC standards achievable by their candidates. As one can see from reading the standards, their supporting explanations, and the expected levels of candidate performance, the expectations are comprehensive and high. NAEYC has taken seriously the body of research about what young children require if they are to learn and develop to their full potential in all areas and about what kinds of skills the practitioners who teach and support them need. The standards ask higher education programs and others to prepare future early childhood professionals to perform in ways that require a high level of skill, insight, and integration. Without stepping away from this complexity or "dumbing down" the standards, professional development specialists and institutions of higher education need to find ways to make these skills, knowledge, and professional dispositions achievable, not overwhelming, for candidates at all levels. As increasing numbers of higher education institutions and other programs reorganize their curricula around these standards, greater numbers of well-sequenced and well-implemented professional preparation programs will be available to serve as examples (Hyson, 2003a).

*Supporting Achievement Among Diverse Students and Potential Students*    Adults enrolled in degree programs and participating in community-based professional development programs in early childhood education are diverse in many ways. They reflect ethnic, cultural, and linguistic diversity. Some are new to early childhood education; others have spent many years in Head Start, child care, or other programs. Some enter these programs lacking strong language and literacy skills and content knowledge; others are highly literate and have strong academic backgrounds. This diversity in backgrounds is a challenge for educators, but when candidates are motivated and supported to enhance their skills, there is potential to meet the challenging NAEYC standards—if programs are able to provide support to build on students' strengths and bridge the gaps in their prior education. Promising approaches to this support exist (Child Care Services Association, 2004; Hyson, 2003b), but they need to be expanded and replicated.

*Creating Pipelines and Pathways*    Along with supporting those currently in early childhood professional development programs, the field urgently needs to focus on recruiting and retaining talented and diverse candidates who will be able and motivated to meet challenging professional standards (Bredekamp, 2004; Hyson, 2002). Given the limited number of early childhood professional preparation programs and current enrollment rates in those programs, and assuming no expansion of that number and access, it would take 10 years to produce enough graduates with bachelor's degrees to meet the demand for prekindergarten settings (Maxwell & Clifford, in press). As of 2005, it is unclear how the field will recruit and retain the number of qualified professionals it needs. Programs and policy makers will need innovative approaches to build the future workforce without sacrificing quality of preparation.

*Enhancing the Professional Development of Faculty and Trainers*    Another challenge is lack of resources or commitment on the part of many 2- and 4-year institutions of higher education to invest in the professional development of their faculty (Bredekamp, 2004; Early & Winton, 2001; U.S. Department of Education, 2000). Many institutions provide inadequate support for faculty professional development, creating the risk that faculty have insufficient knowledge of up-to-date research in critical areas such as literacy and mathematics, inclusion of children with disabilities, and early childhood assessment practices. Pedagogy is a concern as well; some institutions fail to enhance and reward the teaching effectiveness of faculty. Without these skills, faculty members have difficulty teaching evidence- and standards-based content in the most current and effective ways. These challenges parallel those in community-based professional development programs, for which few states have standards for the qualifications, content knowledge, or pedagogical skills of trainers.

***Attending to the Infrastructure***    Improvements will not be possible without attention to public policies at the state and federal levels. Policy makers must help the field build a professional preparation infrastructure to attract, educate, retain, and continuously train early childhood professionals. The minimal teacher qualifications required by most states' child care licensing requirements can be met with almost no attention to the competencies represented in the NAEYC standards. About one third of early childhood program staff leave their jobs every year, creating a revolving door that is unacceptable and that constitutes another major barrier to implementation of the standards. U.S. federal policy should emulate other countries that have created well-financed systems of early care and education, using higher salaries and greater prestige to recruit and retain future practitioners with strong academic credentials and strong professional commitment (Organisation for Economic Co-operation and Development, 2001).

## CONCLUSIONS AND RECOMMENDATIONS

## The Need for Research

Calls for broader use of the NAEYC standards are predicated on an assumption that their use would benefit teachers and children. However, data providing support for this assumption are not yet available. In fact, high-quality studies examining the organization of teacher education programs and delivery of standards-related content and skills in general are not available (Bredekamp, 2004; U.S. Department of Education, 2000). NAEYC and the early childhood field hope researchers soon will provide data on the relationships between standards implementation and teacher quality, program quality, and child and other outcomes. Examples of some key research questions follow.

***Which Supports Allow Higher Education and Other Professional Development Programs to Implement NAEYC Standards?***    As previously suggested, a number of factors may promote or impede the ability of higher education programs to adopt and effectively put into practice the NAEYC professional preparation standards. For example, it would be helpful to know which supports offered to faculty and students (e.g., content- and pedagogy-focused professional development for faculty, release time for faculty to redesign courses and assessment tools in light of the standards, academic or career counseling services for students) have an effect on the program's ability to implement the standards and ultimately to improve candidate outcomes. Researchers could design studies that examine outcomes before and after programs implement such supports.

It would also be valuable to know whether candidate outcomes differ in relation to the pedagogical approaches a program relies on to teach the knowledge and skills related to the standards. For example, do in-depth field experiences and more didactic instruction lead to equal mastery of the standards? Knowing how candidates may best acquire standards-related competencies would assist programs in using their resources most effectively.

### Do Standards-Based Programs Have Positive Effects on Future Teachers' Behavior and Children's Outcomes?

A basic question when evaluating the standards' impact is whether candidate behaviors with children change in predictable ways as a result of participation in a program that is based on the outcomes described in the NAEYC standards. For example, what, if anything, is different about these candidates' relationships with children (the focus of Standard 4a) compared with similar candidates from other programs? What specific teaching strategies do candidates in a standards-based program use in comparison with candidates in other programs? Do these candidates have better skills in planning and implementing effective curriculum, in using appropriate assessment practices, and in communicating with families? Answers to these kinds of questions could profoundly influence the design of early childhood professional preparation.

### What Are the Mediators?

A wide variety of factors may mediate the effects of a standards-based professional preparation program. For example, it is likely that individual or group characteristics—prior education, professional roles and work settings, belief systems, cultural traditions, and other variables—influence the way the knowledge and skills represented in the standards are internalized and practiced. Research could provide better understanding of how these mediating characteristics may affect candidates' learning and of what may be the most effective ways to adapt a program's approaches to support the varied individuals who engage in early childhood professional development.

### What Standards or Key Elements Create the Greatest Impact?

Because institutional resources are not unlimited, which specific competencies should be given the highest priority? These questions go to the heart of the matter, although the answers may be challenging to determine. As discussed, NAEYC has five core standards, each comprised of key elements describing desired outcomes for early childhood professionals. It would be valuable for NAEYC and educators and trainers to know whether certain elements are exceptionally powerful or effective in influencing teacher quality and child outcomes. Research may uncover ripple effects: Having a solid grasp of one key domain (e.g., how to observe and document children's learning) may lead to success in other aspects of teaching (e.g., ability to stimulate oral language through rich conversations) (Reeves, 2002).

However, it may be the case that the whole is greater than the sum of the parts, and that *all* of the expectations, working in tandem, are equally important. If a holistic approach has the best effects, teacher educators would risk neglecting important components by trying to prioritize. Regardless, research could help identify the best approaches to building knowledge and skills, helping to avoid the "mile-wide-and-inch-deep" professional preparation that comprehensive standards can unwittingly promote.

## Working Together

The standards presented in this chapter represent a high level of expectations for what well-prepared teachers of young children should know and be able to do. Yet their very complexity and rigor are reminders of what children need if they are to develop to their full potential. Taking the standards to the next stage—allowing them to have the greatest possible effect on how future teachers are prepared—requires coordinated efforts by researchers, practitioners, and policy makers to construct a shared understanding of the challenging task of teaching the nation's youngest children.

## REFERENCES

American Educational Research Association, American Psychological Association, & National Council on Measurement in Education. (1999). *Standards for educational and psychological testing.* Washington, DC: American Educational Research Association.

Annie E. Casey Foundation. (2003). *KIDS COUNT data book.* Baltimore: Author.

Barnett, W.S. (2003). Better teachers, better preschools: Student achievement linked to teacher qualifications. *Preschool Policy Matters, 2.* New Brunswick, NJ: National Institute for Early Education Research.

Beckman, P.J. (Ed.). (1996). *Strategies for working with families of young children with disabilities.* Baltimore: Paul H. Brookes Publishing Co.

Black, P., & Wiliam, D. (1998). Inside the black box: Raising standards through classroom assessment. *Phi Delta Kappan, 80*(2), 139–148.

Bloch, M. (1992). Critical perspectives on the historical relationship between child development and early childhood education research. In S.A. Kessler & B.B. Swadener (Eds.), *Reconceptualizing the early childhood curriculum: Beginning the dialogue* (pp. 3–20). New York: Teachers College Press.

Bodrova, E., & Leong, D.J. (2003). Chopsticks and counting chips: Do play and foundational skills need to compete for the teacher's attention in an early childhood classroom? *Young Children, 58*(3), 10–17.

Bodrova, E., Leong, D.J., Paynter, D.E., & Semenov, D. (2000). *A framework for early literacy instruction: Aligning standards to developmental accomplishments and student behaviors. Pre-K through kindergarten* (Rev. ed.). Aurora, CO: Mid-continent Research for Education and Learning.

Bornstein, M.H. (Ed.). (2002). *Handbook of parenting* (2nd ed.). Mahwah, NJ: Lawrence Erlbaum Associates.

Bowman, B., Donovan, M.S., & Burns, M.S. (Eds.). (2001). *Eager to learn: Educating our preschoolers.* Washington, DC: National Academies Press.

Bredekamp, S. (2004, June). *Critical issues in early childhood education workforce development.* Cantigny Conference: The Field of Early Childhood Education Professional Development: Implications for Teaching, Research, and Policy, Chicago.

Bredekamp, S., & Copple, C. (1997). *Developmentally appropriate practice in early childhood programs* (Rev. ed.). Washington, DC: National Association for the Education of Young Children.

Cassidy, J., & Shaver, P. (1999). *Handbook of attachment: Theory, research, and clinical applications.* New York: The Guilford Press.

Chafel, J. (Ed). (1997). *Advances in early education and day care: Vol. 9. Families and early childhood education.* Stamford, CT: JAI Press.

Child Care Services Association. (2004). *T.E.A.C.H. Early Childhood® Project.* Retrieved September 15, 2004, from http://www.childcareservices.org/teach/project.html

Council of Chief State School Officers. (2004). *The words we use: A glossary of terms for early childhood education standards.* Retrieved September 15, 2004, from http://www.ccsso.org/eceaglossary

Darling-Hammond, L. (2004). *Examining changes in teachers' classroom assessment practices.* Retrieved September 15, 2004, from http://www.nbpts.org/research/currentres_item.cfm?id=24

Delpit, L.D. (1996). *Other people's children: Culture conflict in the classroom.* New York: The New Press.

Dunst, C.J. (2001). Participation of young children with disabilities in community learning activities. In M.J. Guralnick (Ed.), *Early childhood inclusion: Focus on change* (pp. 307–333). Baltimore: Paul H. Brookes Publishing Co.

Early, D.M., & Winton, P.J. (2001). Preparing the workforce: Early childhood teacher preparation at 2- and 4-year institutions of higher education. *Early Childhood Research Quarterly, 16,* 285–306.

Gesell, A., Ilg, F.L., & Ames, L B. (1974). *Infant and child in the culture of today: The guidance of development in home and nursery school.* New York: Harper & Row.

Goffin, S.G., & Wilson, C. (2001). *Curriculum models and early childhood education: Appraising the relationship* (2nd ed.). Upper Saddle River, NJ: Merrill/Prentice Hall.

Hamilton, S. (2001). The authentic standards movement and its evil twin. *Phi Delta Kappan, 82*(5), 358–362.

Hamre, B.K., & Pianta, R.C. (2001). Early teacher–child relationships and the trajectory of children's school outcomes through eighth grade. *Child Development, 72,* 625–638.

Hart, B., & Risley, T.R. (1995). *Meaningful differences in the everyday experience of young American children.* Baltimore: Paul H. Brookes Publishing Co.

Howes, C., James, J., & Ritchie, S. (2003). Pathways to effective teaching. *Early Childhood Research Quarterly, 18,* 104–120.

Howes, C., & Ritchie, S. (2002). *A matter of trust: Connecting teachers and learners in the early childhood classroom.* New York: Teachers College Press.

Hyson, M. (1996). Theory: An analysis. Part 2. In J. Chafel & S. Reifel (Eds.), *Advances in early education and day care: Vol. 8. Theory and practice in early childhood training* (pp. 41–89). Greenwich, CT: JAI Press.

Hyson, M. (2002, April). *Field of dreams: Higher education and the preparation of early childhood teachers.* Preparing Highly Qualified Prekindergarten Teachers Symposium, Chapel Hill, NC.

Hyson, M. (Ed.). (2003a). *Preparing early childhood professionals: NAEYC's standards for programs.* Washington, DC: National Association for the Education of Young Children.

Hyson, M. (2003b). Putting early academics in their place. *Educational Leadership, 60*(7), 20–23.

Hyson, M., & Duru, M. (2004). Accrediting associate degree programs: NAEYC launches a new system to recognize excellence. *Young Children, 59*(4), 75.

Kagan, S.L., Scott-Little, C., & Clifford, R.M. (2003). Assessing young children: What policymakers need to know and do. In C. Scott-Little, S.L. Kagan, & R.M. Clifford (Eds.), *Assessing the state of state assessments: Perspectives on assessing young children* (pp. 5–11). Greensboro: The University of North Carolina, SERVE.

Kontos, S., Howes, C., Shinn, M., & Galinsky, E. (1995). *Quality in family child care and relative care.* New York: Teachers College Press.

Lombardi, J. (2003). *Time to care: Redesigning child care to promote education, support families, and build communities.* Philadelphia: Temple University Press.

Lynch, E., & Hanson, M. (2004). Family diversity, assessment, and cultural competence. In M. McLean, D. Bailey, & M. Wolery (Eds.), *Assessing infants and preschoolers with special needs* (3rd ed., pp. 71–99). Columbus, OH: Charles E Merrill.

Maxwell, K.L., & Clifford, R.M. (in press). Professional development issues in universal prekindergarten. In E. Zigler, W. Gilliam, & S. Jones (Eds.), *The case for universal preschool education.* New York: Cambridge University Press.

Meisels, S.J., & Atkins-Burnett, S. (2000). The elements of early childhood assessment. In J.P. Shonkoff & S.J. Meisels (Eds.), *Handbook of early childhood intervention* (2nd ed., pp. 387–415). New York: Cambridge University Press.

National Association for the Education of Young Children. (2001). *Standards for early childhood professional preparation: Initial Licensure programs.* Retrieved September 15, 2004, from http://www.naeyc.org/profdev/prep_review/2001.pdf

National Association for the Education of Young Children. (2002). *Standards for early childhood professional preparation: Advanced standards.* Retrieved September 15, 2004, from http://www.naeyc.org/faculty/pdf/2002.pdf

National Association for the Education of Young Children. (2003). *2003 standards at the associate degree level.* Retrieved September 15, 2004, from http://wwwnaeyc.org/faculty/pdf/2003.pdf

National Association for the Education of Young Children. (2005a). *Early childhood program standards and accreditation performance criteria.* Washington, DC: Author.

National Association for the Education of Young Children. (2005b). *NAEYC code of ethical conduct and statement of commitment. A position statement* (Rev. ed.). Washington, DC: Author.

National Association for the Education of Young Children & National Association of Early Childhood Specialists in State Departments of Education. (2002). *Early learning standards: Creating the conditions for success.* Retrieved September 15, 2004, from http://www.naeyc.org/resources/position_statements/creating_conditions.asp

National Association for the Education of Young Children & National Association of Early Childhood Specialists in State Departments of Education. (2003). *Early childhood curriculum, child assessment, and program evaluation: Building an accountable and effective system for children birth through age 8.* Retrieved September 15, 2004, from http://www.naeyc.org/resources/position_statements/pscape.asp

National Association for the Education of Young Children & National Council of Teachers of Mathematics. (2002). *Early childhood mathematics: Promoting good beginnings.* Retrieved September 15, 2004, from http://www.naeyc.org/resources/position_statements/good_beginning.asp

National Association for Nursery Education. (1929). *Minimum essentials for nursery school education.* Chicago: Author.

National Association of School Psychologists. (2002). *Position statement on early childhood assessment.* Bethesda, MD: Author.

National Center on Child Abuse and Neglect. (1997). *Child Maltreatment 1995: Reports From the States to the National Center on Child Abuse and Neglect.* Washington, DC: U.S. Department of Health and Human Services.

National Council for Accreditation of Teacher Education. (2002). *Professional standards for the accreditation of schools, colleges, and departments of education.* Washington, DC: Author.

National Council for Accreditation of Teacher Education. (2004). *Program report for the initial preparation of early childhood teachers/National Association for the Education of Young Children (NAEYC).* http://www.ncate.org/ documents/recognitionReport Forms/NAEYCITPNationalRecognitionReport.doc

Organisation for Economic Co-operation and Development. (2001). *Starting strong: Early childhood education and care. Twelve nation thematic review on early childhood education and care.* Paris: Author.

Osofsky, J.D. (1999). The effects of exposure to violence on young children. *American Psychologist, 50*(9), 782–788.

O'Sullivan, R.G., Hudson, M.L., Orsini, M., Arter, J., Stiggins, R., & Iovachinni, L. (2004). *Investigating the classroom assessment literacy of board certified teachers.* Arlington, VA: National Board for Professional Teaching Standards.

Peisner-Feinberg, E., Burchnal, M., Clifford, R., Culkin, M., Howes, C., Kagan, S., Yazejian, N., Byler, P., Rustici, J., & Zelazo, J. (2000). *The children of the cost, quality, and outcomes study go to school: Technical report.* Chapel Hill: The University of North Carolina at Chapel Hill, FPG Child Development Center.

Phillips, C.B. (Ed.). (2004). *Essentials for child development associates working with young children* (2nd ed.). Washington, DC: Council for Early Childhood Professional Recognition.

Pianta, R.C. (1999). *Enhancing relationships between children and teachers.* Washington, DC: American Psychological Association.

Reeves, D.B. (2002). *The leader's guide to standards: A blueprint for educational equity and excellence.* San Francisco: Jossey-Bass.

Rogoff, B. (2003). *The cultural nature of human development.* New York: Oxford University Press.

Rogoff, B., Mistry, J.J., Goncu, A., & Mosier, C. (1993). Guided participation in cultural activity by toddlers and caregivers. *Monographs of the Society for Research in Child Development, 58*(7, Serial No. 236).

Sandall, S., McLean, M., & Smith, B. (2000). *DEC recommended practices in early intervention/early childhood special education.* Longmont, CO: Sopris West.

Schon, D.A. (1996). *Educating the reflective practitioner: Toward a new design for teaching and learning in the professions.* San Francisco: Jossey-Bass.

Shepard, L., Kagan, S.L., & Wurtz, E. (1998). *Principles and recommendations for early childhood assessments.* Washington, DC: National Education Goals Panel.

Shonkoff, J.P., & Phillips, D.A. (Eds.). (2000). *From neurons to neighborhoods: The science of early childhood development.* Washington, DC: National Academies Press.

Stott, F., & Bowman, B.T. (1996). Child development knowledge: A slippery base for practice. *Early Childhood Research Quarterly, 11,* 16–184.

Tracy, C.O., & Walsh, K. (2004). *Necessary and insufficient: Resisting a full measure of teacher quality.* Washington, DC: The National Council on Teacher Quality.

Turnbull, A.P., & Turnbull, H.R. (2000). *Families, professionals, and exceptionality: Finding a balance* (4th ed.). Upper Saddle River, NJ: Prentice Hall.

U.S. Department of Education. (2000). *New teachers for a new century: The future of early childhood professional preparation.* Washington, DC: Author.

Vacca, J., & Fineberg, E. (2000). Why can't families be more like us?: Henry Higgins confronts Eliza Doolittle in the world of early intervention. *Infants and Young Children, 13*(1), 40–48.

Wozniak, R., & Fischer, K.W. (Eds.). (1993). Development in context: Acting and thinking in specific environments. Hillsdale, NJ: Lawrence Erlbaum Associates.

Yelland, N.J. (Ed.). (2000). *Promoting meaningful learning: Innovations in educating early childhood professionals.* Washington, DC: National Association for the Education of Young Children.

# Economic Perspectives on Early Care and Education

V. Jeffery Evans

Much of the economic research on early childhood care and education has focused on parental decision making regarding choice of a child care setting or early education program. The research indicates that parents are quite sensitive to the price of early childhood arrangements and programs. It also suggests that high-quality care and teaching can be very hard for parents to detect given the wide array of care arrangements available to consumers, ranging from informal care given by family members, friends, and neighbors through small, unlicensed, private arrangements to national organizations providing care and education.

Economic research has been hard pressed to say more about the subject until very recently. This book in general and this section in particular look forward to a time in the not-too-distant future when the problem of individual families finding early childhood care and education will have evolved into the problem of how best to maximize the investment in early childhood from both a public and private point of view.

Why should parents and the public invest in early childhood care and education? There is a growing body of evidence that early childhood development is related to economic success (or failure) later in life and that the early years of life are the most malleable (and vulnerable) periods during the life span. Parents and public policy makers are well advised to take note of the fact that early child care is also early education that can create developmental trajectories that persist throughout life. Similarly, early education programs provide emotional support at a time when children are laying the foundations for their later development through positive and secure early relationships with adults. The developmental trajectories initiated in early childhood precondition learning and economic achievement in later life. They act not only through improved cognitive ability but also by providing values, preferences, and behavior that lead to the motivation to learn and achieve and to avoid self-destructive actions. In economic terms, there are positive human capital returns to investment in early childhood care and education and economic externalities associated with increasing human capital formation. Investment in early care and education pays off in economic success, and private economic success (or failure) can have profound social ramifications.

How can we invest in early childhood care and education? The current options range from simple caregiving arrangements that do not have explicit educational objectives to full-fledged educational programs operated by Head Start or a school system. The trend is to formalize the educational element in these settings, and services are evolving to embrace the idea of universal educational opportunity at early ages. The realization of universal early childhood education is still in the future, but the trend is certainly tending that way—so much so that it is now appropriate to wonder whether there is enough human infrastructure in terms of the early childhood workforce to meet this emergent social demand.

Hence, we are brought to the central questions of this book from an economic perspective. Do we have a stock of early childhood caregivers and teachers with the professional development necessary to meet this demand? How will parents respond in their decision making as the early care and education market evolves? What are the most effective strategies for investing in the development of the early childhood workforce? Economic analysis can indicate which types of early childhood care and education services have long-term effects on children's future and therefore constitute an educational investment in the children's future. It can also identify cost-effective ways of investing in early childhood care education and improve understanding of how the market mechanism will react to alternatives.

Two chapters in Section IV address these questions, and the answers presented in each chapter feed into and inform those of the other chapter. Chapter 12 shows how to pick out effective strategies for investing in the early childhood workforce using cost–benefit analysis. These strategies are the ones that will survive a market test in a price-conscious world and achieve tangible and recognizable effects that parents and policy makers can embrace. Chapter 13 argues that the act of creating and disseminating information that clearly identifies high-quality care and education can itself be an agent of change within the market by providing tangible examples of effective care and education that parents can recognize and then demand. If we as a nation are successful in investing in early childhood care and education along the lines suggested by these two chapters, then we might expect long-term success in achieving our national aspirations in this area.

Both of these chapters are forward looking. Both reveal a mode of economic analysis that can work cooperatively with behavioral science to produce a hybrid type of research that will appeal to both research traditions and the public policy community. Imagine a world in which economist and developmental psychologist can agree on theory, method, and standards of evidence.

In an early meeting sponsored by the Science and the Ecology of Early Development (SEED) consortium in 1998, both disciplines were brought together to begin these deliberations. The topic was child care: how policy can inform research and research can inform policy. The result was a meeting in which the two disciplines did not always communicate well and sometimes conflicted. The meeting did, however, manage to establish lines of communication and eventually resulted in joint work. In the interim, the SEED consortium has consistently fostered collaboration across disciplinary lines, and there are now multiple projects that include developmentalists as well as economists. The meeting that produced this book brought the two disciplines together again, and there was a general consensus that each understood and learned from the other. It was a sign that something important has changed in these fields and that future research could be much better. We have come a long way, as these chapters clearly indicate. The chapters included in Section IV provide a plan for next steps bridging the two disciplines. It will be important to see how this work builds toward analyses of the effects on the early care and education market of making quality ratings widely available to consumers and toward a direct examination of the costs and benefits of different strategies for expanding and investing in the early childhood workforce.

# CHAPTER 12

# A Framework for Cost–Benefit Analysis of Professional Development in Early Care and Education

W. Steven Barnett and Pamela J. Kelley

Cost–benefit analysis (CBA) and related methods of economic evaluation have made a significant contribution to early care and education (ECE) research and policy by providing tools to assess the advantages and disadvantages of specific programs. For example, CBA has provided evidence that high-quality preschool education is a worthwhile public investment, one that can yield a return of $3 to $7 for every dollar invested (Barnett, 1996; Masse & Barnett, 2002). However, for public investment to earn a return of this magnitude, services must be effective enough to produce similar, substantial improvements in children's learning and development.

A number of rigorous longitudinal studies have found that children who received high-quality preschool education made cognitive and social gains that lasted throughout their school years and had important consequences for adult success. Some of these gains included higher grades, less grade retention, lower rates of drug use, and illegitimate births. As children reached adulthood, those who attended preschool had higher rates of graduation, college attendance, and adult employment (Barnett, 1994; Barnett, 1996; Berrueta-Clement, Schweinhart, Barnett, Epstein, & Weikart, 1984; Bowman, Donovan, & Burns, 2001; Bronson, 1985; Consortium for Longitudinal Studies, 1983; Featherstone, 1986; Irvine, 1982; Lazar & Darlington, 1982; Masse & Barnett, 2002; Reynolds, Temple, Robertson, & Mann, 2002). There are several good reviews that provide a more comprehensive account of this research (see Barnett, 1995; Currie 2000; Love, Schochet, & Meckstroth 1996; Shonkoff & Phillips, 2000; Vandell & Wolf, 2000).

Moreover, some studies indicate that high-quality preschool education produces larger gains for children from low-income families than for children from middle- and upper-class families (Barnett, 1995; Burchinal, Ramey, Reid, & Jaccard, 1995). Overall, it is hard to imagine a more positive set of outcomes. If we as a nation truly want no child left behind, then high-quality preschool education is a useful and necessary step toward that goal.

Yet, in spite of all that is known about the benefits of high-quality ECE, studies have consistently rated the quality of care in the United States as substandard. For example, in a 1995 study of 400 centers in 4 states, only 24%

of centers provided quality in the "good" or "above" range (Cost Quality and Outcomes Study Team, 1995). A 1996 study conducted for the National Institute of Child Health and Human Development (NICHD Early Child Care Research Network, 1996) rated 61% of centers in the United States as "fair," 8% as "poor," and 39% as "good" and above. Other studies that have specifically studied the frequency of literacy and math activities have not found a lot of the teacher–child interaction that characterizes high-quality preschool education (Lamy et al., 2004). The evidence to improve quality has guided attention to the quality of the workforce and the potential for preservice education, staff training, and professional development to raise quality.

Economic analysis has great potential to aid program improvement by providing information on the costs and benefits of various approaches to improving teacher quality. To date, the primary application of CBA in ECE has been the evaluation of comprehensive programs rather than specific interventions designed to enhance existing services. This chapter discusses findings from research on professional development and explores how CBA might be applied to evaluate alternatives to enhancing early childhood professional development.

## WHY IS TEACHER QUALITY IMPORTANT?

There is general agreement that the quality of classroom interactions between teacher and child contributes substantially to a child's learning and development (Bowman et al., 2001; Shonkoff & Phillips, 2000). The quality of these interactions is predominantly determined by the classroom effectiveness and general behavior of the teacher. This is, in turn, influenced by the teacher's work environment and his or her general morale (Burchinal et al., 1995; Caughty, DiPietro, & Strobine, 1994; Phillips & Howes, 1987). These characteristics are associated with the teacher's educational qualifications and compensation (Cost Quality and Outcomes Study Team, 1995; Phillipsen, Burchinal, Howes, & Cryer, 1997; Scarr, Eisenberg, & Deater-Deckard, 1994; Whitebook, Howes, & Phillips, 1990; Whitebook, Sakai, Gerber, & Howes, 2001). Teacher quality also has been found to be extremely potent in K–12 education (Goldhaber & Anthony, 2003; Hanushek, Kain, & Rivkin, 1999).

Relatively few studies have focused on the effects of preschool teacher qualifications on child outcomes and even fewer have examined the effects of specific staff development interventions. More research is needed to refine knowledge of the specific contributions of education, training, and experience on child development. Nevertheless, the available research indicates that higher levels of teacher education are associated with greater gains in cognitive and social development in children, more positive teacher behaviors in the classroom, and higher overall classroom quality. These relationships have been associated with both preservice education, such as college degrees and certificate programs, and in-service qualifications, including workshops and training seminars. Particularly relevant studies are reviewed next (see also Chapter 4).

Berk (1985) studied the relationships between caregiver behaviors toward children and caregiver characteristics including qualifications using a sample of 37 caregivers from 12 centers in one Midwestern city. The qualifications measured included college education, child-related preparation, certification, and years of experience. The study found that caregivers with 2- or 4-year college degrees were more responsive and encouraging and offered children more direction and suggestions. They provided emphasis on verbal skills development in their interactions with children almost three times as often as teachers with a high school education. Those with college majors in child-related fields scored significantly higher than those who had not majored in a child-related field on these behaviors. Caregivers with college degrees who had earned certification in early childhood education did not significantly differ from the rest of the college educated caregivers. Experience was not significantly related to behavior. Note, however, that the sample size was quite small.

The Cost, Quality and Child Outcomes Study (1995) used on-site interviews and classroom observations from a sample of more than 400 child care centers in four states to identify the determinants of ECE quality. Of the center characteristics measured, teacher education, staff turnover, staff wages, and child–staff ratios were the strongest predictors of quality. In addition, classrooms taught by teachers with a bachelor's degree or specialized training in ECE were higher in quality than those taught by teachers with less education. Children in classrooms taught by teachers who had more education had greater language and premath skills, greater gains in social skills, and more positive self-esteem and better relationships with their teachers.

The National Child Care Staffing Study (Whitebook, Phillips, & Howes, 1993) studied staff characteristics from 643 classrooms in 227 centers in Atlanta, Boston, Detroit, Phoenix, and Seattle. Teacher qualifications were measured by college education, training, and years of experience. Of these indicators, college education was the strongest predictor of developmentally appropriate practice. Teachers with more years of education exhibited more sensitivity and less harshness when dealing with children and interacted in a less detached manner than did teachers with fewer years of education. Teachers with 4-year degrees in a child-related field scored highest on measures of developmentally appropriate practice. Experience (in years) was not a significant predictor of teacher behavior.

The National Day Care Study (NDCS; Ruopp, Travers, Glantz, & Coelen, 1979) was commissioned by the federal government to determine which characteristics of child care quality had the largest influence on child development. The sample included more than 3000 directors of ECE programs in seven states. A subsample of 49 centers participated in an experiment in which children were assigned to classrooms of varying teacher qualifications and tested using standardized measures of cognitive development. The results indicated that college education, regardless of area of specialization, was not significantly related to child test score gains. However, teachers with higher levels of education who had also received specialized training in a child-related field engaged in significantly more social interactions with children than did caregivers who did not have this training. These types of interactions included questioning, instructing, responding, praising, and comforting. The frequency of these interactions occurred 30% more in classrooms in which the teacher had specialized training. The children in these classrooms were more cooperative and compliant with teachers and peers, were more involved in class activities, and showed more persistence in working at class activities and tasks than children whose teachers did not have specialized training. Furthermore, these children experienced a 25% advantage in growth rate on cognitive test scores compared with children whose teachers did not have specialized training. These results indicated that college education with specialized training in ECE is a critical ingredient for creating a high-quality learning environment.

Arnett (1989) observed 159 child care teachers in Bermuda with four different levels of specialized education ranging from no training to a college degree in early childhood education. Teachers with college degrees showed more warmth and were less punitive and detached than teachers in the other three groups. Teachers who had received some training but who did not earn a college degree in child development were more positive and less punitive and detached than teachers with no training.

The Florida Child Care Quality Improvement Study (Howes, Smith, & Galinsky, 1995) took advantage of changes imposed by the state of Florida on child–teacher ratios and teacher education requirements to study the effect of these characteristics on quality and child outcomes in 150 licensed child care centers. The new state regulations required a Child Development Associate (CDA) credential (or equivalent) or higher level of education for all teachers. Data were collected before the legislation was implemented and in two follow-ups conducted 2 years apart following implementation.

A strong association was found between the implementation of the professional development requirements and increases in children's intellectual and emotional development. Children engaged in more complex play, had closer relationships with their teachers, were more proficient with language, and had fewer behavior problems. Teachers with higher credentials were more sensitive and responsive to children and were less negative and harsh. In addition, measures of overall classroom quality improved significantly following the policy implementation. Teachers with an associate's degree, bachelor's degree, or a higher degree in early education or a related field had the highest scores in terms of children's development and classroom quality. However, teachers who had a CDA (or equivalent) were warmer, more sensitive, and more responsive with children and had higher quality classrooms than teachers without a CDA.

Most studies that have examined teacher education in ECE have measured education by the number of years of schooling rather than comparing educational attainment categories to assess the effects of education (e.g., a 2-year degree versus a 4-year degree). Howes, James, and Ritchie (2003) addressed this issue in a re-analysis of the Cost Quality and Child Outcomes Study (1995) and Florida Child Care Quality Improvement Study (Howes et al., 1995) data sets by classifying teachers into five categories: high school diploma with workshops, CDA training, some college with some early childhood education courses, associate's degree in early childhood, and an undergraduate or graduate degree in early childhood. Results from both data sets indicated that teachers with bachelor's degrees (or higher) in early childhood education were the most sensitive and involved teachers compared with all other groups. Teachers with associate's degrees and CDA credentials were more sensitive and involved than were teachers with some college or high school plus workshops.

Another factor that affects teacher quality is the work environment and its effects on teacher turnover. Turnover limits experience and teacher education (obtained over time) and directly affects classroom relationships with children and their resulting benefits for learning and development (Lamb, 1998). Rates of turnover in the ECE workforce are high across all education levels; estimates range from 20% to 42% annually (Whitebook et al., 2001). As would be expected, there is a strong relationship between turnover and wages, even after controlling for training, experience, and child–staff ratios (Phillips, Howes, & Whitebook, 1992; Phillips, Mekos, Scarr, McCartney, & Abbott-Shim, 2000; Scarr et al., 1994; Whitebook, Howes, & Phillips, 1998). Turnover affects staff morale and workplace performance and, consequently, affects child outcomes (Whitebook & Bellm, 1999).

The National Child Care Staffing Study (Whitebook et al., 1993) followed 92 teachers in California over 6 years to assess the effects of teacher education and turnover. Teachers with a bachelor's degree were more likely to leave if the average level of training for teachers at the child care center was low, wages were low, and the overall rate of turnover was high. In 2001, another study of staffing patterns at 75 ECE centers revealed that teachers identified low pay as the primary reason they were leaving the field (Whitebook et al., 2001). Related evidence is provided by the Cost, Quality and Child Outcomes Study (1995), which examined the relationship between teacher compensation and center quality. Lower quality was associated with lower wages, even after controlling for other teacher characteristics, including education and training.

To summarize, research provides substantial evidence that teacher quality matters a great deal and that both preservice and in-service education contribute to quality. Working conditions and teacher compensation also effect teacher quality. Much work remains to be done to provide more precise estimates of the contributions of various approaches to improving teacher quality, to program effectiveness, and child outcomes. In addition, it seems likely that there are important interactions (e.g., raising education requirements requires raising compensation to be successful) that need investigation. As this work proceeds, it will be important that researchers also attend to the costs of these approaches, an aspect of research that has been almost entirely absent to date. Without knowledge of cost, even very precise information on effects will be of limited use to policy makers and administrators.

## ECONOMIC ANALYSIS

Economic analysis provides methods for choosing among alternatives in order to select those alternatives that are able to accomplish a given result most efficiently (Levin & McEwan, 2001), including 1) CBA, 2) cost-effectiveness analysis (CEA), 3) cost-utility analysis, and 4) cost-feasibility analysis. All four types of analysis have the same goal—to assist decision makers who must choose among one or more policy alternatives in the efficient allocation of resources. Although they are related methodologically, each type of analysis has specific features that make it appropriate in specific circumstances (Levin & McEwan, 2001).

   *CBA* refers to the evaluation of policy or program alternatives in which both costs and benefits can be measured in monetary terms (Levin & McEwan, 2001). Alternatives can be compared on their rate of return or on the net gain in benefits over costs. Perhaps the best known example in early childhood research is the CBA of the Perry Preschool Project (Barnett, 1996). This CBA is based on a longitudinal study of the effects of preschool education provided to 3- and 4-year-old children from disadvantaged backgrounds in Ypsilanti, Michigan (Schweinhart, Barnes, Weikert, Barnett, & Epstein, 1993). Detailed data on staffing, facilities, and other resources were obtained from project and school district records and used to estimate the full cost of the program. In addition, attention was paid to potential costs imposed on parents (time and transportation), but these were found to be minimal for this half-day program in the 1960s. Results of the cost analysis are presented in Table 12.1.

   The benefits of the Perry Preschool Program were calculated by estimating the monetary value of program effects measured from the preschool years through age 27 and projected beyond age 27 to age 65. The program provided (minimal) child care benefits to participating families who would otherwise have to pay for services. The program's effects through age 27 include in-

**Table 12.1.**    Ingredient costs of the Perry Preschool Program

| Instructional staff | $198,884 |
|---|---|
| Administrative and support staff | $7,817 |
| Facilities and equipment (annualized depreciation and interest) | $16,109 |
| Classroom supplies | $3,309 |
| Developmental screening | $1,613 |
| School district overhead | $11,870 |
| **Total cost** | $239,602 |
| Number of children | 21 |
| **Cost per child** | $11,410 |

From Barnett, W.S. (1996). *Lives in the balance: Age 27 benefit–cost analysis of the High Scope Perry Preschool Program* (p. 20). Ypsilanti, MI: High/Scope Educational Research Foundation; adapted by permission.
*Note:* This table is based on 2003 dollars.

creased achievement test scores, fewer years of special education, a higher graduation rate, increased employment and earnings, decreased reliance on welfare, decreased delinquency and crime, and fewer abortions. Economic benefits could be estimated for some, but not all, of these effects. For example, it would be difficult to monetize higher test scores. Earnings (and fringe benefits) were found to be higher for the program group through age 27 and, based on educational attainment, higher earnings and fringe benefits were projected to continue beyond age 27. The estimated benefits from crime reduction include both reduced costs to victims and reduced costs to the criminal justice system.

Table 12.2 shows the most recent published results for costs and benefits of the Perry Preschool Program, including estimated benefits based on interviews, public records data through age 27, and forecasts of continued benefits beyond age 27. The columns in Table 12.2 present the disaggregated benefit and cost values, a conventional procedure that permits examination of impacts on program participants and taxpayers separately as well as the total societal impacts. Benefits and costs were "discounted" to calculate their immediate value, a process explained later in this chapter. As can be seen, the estimated benefits greatly exceed costs, even though not all benefits could be valued monetarily. These results were robust to substantial variations in assumptions and methods. Clearly, the program was a worthwhile investment for everyone concerned.

*CEA* is used to compare the costs and outcomes of alternatives that are designed to achieve the same goal or goals. Typically, only one outcome measure is evaluated. For example, CEA might be used to compare different

**Table 12.2.**   Costs and benefits of the Perry Preschool Program

|  | For participant only | For general public (taxpayers/ crime victims) | Total (for society) as a whole) |
|---|---|---|---|
| Preschool cost | 0 | −16,433 | −16,433 |
| Measured preschool benefits |  |  |  |
| Child care | 982 | 0 | 982 |
| K–12 education | 0 | 9,140 | 9,140 |
| Adult education | 0 | 376 | 376 |
| College | 0 | −1,154 | −1,154 |
| Earnings | 13,659 | 5,623 | 19,282 |
| Crime | 0 | 65,229 | 65,229 |
| Welfare | −2,917 | 3,208 | 291 |
| Total measured benefits | 11,724 | 82,423 | 94,145 |
| Projected preschool benefits |  |  |  |
| Earnings | 14,916 | 6,142 | 21,058 |
| Crime | 0 | 28,378 | 28,378 |
| Welfare | −612 | 673 | 61 |
| Total projected benefits | 14,304 | 35,193 | 49,497 |
| Net benefits (measured and projected benefits minus costs) | 26,028 | 101,182 | 127,209 |

Adapted from "Cost-benefit analysis and cost-effectiveness analysis," by W.S. Barnett, in *Advances in educational productivity. Cost analysis for education decisions: Methods and examples* (Vol. 4, p. 267), edited by H.J. Walberg & W.S. Barnett, copyright © 1994 JAI Press, with permission from Elsevier.

approaches to improving school readiness as measured by a summary score computed from teacher ratings. Alternatives could be evaluated on the basis of their cost of raising readiness by a certain amount. CEA is often used when it is not practical to estimate the monetary value of the outcome.

When there is a single outcome of interest, the results of CEA can be summarized in cost-effectiveness ratios computed either as effects divided by costs (outcomes per dollar) or costs divided by effects (dollars per unit of outcome). The alternative with the highest ratio of outcomes per dollar (or lowest ratio of dollars per outcome) provides the greatest gain per dollar invested. For example, a CEA of alternative professional development programs could compare their effects on teacher qualifications, classroom quality, or early language development per dollar spent on the program. An example of CEA can be found in four educational reforms that were promoted as ways to improve student achievement in the primary grades (Levin 1988; Levin, Glass, & Meister, 1987). The approaches for student achievement included a longer school day, computer-assisted instruction (CAI), cross-age tutoring by peers and/or adults, and reduced class size. Levin and colleagues produced the analysis by adding cost estimates to measures of effectiveness (reading and math achievement gains) obtained from reports of previously conducted studies (see Table 12.3). Costs per child per subject (reading and math) were calculated by allocating total costs to each subject area. The effectiveness of each instructional strategy was determined by the test scores of the students involved in the program compared with those in a control group that received no remedial instruction. Table 12.4 reports the results in ratio form (Levin, 1988) and gives the projected annual cost of producing a 1-month gain in student achievement in the two subject areas for each approach. In terms of the cost-effectiveness ratios, peer cross-age tutoring is clearly the best alternative. CAI ranks next, assuming that math and reading scores are considered equally important. Depending on the relative importance assigned to reading or math, either the longer school day or reduced class size follows. The adult component of cross-age tutoring ranks last.

The ultimate choice depends on the school's situation and what happens to the results when the scale of a reform is changed from what was tested. For example, assume that a school system has $500 per pupil to spend on primary school reform. In that case, peer tutoring is the obvious choice. However, suppose a school has only $250 per pupil for reform. If it adopts the peer tutoring program, then it can fund participation for only about half the students. If it adopts the CAI program, then it will be able to fund participation of all the students. One response might be to operate the peer tutoring program in half of the grade levels so that all students would participate at some time. Alternatively, the district might be able to provide all students with math tutoring only or reduce the number of tutoring sessions by half from what the

**Table 12.3.** Annual costs and effects of four primary grade educational reforms

| Reform | Cost per student per subject | Months of achievement gain | |
| --- | --- | --- | --- |
| | | Math | Reading |
| Longer school day | $61 | 0.3 | 0.7 |
| Computer-assisted instruction (CAI) | 119 | 1.2 | 2.3 |
| Peer tutoring | 212 | 9.7 | 4.8 |
| Adult tutoring | 827 | 6.7 | 3.8 |
| Reduce class size from 35 to 20 | 201 | 2.2 | 1.1 |

From Levin, H.M. (1988). Cost-effectiveness and educational policy. *Educational Evaluation and Policy Analysis, 10*(1), 60; adapted by permission.

**Table 12.4.**   Annual cost (per child) of an additional month of achievement

| Reform | Math | Reading |
|---|---|---|
| Longer school day | $203 | $87 |
| Computer-assisted instruction (CAI) | 100 | 52 |
| Peer tutoring | 22 | 44 |
| Adult tutoring | 123 | 218 |
| Reduce class size from 35 to 20 | 91 | 183 |

From Levin, H.M. (1988). Cost-effectiveness and educational policy. *Educational Evaluation and Policy Analysis, 10*(1), 60; adapted by permission.

model tested. However, the school would run the risk that the reduced program would be less effective.

Further consideration of the decision illustrates the limitations of CEA. Whether a school should invest in peer tutoring depends on whether a 9.7-month gain in math and a 4.8-month gain in reading are worth at least $424 per child. This may not be easy to determine. However, even if a school administration (or board) decided that the gains are worth $424 per child, it should then consider whether it should invest in one of the other alternatives. Assuming that the results of the programs are additive, spending another $238 per child would add 1.2 months more to math scores and 2.3 months more to reading scores. If this is judged worthwhile, then the CAI program should be funded as well. This examination of options should continue until it is determined that the next best option is undesirable or additional funds cannot be raised.

*Cost-utility analysis* refers to the evaluation of alternatives by comparing their costs and their "utility." In economics jargon, *utility* refers to the satisfaction individuals derive from an outcome (Levin & McEwan, 2001). Cost-utility analysis requires a method for estimating the utility or satisfaction associated with effects on one or more outcomes. Alternatives are ranked based on the cost of producing a given amount of utility. Levin and McEwan (2001) provided the following example of cost utility analysis.

A school administration is selecting new curricula to improve the teaching of reading. For each of five selected alternatives, the administration found rigorous estimates of the percentile gain of the average student on four measures: reading speed, reading comprehension, word knowledge, and student satisfaction with reading. In addition, the cost per student for each alternative was estimated (see Table 12.5).

If a single alternative scored highest on all measures of effectiveness and was the least costly, then the best alternative would be obvious. However, the five alternatives vary widely in their measured effectiveness and costs. Cost-utility analysis provides a summary measure of the value of the outcomes that reflect the overall utility, or satisfaction, derived from each alternative. This greatly simplifies the comparison of the alternatives.

**Table 12.5.**   Costs, utilities, and cost-utility ratios of strategies for improved reading

| | | Measure of effectiveness | | | | |
| Alternative | Cost per student | Speed | Compre-hension | Word knowledge | Student satis-faction | Overall utility (weighted sum) | Cost–utility ratio |
|---|---|---|---|---|---|---|---|
| A | $177 | 8 | 6 | 6 | 7 | 6.7 | $26.41 |
| B | $161 | 5 | 4 | 6 | 3 | 4.5 | $35.78 |
| C | $222 | 6 | 9 | 7 | 7 | 7.6 | $29.21 |
| D | $206 | 4 | 9 | 9 | 5 | 7.2 | $28.61 |
| E | $294 | 9 | 6 | 4 | 6 | 6.4 | $46.00 |
| *Importance weight* | | 0.25 | 0.40 | 0.20 | 0.15 | | |

From Levin, H.M., & McEwan, P.J. (2001). *Cost effectiveness analysis* (2nd ed., p. 23). Thousand Oaks, CA: Sage Publications; adapted by permission.
*Note:* This table uses 2003 dollars.

The school administration could consult with parents and school personnel to derive a set of four utility weights. These are also called "importance weights" because they reflect the relative contribution of each outcome measure of effectiveness to overall utility. In this example, the weight assigned to reading comprehension is 0.40, indicating that it is twice as important as word knowledge, which has a weight of 0.20. After weighting each outcome measure by the corresponding importance weight, the results are summed. The final columns of Table 12.5 show cost-utility ratios that were derived by dividing the cost per student by the appropriate utility score. The lowest cost-utility ratios imply the lowest cost for obtaining a given level of utility, and the highest cost-utility ratios imply the highest cost.

*Cost-feasibility analysis* entails estimating only the costs of an alternative in order to ascertain whether it is realistic given the decision maker's budget. If the cost of an alternative exceeds the available resources, then it is not practical under current circumstances. For example, if a program is allocated $400 per child for professional development, then any alternative that costs more than $400 per child would not be feasible without additions to the budget. Cost-feasibility analysis can determine whether alternatives are within a budget constraint. Cost alone is not an adequate basis for deciding among affordable options. In some cases, the appropriate response may be to change the budget constraint—shifting resources within a budget or expanding a budget—if none of the currently affordable options are believed to be very effective.

King (1994) provided an example comparing the costs of three programs (Comer, Levin, and Slavin) for students who were at risk and attending elementary school and estimating marginal costs (i.e., the cost of the additional or incremental services required by each program beyond the cost of the "standard" elementary school operation). The analysis focused on personnel costs, which constitute the vast majority of program resources and included additional staff salaries and benefits and any training/development expenditures for program implementation. King also estimated the opportunity costs of student, parent, and staff resources, which accounted for additional responsibilities required of teachers, parents, administrators, and students. King chose to measure the opportunity cost of time in units of hours per week because of the difficulty of estimating the monetary value of parent and student time. King's results are summarized in Table 12.6. A low and high cost was estimated for each model to allow for various uncertainties.

When analyzing only direct expenditures, King's (1994) comparison indicated that Slavin's Success for All program was most costly, followed by the Comer and Levin programs. Regarding the opportunity cost of participant time, Levin's model required the most additional time from teachers and principals, whereas Comer's required the most parent time. Such an analysis provides useful information to policy makers about the resources they must have to successfully implement a program. It is not a complete basis for choosing a model but is one consideration. Moreover, once a model is chosen, the administrators are forewarned about the time, money, and staff commitments that must be made.

**Table 12.6.**  Cost-feasibility analysis: Comparing cost estimates of three educational interventions

| Expenditure | Low estimates | | | High estimates | | |
|---|---|---|---|---|---|---|
| | Slavin | Levin | Comer | Slavin | Levin | Comer |
| Additional budget expenditures (in dollars) | | | | | | |
| Additional staff | 260,190 | 0 | 66,500 | 704,900 | 199,500 | 199,500 |
| Training | 87,860 | 63,840 | 70,220 | 154,950 | 154,280 | 170,440 |
| Total | 348,050 | 63,840 | 136,720 | 859,850 | 353,780 | 369,940 |
| Additional time requirements of existing personnel (hours per week) | | | | | | |
| Teachers | | | | | | |
| All | 0.5 | 3.5 | 1.0 | 1.5 | 7.0 | 3.0 |
| Partial | 4.0 | 1.0 | 1.0 | 11.5 | 12.0 | 12.0 |
| Principals | 1.0 | 1.0 | 1.0 | 2.0 | 8.0 | 3.0 |
| Parents | | | | | | |
| All | 0.25 | 1.0 | 1.5 | 1.0 | 2.0 | 6.25 |
| Partial | 1.0 | 0 | 1.0 | 2.0 | 0 | 2.0 |

From King, J.A. (1994). Meeting the educational needs of at-risk students: A cost analysis of three models. *Educational Evaluation and Policy Analysis, 16*(1), 14; adapted by permission.

*Note:* This table uses 2003 dollars.

## Choosing a Method of Economic Analysis

Choosing an appropriate method will depend on circumstances, including the information available, the resources that can be devoted to the analysis, the nature of the alternatives to be evaluated and their outcomes, and the available time. How much to invest in an economic evaluation is itself an economic question subject to analysis. The evaluator needs to determine whether the alternatives seem likely to be feasible in light of current or future budget constraints, and the costs of the analysis should be weighed against the costs of poor decisions. Obviously, there are large benefits to economic analyses that can broadly inform many decisions. It typically makes little sense for individual centers or programs to invest heavily in such analyses. This also suggests the need for national or state sponsorship of economic analyses that have broad applicability. Nevertheless, some economic analyses can be useful even at a local or program level. The estimation of the unique costs of various alternative programs and policies is one example.

When planning analyses, it is generally important to consider the nature and number of outcomes involved. When outcomes are limited and the project timeline is short, either cost-utility analysis or cost-feasibility analysis are good choices due to their flexibility with regard to both of these constraints. The disadvantage of using cost-utility analysis is it can only be used to determine which alternatives are within the boundaries of consideration, it cannot be used to determine which one should be selected. The disadvantage of using cost-feasibility is that it relies more on subjective judgment than the other methods because its information is based on the opinions of the primary audience.

CEA is most satisfactory when there is a single outcome of interest. When there are multiple effects, CEA rarely indicates a clear "winner." In such cases, it may be worth investing in CBA to produce a single measure of benefits based on a variety of different outcome measures. The problem with CBA is that all too frequently it is impractical to produce accurate estimates of the dollar value of proximal educational outcomes. CBA may require more extensive research to follow through to outcomes that have economic consequences that can be estimated given current knowledge.

## CONDUCTING ECONOMIC ANALYSIS OF PROFESSIONAL DEVELOPMENT PROGRAMS OR POLICIES

The remainder of this chapter explains the process of CBA as applied to professional development issues. Potential issues that may arise when conducting such an analysis are addressed and implications for policy analysis are presented. As CBA encompasses most of the work required for other types of economic analysis, it provides a useful overarching example. The process is described as a series of seven steps.

## Step 1: Frame the Analysis

The first step in CBA (and any economic analysis) consists of problem identification, identification of the alternatives, and identification of the audience (Barnett, Frede, Cox, & Black, 1994; Levin & McEwan, 2001). When starting out to conduct a CBA, the evaluator should clearly identify the problem or question under consideration to ensure that the most relevant alternatives are assessed. Next, the evaluator must identify the alternatives, which are the potential solutions to the problem addressed. For example, the alternatives in a CBA that identifies the best approach for improving current teachers' effectiveness through professional development might include the following:

- Funding teachers to take specific courses provided by colleges and universities
- Funding teachers to obtain degrees (associate's degree, bachelor's degree) and tying their salaries to the degrees
- Funding teachers to obtain CDAs and tying their pay raises to the CDA
- Having teacher coaches to work with current teachers
- Tying pay raises to length of service
- Funding teachers to attend workshops of their choice for 100 hours over 4 years
- Purchasing curriculum materials for teachers to use on their own
- Tying pay raises to teacher performance and/or child outcomes

In this CBA, the audience would be any individuals or institutions with an interest in the results, including school administrators, policy makers, taxpayers, and teachers. The analysis should take into account their information needs and how they will judge the framing of the problem, identification of alternatives, and methods. Ideally, the desired outcomes will benefit not just local stakeholders but also extend to others. It may be necessary to examine cost and benefits separately for different stakeholders whose cooperation is necessary to successful implementation of the alternative eventually chosen.

## Step 2: Estimate Costs

Education and training are costly whether they involve attending classes and workshops or take place on the job, such as mentoring or learning by doing. They have direct costs such as the costs of instructors and facilities, books and materials, and (when off-site) transportation to and from the training. There are indirect costs, primarily the time and energy of the staff receiving education and training, as well.

The standard method of cost analysis is the ingredients, or resource cost model (Chambers & Parrish, 1994; Levin & McEwan, 2001), which identifies and quantifies all resources necessary to produce each alternative for a given period of time. Although costs may be calculated on a daily, weekly, or even annual basis (whatever makes sense), it is essential to include the full costs of each alternative from beginning to end.

Identification of ingredients is essentially accomplished by writing out a recipe for each policy or program that specifies all of the ingredients and the amount needed. Ingredients are included regardless of who pays for them and whether they are "free." The ingredients that constitute the costs of administration and overhead are included as well as the ingredients employed in direct service. Ingredients include capital (e.g., facilities that were paid for long ago) as well as items that show up in current expenditures. A common classification that can help to ensure that all costs are included is: 1) personnel, 2) facilities, 3) equipment and supplies, 4) miscellaneous inputs, and 5) client-provided inputs. Another approach is to classify resources by function: 1) administration and support, 2) direct services, 3) transportation, 4) buildings and grounds, 5) communications, 6) transportation, 7) students/trainees, and 8) other.

The list of program ingredients for an ECE teacher education or professional development program will depend on the form of delivery, location, duration, and intensity of the program. These vary widely. The list of ingredients for courses at 2-year or 4-year colleges is quite different from the list of ingredients for an 8-week training program over 2 years provided by a curriculum developer, which is, in turn, quite different from 3 half-day seminars during the school year provided by a center's education coordinator.

One of the most useful economic concepts to be encountered in cost analysis is "marginal cost," which refers to an addition to current costs attributable to a new program or policy. The relevant cost for decision making is the extra cost incurred by adding a new education or professional development program or expanding an existing one. For example, it may be possible to expand a professional development operation without adding a program director or other administrative capacity. No additions to facilities might be required if there is space already available. Practical experience suggests that such circumstances are not as common as one might think and that average cost sometimes is equal to marginal cost, but the potential for the two to differ should be kept in mind.

Once all of the ingredients have been specified, the cost of each ingredient must be estimated. The appropriate cost of any resource is its "opportunity cost," which is the value of that resource in its best alternative use. In most instances, the market price of a resource provides a good estimate of "opportunity cost." Thus, for example, the best estimate of the value of people's time often is given by what their employers pay to hire them, their total salary and benefits (including those paid to the government such as the employer's share of Social Security and Medicare taxes). Thus, budgets and fees or other payments can sometimes provide good estimates of costs—or at least part of costs, as will be explained next. Thus, if an organization purchases a training package from a commercial organization or buys training materials, then the cost is best estimated by the price paid.

Unfortunately, market prices and budgets do not always provide all of the information needed to estimate costs. Consider the example of preservice teacher education. The costs paid by the student will not, in most cases, provide an accurate estimate of the costs of the education. First, tuition and fees frequently cover only a portion of the costs of higher education because of government and private philanthropic subsidies to higher education. Thus, it is necessary to obtain estimates of the costs of higher education—typically these can be obtained from published studies or from government statistics on the costs of higher education. Second, student payments for room and board should not be included, as the student would incur living costs independent of the decision to attend college. Third, the opportunity costs of the time devoted to college education must be taken into account. As a first approximation, this opportunity cost can be estimated as the difference between the student's earnings (and benefits) and the earnings (and benefits) of a comparable person who did not enroll in college.

Estimating the opportunity costs of the participants' time is easier said than done, whether it is for college attendance or on-the-job training. Many college students work part- or full-time while going to school, and identifying comparable people who chose not to enter college is not a simple task. For those who work full-time while going to school (a common practice for teachers seeking to add to their education), the opportunity cost is likely to be less time with friends and family and in other leisure activities but could include less time preparing to teach their own classes. Generally, it is acceptable to use market compensation (per hour) to estimate the value of time withdrawn from all of these activities. However, it is necessary to estimate how much time is required by the education and training. Use of a market rate would tend to overestimate cost in one case: when a person would have been involuntarily unemployed (cannot find work) otherwise. This should not be confused with the case of parents who choose to stay home to care for children and engage in other unpaid (but valuable) activities. Market compensation is a reasonable guide to the value of their time.

One complexity in estimating the costs of in-service training arises when the training is provided by the employer. In such cases, part or all of the cost may actually be paid for by the employee through lower compensation. This tends to be true to the extent that the training is not specific to the individual center or school and is valuable to other employers so that the original employer fears that high turnover will result in the loss of the investment in training. The employee would be "repaid" for the value of the training through higher compensation after completing the training. The cost of such training is likely to be best estimated by calculating the employer's costs in terms of administrative and staff time including any time "off-task" by the "trainee" and any direct expenditures on such items as materials, supplies, and transportation. Space may or may not be dedicated to this type of training activity. In practice, it may be difficult to ascertain how much time is spent on these kinds of training activities— a time diary (providing a history of all activities during the day) is one approach that has proved useful. From a policy perspective in which it may be necessary to predict the response to policy changes intended to induce increased training, it is important to remember that the cost is at least partly "paid for" by the employee even if the cost is estimated based on employer expenditures.

For resources other than personnel, the prices paid usually provide an adequate and straightforward guide to costs. Useful prices include private sector fees for consultants and training programs (public sector organization fees may or may not be subsidized) and prices paid for textbooks and curriculum materials, equipment and supplies, and transportation. Facilities cost is another exception in which the prices paid may not adequately reflect cost, although market prices can have a role to play in estimating costs.

Early childhood programs, teacher training, and education organizations may be located in facilities that are operated by another organization and may not be of optimal size. These other organizations may charge rent that is lower or higher than the fair market rate—either providing or receiving a subsidy. Frequently, there is not a charge for facilities in the budget of the educational or child care organization that is the focus of the cost study. In addition, the determination of opportunity cost can be somewhat complicated. When faith-based organizations provide facilities, that space may be unused if not occupied by the early childhood program and many have few acceptable alternative uses when it also is used for faith-based purposes on weekends and evenings. These and other circumstances can make it difficult to determine the opportunity cost of using a space.

Facilities cost can be estimated based on the average cost of commercial space of similar quality in the area and the square footage actually used by the program. However, the best estimate would be the amount of rent the organization would generate from the space if they did not lease or donate it to the early childhood (or teacher education and training) program. Unfortunately, this can be difficult to determine. Because facilities tend to account for only about 10% of the total cost of most operations, even a 30% error in estimating facilities cost would throw off the total cost estimate by only 3%. Any extra costs generated for up-keep, utilities, insurance, and other items related to the program's use of the facilities must be added as well—here market prices are again a good guide.

## Step 3: Identify Program Effects

Any analysis of the benefits of a professional development program or policy will require a study or analysis of its effects on teachers and children. In some cases, it will be useful to examine broader effects on programs and systems that take into account the responses of consumers and producers (owners and operators) as well. The most straightforward questions to be addressed are the most basic ones: Did the policy or program produce an increase in the knowledge and skills of teachers, and did the experiences, learning, and development of young children improve? Research has demonstrated that improvements in proximal child outcomes can lead, in turn, to gains with respect to school achievement, special education placements, grade retention, educational attainment, employment and earnings, crime and delinquency, health, and adult social status and life circumstances. Thus, it may be possible to estimate the economic value of effects on children's learning and development based on their ultimate consequences.

## Step 4: Estimate Monetary Value of Benefits

Moving beyond effects to estimates of the dollar value presents a challenge. When only proximal effects on child outcomes have been measured, direct estimates of economic benefits are difficult to produce. One strategy might be to make use of estimates from prior CBAs of early childhood programs. For example, the improvement in child outcomes produced by a professional development program could be compared with the improvements produced in these studies and then tied to the estimated economic benefits of the improvements. Thus, if a professional development program improved outcomes for children 1/10th as much as the Perry Preschool program (or Chicago Child Parent Centers) improved child outcomes, one might infer that the benefits were 1/10th as large as the Perry (or Chicago) program. This would be plausible only to the extent that the population of children and their circumstances were reasonably comparable with the population in the Perry (or Chicago) program.

When more distal outcomes have been measured—special education placements, grade retention, delinquency and crime, and graduation—then it is possible to construct estimates of the dollar value of benefits specific to the professional development study. To produce such benefit estimates, it would be necessary to obtain estimates of the average costs of a year of school and a year of special education, the lifetime value of earnings and fringe benefits for people with various levels of educational attainment, and the costs of crime. The time and effort devoted to obtaining precise estimates of the economic value of such outcomes should be proportionate to the quality of the underlying data and estimates and the importance of the application. Is this a decision by a single program, a city, a state, or the nation? Does it involve a high-cost or low-cost program?

## Step 5: Calculate Present Value

Every CBA that deals with costs and benefits over 1 year has to make adjustments for differences in the value of money over time. This may be done in two steps—one for inflation and the other for the opportunity cost of money—or both parts of the adjustment may be made at once. The adjustment for inflation is necessary because increases in the general price level over time means that prices rise over time even if the real value of a resource does not change. Inflation-adjusted dollars are called "real" or "constant" dollars in contrast to "current" dollars that are not adjusted for inflation. The second adjustment is required to take into account that there are alternative uses of resources in consumption or investment so that a real dollar today is more valuable than one that will be received only after 5, 10, or 20 years.

The present value of a dollar is calculated to transform real dollars from different years into comparable figures. Present value is the value of a dollar from any year expressed in terms of the value of a dollar at the beginning of the program or policy. If multiple policies or programs are being compared, then present value is calculated by discounting all projects to the date of the one starting first. The formula for discounting constant dollars (i.e., inflation adjusted) to calculate present value is:

$$PV = \$BEN_t/(1 + r)^{t-1}$$

In this equation, *PV* stands for present value, *$BEN_t* stands for the value of benefits in year *t* in real dollars, and *r* is the real discount rate. The discount rate is essentially an interest rate that indicates the tradeoff rate between dollars in one year and dollars in the next year (Barnett, 1994). All economists do not agree on a single discount rate for all purposes, but real rates in the range of 3%–7% have wide acceptance.

Omitting the discounting step will tend to make programs or policies appear more economically sound than they really are and leads to inaccurate comparisons of alternatives that differ in their patterns of costs and benefits over time. After present value has been calculated, all the costs and benefits can be combined to calculate net present value (benefits–costs) or a benefit–cost ratio, which can be used to rank alternatives. A third alternative that is sometimes used is to calculate the (internal) rate of return, which is the discount rate at which the present value of benefits and costs equal each other. Projects can then be ranked according to their net present value, benefit–cost ratio, or internal rate of return. There is no simple rule that can be applied to select the best alternatives in every situation (Barnett, 1994). However, a positive net present value is a clear indicator that a program or policy can make a positive economic contribution to society and may be a sound public investment (Barnett, 1994).

## Step 6: Estimate the Distribution of Costs and Benefits

In the real world, people are concerned with who gains and who loses, not simply whether the sum of all costs and benefits leads to a net gain for society as a whole. Thus, it is generally useful to examine the distribution of costs and benefits to different parts of the population. For example, a common concern with public policies and programs is the extent to which they produce costs and benefits for taxpayers and for the policy or program's target population. With professional development programs, it often is desirable to know what the costs and benefits are to teachers and their employers as their response to a program can determine its feasibility. For example, a requirement that teachers obtain more preservice education in order to teach will raise costs to teachers entering the field. It may also raise the costs to programs of hiring teachers. If salaries are higher, then this benefits teachers who enter the field. If fewer teachers are hired because of higher salaries, then this imposes a cost on the teachers who are not hired and must take less satisfying or lower-paying jobs (*compared with* the jobs they would have at the old salaries). As these examples suggest, identifying the distribution of costs and benefits can be a complicated task, and precise estimates can be difficult to produce.

The cost of professional development may or may not be borne by the person or organization responsible for the expenditure of time or money. With no government subsidy, cost will be split between teachers and employers. They may be fully or partially compensated for this cost on the benefit side by way of increased compensation (e.g., nonmonetary compensation to teachers in the form of increased autonomy or status) or higher fees. Ultimately, consumers may pay part or all of the cost through higher fees. The consumers may be private or public (and so costs would be passed on to taxpayers in the latter case). There are no simple rules for allocating costs in a field such as education in which both public and private sectors are involved on both the supply and demand sides.

To further complicate the analysis, some of the costs of professional development may not be "paid" by anyone in an obvious manner. For example, training might be provided by program administrators to teachers by reallocating the time of each away from direct service (by having more professional development days when preschool programs serve no children). Most of the costs would be imposed on the children and their families in the form of reduced services, which may impose costs on families for alternative child care arrangements and on the children in the form of less pleasant activities (or more pleasant, transforming this into a benefit from the child's perspective) and poorer outcomes. The last of these is effectively netted out in estimates of the training's impact on child outcomes. If there is no net effect of the training on child outcomes, then the cost is primarily to parents for increased child care. Whether the cost of staff salaries is properly considered a cost in this case depends on the alternative under consideration: Is the alternative to reduce the number of days and pay staff less or to deliver services for additional days at the same salaries?

## Step 7: Conduct Sensitivity Analysis

There is always some uncertainty surrounding cost, effects, and benefits esti-mates. One way to deal with the uncertainty is to conduct a sensitivity analy-ses in which assumptions about costs, effects, and benefits are varied to pro-duce a range of estimated costs, effects, and benefits. Two commonly varied assumptions are the discount rate used to calculate present value and the growth rate of future productivity of workers. Confidence intervals around estimated effects can provide another source of variation to examine. When there is a great deal of uncertainty about outcomes and their value, studies may wish to ask just how small effects and benefits can be if the program or policy is to remain a good investment. Studies can also vary assumptions about cost. For example, a large increase in demand could raise the cost of training—would plausible increases in cost still leave training a good invest-ment? Sensitivity analysis can be especially useful for estimating the distribu-tion of costs and benefits when there is considerable uncertainty regarding the responses of consumers, teachers, and producers to the program or policy.

## CONCLUSIONS AND RECOMMENDATIONS

Many kinds of decisions about professional development can benefit from the application of CBA. It can be useful as a framework for thinking about the implications of alternative policies and programs, even if there is not sufficient information to make complete application feasible. Examples of the kinds of questions that could be usefully addressed by economic analysis include the following:

- What are the consequences of requiring various levels of preservice educa-tion for preschool teachers including various credentials and degrees? How much must teachers be paid to induce them to acquire the required educa-tion? To what extent would subsidies for higher education induce teachers to acquire the required education at current or anticipated salaries?

- If preservice or in-service requirements for licensed programs are increased, then to what extent might this 1) drive up the required public subsidies to sustain the programs, 2) lead to reallocations of program expenditures toward teacher compensation, and 3) lead parents to shift to unlicensed substitutes because they are unwilling to pay higher fees?

- How much should be allocated to alternative types of in-service and pre-service professional development? To what extent should programs subsi-dize teachers' acquisition of additional coursework in early childhood edu-cation or the attainment of advanced degrees?

- How much should teachers be paid to start, and how much should pay rise with longevity?

- To what extent might the costs of increased preservice training and higher compensation be offset by reduced costs of hiring and in-service training associated with lower turnover rates?

- What is the value of teacher coaches when launching new programs with many new teachers or when the demands on early childhood teachers with respect to teaching have been dramatically increased?

- How much additional teacher effectiveness can be purchased by an additional $1000 or $5000 in teacher compensation? How much additional teacher effectiveness can be purchased by an additional $1000 or $5000 per teacher spent on professional development (keeping in mind that teachers must stay for the program and its clients to benefit)? Is there an interaction between the two?

These are all important questions for which CBA would be useful. Answering them will require studies of the impacts of alternative policies and programs relating to professional development. At least some of those studies would have to be of sufficient size to address questions of the market responses over time. The field is more or less in its infancy with respect to such studies. Even a few strong studies would contribute significantly to increased understanding of what works best under what circumstances. It is hoped that the exposition of CBA here might help inform the development and design of such studies.

## REFERENCES

Arnett, J. (1989). Caregivers in day-care centers: Does training matter? *Journal of Applied Developmental Psychology, 10*(4), 541–552.

Barnett, W.S. (1994). Cost-effectiveness cost-benefit analysis. In H.J. Walberg & W.S. Barnett (Eds.), *Advances in educational productivity. Cost analysis for education decisions: Methods and examples* (Vol. 4, pp. 257–276). Greenwich, CT: JAI Press.

Barnett, W.S. (1995). Long-term effects of early childhood programs on cognitive and school outcomes. *The Future of Children, 5*(3), 25–50.

Barnett, W.S. (1996). *Lives in the balance: Age 27 benefit-cost analysis of the High Scope Perry Preschool Program.* Ypsilanti, MI: High/Scope Educational Research Foundation.

Barnett, W.S., Frede, E., Cox, J.O., & Black, T. (1994). Using cost analysis to improve early childhood programs. In W.S. Barnett (Ed.), *Cost analysis for education decisions: Methods and examples* (pp. 145–182). Greenwich, CT: JAI Press.

Berk, L.E. (1985). Relationship of caregiver education to child-oriented attitudes, job satisfaction, and behaviors toward children. *Child Care Quarterly, 14*(2), 103–129.

Berrueta-Clement, J.R., Schweinhart, L.J., Barnett, W.S., Epstein, A.S., & Weikart, D.P. (1984). *Changed lives: The effects of the Perry Preschool Program on youths through age 19.* Ypsilanti, MI: High/Scope Press.

Bowman, B.T., Donovan, S.M., Burns, S.M. (2001). *Eager to learn: Educating our preschoolers.* Washington, DC: National Academy Press.

Bronson, W.C. (1985). Growth in the organization of behavior over the second year of life. *Developmental Psychology, 21*(1), 108–117.

Burchinal, M.R., Ramey, S.L., Reid, M.K., & Jaccard, J. (1995). Early child care experiences and their association with family and child characteristics during middle childhood. *Early Childhood Research Quarterly, 10,* 33–61.

Caughty, M., DiPietro, J., & Strobine, D.M. (1994). Day care participation as a protective factor in the cognitive development of low income children. *Child Development, 65,* 457–471.

Chambers, J., & Parrish, T. (1994). Modeling resource costs. In H.J. Walberg & W.S. Barnett (Eds.), *Advances in educational productivity. Cost analysis for education decisions: Methods and examples* (Vol. 4, pp. 7–21). Greenwich, CT: JAI Press.

Consortium for Longitudinal Studies. (1983). *As the twig is bent: Lasting effects of preschool programs.* Mahwah, NJ: Lawrence Erlbaum Associates.

Cost Quality and Outcomes Study Team. (1995). *Cost, quality and outcomes in child care centers.* Denver: Economic Department, University of Colorado.

Currie, J. (2000). *Early childhood intervention programs: What do we know?* Los Angeles: National Bureau of Economic Research, University of California.

Featherstone, H. (1986). Preschool: It does make a difference. Special report: Early childhood education. *Principal, 65*(5), 16–17.

Gersten, R. (1986). Response to "consequences of three preschool curriculum models through age 15." *Early Childhood Research Quarterly, 1*(3), 293–301.

Goldhaber, D., & Anthony, E. (2003). *Teacher quality and student achievement.* New York: ERIC Clearinghouse on Urban Education.

Gray, S.W., & Klaus, R.A. (1970). The early training project: A seventh year report. *Child Development, 41*(4), 909–924.

Hanushek, E.A., Kain, J.F., & Rivkin, S.G. (1999, January). *Do higher salaries buy better teachers?* Paper presented at the Annual Meeting of the American Economic Association, New York.

Howes, C., James, J., & Ritchie, S. (2003). Pathways to effective teaching. *Early Childhood Research Quarterly, 18,* 104–120.

Howes, C., Smith, E., & Galinsky, E. (1995). *The Florida Child Care Quality Improvement Study.* New York: Families and Work Institute.

Irvine, D.J. (1982). *Evaluation of the New York State Experimental Prekindergarten Program.* Albany: New York State Department of Education.

King, J.A. (1994). Meeting the educational needs of at-risk students: A cost analysis of three models. *Educational Evaluation and Policy Analysis, 16*(1), 1–19.

Lamb, M.E. (1998). Nonparental child care: Context, quality, coorelates. In W. Damon, I.E. Siegel, & K.A. Renniger (Eds.), *Handbook of child psychology* (Vol. 4, pp. 73–133). New York: John Wiley & Sons.

Lamy, C.E., Frede, E., Seplocha, H., Strasser, J., Jambunathan, S., Ferrar, H., Wiley, L., & Wolock, E. (2004). *Inch by inch, row by row, gonna make this garden grow: Classroom quality and language skills in the Abbott Preschool Program.* Retrieved June, 2004, from http://nieer.org/resources/research/AbbottReport.pdf

Lazar, I., & Darlington, R. (1982). Lasting effects of early education: A report from the consortium for longitudinal studies. *Monographs of the Society for Research in Child Development, 47*(2–3).

Levin, H.M. (1988). Cost-effectiveness and educational policy. *Educational Evaluation and Policy Analysis, 10*(1), 51–59.

Levin, H.M., Glass, G.V., & Meister, G.R. (1987). Cost-effectiveness of computer assisted instruction. *Education Review, 11*(1), 50–72.

Levin, H.M., & McEwan, P.J. (2001). *Cost effectiveness analysis (2nd ed.).* Thousand Oaks, CA: Sage Publications.

Love, J., Schochet, P., & Meckstroth, A. (1996). Are they in any real danger? What research does—and doesn't—tell us about child care quality and children's well being. *Child care research and policy papers: Lessons from child care research.* Princeton, NJ: Mathematica Policy Research, Inc.

Masse, L.N., & Barnett, W.S. (2002). A benefit-cost analysis of the Abecedarian early childhood intervention. In H. Levin & P. McEwan (Eds.), *Cost effectiveness and educational policy: 2002 yearbook of the American Education Finance Association* (pp. 157–176). Larchmont, NY: Eye on Education.

NICHD Early Child Care Research Network. (1996). Characteristics of infant childcare: Factors contributing to positive care giving. *Early Childhood Research Quarterly, 11,* 269–306.

Phillips, D., & Howes, C. (1987). *Indicators of quality in child care: Review of the research.* Washington, DC: National Association for the Education of Young Children (NAEYC).

Phillips, D.A., Howes, C., & Whitebook, M. (1992). The effects of regulation and auspice on child care quality. *American Journal of Community Psychology, 20,* 25–51.

Phillips, D.A., Mekos, D., Scarr, S., McCartney, K., & Abbott-Shim, M. (2000). Within and beyond the classroom door: Assessing quality in child care centers. *Early Childhood Research Quarterly, 15*(4), 475–496.

Phillipsen, L.C., Burchinal, M.R., Howes, C., & Cryer, D. (1997). The prediction of process quality from structural features in child care. *Early Childhood Research Quarterly, 12*(3), 281–303.

Powell, D.R. (1986). Research in review. Effects of program models and teaching practices. *Young Children, 41*(6), 60–67.

Reynolds, A.J., Temple, J.A., Robertson, D.L., & Mann, A.E. (2002). Age 21 cost-benefit analysis of the title I Chicago Child Parent Center Program. *Educational Evaluation and Policy Analysis, 24*(4), 267–303.

Ruopp, R., Travers, J., Glantz, F., & Coelen, C. (1979). *Children at the center: Final report of the National Day Care Study.* Cambridge, MA: Abt Associates.

Scarr, S., Eisenberg, M., & Deater-Deckard, K. (1994). Measurement of quality in child care centers. *Early Childhood Research Quarterly, 9,* 131–151.

Schweinhart, L.J., Barnes, H.V., & Weikart, D.P., with Barnett, W.S., & Epstein, A.S. (1993). *Significant benefits: The High/Scope Perry Preschool Study through Age 28.* Educational Research Foundation, No. 10. Ypsilanti, MI: High/Scope Press.

Shonkoff, J.P., & Phillips, D.A. (2000). *From neurons to neighborhoods: The science of early childhood development.* Washington, DC: National Academy Press.

Stallings, J.A., & Stipek, D. (1986). Research on early childhood and elementary school teaching programs. In M.C. Wittock. (Ed.), *Handbook of research on teaching* (3rd ed., pp. 727–753). New York: American Educational Research Association.

Stevens, M. (1994). A theoretical model of on-the-job training with imperfect competition. *Oxford Economic Papers, 46*(4), 537–562.

Vandell, D.L., & Wolf, B. (2000). *Child care quality: Does it matter and does it need to be improved?* Retrieved September, 2004, from http://aspe.hhs.gov/hsp/ccquality00/ccqual.htm

Whitebook, M., & Bellm, D. (1999). *Taking on turnover: An action guide for child care center teachers and directors.* Washington, DC: Center for the Child Care Workforce.

Whitebook, M., Howes, C., & Phillips, D. (1990). *Who cares? Child care teachers and the quality of care in America. Final report of the National Child Care Staffing Study.* Oakland, CA: Child Care Employee Project.

Whitebook, M., Howes, C., & Phillips, D. (1998). *Worthy work, unlivable wages: The National Child Care Staffing Study, 1988–1997.* Washington, DC: Center for the Child Care Workforce.

Whitebook, M., Phillips, D., & Howes, C. (1993). *National Child Care Staffing Study revisited: Four years in the life of center-based child care.* Oakland, CA: Child Care Employment Project.

Whitebook, M., Sakai, L., Gerber, E., & Howes, C. (2001). *Then & now: Changes in child care staffing. 1994–2000.* Washington, DC: Center for the Child Care Workforce. Retrieved August 2004, from http://www.ccw.org/pubs/Then&Nowfull.pdf

# CHAPTER 13

# Early Childhood Professional Development Programs

## *Accounting for Spillover Effects and Market Interventions*

H. Elizabeth Peters and Barbara Bristow

$\mathbf{M}$ost of the programs described in this book try to affect early childhood professional development by providing education or training directly to providers. This chapter outlines several mechanisms through which programs not directly targeted at professional development can indirectly affect these outcomes. Specifically, it focuses on the possibility that certain interventions in the child care market may change parents' demand for quality child care and indirectly affect the willingness of providers to undertake additional training, and the willingness of the public to pay for that training. The chapter discusses how modeling the child care market as a whole can help us understand how interventions in one part of the market (e.g., subsidies, regulations, information) can have feedback effects that influence other parts of the market (e.g., the supply of child care providers, training, compensation). We call these *spillover effects.*

In addition, researchers are becoming increasingly aware that the evaluation of small-scale interventions or programs may not fully capture the long-run effects of such a program were it to be implemented more widely (Garfinkel et al., 1992; Harris, 1985). Distinguishing the direct and short-run effects of a particular intervention from the full long-term effects of an intervention is an important focus in the recent evaluation literature (Heckman, LaLonde, & Smith, 1999). This focus suggests that when we as a field look at program interventions, both our lens and time frame are often too narrow. Finally, the chapter describes one specific intervention in the child care market—disseminating information to parents about the quality of child care providers in a local area—and discusses how that intervention might affect the incentives of providers to get additional training and education.

The next section of the chapter discusses the literature on spillover and market interaction effects and provides several brief examples of child care

The research described in this chapter has been supported, in part, by a grant from the Child Care Bureau, Administration for Children and Families, U.S. Department of Health and Human Services, and a Research-Extension Integration grant from the U.S. Department of Agriculture.

interventions that might be expected to have these types of effects. The third section describes our child care consumer information project, outlines the types of indirect effects this project might be expected to have on early childhood professional development, and presents our evaluation design and preliminary results. The chapter concludes with a discussion of how the child care field can benefit from taking a broader view of child care interventions and evaluating how these interventions can affect professional development as well as other aspects of the child care market.

## SPILLOVER AND MARKET EQUILIBRIUM EFFECTS

Indirect, or spillover, effects occur when a program intervention has an impact on outcomes beyond what was directly targeted. Garfinkel et al. (1992) suggested that spillover effects are due to both *market* interactions and *social* interactions (these terms are defined briefly next). These interactions can also cause the short-run effect on behavior that was directly targeted to be different from the long-run effect because they lead to iterations in outcomes that may take time to evolve.

Market interaction effects exist when an intervention in one part of the market has feedback effects on another part of the market because of the interaction between supply and demand. For example, if parents' demand for child care increases, then they will be willing to pay more for child care, and more providers may enter the market because the compensation they can receive has increased. Events or policies leading to an increase in the demand for child care could include work requirements for welfare mothers (and subsidies to help them pay for child care) or public information campaigns promoting preschool as a way to enhance school readiness for 3- and 4-year-olds. One study that examined changes in child care prices in California (Marrufo, O'Brien-Strain, & Oliver, 2003) concluded that the increase in demand for child care caused by the decline in welfare caseloads (and the increase in labor supply due to women who left welfare) resulted in an increase in both center and family child care prices. The study also found that the increased availability of child care subsidies increased the demand for child care and subsequently increased prices. So, demand increases both because of the increased need for child care when more women work and because subsidies make it cheaper for parents to purchase child care. Market prices then increase because scarce suppliers of child care need to receive higher compensation to meet the increased demand.

Similarly, changes in the supply of child care can affect child care prices and wages of child care providers. The supply of child care can change if some policy or other event changes the number of providers willing to supply their services at a given wage. For example, a change in Medicaid rules that caused an increase in the demand for nursing home aides, who have skills similar to those of child care providers, would decrease the supply of potential child care providers. Child care workers would need to receive higher wages to keep them from switching occupations.

The simple supply and demand analysis is predicated on the assumption that the supply of child care workers is responsive to wages (i.e., higher wages are needed to induce increased numbers of providers to supply their services). Historically, the supply of child care was not very responsive to wages, primarily because the supply of child care was not scarce. Specifically, there was a large number of women willing to provide child care at a low price (Blau, 1992). This may have resulted from the view that providing child care was an enjoyable activity, was often compatible with providing care for one's own children, or was a good option for women who did not have higher paying jobs. However, as women's market opportunities have increased and as the field of child care is increasingly professionalized, the supply of child care becomes more responsive to wages, and market interventions are more likely to have an impact on wages. Higher wages may, in turn, translate into a better educated workforce because a narrowing of the pay gap between the child care profession and other occupations that require an education background will enable the child care field to more easily compete for better educated workers.

Interventions in the child care market can have unintended consequences if the operation of the market is not fully understood (Queralt & Witte, 1999). One specific example of unintended consequences is described by Chipty and Witte (1997) who showed that regulations that increase minimum licensing requirements (additional training, increased child–staff ratios, and group size) reduce the supply of child care because they also raise costs. Higher costs shift the supply of child care and increase the price that providers must charge. At the higher price, parents reduce their demand for child care, and the total amount of care provided in the market falls. Although higher training and the concomitant higher compensation could make the child care profession more attractive to providers, the bottom line could be a lower supply of trained providers. In addition, the higher costs in the regulated child care sector could provide incentives for parents to move to the less expensive and unregulated sector. Chipty and Witte emphasized that understanding the effect of regulations on the child care market means measuring changes in both the regulated and unregulated sectors because parents can choose to move from one sector to the other.

Another area where choice is important is in the production of child care services. For example, if child care is produced by various combinations of quantity (e.g., numbers of staff) and quality (e.g., training, education), then regulations that increase the cost of one of the inputs may cause child care providers to choose to use less of that input and more of the other input. Similarly, if regulations mandate an increase in the amount of one input, then providers may choose to lower total costs by reducing the amount of the other input. So, if regulations require an increase in training, then it is possible that providers will try to minimize costs by lowering the quantity input (e.g., number of additional classroom aides; Queralt & Witte, 1999).

Another example of the importance of understanding market interactions is the question of how scholarships for training and education of child care providers (here referred to as *education and training subsidies*, which should not be confused with child care subsidies to families for the cost of child care) will affect their wages. Providing education and training subsidies is likely to increase the number of providers who receive additional professional development, which, in turn, will increase their wages (because more highly educated and trained workers can command higher wages). However, as the supply of workers with education and training in early childhood development increases, these workers become less scarce and the wage premium they are able to command will be lower.[1] Thus, the long-run effect of education and training subsidies on wages will be smaller than the short-run effect. Similarly, the long-run effect of education and training subsidies on the supply of trained child care workers is also smaller than the short-run effect because the reduced wage premium for workers with further professional development will cause fewer additional workers to get training. Analysis of the total impact of education and training subsidies on the economic well-being of child care workers also needs to account for the effects of the increased taxes needed to fund the increase in such subsidies. If this cost falls disproportionately on those most likely to get the education and training (e.g., through a regressive tax), then the total impact of professional development subsidies on the income of child care providers will be even smaller.

This example is similar to the work on the effect of tuition subsidies on rates of college attendance. Heckman, Lochner, and Taber (1998) found that the short-run effects are 10 times larger than the long-run effects because, in the long run, the increase in the supply of college educated workers reduces the wage premium for attending college.

The second type of indirect or spillover effect of an intervention discussed by Garfinkel et al. (1992) is due to social interactions. One way that social interactions affect outcomes is through changes in social norms. For example, changes in divorce laws making it easier to get divorced may have increased divorce rates both by lowering the direct cost of divorce (e.g., court costs, lawyers' fees) and indirectly by decreasing the social stigma attached to divorce as divorce became more commonplace (Becker, 1991; Cherlin, 1992). Similarly, welfare reform policies have directly reduced welfare caseloads by making welfare eligibility requirements stricter and possibly indirectly by increasing the stigma of being on welfare.

---

[1]Of course, there is a delicate balance between demand and supply. If additional education and training allowed these workers to move to the K–12 system, particularly as it extends downward to prekindergarten, then more educated and trained early childhood workers would still remain relatively scarce, commanding a wage premium large enough to attract additional workers into the profession.

Social norms in the child care field have also undergone dramatic changes over time. In the past, child care was frequently thought of as "babysitting," and the primary goal was to keep a child safe from physical harm while the mother worked in the labor force. As the importance of the early years for child development has become increasingly understood (e.g., as documented in Shonkoff & Phillips, 2000), child care is being viewed as an opportunity to enhance that development by providing a high-quality environment and stimulating inputs. Perhaps as a consequence of becoming more closely associated with the education field, child care is becoming recognized as a profession with specific education, training, and competencies. Child care programs and policies such as universal prekindergarten may have been stimulated by those changes in norms and, in turn, may reinforce those norms. For example, in the universal prekindergarten program in the state of New York, prekindergarten teachers are required to have the same credentials as K–12 teachers. These requirements are likely due to the increasing professionalization of the early care and education field and may also lead parents to begin to expect those types of credentials in the child care they use.

It is important to take into account these indirect or spillover effects when evaluating any policy or intervention. For example, the standard cost–benefit analysis tends to focus on the outcomes that were targeted by a specific intervention and may miss benefits or costs that are due to unanticipated outcomes. An understanding of the full consequences of an intervention can allow researchers to collect data on a broader set of outcomes when designing any evaluation. For example, to understand the consequences of the requirement that universal prekindergarten teachers have the same credentials as K–12 teachers, it would be useful to measure the supply of universal prekindergarten teachers as well as the supply of K–12 teachers. If K–12 teachers are better paid than universal prekindergarten teachers, then there is an incentive for universal prekindergarten teachers who get the necessary credentials to look for jobs as K–12 teachers. To understand the universal prekindergarten market, it is necessary to observe the supply in a related occupation, in this case, K–12 teachers. As the previous examples illustrate, the stimulus for spillover effects can be thought of as being initiated either through changes in the child care market or in social norms. Market oriented stimuli include 1) subsidies to parents to help pay for child care, 2) subsidies to help pay for education and training in early child development, 3) regulations that require minimum standards, 4) welfare work requirements that increase the demand for child care, and 5) change in the demand for other occupations that compete for workers who might enter or be in the child care field. All of these stimuli, then, have cascading effects that can eventually impact the professional development and wages of child care providers. Other stimuli begin with changes in social norms that can lead parents to increase their demand for higher-quality child care. These changes, which occur outside the market, then have an impact on the choices that parents make. Subsequently, these choices have further impacts on incentives for providers to get education and training that operate through the market.

## CHILD CARE PROGRAMS OF EXCELLENCE

This section describes a specific intervention—Child Care Programs of Excellence—that is designed to affect parents' child care choices. Because the intervention is implemented at the community level, there is a large potential for spillover effects due to both social and market interactions. It outlines the potential indirect effects this intervention may be expected to have on various parts of the child care market, and specifically on the quality of child care, with professional development as one component of quality. It then describes how our evaluation is designed to capture these indirect effects and presents some preliminary results.

Lack of information about the available options for child care and their quality is one barrier for parents in seeking child care. Child Care Resource & Referral (CCR&Rs) agencies in each county provide some information about child care but generally do not make specific recommendations. A report on the Economics of Child Care by the Council of Economic Advisors (1997) discussed the general problem of information in the child care market. Lack of information can reduce the competitiveness of the child care market, allowing variations in price that are not related to quality and the cost of care. Better information should make selecting quality child care simpler for parents and may increase the demand for quality when the cost of ascertaining quality is less. The Cost, Quality, and Child Outcomes Study Team (1995) provided evidence that parents may not have good information about quality. Specifically, they found that parents consistently overestimate the quality of care their child receives, implying that it is difficult for them to evaluate quality. In a survey of parents in eight upstate New York counties, we found that 82% of parents with young children say that they would be interested in a quality rating report that provided information about the quality of child care options that are available in their county, and 94% of those parents stated that they would be willing to pay for that information (Peters, Bristow, & Lim, 2002).

To address the issue of lack of information about quality, we developed the Child Care Programs of Excellence (CCPOE), an intervention that provides parents with information about high-quality licensed child care programs in their local area.[2] It was developed through a collaboration between researchers and faculty at Cornell University and staff of participating

---

[2]This intervention and its evaluation is funded through grants from the United States Department of Health and Human Services Child Care Bureau and the United States Department of Agriculture.

CCR&Rs in five pilot counties of New York State (Albany, Rensselaer, Onondaga, Ontario, and Yates; see http://www.ccstars.org for more information about CCPOE). The program has three primary objectives:

1.  To collect information about the quality of child care providers for children who are under 5 years old in these regions using well-established rating systems

2.  To communicate the quality ratings of each provider to parents by developing and disseminating a Child Care Quality Rating Report

3.  To evaluate the impact of the program on choices made by parents and on the child care market in terms of quality, cost, and availability of child care

As part of the first objective, we designed a rating system that has three components: 1) program standards, 2) teacher qualifications, and 3) health and safety compliance. To assess program standards, we observed each participating child care provider using the Early Childhood Environment Rating Scale (ECERS), the Infant-Toddler Environment Rating Scale (ITERS), and Family Day Care Rating Scale (FDCRS) (Harms & Clifford, 1989; Harms, Clifford, & Cryer, 1998; Harms, Cryer, & Clifford, 1990). We trained master observers to administer those instruments with a reliability of an 85% exact match. To assess teacher qualifications, we gave programs higher scores when teachers had 1) annual training hours in excess of the minimum required by New York state; 2) advanced degrees; and 3) specific training in early childhood education, such as a Child Development Associate (CDA) credential. We also reviewed each applicant's history of compliance. Higher scores reflected a longer history with no serious, substantiated violations.

With help from the local CCR&Rs, we recruited local providers to participate in the program. Participation is voluntary, but the possibility of obtaining a CCPOE designation was attractive to many providers. Overall, 29% of centers participated in the program and agreed to be assessed.[3] Prior to the assessment, we gave providers a copy of the environmental rating scale relevant to their child care setting so they would be able to understand the criteria on which our ratings were based. To be designated a Child Care Program of Excellence, a provider must exceed minimum licensing requirements, and the levels of excellence range from two to five stars.[4] Only programs that achieve two or more stars are actually listed in our quality rating report. This procedure provided some insurance for the down-side risk that some providers might not be rated as highly as they had anticipated.

---

[3]Note that the willingness to participate among family child care providers has been significantly lower.

[4]One star indicates programs that just meet minimum licensing standards, and they are not eligible for the CCPOE designation. Of the providers who participated in our program, 24% received five stars, 27% received four stars, 24% received three stars, 3% received two stars, and 22% did not exceed minimum licensing requirements.

The Child Care Quality Rating Report is available on the web (http://www.ccstars.org/parents/qualityratingreport.asp), and each provider who meets our CCPOE criteria is listed along with a rating for each of the three components and a description of distinctive features of specific providers. Our web site also includes information about why quality child care matters and why the specific criteria that we use for our rating are important and lists steps that parents can take on their own to search for and assess high-quality child care. In the summer of 2003, we conducted a parent education campaign. Information about the program was widely distributed throughout each of the pilot areas through the media and through brochures available at pediatricians' offices, community organizations, and social services agencies. As evidence that parents place some value on information about the quality of child care options available them, we have calculated the number of unique visits to our web site over time. The number of visits grew from about 150 per month at the beginning of the parent education campaign to more than 350 at the end of the campaign, and the number has fluctuated around that level since that time.

Although the intervention is focused on consumer information and educating parents, we expect its impact to operate, in part, through the child care market. Specifically, we expect that better information will increase parents' demand for high-quality child care and this, in turn, will increase the incentives for child care providers to supply that care. One important way to increase quality is to increase the education levels and professional development for child care staff. Parents' demand is influenced through two pathways. First, some research has indicated that parents do not appear to be willing to pay more for higher-quality child care (Blau, 2001). By educating parents about the importance of child care quality, we may be able to increase their willingness to pay for quality. In addition, when parents do not know the quality of a given provider, they may assume that the provider has the average quality in the market and will base their willingness to pay on that average level of quality. Providing information about quality will allow differences in prices to more closely match differences in quality. Parents who do want higher-quality care are willing to pay more for that care when they can be assured of its quality.

One might ask why a voluntary rating system that lists only higher-quality providers rather than all providers is likely to affect the market. Theory suggests that parents may use the listing as a signal (Grossman, 1981). If parents interpret not being listed as a signal of low quality, then all high-quality providers have an incentive to participate, and this process would continue until all but the very lowest quality providers are participating. Of course, this takes time to unfold, and the short-run impact of our program is likely to be different from the long-run effect. There was an initial burst of interest when the program started, and over time, more programs have slowly but steadily signed on. For example, in Albany, about one third of the total participants were assessed in the first 3 months of the program (April 2002– June 2002), whereas the remaining two thirds signed on over the next 2 years. In our pilot counties, approximately 29% of all centers participated in the program, but only 4% of family child care providers participated. There is some evidence that the higher-quality programs were more likely to participate. For example, accredited centers were more likely to participate than nonaccredited centers. However, we also found some contrary evidence showing that centers that paid lower wages were more likely to participate. It is difficult to explain the latter result.

Identifying the mechanisms through which consumer information can affect the quality of child care through a standard evaluation design is difficult. Because our intervention is at the community level, we cannot compare the choices of parents who were subject to a given intervention with those who were not because all parents in the community can potentially receive the information about child care quality. This is a standard problem for the evaluation of any type of community intervention (Hollister & Hill, 1995). One solution to this problem is to compare parents' choices and other outcomes in the child care market before and after the intervention. To account for the possibility that other factors might effect changes over time independent of the intervention, we can compare these changes in intervention counties with changes in similar counties that did not receive the intervention. This evaluation techniques is sometimes referred to as *difference-in-differences*.

Our model of the child care market and parents' responses to information about quality suggests that we need to collect data about parents' choices (i.e., the providers they chose and the providers they did not choose), the dispersion and average level of quality in the market, prices, and the correlation between prices and quality. One indicator of quality that has been shown to be important and is straightforward to collect is the education and training of providers. Unfortunately, data on these types of market outcomes are limited. As a starting point, our study collected survey data on parent choices and attitudes in participating and comparison counties, both before and after implementing our consumer education intervention. We hope to extend the evaluation to focus on dispersion of quality (including the professional development component) and relation of price and quality.

Our parents' survey collected information on parents' current child care choices, the attributes of child care that were important in that choice, which sources of information they used to find their child care provider, their knowledge about other options in the community, and their view of whether those options were limited. As has been found in other studies (Hofferth, Brayfield, Deich, & Holcomb, 1991), the vast majority of parents in the preintervention data (more than two thirds) found out about their child care provider through friends and neighbors. Although 85% of parents rated the quality of their child care providers as an A or A+, 35% said that they had difficulty finding the child care they wanted, and 17% said they took whatever they could get. If provision of information helps the operation of the child care market to work more smoothly, then we would expect that in the period after the intervention, parents would rely less on friends and neighbors and might be less likely to say they had difficulty in finding the child care they wanted. Our results comparing the change in these reports over time for both pilot and comparison counties were consistent with these expectations. We found that parents in the pilot counties were seven percentage points less likely to report that they found their child care provider through friends and neighbors in the postintervention period and five percentage points less likely to report that they had difficulty in finding the child care they wanted relative to the change over a similar time period in comparison counties.

In addition to predictions about market outcomes from standard economic theory, sociologists and others might predict our intervention could change social norms or help to enforce social norms that already exist. Our intervention may also have educated some providers about the types of characteristics that signal high quality. To understand providers' responses to our program, we developed an open-ended questionnaire and interviewed providers who had participated in CCPOE. We obtained interviews from 20 centers and 12 family or group care homes.

Ten out of the 12 family child care and group family care (FDC) providers described making significant improvements to the child care program or facilities in preparation for the on-site visit by a trained Master Observer. For child care centers, 16 out of 20 said the assessment tool was used to make improvements. These included 1) purchasing new materials and furnishings (5 FDC and 12 centers); 2) rearranging the child care space (2 FDC and 3 centers); 3) labeling of materials more clearly (3 FDC and 4 centers); 4) adding additional features to the child care program (4 FDC and 3 centers); 5) improving interactions/communication with children or parents (1 FDC and 2 centers); and 6) improving routine child care practices (2 FDC and 1 center). The motivation for these changes is reflected in the comments about why providers chose to participate in the program and what benefits they perceived would come from participation. In particular, they cited reasons such as the external recognition they would receive from parents and others. Although the initial steps providers have taken relate to aspects of quality that are easily changed, these short-run responses give us some expectation that longer-run changes, including increases in education and training of staff, may also occur.

Related finding were reported by Witte and Queralt (2004). They found that the average quality of center care in Broward County, Florida, increased after inspection reports were published on the Internet. They also found that the ratings provided by licensing inspectors changed, and that the number of reported violations increased. Although there was a substantial increase in consumer "hits" to the web site providing inspector reports after a public information campaign about the usefulness of the information and how to access it, no indication was found of diminished enrollment in facilities for which problems had been noted by licensing inspectors. A more detailed examination of parent use of the information is warranted. For example, although enrollment may not have changed overall, informed parents (those who had accessed the web site) may have altered their behavior, and the slots may have been filled by uninformed parents.

It has been 2 years since our first providers received the CCPOE designation. We have completed a preintervention and postintervention survey of parents in pilot and comparison counties. We have also conducted a qualitative survey of providers to understand their motivations for participation and for making quality enhancements. In the future, we plan to do a qualitative survey of parents whose children are attending one of the CCPOE programs to better understand how information can alter parents' choices. In turn, we will continue to interview both new and continuing CCPOE providers to understand their motivations for participation; changes in reasons for participation as CCPOE becomes more widespread; whether consumer pressure for increased quality influences these providers to improve aspects of quality; and what types of quality enhancements, including increases in staff salaries and training and education, providers undertake in the short and long run.

## CONCLUSIONS AND RECOMMENDATIONS

There are numerous programs that are targeted at increasing professional development in the child care field. This chapter, however, examined ways in which programs that are not directly focused on professional development may have indirect effects primarily through changing parents' demand for quality child care or through changing social norms and expectations. It emphasized that understanding the interaction of supply and demand in the child care market is critical to assessing the indirect consequences of any intervention. In addition, evaluating the broader and long-term impacts of any intervention in the market will require a different type of research design. The chapter then described one specific intervention in the child care market designed to provide information about child care quality to parents and presented evidence that this intervention has had some indirect effect on the quality of child care. Future work will examine the implications that the intervention is having on professional development as one component of quality. In sum, economic theory and our work in New York suggest the potential importance not only of interventions targeting professional development specifically but also of market interventions for changing the professional development of the early childhood workforce.

## REFERENCES

Becker, G.S. (1991). *A treatise on the family.* Cambridge, MA: Harvard University Press.
Blau, D. (1992). The child care labor market. *Journal of Human Resources, 27*(1), 9–39.

Blau, D. (2001). *The child care problem: An economic analysis.* New York: Russell Sage Foundation Publications.

Cherlin, A.J. (1992). *Marriage, divorce, remarriage.* Cambridge, MA: Harvard University Press.

Chipty, T., & Witte, A.D. (1997). *An empirical investigation of firms responses to minimum standards regulations.* (National Bureau of Economic Research Working Paper No. 6104). Cambridge, MA: National Bureau of Economic Research.

Cost, Quality, and Child Outcomes Study Team. (1995). *Cost, quality, and child outcomes in child care centers: Public report.* Denver: University of Colorado.

Council of Economic Advisers. (1997) *The economics of child care.* Retrieved September 16, 2004, from http://clinton4.nara.gov/WH/EOP/CEA/html/childcare.html

Garfinkel, I., Manski, C.F., & Michalopoulos, C. (1992). Micro experiments and macro effects. In C. Manski & I. Garfinkel (Eds.), *Evaluating welfare and training programs* (pp. 253–273). Cambridge, MA: Harvard University Press.

Grossman, S.J. (1981). The information role of warranties and private disclosure about product quality. *Journal of Law and Economics, 24,* 461–489.

Harms, T., & Clifford, R.M. (1989). *Family Day Care Rating Scale (FDRS).* New York: Teachers College Press.

Harms, T., Clifford, R.M., & Cryer, D. (1998). *Early Childhood Environment Rating Scale–Revised Edition (ECERS-R).* New York: Teachers College Press.

Harms, T., Cryer, D., & Clifford, R.M. (1990). *Infant/Toddler Environment Rating Scale (ITERS).* New York: Teachers College Press.

Harris, J.E. (1985). Macroexperiments versus microexperiments for health policy. In J. Hausman & D. Wise (Eds.), *Social experimentation* (pp. 145–186). Chicago: University of Chicago Press.

Heckman, J.J., LaLonde, R.J., & Smith, J.A. (1999). The economics and econometrics of active labor market programs. In O. Ashenfelter & D. Card (Eds.), *Handbook of labor economics* (Vol. 3, pp. 1865–2097). New York: Elsevier Science.

Heckman, J.J., Lochner, L., & Taber, C. (1998). General-equilibrium treatment effects: A study of tuition policy. *The American Economic Review, 88*(2), 381–386.

Hofferth, S.L., Brayfield, A., Deich, S., & Holcomb, P. (1991). *National child care survey, 1990.* Washington DC: The Urban Institute Press.

Hollister, R.G., & Hill, J. (1995). *Problems in the evaluation of community-wide initiatives* (Russell Sage Foundation Working Paper #70). New York: Russell Sage Foundation.

Marrufo, G., O'Brien-Strain, M., & Oliver, H. (2003). *Child care price dynamics in California.* San Francisco: Public Policy Institute of California.

Peters, H.E., Bristow, B., & Lim, Y. (2002, April). Poster presented at the Child Care Bureau Research Meeting, Washington, DC.

Queralt, M., & Witte, A.D. (1999). Child care regulations: A method to pursue social welfare goals? *Children and Youth Services Review 21*(2), 111–146.

Shonkoff, J.P., & Phillips, D.A. (Eds.). (2000). *From neurons to neighborhoods: The science of early childhood development.* Washington, DC: National Academies Press.

Witte, A.D., & Queralt, M. (2004). *What happens when child care inspections and complaints are made available on the Internet?* (National Bureau of Economic Research Working Paper 10227). Cambridge, MA: National Bureau of Economic Research.

# Charting a Course for Improved Professional Development Across Varying Programs and Policies

MARTHA ZASLOW

A strong theme in the final section of this book is the importance of making progress toward improved early childhood professional development in the context of a wide range of different programs and policies for early care and education in the United States. Challenges include the fact that there are multiple federal and state programs and policies with different goals; furthermore, these have different requirements for professional development and different mechanisms and levels of support for professional development.

Despite these challenges, there are important common denominators that provide a basis for improving professional development and measuring its impact. The concluding chapters of the book present views of how to make progress in a way that has the potential to affect all types of early care and education and yet takes into account the substantial and meaningful variation across programs and policies.

Chapter 14 identifies three common denominators that the authors see as providing the basis for an approach to improving early professional development across early childhood programs and settings.

First, the chapter authors hold that there is much greater consensus regarding the components of high quality early childhood care and education than is widely acknowledged. They view the research as strongly supporting four core components that apply, irrespective of the particular program and whether it is home or center based. These components include healthy and safe care environments; frequent, warm, and responsive caregiver–child interactions; frequent experiences that support early language development and learning; and frequent family–caregiver communication.

Second, the authors view it as a priority to go beyond requiring degrees, specified amounts of training completed, and certifications to measure professional development. They recommend focusing on observable practices and caregiver knowledge within the care and education setting that contribute to these core components of quality. They propose field testing different approaches to the direct observation and assessment of educator/care provider practices, with the aim of eventually reaching agreement on components to be used universally to measure professional development directly.

Third, the authors hold that a system of supportive monitoring should be put in place, involving both direct observation of early educator/care provider practices and assessments of children's progress during the course of a year of early care and education. Such a monitoring system could be used to help programs reach the agreed-on goals for directly observed educator/caregiver practices.

Chapter 15 describes the multiple federally funded programs that have specific components bearing on early childhood professional development. The authors begin with a historical perspective, noting that one reason for the range of federally funded programs is a set of differing underlying goals: supporting parental employment, enhancing the development of children with economic or developmental risks, or fostering early learning more universally. Knowledge of these different federal programs and policies and their professional development goals and provisions is an important starting point for determining how early childhood professional development can be fostered across them.

Chapter 15 provides the details for eight programs with provisions related to early childhood professional development: the Child Care and Development Fund (CCDF), Head Start and Early Head Start, prekindergarten programs with Title I funding, Even Start, Early Reading First, the Early Childhood Educator Professional Development Program, the Individuals with Disabilities Education Act (IDEA) Amendments of 1997 (PL 105-17) and the Individuals with Disabilities Education Improvement Act of 2004 (PL 108-446), and state-funded prekindergarten programs. These programs vary substantially in terms of goals, funding levels, explicit requirements, and degree of decision making at federal, state, and local levels regarding professional development. For example, the CCDF leaves it to states to determine the requirements for the education or training of those who care for children receiving child care subsidies, whereas the Head Start program has requirements at the national level—specifically, as of the last reauthorization (PL 105-285), that 50% of all Head Start teachers will have an associate's degree or higher in early childhood education or a related field.

Yet it is interesting to note that despite the substantial differences across programs and policies, the chapter also identifies important elements that the programs share or coordinate with other programs:

- All of the programs have a focus on early childhood professional development and provide a mechanism for supporting it. Across programs there is an emerging emphasis on this facet of program quality.

- There is a growing tendency to coordinate professional development efforts across specific programs. For example, one of the federal programs, the Early Childhood Educator Professional Development Program, is a competitive grant program designed to improve teacher quality, with grants made directly to entities such as higher education institutions. Professional development activities funded by this program must be coordinated with the professional development components of the early child-hood programs funded through the U.S. Department of Education (e.g., prekindergarten programs funded through Title I) and the U.S. Department of Health and Human Services (e.g., Head Start).

• The No Child Left Behind (NCLB) Act of 2001 (PL 107-110) provides a common set of professional development requirements for early childhood programs that are implemented in public schools. For example, although federally funded prekindergarten programs in the states vary in a number of ways, those implemented in public schools must meet the NCLB teacher requirements of a bachelor's degree, a state certificate or teaching license, and demonstrated competence in all subject areas taught.

• The *Good Start, Grow Smart* initiative provides a framework for looking at professional development across types of early care and education. In particular, it encourages states to create professional development plans that apply across early care and education programs.

Chapter 15 concludes with a discussion of research needs that apply across programs and policies. The authors highlight characteristics of research that they see as having the greatest utility. For example, they discuss the importance of using an appropriate and rigorous research design, including the use of random assignment evaluations when possible and conducting direct observations of provider practices and children's outcomes. In addition, they illustrate the types of research questions that are associated with different points in a policy cycle, such as the initial consideration of a policy, the implementation of a policy, or the reauthorization of legislation.

In short, the chapters in Section V, although different in focus, present complementary views of improving early childhood professional development. One envisions a set of standards for professional practice that could be applied across differing programs and used for program monitoring and improvement. The other describes differences across federally funded programs as a context for building on emerging commonalities and determining how best to strengthen professional practices and children's outcomes in each early child-hood setting. Both chapters focus on the types of resources that are available or needed for professional development, the need to clarify professional development goals, and the importance of grounding early childhood professional practices in methodologically sound research.

## REFERENCES

Coats Human Services Amendments of 1998, PL 105-285.
Individuals with Disabilities Education Act (IDEA) Amendments of 1997, PL 105-17, 20 U.S.C. §§ 1400 *et seq.*
Individuals with Disabilities Education Improvement Act of 2004, PL 108-446, 20 U.S.C. §§ 1400 *et seq.*
No Child Left Behind (NCLB) Act of 2001, PL 107-110, 20 U.S.C. §6301 *et seq.*

# Creating and Sustaining a High-Quality Workforce in Child Care, Early Intervention, and School Readiness Programs

Sharon Landesman Ramey and Craig T. Ramey

$T$his chapter presents our perspective on the salient themes to emerge from the meeting that Science and the Ecology of Early Development (SEED) sponsored on professional development of the early childhood workforce. In numerous instances, the themes that were identified at the meeting center on challenges: defining and measuring the workforce, attracting and retaining a well-qualified workforce, and providing appropriate professional development for this workforce. We react to the themes presented, providing our reading of the research and of how best to respond to the challenges.

To a large degree, the success of child care and other early childhood programs depends on attracting and supporting well-qualified, dedicated caregivers and teachers, as well as effective program leaders and administrators. There are many distinct, as well as overlapping, early childhood programs intended to enhance the education and health of young children and their families. Many of these programs target children judged to be "at risk" or known to already have experienced serious difficulties and delays in their development. Other programs seek to provide universal community-based services and aspire to meet the needs of a diverse group of children and families. Some private and public preschool programs cater to families that seek early academic enrichment and a competitive academic edge for their young children. Regardless of the administrative authority, funding source, or stated objectives, all forms of child care and all types of early childhood programs should be responsible for promoting the health and development of the children in their care. Accordingly, the individuals who work in these settings and provide care for children need to have a common base of knowledge, skills, and positive behavior.

We have identified three crucial issues for the closely related fields of early child development, child care, early intervention, and school readiness based on the papers and discussions at the SEED meeting and our broader understanding of the research:

1. Defining *quality* and desired outcomes in early childhood programs

2. Attracting, training, and sustaining a high-quality early childhood workforce

3. Developing strategies to use monitoring data and research findings in a timely way to drive up the quality of the workforce and to inform policy changes.

These issues are highly interrelated. Although the chapter begins with a discussion of the issue of defining *quality* and gathering data on quality as well as child outcomes, it notes the centrality of definitions and measurement to the second and third issue of recruiting and retaining a workforce that provides high-quality care and monitoring quality on an ongoing basis. Where appropriate, the discussion identifies steps that have been taken following the SEED meeting and further steps that need to be taken.

## DEFINING *QUALITY* AND DESIRED OUTCOMES IN EARLY CHILDHOOD PROGRAMS

Since the 1980s, there has been a widespread perception—with which we disagree—that there is *not* a clear consensus about what comprises a high-quality program or high-quality child care for young children. This apparent lack of resolution about what *quality* really means has prevented moving forward with crucial policy decisions about a wide array of topics, from setting standards to monitoring quality and measuring outcomes. This misguided perception states that *quality* is mostly a subjective judgment. Furthermore, *quality* is not *sensitive* to cultural and family values and does not consider economic and practical realities. We strongly disagree. We think there are remarkably high levels of agreement among parents and professionals about what represents high-quality child care. Quite frankly, much of the pseudo-debate about how to improve the current situation of woefully widespread substandard care—which exists in almost all types of early childhood programs, public and private and regulated and unregulated—is fueled by the fact that some programs and forms of care are, in fact, consistently worse than others. If a vigorous commitment to overhaul child care and early education moves forward, then there is no doubt that some providers and programs will face implementing major changes to achieve quality programs and outcomes; others are likely to be closed down. This fear of change has contributed to concealing some horrific child care and educational practices that are undoubtedly harming children (S.L. Ramey, 2005). By continuing to act as though there is no agreement about what constitutes high-quality care and early childhood education, society becomes complicit in the maltreatment of children. Poor quality child care and substandard preschool education affect not only the children in these programs, but also public K–12 education as well because children who have received substandard care will be less ready for school (National Institute of Child Health and Human Development [NICHD] Early Child Care Research Network, 2005). We see school readiness as encompassing the inter-related domains of cognitive and social-emotional development, and early childhood care and education experiences as contributing to development across these domains.

Given the longstanding awareness of substandard care and education in the United States, and the lack of major progress in monitoring and improving the quality of care children receive, we propose that new alliances among professionals and families be created to advocate for a unified system of standards and a definition of high-quality care that can be achieved for all children and in all places. The goal needs to be the improvement of care and education for very young children, and the effort must encompass the full range of types of care and programs that families want to have available. We argue that there is an urgent need for a consensus that children's care be actively monitored and that this monitoring be guided by a common definition of *quality*. Specifically, the focus must be one in which it is the actual and observable care, day in and day out, that children and their families receive that matters. This means that quality *cannot* be simply equated with factors such as program structure (e.g., staff-to-child ratios, group size, accreditation), formal staff credentials (e.g., earning certificates and degrees at colleges and universities, receiving fixed hours of training per year), and administrative indicators (e.g., detailed recordkeeping, compliance with program regulations for a given program), and level of resources (e.g., the square footage per child, the presence of "learning centers," equipment and supplies). Instead, quality will be directly measured by a common metric—that is, observable features of how the staff and children behave throughout the day and the safety and health of the environment—that can be achieved by all types of care for children from birth through school entry age. What would these observable features be? What is the basis for asserting that these features make a difference in children's lives?

## TOWARD A UNIVERSAL UNDERSTANDING OF *QUALITY:* BEYOND OPINION AND PROGRAM TERRITORIALITY

Based on an extensive multidecade review of the scientific and professional articles and books, as well as conference proceedings, reports of legislative and foundation studies, and the 10-site NICHD study of early child care, we formulated and then field-tested a model of child care and education that includes four major dimensions (Ramey, Ramey, & Cotton, 2002). We developed the Ramey and Ramey "Four Diamond" Model of Quality of Child Care and Early Education to apply to all forms of care, encompassing home-based and center-based care, public and private, and for typically developing children as well as for children who are at risk or with special needs. Figure 14.1 illustrates these four closely related major dimensions of high-quality care:

1.  Health and safety practices: practices that seek to prevent all major problems and promote physical and mental health and safety; consistently implemented at all times

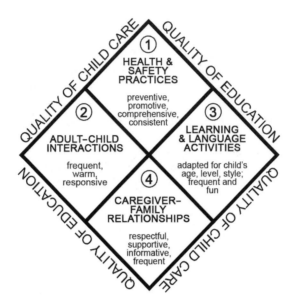

Figure 14.1.    "Four Diamond" Model of Quality of Child Care and Early Education.

2.   Adult–child interactions: frequent, warm, and responsive

3.   Learning and language activities: adapted for the child's age, level, and style; frequent and enjoyable

4.   Caregiver–family relationship: respectful, supportive, informative, and frequent communication between caregiver and family members

The elements in the "Four Diamond" Model are well established by extensive research by many investigators, are not highly controversial, and provide a simpler definition of *quality* than many previous efforts. In addition, the "Four Diamond" Model uses words that are familiar to parents and informal caregivers, rather than specialized professional terms. This effort to promote the widespread use of a practical definition of *quality*—that transcends any particular type of care or educational program—is intentional. Three of the four key elements (diamonds) in this model are endorsed by extensive research indicating that these factors result in measurable benefits for children—health and safety, adult–child interactions, and learning and language activities. For example, in terms of health and safety practices, programs that consistently implement proper hand-washing programs spread fewer illnesses to children; similarly, environments that have child safeguards on doors, windows, poisonous substances, and dangerous objects have fewer child injuries; and caregivers placing infants on their backs or sides to nap is a vital practice to lower rates of Sudden Infant Death Syndrome (SIDS). Regarding learning and language activities, the environments where children receive more frequent and stimulating language, on a daily basis, are those where children's vocabularies and language competencies are higher than environments that provide low levels of these activities; and frequent caregiver–child interactions that are positive and responsive are associated with children who are more socially and emotionally capable (Borkowksi, Ramey, & Bristol-Power, 2002; NICHD Early Child Care Research Network, 2005; C.T. Ramey & Ramey, 1999; S.L. Ramey & Ramey, 2000; Shonkoff & Phillips, 2000).

The fourth and somewhat novel element in the "Four Diamond" Model is the caregiver–family relationship, which is based on practical considerations to foster frequent two-way communication about a child and what is happening in all aspects of a young child's life. For young children, the failure to have positive continuities across the major places where the child spends time serves to increase the probability that the special needs and issues affecting the child may not be addressed adequately by the key individuals in the child's life. The potential benefits of caregiver–family communication in the first 5 years of life are many, although there has been remarkably little research about this topic.

The "Four Diamond" Model of quality assumes that in all places where children live, play, learn, and receive care and education—whether the care and education are brief or extended, regulated or informal, planned for a special purpose or not—that these four features are vital to protect children and to promote their positive development. None of these four features is considered optional or merely desirable. That is, children always must have responsible individuals who have the knowledge, skills, and motivation to provide them with the content of what the Four Diamonds represent. Thus, caregivers must be knowledgeable and up-to-date about what is essential for children to be healthy and safe at any given age; skilled in providing the type of responsive, warm, and frequent interactions that are needed to promote young children's sense of social connectedness, trust, emotional responsiveness, and caring; and able to teach children new things and language in ways that are fun, increasingly more complex, and mature. Furthermore, the caregiver must be capable of and motivated to develop a close working relationship with the key individuals in a child's family. Under some conditions, caregivers may sometimes need additional outside help (e.g., professional expertise, information, equipment) when children or their families have special needs or when the typical ways of providing high-quality care and education do not result in the expected progress for a given child.

To use the "Four Diamond" Model in a way that will help to recruit, train, and sustain a highly competent workforce in child care and early education, we find it informative to view the Four Diamonds within a broad social, political, economic, community, and family context. This builds on the popular and well-accepted idea that a child spends time in multiple settings that are simultaneously influenced by many factors, as well advanced by Bronfenbrenner and many other developmental scientists (Bronfenbrenner, 1979; C.T. Ramey & Ramey, 1998; S.L. Ramey & Ramey, 2000; Shonkoff & Phillips, 2000). Figure 14.2 places the "Four Diamond" Model within other contexts, including the immediate supportive child care context, which is influenced by the economic and political climate. Many of the presentations at the SEED conference focused on the supportive environment—trying to improve structural and training aspects of the child care and educational setting. In addition, the centrality of the family is essential to recognize, including the fact that children need the same high-quality care from home that they need when in the care of others. Ideally, the child's family and other caregivers and educators will coordinate and mutually enhance their ability to support positive child outcomes, as Figure 14.2 indicates.

The national concern about "child outcomes" has been closely linked to school readiness and academic achievement. Of equal concern to society is a child's social and emotional development, including a child's happiness and sense of overall adjustment. Children should be actively engaged and thriving wherever they are—in the care of their family and in the care of others. Similarly, children should demonstrate good progress in their development in the areas that relate directly to the Four Diamonds. Positive health and safety practices, provided in the child's family and the child care and education environments, should contribute to children being physically and emotionally healthy, displaying appropriate safety behavior in given environments, and receiving needed health care and screening for prevention and early detection of problems. In the area of adult–child interactions, the receipt of frequent, warm, and responsive care should lead to an outcome of children who are securely attached and trusting of adults, appropriate in their social and emotional self-regulation, able to "read" the feelings of others as they become older, and interested in sharing and helping others. In the area of learning and language activities, when children receive frequent, stimulating, and fun learning-language experiences, their outcomes will include age-appropriate progress (or better) in language (e.g., skills in comprehension, vocabulary, expressive language, understanding of signs and symbols, and early literacy skills) and learning (e.g., basic math concepts, reasoning about everyday problems, self-help skills, general knowledge about the world). Finally, when there is frequent, two-way communication between caregivers and families, children are more likely to have positive feelings about their child care or preschool experiences and about themselves and feel comfortable sharing information about what is happening in their lives. Collectively, the provision of high-quality child care and education, when conjoined with positive family environments that also offer high-quality supports in the same "Four Diamond" model, is expected to strengthen a child's overall sense of well-being, including realizing the important but difficult-to-measure outcomes such as

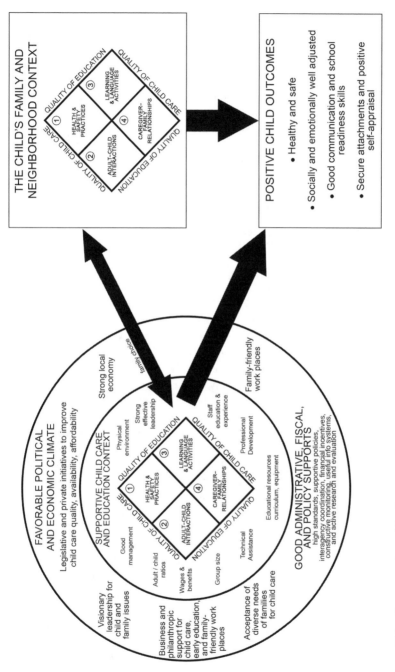

**Figure 14.2.** The community and family contexts that contribute to quality of care and education and to child outcomes.

positive self-esteem, interest in life and learning, and the ability to form and maintain positive social relationships with other children and adults.

As Figure 14.2 illustrates, creating a trans-environmental definition of *high-quality* and what young children need from their caregivers—whether their caregivers are family, paid professionals, or informal caregivers—opens up the possibility for new approaches to recruiting, training, and sustaining the child care workforce. At the same time, this model facilitates providing a common vocabulary for families, caregivers, and educators to discuss their activities on behalf of young children. Study after study has reported that parents from all walks of life and all cultures express strong support for children doing well in school, as well as for acquiring social skills to help them get along with peers, teachers, and family members. These are universal values, not culture-specific or unique to a particular generation of children or parents.

## ATTRACTING, TRAINING, AND SUSTAINING A HIGH-QUALITY EARLY CHILDHOOD WORKFORCE

Historically, there have been many obstacles to the provision of high-quality child care and education. Today, the use of nonparental care in the first 5 years of life has become almost universal, at least for some time prior to entering kindergarten—even for children with a parent who does not work outside the home, there are strong incentives to create efficient and sustainable community-based systems of care that meet the needs of families, children, and society at large. It is important to note that poor quality child care not only potentially harms children (e.g., resulting in lower levels of language development and school readiness, lack of positive social-emotional connectedness to others, disruptive behavior), but also can negatively impact the family unit (e.g., altering parental employment opportunities, causing emotional distress for the parents) and affect the subsequent competency of children in a community (e.g., lowering academic progress of children in public schools, creating social turmoil in school and recreational settings, having higher rates of later substance abuse and crime).

The conventional wisdom seeks to keep a stable workforce. Accordingly, many systems have designed incremental incentives, such as pay increases and increased employee benefits for remaining in the childcare workforce. We caution, however, that it is neither desirable to have a stable *unskilled* workforce, nor does high staff turnover absolutely prevent providing high-quality care and education. *The key is that the highest priority has to be placed on the direct provision of high-quality care at all times, in all settings, for all children.* Young children can adjust well to some planned transitions in their caregivers and care settings, as long as they receive support for the changes and the care continues to be of high-quality. This is another instance of why caregiver–family relationships are so important for the child's well-being.

We think there are many possible sources for recruiting individuals for the early child care and education workforce—some of which have not been fully explored in the past, including greater utilization of young people while they are enrolled in higher education or when they are in transitions, such as after graduation and before they continue further education or long-term employment. Similarly, older men and women, perhaps retired or working only part-time, may be eager to receive training to help improve the quality of child care and early education. More national service programs might be fostered in this area, such as the AmeriCorps program (some already exist with a focus on young children), and more carefully supported volunteer opportunities could be developed. By expanding the recruitment net, there is likely to be an additional benefit for society: namely, as more types and ages of individuals join in caring for young children, these individuals will acquire greater knowledge and skills related to the care and education of young children, which in turn will help them to be better parents, grandparents, and citizens.

One of the most difficult and sensitive issue to address is how to deal with those people already providing care whose knowledge, skills, and performance are below acceptable levels of quality. This issue, in our judgment, has contributed substantially to the presumed "opinion wars" about what "quality" really is. Many informally trained women, often from low-income backgrounds, have become the backbone of child care in some communities throughout the United States. To only criticize and discount them is unacceptable. To ignore the seriousness of this problem, however, would be to marginalize the children and their future. It is encouraging and important that data on the Head Start program (collected both through the Family and Child Experiences Survey and through Program Information Report data) indicate that educational credentials of teachers are increasing and national targets for the proportion of teachers with an associate's degree have been met.

Since the 1980s, there has been a singular approach to this problem— namely, to provide more training and incentives for these individuals. For example, Head Start has established goals for the proportion of Head Start teachers who will have an associate's degree by certain time periods. Some states have required increased amounts of annual training for workers in child care centers; and many public school prekindergarten programs offer professional development for both teachers and paraeducators or teaching assistants. The presumption has been that more training will necessarily lead to improved quality of care, largely based on the finding of correlations between the educational levels of caregivers and the observed quality of care children receive. We note that there are exceptions to this generalization: well-trained teachers with high-level credentials do not always provide consistently high-quality care; conversely, there are some excellent caregivers who have never been formally trained. Although we endorse efforts to increase the knowledge and skills of the child care and education workforce, such as encouraging caregivers to complete credential and other college degree programs, we recognize that there are many paths by which knowledge and skills can be improved. We emphasize that the variables such as caregiver education cannot be used alone as indicators for high quality. Rather, as the "Four Diamond" Model of Quality of Child Care and Early Education indicates, the measure of quality must rely on actual practices, although these practices may be more likely to thrive within a supportive child care and educational context. Similarly, efforts to increase the pay and benefits for those in the early child care and education workforce are admirable and long overdue, but once again, these changes in the supportive context cannot be relied on as guarantees that the quality of care will be high.

In addition to widening the net for recruitment into the child care workforce, we advocate training that goes beyond the conventional formats that are currently popular. These conventional formats are usually group-based, involve lectures and demonstrations by "experts," sharing and "networking" among caregivers, and handing out a lot of print materials. Other innovative approaches that now are being tested in the field include the consultation model that individualizes goals and strategies for improving care with the caregivers over an extended period of time; a highly intensive form of coaching, called "immersion training," that is coupled with videotaped examples of desired caregiver–child interactions; and web-based, computer-assisted training programs that can be self-administered by caregivers and teachers. Remarkably, there are no standardized tests for assessing what has been learned in training, although almost all training now provided is rated by the participants in terms of their satisfaction with the training they received. More important, even if caregivers and teachers learn new knowledge, there needs to be a way to evaluate whether this knowledge is applied in the caregiving and educational setting. Currently, there is no entry-level assessment tool for estimating a caregiver's or teacher's knowledge and skills, so that when additional training is provided, it can be tailored to fill in the gaps and to increase skills in needed areas.

There is an urgent need to develop such tools for the child care workforce. Ideally, these would be designed so that practical demonstration of competency can be expressed in multiple formats, not just paper-and-pencil tests or oral questions and answers because these would unduly favor caregivers with formal education experience.

## Gathering Trustworthy, Accurate, and Ongoing Information About the Actual Performance of Caregivers and Teachers and Child Outcomes

There are few systems of data collection and monitoring that involve actual visits to places where children receive care. Initial licensing, updating or relicensing, and accreditation activities often involve an on-site visit, but many states and programs are burdened with heavy schedules and are late or unable to keep up with planned monitoring. In the past, many such visits involved identification of noncompliance issues and the need for plans of correction but did not provide overall assessments and feedback regarding all of the dimensions identified by the "Four Diamond" Model. In order for monitoring or surveillance systems to be effective, there needs to be a system for feedback and for constructive exchange between the regulatory entities and the care providers or teachers. Furthermore, the consequences of these regulatory visits were high, and often much preparatory activity preceded the visits so that the data gathered were not necessarily considered to be truly representative of what typically happens in the setting on an everyday basis. Another serious and still unanswered question is how often and for how long a child care or educational setting needs to be observed to yield a true picture of the care that children receive? Almost everyone agrees that a 1- or 2-hour visit, or even just a 1-day visit, is unlikely to be sufficient. What then are the alternatives that are feasible to test in developing a trans-setting system of data gathering and constructive monitoring for places that care for and educate young children?

We propose that there should be a coordinated effort to conduct field trials of different types of data collection and monitoring strategies to provide practically useful information for caregivers and program directors. Ideally, parents and professionals with different disciplinary backgrounds would contribute to the design of these field trials. We propose that direct observations of adult–child and caregiver–parent interactions occur; in addition, interviews with family members and caregivers could be designed to provide feedback that would help to improve quality. Finally, direct assessment and ratings of children, twice per year, could be implemented to provide indicators of child outcomes in key domains related to health and health care, social-emotional development, language and cognition, and self-appraisal and relationships with key caregivers.

There have been several major reasons advanced as to why data collection and monitoring have been lax in the field of child care and early childhood education, including the high cost of making visits, the lack of consensus about what to measure, and the invasiveness or disruption caused by visits. In fact, if data collection and monitoring activities were planned as part of continuous quality improvement and served to help identify areas for training and professional development, then the costs could be well justified. Parents might serve as data collectors if they received sufficient training, and caregivers (also trained in the procedures) might have an opportunity to become observers for other programs—thus acquiring new ideas from their visits to other child care and education settings. Finally, technology affords some innovative opportunities to use systems such as video-monitoring, which has been voluntarily adopted in some high-end preschool programs to permit parents to observe their young children during the day.

Administrative data also warrant collection and could become part of systems that identify places where there may be problems, such as when there is high turnover in either the children served or the staff. The goal is to include data from a variety of sources, collected frequently, as part of a systematic and open endeavor to improve the quality of care and education for young children. The cost of maintaining such systems could be factored in as part of regular program costs. Conversely, the costs to children, families, and society of failing to actively monitor the quality of child care and educational programs are far too high to continue to pay.

## Developing Strategies to Use Monitoring Data and Research Findings in a Timely Way to Drive Up the Quality of the Workforce and to Inform Policy Changes

One of the most surprising facts is that there is regular data collection about programs at the federal, state, and local community level, but the information is not used in a timely way to inform policy or identify areas in need of improvement. The SEED endeavor, supported by multiple federal agencies and private foundations, could provide much needed leadership to promote the active use of data in improving the quality of care and education.

We recommend that alternative systems for use of data be pilot tested in diverse types of child care and educational settings with a nationally representative sample. Chapters in this book point to pilot testing of rating systems at a local level. For instance, in one current pilot, ratings and observations of child care environments are being converted to an overall score that is publicly displayed. Alternatively, guided sessions in which caregivers, as well as administrators, have an opportunity to review the observational data and make suggestions for improvements could be tried to see whether changes would be voluntarily implemented. Linking these efforts to communitywide initiatives to promote school readiness and to improve children's health outcomes would provide natural roles for many service providers as well as for families to become engaged locally in these efforts to use data about quality.

Some thorny issues that warrant consideration include how to engage those who provide care informally and who are not subject to regulatory mechanisms or external funding; how to prevent families from becoming alarmed when they learn that their child's care may be below an acceptable threshold for quality; how to encourage certain agencies or programs to be open to revising their own regulations that may now be out-of-date or unnecessary to ensure quality; and how to offer technical assistance and remedial actions that will allow some settings to achieve high quality within a short period of time.

## CONCLUSIONS AND RECOMMENDATIONS

In our conference summary, we originally advanced five major ideas as "next steps for the field," which have already been initiated by the leaders of the SEED group. This concluding section reiterates these next steps in the hope that they will provide an opportunity for almost everyone to consider joining this coalition of individuals and groups seriously committed to improving the workforce quality on behalf of young children and their families. The next steps that we propose are as follows:

1. To use the SEED model to facilitate greater coordination among investigators and practitioners regarding early school success. This extension could include regional and local efforts and could be aligned with other national meetings.

2. To share the knowledge from this meeting in a timely and strategic fashion (this book is one such example). Ideally, different forms of information dissemination would be used to reach the media, educators, decision makers, scientists, and parents.

3. To agree to adopt an initial set of terms, definitions, and measures that can be widely shared, compared, and subsequently refined.

4. To destroy the myths that have been so divisive to the field and harmful to children (e.g., "early learning is stressful for children"; "language learning is a Caucasian, middle-class value"; "caregivers do not need to be highly knowledgeable to care for infants").

5. To coordinate even more vigorously, the federal research initiatives and evaluations (contracts) in the fields of early childhood, child care, Head Start, Even Start, early intervention, curriculum testing, welfare reform, child neglect and abuse, and other school readiness initiatives.

## REFERENCES

Borkowski, J.G., Ramey, S.L., & Bristol-Power, M. (Eds.). (2002). *Parenting and the child's world: Influences on academic, intellectual, and social-emotional development.* Mahwah, NJ: Lawrence Erlbaum Associates.

Bronfenbrenner, U. (1979). *The ecology of human development: Experiments by nature and design.* Cambridge, MA: Harvard University Press.

National Institute of Child Health and Human Development Early Child Care Research Network. (Ed.). (2005). *Child care and child development: Results from the NICHD Study of Early Child Care and Youth Development* (pp. 427–436). New York: The Guilford Press.

Ramey, C.T., & Ramey, S.L. (1998). Prevention of intellectual disabilities: Early interventions to improve cognitive development. *Preventive Medicine, 27,* 224–232.

Ramey, C.T., & Ramey, S.L. (1999). Beginning school for children at risk. In R.C. Pianta & M.J. Cox (Eds.), *The transition to kindergarten* (pp. 217–251). Baltimore: Paul H. Brookes Publishing Co.

Ramey, S.L., & Ramey, C.T. (2000). Early childhood experiences and developmental competence. In J. Waldfogel & S. Danziger (Eds.), *Securing the future: Investing in children from birth to college* (pp. 122–150). New York: Russell Sage Foundation.

Ramey, C.T., Ramey, S.L., & Cotton, J. (2002). Early interventions: Programs, results, and differential response. In A. Slater & M. Lewis (Eds.), *Introduction to infant development* (pp. 317–336). Oxford, England: Oxford University Press.

Ramey, S.L. (2005). Human developmental science serving children and families: Contributions of the NICHD Study of Early Child Care. In NICHD Early Child Care Research Network (Ed.), *Child care and child development: Results from the NICHD Study of Early Child Care and Youth Development* (pp. 427–436). New York: Plenum Press.

Ramey, S.L., Ramey, C.T., & Lanzi, R.G. (2004). The transition to school: Building on preschool foundations and preparing for lifelong learning. In E. Zigler & S.J. Styfco (Eds.), *The Head Start debates* (pp. 397–413). Baltimore: Paul H. Brookes Publishing Co.

Shonkoff, J.P., & Phillips, D.A. (Eds.). (2000). *From neurons to neighborhoods: The science of early childhood development.* Washington, DC: National Academy Press.

# CHAPTER 15

# Improving Connections Between Professional Development Research and Early Childhood Policies

Melissa Welch-Ross, Anne Wolf,
Martha Moorehouse, and Colleen Rathgeb

The preparation of early childhood education providers in the United States is a patchwork of preservice degrees, specialized training opportunities, and credentials. The type of preparation a provider must have depends on the state, locale, auspice, and type of early childhood program. Many providers pursue certificates such as the Child Development Associate (CDA) or various state or local credentials, whereas others seek formal education, such as a 2-year associate's degree or a 4-year bachelor's degree in child development or early childhood education. In addition to these formal preservice experiences, early childhood providers may be required to attend training, including an assortment of conferences, workshops, and other technical assistance offerings. Federal agencies are among those that give technical assistance and funding to improve professional development in Head Start, child care, and prekindergarten settings, including programs funded by Title I and the Individuals with Disabilities Education Act (IDEA) that serve children who are poor or who have special needs.

The content of these educational experiences varies widely, although some efforts are being made to make the quality of early childhood professional training more uniform. For example, many associate and baccalaureate degree programs seek accreditation from the National Association for the Education of Young Children (NAEYC), which evaluates degree requirements against their standards. (See Chapter 11 for more information about the NAEYC and accreditation.) Many states also either have their own accreditation systems for early childhood professionals or are in the process of developing their own systems.

Efforts to improve the quality of early childhood professional preparation focus primarily on teachers of preschoolers, especially those working in center-based settings, including Head Start and prekindergarten programs. A few

This chapter was completed while the first author served as Research and Policy Analyst in the Office of the Assistant Secretary for Planning and Evaluation at the U.S. Department of Health and Human Services. The views expressed are those of the authors and do not necessarily reflect positions of the Office of the Assistant Secretary for Planning and Evaluation or the U.S. Department of Health and Human Services.

public programs, such as Early Head Start and early interventions funded through Part C of IDEA, are working to improve the preparation of providers serving infants and toddlers. However, such efforts for this population of providers, as well as for providers in mostly unregulated, informal home-based child care, are not very widespread.

Despite all of these long-standing and more recent efforts to educate and train the early childhood workforce, there is no consensus on the knowledge and skills that providers need to promote children's early learning and development or on the best methods for training diverse groups of providers in different early childhood settings. Many empirical questions remain about how best to prepare early childhood professionals. As researchers attempt to answer these questions, greater attention to the history of early childhood programs and to the current policy context can strengthen the applied value of their contributions.

This chapter describes historical trends in early childhood programs and policies. Furthermore, it highlights current policy provisions and mechanisms for offering professional development in the context of federally supported early childhood care and education programs. It then offers suggestions for improving the usefulness of professional development research to practice and policy. Specifically, it describes how professional development research can be helpful at various points in the cycle of policy formulation and policy implementation. Next, it suggests broad directions for research with potential to advance useful knowledge about professional development practices and policies. The chapter concludes with a discussion of practical issues that can influence the application of research findings.

## HISTORICAL TRENDS IN EARLY CHILDHOOD PROGRAMS AND POLICIES

It is important to look historically at the origins of early childhood programs before discussing current early childhood policies. Programs initially emerged to serve different functions (see Kamerman & Gatenio, 2003). Many programs were designed as child care support for working parents, whereas others were designed to enhance young children's development and learning. In the 1830s, under the auspices of private charities, day nurseries provided custodial care for young children while their mothers worked. At the same time, private, fee-for-service nursery schools offered social and cognitive enrichment primarily for children from middle-class families.

In the 1960s and 1970s, each type of program began to expand considerably. As part of the War on Poverty, compensatory education programs were developed to prepare preschool children who were disadvantaged for school, as well as to provide access to health care and improved nutrition. The emergence of these comprehensive intervention programs culminated with the federal establishment of Head Start in 1965. Federal support to states for programs educating children with special needs was also expanded through the Education for All Handicapped Children Act of 1975 (PL 94-142; most recently reauthorized as the Individuals with Disabilities Education Improvement Act of 2004, PL 108-446). Following the growth in early education programs serving children in poverty and children with special needs, the increase of middle-class mothers in the labor force resulted in the expansion of child care programs for working parents and subsequent push for quality care in all settings (Kamerman & Gatenio, 2003). With these changes, previous boundaries between child care as an educational enrichment program and child care as a support for working families have blurred (Shonkoff & Phillips, 2000).

Nonetheless, because early childhood programs have evolved out of different traditions (developmental enrichment, support for working families, compensatory education for children who are disadvantaged, interventions for children with special needs), child care and education for young children in the United States currently consists of a diverse array of public and private programs in a wide range of settings, including center-based child care, Head Start, prekindergarten, part-day preschool, family child care (both regulated and unregulated), relative care, and nonrelative baby sitters. Professional development opportunities and varying credentialing requirements for providers have developed along the lines of these different traditions. For example, early education programs tend to require higher levels of education for providers than child care programs designed primarily to support working parents. As noted earlier, efforts to improve the quality of provider preparation focus primarily on teachers in center-based programs for preschoolers rather than on providers in informal, home settings or other programs serving infants and toddlers. Because there are fewer public programs for infants and toddlers than for preschoolers and because these younger children are more often cared for in homes than preschoolers, many providers serving infants and toddlers have no required preservice qualifications.

Regardless of uneven preservice and credentialing requirements for early childhood providers, the trend for programs from all traditions both to foster children's school readiness and support working families has led to a strong desire to better integrate programs. For example, efforts to coordinate part-day Head Start and prekindergarten programs with existing full-day child care programs can increase the efficiency of current systems by making more effective use of existing federal, state, and local resources. Integrating programs presents challenges, however, for coordinating quality standards because programs have disparate traditions and providers with a diverse range of education and training.

## CURRENT POLICY CONTEXT

Although there are ongoing attempts to integrate services and coordinate standards across early childhood programs, a unified child and family policy does not exist in the United States. Instead, as noted previously, an array of early childhood programs and policies has been designed to serve different functions. The federal government offers services to children who are disadvantaged economically, socially, and physically and helps provide child care services to enable mothers who have low incomes to work. Federal assistance also supports working parents who have middle incomes through the nonrefundable Child and Dependant Care Tax Credit, which facilitates parents' choice in selecting child care services.

Most federal programs serving children and families (with the notable exception of Head Start) are implemented through state and local governments in order to better meet local preferences and needs. At the federal level, broad boundaries and general guidelines are offered, enabling states tremendous flexibility in implementing programs. The federal child care subsidy program (Child Care and Development Fund [CCDF]), for example, gives states broad discretion in how they determine eligibility, reimbursement rates, program standards, and teacher qualifications.

States differ widely in their approaches to implementing federal programs and in their levels of investment in state early childhood programs. For example, some states are actively building prekindergarten programs in their public school systems and expanding early intervention programs and other services for children from birth through age 5, whereas other states choose to undertake none or only some of these activities. States also vary in the extent to which they encourage local governments and communities to participate in the development of early childhood policies (Kamerman & Gatenio, 2003).

Recent federal initiatives encourage states to improve young children's learning opportunities across early childhood settings. States are encouraged, for example, to develop guidelines for quality early childhood programs, including early learning goals that align with K–12 standards and with professional development options. The No Child Left Behind (NCLB) Act of 2001 (PL 107-110) asks states to set standards for student performance and teacher quality and holds public elementary and secondary schools accountable for achieving standards, beginning with the testing of third-grade students, by linking funding to school performance. With the recent federal early childhood initiatives, such as *Good Start, Grow Smart* (see Chapter 1), efforts to achieve the goals of NCLB have been extended to early childhood programs.

## PROFESSIONAL DEVELOPMENT PROVISIONS AND FUNDING FOR PUBLIC EARLY CHILDHOOD PROGRAMS

Chapter 1 gives background on current public investments specific to early childhood education and describes funding mechanisms for and services offered through the CCDF, Head Start and Early Head Start, and state-administered prekindergarten programs. This chapter extends that discussion by describing legislative provisions specific to provider qualifications and professional development for major federal programs and funding streams administered by the U.S. Department of Health and Human Services and the U.S. Department of Education, and it concludes with an overview of state-administered prekindergarten programs.

## U.S. Department of Health and Human Services

***Child Care and Development Fund***    The CCDF is administered by the Child Care Bureau under the Administration for Children and Families. The CCDF gives grants to states to operate child care subsidy programs to help families with low incomes obtain child care. Federal law sets the maximum eligibility level at 85% of the state median income (SMI) for a family of the same size. On average, states set the eligibility level at 62% of SMI (Child Care Bureau, 2003). However, states may set eligibility guidelines at any level below the federal maximum because they have broad discretion in operating their child care programs. For this reason, states vary widely not only in eligibility guidelines but also in reimbursement rates and co-payment amounts. Under CCDF, subsidized child care services are available to eligible parents through certificates, cash reimbursement, or contracted programs, enabling parents to select any legally operating child care provider. The original authorization of CCDF (together with Temporary Assistance for Needy Families [TANF]) expired in September 2002 (Personal Responsibility and Work Opportunities Reconciliation Act of 1996, PL 104-193). The program has continued to operate through a series of short-term extensions approved by Congress; however, CCDF is currently due for reauthorization. Once passed by Congress, a new law will reauthorize CCDF for an additional 5 years.

The CCDF legislation offers no specific provisions regarding provider preservice qualifications or ongoing professional development. With guidelines left entirely to states' discretion, state requirements for provider qualifications and in-service training are quite variable (see LeMoine, 2004, for a summary). Thirty-seven states do not require center-based teachers to have any preservice training in early childhood education. Three states require center teachers to complete vocational child care provider training. Three states require 8–90 clock hours of training in early childhood education. One state requires six courses in early childhood education or child development. Six states and the District of Columbia require a CDA or other type of credential, such as a Certified Child Care Professional (CCP) credential, awarded by the National Child Care Association, or a state or local certificate in early childhood education. In addition to preservice training, five states and the District of Columbia also require that center-based teachers have experience working in an early childhood setting.

Although the CCDF legislation does not specify provider qualification requirements, it does require states to spend at least 4% of CCDF funds to improve the quality and availability of child care. Quality funds may also be used to promote comprehensive consumer education and to increase parental choice. In achieving these goals, states may use quality funds for a range of activities, including training and technical assistance to providers serving infants and toddlers; grants for improving provider wages; tiered reimbursement systems to pay higher reimbursement rates to higher-quality providers; enhancement grants to programs for purchasing equipment, developing curricula, or pursuing accreditation; specialists to consult with programs on the health and developmental needs of infants and toddlers; and state monitoring of compliance with licensing and regulatory requirements (Child Care Bureau, 2003). In fiscal year 2001, approximately 9% of combined federal and state child care expenditures were used for quality enhancement (Child Care Bureau, 2003).

States have invested quality improvement funds in a range of innovative initiatives (see Child Care Bureau, 2004). For example, 29 states use quality funds to support or build a career development system for early care and education. Pennsylvania Pathways is one such system, and it delivers free and low-cost training/education, technical assistance, and on-site mentoring opportunities. Professional development offered through this system is coordinated with the Keystone Stars performance standards, a quality rating system that provides information to parents on each program's quality. As of October 2004, quality rating systems such as this one or tiered reimbursement systems were established by 13 states using CCDF quality funds. States with tiered reimbursement systems not only indicate a rating of child care quality but also provide parents with a higher reimbursement rate for use of a provider with a higher rating.

Even states that have not established large professional development or tiered reimbursement systems are investing in smaller-scale initiatives to improve provider training and program quality. For example, Montana provides grants to mentoring programs that match experienced caregiver mentors with novice caregivers. Eight other states support similar mentoring programs. In addition, seven states provide support for training unregulated child care providers. Missouri offers incentives to aides and relative care providers who pursue additional child care training. Initiatives to train providers in promoting children's early language, literacy, and mathematics development have been implemented with quality funds in 23 states. Eight states have also funded train-the-trainer programs to help improve such training initiatives (Child Care Bureau, 2004).

In addition to quality improvement funds, federal regulation reserves one quarter of 1% of total annual CCDF funds to provide technical assistance. The Child Care Bureau used these funds to establish the Child Care Technical

Assistance Network (CCTAN) to address the needs of states, territories, and tribes administering the CCDF. CCTAN assesses states' needs, identifies innovations in child care administration, and supports the dissemination and replication of these innovations. CCTAN provides technical assistance to CCDF administrators through consultation, conferences, and training sessions. Technical assistance funds have been used to establish the National Child Care Information Center (NCCIC) and more specialized information centers focused on key issues such as administering programs; reporting of child care data; increasing the availability, quality, and accessibility of child care in tribal communities; promoting children's social and emotional competence; building partnerships among child care, Head Start, and other early childhood organizations; and improving the health and well-being of children in child care, including children with disabilities. In addition to providing technical assistance to state child care administrators, technical assistance funds are used to provide information to parents through a national network of local child care resource and referral agencies (Child Care Bureau, 2003).

*Head Start*    The Head Start program is administered by the Head Start Bureau under the Administration for Children and Families. According to the Head Start Act (part of the Omnibus Budget Reconciliation Act of 1981, PL 97-35), a child is eligible for Head Start if his or her family income is below the federal poverty line or if the family is eligible for public assistance or would be eligible without child care. Grantees may enroll up to 10% of children whose family income is above the poverty line. Since 1965, Head Start has been delivering comprehensive services to support the healthy development of 3- to 5-year-old children from families with low incomes. In addition to early childhood education, Head Start provides a range of individualized services to meet children's nutritional, medical, dental, and mental health needs and to offer parenting support. The Head Start Bureau awards grants directly to local public agencies, private organizations, Indian tribes, and school systems, which enables Head Start programs to operate at the community level. The Head Start Act was last reauthorized in 1998 through fiscal year 2003 (PL 105-285) and currently requires reauthorization. Once passed by Congress, a new law will reauthorize Head Start for an additional 5 years.

As noted in Chapter 1, the 1998 reauthorization of Head Start required that, by September 30, 2003, at least 50% of all Head Start teachers have an associate's degree or higher either in early childhood education or in a related field with experience teaching preschool children. Teachers who do not meet these criteria are required to have a CDA credential or a state certificate that meets or exceeds the CDA requirements. Head Start has met this goal. In program year 2003–2004, 65% of Head Start teachers had an associate's, bachelor's, or higher degree in early childhood education or a similar field (Head Start Bureau, 2004).

Head Start's authorizing legislation allocates a minimum of 2% of annual funding for training and technical assistance activities to improve program quality and management, to ensure program responsiveness to local needs, and to help resolve barriers to collaborating with other programs in providing wrap-around care. Specified priorities include assisting programs in ensuring children's school readiness and in meeting educational performance measures, as well as addressing training and career development needs of staff.

In 2004, the Head Start Bureau redesigned the national training and technical assistance (T/TA) system. A regional T/TA network was created to focus on the local needs of grantees. Although T/TA funds support the new regional network, some funds are retained for national activities, such as the national T/TA system and the Summer Teacher Education Program (STEP) literacy trainings that occurred in 2002 and 2003. The Bureau also awards training and technical assistance funds directly to grantees.

In addition to technical assistance, some Head Start funds are reserved for improving program quality. The Head Start program is designed so that overall increases in funding provide for increases in funding designated for quality improvement. Specifically, 25% of any annual increase in Head Start funding, after cost of living adjustments, is reserved for improving program quality. Each year since fiscal year 2003, 25% of overall funding increases have been used for quality improvement purposes. Congress mandated that a portion of overall funding increases be used for quality improvement for the first time in fiscal year 1999. At that time, 60% of the overall annual increase in funding was reserved for quality improvement. Every year since, the percentage of overall increases designated for quality improvement has been gradually declining from the initial 60% in 1999 to the current 25%. When the Head Start program receives increased funding in a given year, the increase remains part of its budget in subsequent years. Similarly, increases in funds reserved for quality improvement remain part of the budget for quality improvement in subsequent years. As a result, even with the gradual decline in the proportion of overall increases reserved for quality improvement, the funds available for quality improvement have still increased each year since fiscal year 1999.

The Head Start Act of 1998 (under the Coats Human Services Amendments of 1998, PL 105-285) specifies that quality improvement funds may be used to accomplish any or all of the following goals: enabling Head Start programs to meet and exceed performance standards; ensuring that programs have adequate numbers of qualified staff; providing staff with adequate training, including skills to work with English language learners and children with disabilities; offering salary levels and benefits sufficient to attract and retain qualified staff; improving staff qualifications through salary increases; implementing career development programs; encouraging staff to use federal and state incentive and loan forgiveness programs for professional development; ensuring that qualified staff can promote children's language and literacy growth and "provide children with a variety of skills that have been identified, through scientifically based reading research, as predictive of later reading achievement"; improving collaboration with community programs; ensuring adequate physical environments, including accessibility for children with disabilities; and providing any other needed quality improvements.

In an effort to accomplish these goals, Head Start legislation specifies that at least half of the amount reserved for quality improvement must be used to improve salary and benefits of teachers and other staff in order to encourage recruitment and retention of qualified staff. Teachers and staff who obtain additional training or education must be given preference for salary increases above cost-of-living allowances.

Furthermore, the legislation specifies that the greatest priority for the remaining quality improvement funds is training teachers and staff to meet education performance standards, including promoting children's language and literacy growth, promoting English among second language learners, fostering children's school readiness, and providing training to improve staff qualifications. Additional quality improvement funds may be used to employ additional staff and provide employee benefits.

***Early Head Start***    With the reauthorization of the Head Start Act (under the Human Services Amendments of 1994, PL 103-252), Congress established the Early Head Start program to serve low-income families with infants and toddlers, as well as pregnant women. Income eligibility guidelines are the same as those for Head Start. This program provides early, intensive comprehensive child development and family support services to enhance children's development, promote positive parent–child interactions, support parenting, and help families move toward self-sufficiency.

A percentage of the total funding for the Head Start program is designated for Early Head Start; in fiscal year 2003; this amount was 10%, a gradual increase from 7.5% in fiscal year 1999. From the amount set aside for Early Head Start, between 5% and 10% of funds are reserved for training and technical assistance. These funds may be used for a range of activities, including making grants to or contracts with organizations with expertise on infants, toddlers, and families to provide direction for training and technical assistance; providing training and technical assistance to staff who monitor and administer Early Head Start programs; providing training and technical assistance to Early Head Start grantees to support program planning and implementation; and providing professional development and training for the recruitment and retention of qualified staff (Head Start Act, under the Coats Human Services Amendments of 1998).

## U.S. Department of Education

***Title I Preschools***    Title I of the Elementary and Secondary Education Act (ESEA) authorizes the Office of ESEA to award federal grants to states and school districts with large numbers of students who are poor[1] in order to meet the educational needs of students who are low achievers. Title I is a funding stream for early childhood programs rather than an early childhood program itself, such as Head Start. State-administered prekindergartens serving children who are poor can be funded in part through Title I. Other examples of Title I-funded programs serving preschool children include Even Start and Early Reading First, which are described in the next section.

Title I was reauthorized as part of the NCLB Act of 2001,[2] which requires that by the end of the 2005–2006 school year, all public school teachers be "highly qualified" (ESEA, Title I, Section 1119[a][2]), which is defined as having a state teaching certification or license, a bachelor's degree, and a demonstrated competency in all subject areas taught (ESEA, Title IX, Section 9101[23]). This qualification applies to teachers in Title I-funded preschools that are part of a state's public elementary education. If the preschool or prekindergarten is not part of the state's school system, then teachers in Title I-funded preschools are not required to meet this qualification (U.S. Department of Education, 2004).

Title I funds can be used for professional development for teachers and paraprofessionals working with children funded through Title I. According to nonregulatory guidance[3] for serving preschool children under Title I (U.S. Department of Education, 2004), the following professional development activities listed in the ESEA statute are most applicable to preschool teachers: high-quality sustained, intensive, and classroom-focused activities for a positive and lasting impact on classroom instruction; activities that advance teachers' understanding of effective instructional strategies that are based on scientific research; activities that align with applicable state content standards; methods to improve the teaching of children with special needs; and activities that are regularly evaluated for effectiveness. One-day or short-term workshops are not encouraged. The guidance especially advocates mentoring and coaching strategies for providing ongoing training to preschool teachers. For example, a coach might model effective teaching strategies for the teacher, and/or observe the teacher's instruction, which is followed by discussion and reflection on the effectiveness of instructional strategies and how they support young children's progress (U.S. Department of Education, 2004).

---

[1]In addition to poverty, school systems can qualify for Title I funds for children who participate in TANF, live in foster homes, or live in other facilities for children removed from their homes due to abuse and neglect.

[2]The Elementary and Secondary Education Act is scheduled to be reauthorized in 2007.

[3]Through nonregulatory guidance, the U.S. Department of Education (or the appropriate administrative agency) offers assistance with interpreting and applying the law (ESEA, in this case). However, nonregulatory guidance does not carry legislative authority.

*Even Start*    Even Start was created in 1989 to improve the literacy of both children and parents through early education, parenting education, adult education, and joint parent–child literacy activities. The 2004 appropriation for Even Start was nearly $249 million. Each year, approximately 50,000 families are served through the program's 1000 partnerships of local education agencies and community-based organizations. By December 2004, a majority of all Even Start staff providing instruction are supposed to obtain at least an associate's degree in a field related to early childhood education, elementary school or secondary school education, or adult education and meet state qualifications for the program. *All* new staff hired since the passage of the NCLB Act must meet the requirements, and states may establish even more stringent qualifications.

*Early Reading First*    Title I, Part B of the NCLB Act authorized the Early Reading First competitive grants program for the first time to address the concern that many children begin kindergarten without the necessary foundation to fully benefit from formal school instruction. Funds are given to local education agencies and public or private organizations that serve children from low-income families. Grantees receive funding for 3 years and must seek to enhance children's language and cognitive development by providing high-quality instruction and ongoing professional development grounded in scientifically based research. Public, nonprofit, and private organizations, including faith-based organizations, have competed for the grants. In 2004, 32 new grantees received a total of more than $90 million. During each of the 2 prior years, 30 new grantees received a total of $72–$74 million (http://www.ed.gov/programs/earlyreading/awards.html).

States and programs can use funds to offer professional development for teachers. Although no explicit staff qualifications are required to receive Early Reading First grants, the law requires programs to report levels of staff qualification for future evaluation.

### *Early Childhood Educator Professional Development Program*

The Early Childhood Educator Professional Development program, first authorized by Title II of the NCLB Act of 2001, is a competitive grants program designed to improve teacher quality. The program was created to "enhance the school readiness of young children, particularly disadvantaged young children" and "to prevent young children from encountering difficulties once the children enter school, by improving the knowledge and skills of early childhood educators who work in communities that have high concentrations of children living in poverty" (http://www.ed.gov/programs/eceducator/index.html). Grants are made directly to local partnerships, such as higher education institutions or other public or private entities that provide professional development to early childhood educators. The statute requires that professional development activities carried out through this grant be coordinated with the professional development components of other early childhood programs administered through either the U.S. Department of Education (e.g., Title I preschools) or the U.S. Department of Health and Human Services (e.g., Head Start).

After $10 million was appropriated for the first program year (fiscal year 2001), the amount appropriated the following year (fiscal year 2002) increased by 50% to $15 million. Appropriations were $14.9 million in fiscal year 2003 and $14.8 million in fiscal year 2004 (http://www.ed.gov/programs/eceducator/funding.html).

The federal legislation indicates that funds may be used for training providers to apply recent child development research to teaching practices; to collaborate with parents on promoting children's school readiness; to work with children with limited English proficiency, disabilities, or other special needs; to identify and prevent behavioral problems; to work with children who have been identified as or suspected of being victims of abuse; to improve preparation during their first 3 years in the field; to use assessments to improve teaching; and to meet accountability requirements. Grant funds may also be used to develop and implement distance learning and other technologies in professional development programs (e.g., ESEA).

According to the legislation, professional development activities funded under this grant program must conform to accountability standards. In other words, professional development activities must be evaluated for their quality, accessibility, and impact on teaching.

***IDEA Early Education Programs***    IDEA was passed in 1975 to provide states with federal funding for educating children with disabilities. Under the law, which was reauthorized in 2004 for the standard 5-year cycle, states are required to provide access to a free, appropriate public education for children with disabilities. A child with a disability is defined as one with mental retardation; a hearing impairment or deafness; a speech or language impairment; a visual impairment, including blindness; emotional disturbance; an orthopedic impairment; autism; traumatic brain injury; any other health impairment; a specific learning disability; deaf-blindness; or multiple disabilities.

Early intervention and preschool programs funded through IDEA in 2003 served more than 260,000 infants and toddlers (http://www.nectac.org/partc/partcdata.asp) and nearly 650,000 preschoolers (http://www.nectac.org/sec619/619overview.asp). In 2004, $444 million was appropriated for early intervention services to children from birth through age 2 years; $388 million was appropriated for special education services to children from ages 3 to 5 years.

In the newly reauthorized IDEA (Individuals with Disabilities Education Improvement Act of 2004, PL 108-446), language on personnel qualifications was made more consistent with the NCLB Act. All special education teachers teaching in a public school system must also be "highly qualified," as defined in Section 9101(23) of the ESEA, by the end of the 2005–2006 school year. For special education teachers, being "highly qualified" means having a bachelor's degree and a state special education certification or license. Some advocacy groups oppose the licensing exam as the only standard by which teachers can achieve "highly qualified" status. Instead, they prefer the use of performance evaluations to assess teachers' expertise in altering instruction to meet individual learning needs (Council for Exceptional Children, 2004).

The new law directs states to require local school systems to "take measurable steps to recruit, hire, train, and retain highly qualified personnel to provide special education and related services . . . to children with disabilities" (IDEA 2004). The law no longer requires states to maintain "a comprehensive system of personnel development that is designed to ensure an adequate supply of qualified special education, regular education, and related services personnel" (Individuals with Disabilities Education Act Amendments of 1997, PL 105-17).

The 2004 reauthorization creates the State Personnel Development Grants program (replacing the previous State Improvement Grants) to assist states in "improving their systems for personnel preparation and professional development in early intervention, educational, and transition services in order to improve results for children with disabilities" (IDEA, 2004). States have broad flexibility in designing professional development activities for improving the knowledge, skills, and effectiveness of special education teachers and general educators serving children with disabilities. No more than 10% of funds can be used for activities other than delivering training, such as reforming certification or licensing requirements or developing mechanisms to recruit and retain teachers. Grants may be used for professional development activities that provide support to teachers, such as mentoring, collaboration, or other intensive professional development; encourage effective use and integration of technology; improve knowledge of effective instructional practices; foster skills for involving parents; encourage responsiveness to children's varied learning styles and developing English skills; and provide training in methods of positive behavioral interventions, scientifically based reading instruction, early and appropriate interventions, instruction for children with low-incidence disabilities, and instruction for children with significant health, mobility, or behavioral needs.

## State-Administered Prekindergarten

About 19,000 public elementary schools (35%) offered prekindergarten classes in 2000–2001 (U.S. Department of Education, National Center for Education Statistics [NCES], 2003). Local school districts operate prekindergarten programs primarily in public elementary schools, though state-administered prekindergarten may also operate in Head Start and community-based early childhood programs. Implementation usually involves integrating diverse federal, state, and local funding streams and offering programs in a variety of center-based and school settings.

State funding for prekindergarten programs generally ranges between $1.4 million for a program serving 1,081 children in Vermont (in fiscal year 2001) to $322 million for a program serving 153,568 (43%) children in Texas (in fiscal year 2002), with a low of $150,000 for a small program serving 414 children (in fiscal year 2000) in Nevada (Education Commission of the States, 2002). Variations in funding levels primarily reflect the number of children served, but they also result from other forces on per-pupil expenditures, such as state eligibility guidelines, co-payment amounts, and teacher qualifications and compensation.

For preservice education, 86% of prekindergarten teachers in public school programs have a bachelor's degree or higher (U.S. Department of Education, NCES, 2003). Of the 44 state prekindergarten initiatives in 39 states in 2002–2003, only 13 required teachers to have both a bachelor's degree and specialized training in early childhood education. Ten state initiatives required only a bachelor's degree, and an additional eight required a bachelor's degree only for preschool teachers in public school settings. Twelve state initiatives required teachers to have specialized training in early childhood education but not a bachelor's degree. New Mexico is the only state that did not require preschool teachers to have either a degree or specialized training (Barnett, Hustedt, Robin, & Schulman, 2004).

State-administered prekindergarten programs also vary widely in their requirements for in-service training. In 2002–2003, 27 of the 44 initiatives required teachers to participate in at least 15 hours of in-service training per year. Alabama required the most in-service training (40 hours per year), and six states did not require any annual in-service training (Barnett et al., 2004).

## IMPROVING THE APPLIED VALUE OF PROFESSIONAL DEVELOPMENT RESEARCH

Strengthening the scientific integrity of professional development research and becoming aware of practical issues that affect whether or how research is applied can improve the usefulness of research to practice and policy. Before discussing these points, however, the next section describes more generally how research can be useful at various points in the cycle of policy formulation and policy implementation.

## Research in the Policy Formulation and Implementation Cycle

A bidirectional relationship between research and policy, whereby each influences the other, operates in the cycle that moves from policy formulation to the implementation of policies and programs and back again to policy formulation.

At the policy formulation phase, federal legislation is developed to guide program regulations in the executive branch, program administration and monitoring, and technical assistance to those who administer and implement programs. Research findings alone typically do not stimulate or guide these policies because many political, cultural, and economic factors affect whether an issue is addressed through policy and the specific policy decisions that are made. Research is often useful, however, for framing the extent of a problem and assessing the feasibility and potential consequences of different policy strategies. During the policy implementation process, questions about how best to implement policies to maximize effectiveness and resources can stimulate research that is useful for informing implementation, as well as new policy directions. Research on how policies and programs were actually implemented and whether desired outcomes were achieved is especially important for informing subsequent policy decisions.

At all points in the policy formulation and implementation cycle, an inherent tension exists among federal, state, and local roles, which involves balancing federal legislative and regulatory prescriptiveness with state or local control. As described earlier, the current federal legislative trend is toward local administration and decision making. Again, with the exception of Head Start, the primary federal role is increasingly to provide guidance in the form of technical assistance and to set requirements for results-based accountability as well as the use of evidence-based practices and program models. This approach allows states and localities maximum flexibility in meeting locally identified needs while accounting for results.

Because many policy decisions are made at state and local levels, state policy makers have a strong interest in research on the effectiveness of various approaches to enhancing professional development and other ways of improving the quality of early childhood settings. As a result, research is often used to inform policy and practices at state and local levels. Often, innovative state and local early childhood policies and programs can lead to studies of implementation and effectiveness that inform subsequent policy formulation at all levels. For example, as states implement tiered reimbursement systems, research can begin to examine the extent to which such systems are successful in providing an incentive for improving program quality.

State and local policy makers are invested in discovering what policies are effective, and their questions can stimulate research. For example, Washington state's Child Care Coordinating Committee requested a study of family, friend, and neighbor care, including input on how to structure training for this group. Also the Minnesota Department of Human Services, through participation in the Minnesota Child Care Policy Research Partnership, has supported observational study of quality in centers; licensed family child care homes; and care provided by family, friends, and neighbors. Quality improvements are being developed based on study findings.

At the federal level, research investments often address questions of interest to both federal and state and local policy makers. Although major federal studies of early care and education programs are conducted to answer federal policy makers' questions about overall effectiveness, they are also designed to take into account local variations such as state and local policies; the services offered; and the characteristics of children, families, and providers. The Early Head Start Research and Evaluation Project, funded by the Administration for Children and Families, and the Quality Interventions for Early Care and Education (QUINCE), funded by the Child Care Bureau and the Office of the Assistant Secretary for Planning and Evaluation, are two examples of research from the U.S. Department of Health and Human Services that include the professional development of early childhood providers as a key component. The study of Early Head Start evaluates overall short and long-term effects of the program on infants, toddlers, and their families, whereas sub-studies embedded within the larger evaluation address issues relevant to particular localities. The QUINCE study, which is being conducted in six states, evaluates intensive, on-site strategies for training family child care providers and entry-level center care teachers. The results will give state-specific information on effectiveness in addition to an overall picture of program effectiveness in different policy and demographic contexts.

Although policy makers' questions are generating research, field-initiated studies generated by researchers' questions can also influence policy makers' decisions about policy development and implementation. States and local communities vary widely in their efforts to improve program quality and enhance professional development, providing a valuable opportunity for researchers to examine the effectiveness of alternative approaches to improving quality and better training providers. Regardless of whether research questions come from state and local policy makers, federal policy makers, or researchers, coordinating research agendas at federal and state levels can be one strategy for effectively answering questions that are common to all states and that address state-specific needs.

A key time for federal and state policy makers to review research findings is when programs require reauthorization by Congress or the state legislature. At reauthorization, research on the implementation and effectiveness of existing policies and programs, findings from new early education interventions, and discoveries about children's learning and development from basic research may all stimulate thinking about new policy directions. A direct line does not always exist, however, from research findings to the formulation of new policies. When policy makers attempt to use the results of basic research that was not designed to directly inform policy decisions, research can be applied in ways that go beyond the actual results. This leap is especially likely when policy makers seek to remedy a problem, but research findings are not available that speak directly to the issue.

In early childhood education and professional preparation, basic research findings on child development sometimes have been used to specify desired program outcomes for children and provider qualifications without having direct evidence on how best to prepare diverse groups of providers to support children's progress in all areas essential to their healthy development and school readiness. For example, in the past, policy makers interpreted the findings of basic research as showing that knowing a certain number of letters is important for later reading. Policy makers subsequently learned of additional research showing associations between reading ability and early rich language environments and other early literacy experiences. They also learned of research showing that children often were not receiving these experiences. As a result, interest has been renewed in determining how best to define and promote children's progress in areas associated with reading achievement and school readiness. Chapter 1 describes a set of federally funded studies underway across the U.S. Department of Health and Human Services and the U.S. Department of Education that are intended to address issues of how to educate providers to promote children's progress in language, literacy, and other areas that prepare children for school. The next section highlights broad research directions for further bridging this gap between research and policy questions on provider preparation.

## Research Directions for Advancing Practice and Policy

Designing and delivering effective early childhood preparation depends, in part, on having a scientifically sound and practically relevant knowledge base. Three key overarching goals for professional development research are to identify the necessary and sufficient components of early childhood practices and provider preparation that produce desired outcomes; inform choices about which professional development opportunities and policies should be implemented; and provide data to continually improve approaches to professional development (see Chapter 14).

Existing scientific knowledge on how best to prepare diverse groups of early childhood professionals and implement effective professional development systems cannot yet address most questions central to practice and policy. One persistent question in early childhood policy contexts is, "What level of formal education and training does the early childhood workforce need to implement effective teaching and care-taking practices?" Chapters 2 and 4 highlight limitations of existing data that prevent knowing the answer, although others have concluded that it is especially a baccalaureate degree with specialized training in early childhood education that contributes to higher-quality early childhood programs and better child outcomes (e.g., National Research Council, 2001; Whitebook, 2003).

Several issues need to be addressed before drawing firm conclusions about the optimal education level for providers, including the following:

• More detailed and systematic collection, reporting, and analysis is required to determine what providers are learning in formal education settings, including information about the availability and quality of assisted teaching or expert mentoring opportunities. To assess quality of preparation, most research has focused on types of teacher credentials; use of curricula or educational materials; and the number of courses, workshops, or other training activities that providers have attended. The content of these experiences varies widely, including the content of baccalaureate and associate-level coursework, as well as what is often referred to as "specialized training in early childhood education." Because little information about the content of these experiences has been reported and analyzed (see Chapter 2), it is not yet clear from this body of research what type and level of education results in promoting desired child outcomes.

- To examine the extent to which increasing levels of education and training results in improved teaching practices, researchers also need to control for personal characteristics and skills, such as motivation or verbal ability, that providers have in common that may make them good teachers and caregivers, regardless of whether they have a particular college degree.

- Better observational evidence is needed to determine if teachers with certain education levels actually interact with children using strategies that result in desired outcomes in key areas of learning and development, such as language, literacy, mathematics, problem solving, self-regulation, and social skills. Many studies assess only providers' reported satisfaction with training experiences or their caregiving beliefs and philosophies. Although a number of studies show associations between observations of program and teacher quality and provider qualifications, these quality measures focus mainly on general aspects of caregiving, such as warmth and responsiveness; the availability of educational and play materials; and selected observations of language and literacy interactions that do not represent the breadth and depth of interaction that research shows to be important for promoting children's progress. Thus, higher scores on these more global measures of quality do not necessarily mean that providers are engaging in specific interactions needed to support children's learning and development in specific areas.

- Comprehensive assessments of not only teacher outcomes but also children's outcomes are critical for determining the impact of increasing levels and types of education for promoting children's learning and development.

From a practical perspective, many providers do not have bachelor's degrees and need help acquiring the knowledge and skills essential for promoting children's early learning and development. As a result, professional development practices and policies can benefit from a shift in research focus. Rather than attempting to identify an optimal level of formal education and training for providers by comparing the bachelor's degree with other education levels, research is needed to better understand the education and training content and the delivery methods that best prepare diverse groups of providers to meet children's needs in each early childhood setting.

With this perspective in mind, policies and practice can benefit from research that focuses on the following broad questions.

- *What works for whom?* What knowledge and skills do providers need to promote desired outcomes for diverse groups of children in different early childhood settings? Does acquiring this essential knowledge and skill require a specific formal educational background, or can all subgroups of providers acquire these through particular types of focused training, mentoring, and other follow-up supports? What are the characteristics of providers who are willing to progress through the necessary education and training? What incentives are most effective for motivating the most qualified providers to continue in the field? What are the most effective and cost-efficient delivery methods for addressing financial, personal, physical, and geographic barriers to receiving essential education and training?

- *How does context influence effectiveness?* How do providers' work environments affect their professional development? In other words, how do organizational, administrative, and policy contexts in various early childhood settings affect providers' ability to develop and apply their knowledge and skills?

- *What is the best use of funds?* To what degree does each approach to provider preparation affect children's early outcomes and later school achievement? How do different approaches to preparation compare with one another? That is, to what degree do different approaches lead to similar or different provider and child outcomes? How much time is needed and what is the entire cost (including initial and ongoing training costs, costs of large-scale implementation, salary costs resulting from increased education and training levels, and so forth) of moving each segment of the early childhood workforce to the desired level of competency? What would be the primary facilitators or impediments to implementing each approach? Would costs be offset, and would there be quantifiable benefits? For example, would the cost of improved preparation reduce turnover rates, resulting in a net savings?

To be both rigorous and relevant, research programs on professional development must be sophisticated and detailed enough to answer these and other complex questions: How does an approach exert its effect? Why is the approach effective or ineffective? Why do some providers and children benefit more than others? What additional knowledge, skills, and resources are required to help all subgroups of teachers and children reach desired goals? What factors, if any, affect the feasibility of implementing the approach on a large scale?

In addressing these questions, we see several ways to strengthen the scientific integrity and policy relevance of individual studies, as well as the entire body of professional development research. Our intent is to highlight specific issues that seem to persistently limit the application of research to practice and policy. These issues are categorized into theory and conceptual models, research design, data analysis, measures, research samples, and data interpretation (see Chapter 14).

***Theory and Conceptual Models***     More systematic progress in answering complex questions will be made if detailed conceptual models, supported by existing basic or applied research, are used to explain how and why an approach is expected to affect specific desired outcomes for particular providers and children. The knowledge that accumulates from model-driven research is more likely to give increasingly accurate information about which professional development policies and practices are most effective and for whom.

***Research Design***     Randomized experiments, in combination with other methods, can best identify the components of professional preparation that are necessary and sufficient for promoting children's development and learning. Other useful approaches for evaluating the effectiveness of professional development for providers and children include planned variations that can specify the added value of different training components; longitudinal studies that track improvements or decrements over time in provider practices and children's outcomes following provider education and training; and embedded implementation studies that use quantitative and qualitative methods that together show which training procedures and other supports were needed to benefit from the approach.

Studies must be ecologically valid in order to inform decisions about practice and policy. One approach to improving ecological validity requires that researchers establish truly collaborative partnerships with early childhood service providers or administrators at state or local levels. Researchers with experience in developing such partnerships (e.g., Fantuzzo, McWayne, & Childs, in press) have discussed, for example, the importance of understanding the problems to be solved from the providers' or administrators' perspectives. Practitioners and researchers can then establish a common language for how research can meaningfully address the problem. The partners work together to establish a research agenda and to identify or develop measures and procedures that each believes are appropriate for answering the research questions. The Head Start Quality Research Consortium is an example of one effort to create researcher–practitioner partnerships (http://www.acf.hhs.gov/programs/opre/hs/qrc_two/). The Child Care Bureau has also funded state administrator–researcher collaborations (http://www.acf.hhs.gov/programs/ccb/research/ccprc/partner/index.htm#ind).

***Data Analysis***    Approaches to analyzing data from professional development research could be strengthened in several ways. Correlational studies, for example, often focus on testing the unique effect of an intervention by controlling statistically for associations between measured outcomes and measured child, family, and other background characteristics. Although this approach can help control for selection bias, it cannot show how an intervention or training method affects different subgroups, which is essential for the effective delivery of programs (see Newcombe, 2003, for a related discussion). As professional development research moves from small to large-scale studies, researchers need to test complex interactions with sufficient numbers of participants from diverse subgroups and settings.

In general, more complex questions should be addressed in professional development research using more sophisticated analytic techniques that produce more reliable data and that take full advantage of the research design. For example, longitudinal analyses, such as individual growth modeling, would be useful for identifying how participating in a particular type of training relates to changes over time in provider behavior and child measures. Structural equation modeling could be used with either longitudinal or cross-sectional designs to test ideas about pathways through which training might influence provider practices and ultimately child outcomes. Multilevel modeling is also appropriate for examining how characteristics of programs, providers, or classroom environments affect aspects of training and the effects of training on provider practices.

Research reports should include information about the magnitude of obtained effects and a discussion of what the effect sizes mean for professional development practices and policies. Although general rules are sometimes used to label obtained effect sizes as small, moderate, or large, the field could benefit from strategies for making a priori estimations of expected effect sizes specific to professional development research. When researchers more consistently report and interpret the magnitude of observed effects, these data can be used to develop an informed standard for expected effect sizes.

***Measures***    Studies are needed that directly assess relations among the content of provider preparation, provider knowledge and skills, and desired child outcomes. Usually, studies lack information about the preparation providers actually received (referred to also as *measures of intervention fidelity*). They also typically lack measures of provider–child interactions that were the target of preparation and that were expected to affect certain child outcomes. Measures in these three areas—provider preparation, provider knowledge and skill, and child outcomes—should also be linked in a theoretically meaningful way. Often, the measures selected relate only loosely to underlying constructs, making the data difficult to interpret and apply in improving provider preparation.

In general, better measures are needed of provider practices and child outcomes (see Chapter 14). As mentioned earlier, studies too often rely on measuring general aspects of teacher behavior or classroom environments. The field especially lacks criterion-referenced measures for both providers and children that can be used to measure growth against an objective standard. Other chapters in this book describe programs of research in which new measures of provider practices are being developed to assess those provider–child interactions believed to support specific desired outcomes for children. A new joint initiative of the U.S. Department of Health and Human Services and the U.S. Department of Education, led by the National Institute of Child Health and Human Development, is also encouraging the development of child measures. Knowledge of how best to educate and train early childhood professionals will remain limited until conceptually driven and psychometrically sound measures are developed for directly observing provider practices and assessing children's progress. (See National Institute of Child Health and Human Development [NICHD], 2002, for a discussion of practical and research issues relating to child measures.)

*Research Samples*    More consideration should be given to the diversity of providers' background characteristics and needs when selecting and describing research samples. More detailed descriptions of participating providers and of early childhood settings are needed in research reports, including the administrative and policy contexts in which providers work. Studies typically do not document aspects of the administrative, policy, and program environments that may support or interfere with teachers' ability to apply their knowledge and skills. These environments would be expected to differ in systematic ways across early childhood settings, which in turn are typically associated with certain provider characteristics and levels of education and training. Detailed descriptions of the broader service environment are typically not collected, reported, or their effects analyzed.

Similarly, greater attention should be paid to policy-relevant factors when selecting and describing child samples. For example, selecting or describing child samples with respect to eligibility requirements of early childhood programs can strengthen the relevance of the findings to policy.

*Data Interpretation*    When discussing research results, researchers aim to give objective summaries of the findings that do not go beyond the data. Too often, however, this goal goes unrealized. To be most useful for policy, every aspect of the research—the design, samples, procedures, measures, and statistical analyses—needs to be considered in drawing conclusions and implications for policy. Caution is especially called for when making causal claims about the level and content of teacher preparation needed to achieve high-quality programs and specific child outcomes from designs that do not directly test causation or that do so for a select sample. Policy makers rely on researchers to make clear the extent to which findings can be generalized to various early childhood settings and populations of children and providers. It is important to be explicit about the strengths and limitations of the research and not to assume that policy audiences will know what caveats would apply. Finally, researchers can help ensure the appropriate use of research findings by situating their results within the broader body of knowledge and explaining how they contradict, confirm, or otherwise build on existing research.

## Practical Considerations in Applying Research Findings

In addition to scientific issues, it is important to be aware of practical factors that potentially influence the usefulness of professional development research. For example, when developing a research agenda, it is helpful to become familiar with the content of a program's authorizing legislation and to understand which policy makers at federal, state, or local levels are the audience for the findings. This familiarity with legislative and administrative processes can lead to better decisions about which types of data might be useful at each point along the cycle from policy formulation to policy implementation and policy reformulation.

Research findings are needed that can offer practical solutions concerning the best and most feasible ways to improve professional preparation and early childhood programs. This practical approach requires becoming familiar with existing mechanisms for delivering new methods of professional development and identifying adaptations that may be necessary within existing organizational structures and policy contexts. When designing a program of research and discussing the potential application of the results, it is also helpful to know whether new funds will be needed to implement the approach given current budgets, and if so, how much. As they consider professional development alternatives, policy makers want information about relative costs in relation to the expected impacts. However, it is necessary to be aware of the kinds of general tradeoffs policy makers tend to weigh, such as whether funds should be used to improve program quality by investing in certain kinds of provider preparation or to improve access to an existing program by paying for greater numbers of children.

Becoming familiar with issues raised during previous cycles of program reauthorization can help focus research agendas in useful ways. Aside from giving historical context, knowing which issues were considered but did not become part of legislation can help forecast policy questions in upcoming cycles that could be addressed through research. As mentioned earlier, the demand for research data is usually greatest when legislation is ready to be reauthorized. Keeping track of policy reauthorization cycles for programs with professional development components can inform planning for a research timeline that makes it more likely that the results will be available when the data are most needed.

Finally, the values held by researchers and funding institutions affect which research questions are asked, the methods used, the conclusions drawn, and ultimately the potential contribution of a single study or entire program of research. As Shonkoff (2000) framed it, "Value-free social science and human service delivery are an illusion" (p. 182). In the field of early childhood education, research on how best to support children's learning and development has been embedded in cultural and ideological differences and long-held assumptions about methods and settings for child rearing and expectations for children, especially as they prepare for school. Debates linger, for example, about whether social and emotional or cognitive and language development should be the primary target of early childhood education, although child development research shows that adult guidance in all areas supports children's well-being, a positive transition to school, and early school success. From our perspective, producing research with promise for advancing practice and policy requires acknowledging personally held values and preconceptions, becoming thoroughly familiar with the policy and program context, using appropriate and rigorous methods to empirically evaluate all untested assumptions (at least those that are possible to evaluate with scientific methods), and presenting unbiased results that do not go beyond the data.

## CONCLUSIONS AND RECOMMENDATIONS

This chapter offered one policy-based perspective on professional development research and made suggestions for future study. We hope that these observations will be useful as researchers work to produce data with greater potential to bear directly on the preparation of early childhood professionals. Early childhood education practices and policies are derived from many sources other than findings from empirical research. Yet, professional development research, if sound, timely, and relevant, is critical to giving the early childhood workforce the knowledge, skills, and other tools required for promoting the healthy development and early learning of young children.

## REFERENCES

Barnett, S.W., Hustedt, J.T., Robin, K.B., & Shulman, K.L. (2004). *The state of preschool: 2004 state preschool yearbook.* New Brunswick, NJ: National Institute for Early Education Research (http://nieer.org/yearbook/pdf/yearbook.pdf).

Child Care Bureau. (January, 2003). *Child Care and Development Fund {CCDF} report to Congress.* Washington, DC: U.S. Department of Health and Human Services, Administration for Children and Families.

Child Care Bureau. (October, 2004). *Child Care and Development Fund {CCDF} report of state plans FY 2004–2005*. Washington, DC: U.S. Department of Health and Human Services, Administration for Children and Families.

Coats Human Services Amendments of 1998, PL 105-285.

Council for Exceptional Children. (November, 2004). *The new IDEA: CEC's summary of significant issues*. Retrieved April 4, 2005, from http://www.cec.sped.org/pp/IDEA_120204.pdf

Education Commission of the States. (2002). *State-funded pre-kindergarten programs: State funds and number of children served*. Retrieved April 4, 2005, from http://www.ecs.org/dbsearches/EarlyLearning_Reports.htm

Education for All Handicapped Children Act of 1975, PL 94-142, 20 U.S.C. §§ 1400 *et seq.*

Fantuzzo, J., McWayne, C., & Childs, S. (in press). Scientist-community collaborations: A dynamic tension between rights and responsibilities. In J. Trimble & C. Fisher (Eds.), *Handbook of ethical research with ethnocultural populations and communities*. Thousand Oakes, CA: Sage.

Head Start Bureau. (2004). *Head Start program information report*. Washington, DC: U.S. Department of Health and Human Services, Administration for Children and Families.

Human Services Amendments of 1994, PL 103-252, 42 U.S.C. §§ 9801 *et seq.*

Individuals with Disabilities Education Act (IDEA) Amendments of 1997, PL 105-17, 20 U.S.C. §§ 1400 *et seq.*

Individuals with Disabilities Education Improvement Act of 2004, PL 108-446, 20 U.S.C. 1400 *et seq.*

Kamerman, S.B., & Gatenio, S. (2003). Overview of the current policy context. In D. Cryer & R.M. Clifford (Eds.), *Early childhood education and care in the USA*. Baltimore: Paul H. Brookes Publishing Co.

LeMoine, S. (August, 2004). *Summaries of child care licensing requirements: Minimum preservice qualifications and annual/ongoing training hours in early childhood education*. Retrieved April 4, 2005, from http://nccic.org/pubs/licensingtables

National Institute of Child Health and Human Development. (June 17–18, 2002). *Early childhood education and school readiness: Conceptual models, constructs and measures. A workshop summary*. Retrieved April 4, 2005, from http://www.nichd.nih.gov/crmc/cdb/Kyle-workshop.pdf

National Research Council. (2001). *Eager to learn: Educating our preschoolers*. Committee on Early Childhood Pedagogy. Washington, DC: National Academy Press.

Newcombe, N.S. (2003). Some controls control too much. *Child Development, 74*(4), 1050–1052.

No Child Left Behind (NCLB) Act of 2001, PL 107-110, 20 U.S.C.

Personal Responsibility and Work Opportunities Reconciliation Act of 1996, PL 104-193, 42 U.S.C. 211 *et seq.*

Omnibus Budget Reconciliation Act of 1981, PL 97-35, 42 U.S.C. §§ 9801 *et seq.*

Shonkoff, J.P. (2000). Science, policy, and practice: Three cultures in search of a shared mission. *Child Development, 71*(1), 181–187.

Shonkoff, J.P., & Phillips, D.A. (Eds.). (2000). *From neurons to neighborhoods: The science and ecology of human development*. Washington, DC: National Academy Press.

Technology-Related Assistance Act for Individuals with Disabilities of 1993, PL 103-218.

U.S. Department of Education. (March 4, 2004). *Serving preschool children under Title I: Non-regulatory guidance.* Retrieved April 4, 2005, from http://www.ed.gov/policy/elsec/guid/preschoolguidance.doc

U.S. Department of Education, National Center for Education Statistics. (2003). *Prekindergarten in U.S. public schools: 2000–2001.* Washington, DC: Author.

Whitebook, M. (2003). *Early education quality: Higher teacher qualifications for better learning environments. A review of the literature.* Retrieved April 4, 2005, from http://www.iir.berkeley.edu/cscce/pdf/teacher.pdf

# Index

Page numbers followed by *f* indicate figures; those followed by *t* indicate tables; those followed by *n* indicate footnotes.